Adobe® Photoshop® CS6
The Professional Portfolio

AGAINST THE CLOCK
mastering graphic technology

Managing Editor: Ellenn Behoriam
Cover & Interior Design: Erika Kendra
Copy Editor: Angelina Kendra
Printer: Prestige Printers

10   9   8   7   6   5   4   3   2   1   978-1-936201-09-9

4710 28th Street North, Saint Petersburg, FL 33714
800-256-4ATC • www.againsttheclock.com

Acknowledgements

ABOUT AGAINST THE CLOCK

Against The Clock, long recognized as one of the nation's leaders in courseware development, has been publishing high-quality educational materials for the graphic and computer arts industries since 1990. The company has developed a solid and widely-respected approach to teaching people how to effectively utilize graphics applications, while maintaining a disciplined approach to real-world problems.

Having developed the *Against The Clock* and the *Essentials for Design* series with Prentice Hall/Pearson Education, ATC drew from years of professional experience and instructor feedback to develop *The Professional Portfolio Series*, focusing on the Adobe Creative Suite. These books feature step-by-step explanations, detailed foundational information, and advice and tips from industry professionals that offer practical solutions to technical issues.

Against The Clock works closely with all major software developers to create learning solutions that fulfill both the requirements of instructors and the needs of students. Thousands of graphic arts professionals — designers, illustrators, imaging specialists, prepress experts and production managers — began their educations with Against The Clock training books. These professionals studied at Baker College, Nossi College of Art, Virginia Tech, Appalachian State University, Keiser College, University of South Carolina, Gress Graphic Arts Institute, Hagerstown Community College, Kean University, Southern Polytechnic State University, Brenau University, and many other educational institutions.

ABOUT THE AUTHOR

Erika Kendra holds a BA in History and a BA in English Literature from the University of Pittsburgh. She began her career in the graphic communications industry as an editor at Graphic Arts Technical Foundation before moving to Los Angeles in 2000. Erika is the author or co-author of more than thirty books about Adobe graphic design software. She has also written several books about graphic design concepts such as color reproduction and preflighting, and dozens of articles for online and print journals in the graphics industry. Working with Against The Clock for more than 12 years, Erika was a key partner in developing *The Professional Portfolio Series* of software training books.

CONTRIBUTING AUTHORS, ARTISTS, AND EDITORS

A big thank you to the people whose artwork, comments, and expertise contributed to the success of these books:

- John Craft, Appalachian State University
- Brian McDaniel, Central Georgia Technical College
- Chris Hadfield, Doane College
- Michael Watkins, Baker College of Flint
- Jennifer Hair, Shawnee Mission East High School
- Debbie Davidson, Sweet Dream Designs
- Charlie Essers, photographer, Lancaster, Calif.

Finally, thanks also to **Angelina Kendra**, editor, for making sure that we all said what we meant to say.

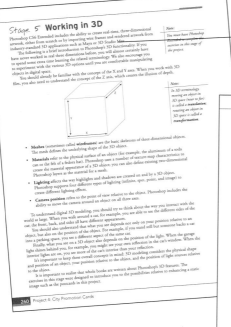

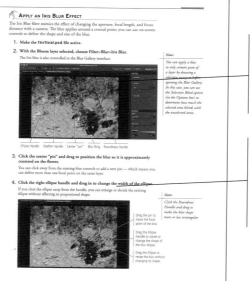

Project Goals

Each project begins with a clear description of the overall concepts that are explained in the project; these goals closely match the different "stages" of the project workflow.

The Project Meeting

Each project includes the client's initial comments, which provide valuable information about the job. The Project Art Director, a vital part of any design workflow, also provides fundamental advice and production requirements.

Project Objectives

Each Project Meeting includes a summary of the specific skills required to complete the project.

Real-World Workflow

Projects are broken into logical lessons or "stages" of the workflow. Brief introductions at the beginning of each stage provide vital foundational material required to complete the task.

Step-By-Step Exercises

Every stage of the workflow is broken into multiple hands-on, step-by-step exercises.

Visual Explanations

Wherever possible, screen shots are annotated so you can quickly identify important information.

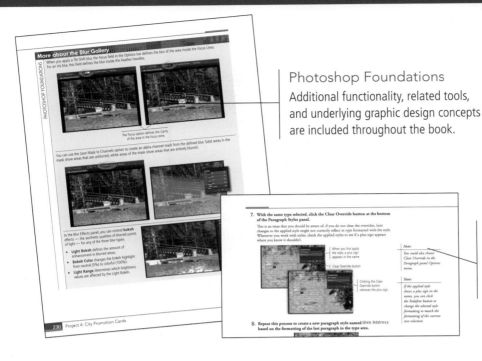

Photoshop Foundations
Additional functionality, related tools, and underlying graphic design concepts are included throughout the book.

Advice and Warnings
Where appropriate, sidebars provide shortcuts, warnings, or tips about the topic at hand.

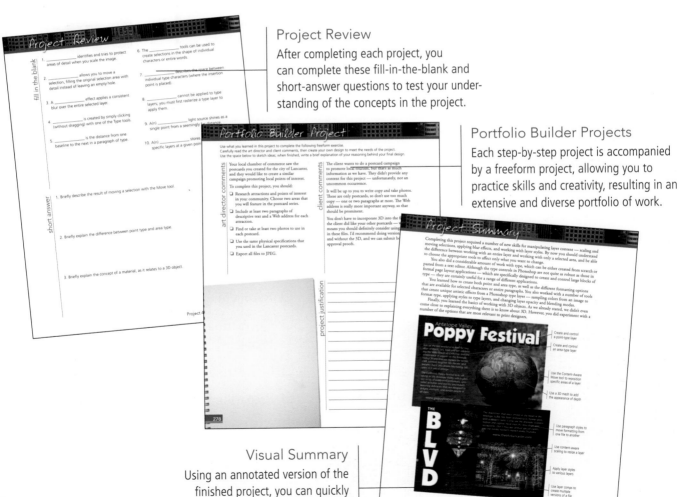

Project Review
After completing each project, you can complete these fill-in-the-blank and short-answer questions to test your understanding of the concepts in the project.

Portfolio Builder Projects
Each step-by-step project is accompanied by a freeform project, allowing you to practice skills and creativity, resulting in an extensive and diverse portfolio of work.

Visual Summary
Using an annotated version of the finished project, you can quickly identify the skills used to complete different aspects of the job.

The Against The Clock *Portfolio Series* teaches graphic design software tools and techniques entirely within the framework of real-world projects; we introduce and explain skills where they would naturally fall into a real project workflow.

The project-based approach in *The Professional Portfolio Series* allows you to get in depth with the software beginning in Project 1 — you don't have to read several chapters of introductory material before you can start creating finished artwork.

Our approach also prevents "topic tedium" — in other words, we don't require you to read pages and pages of information about text (for example); instead, we explain text tools and options as part of a larger project (in this case, as part of a postcard series).

Clear, easy-to-read, step-by-step instructions walk you through every phase of each job, from creating a new file to saving the finished piece. Wherever logical, we also offer practical advice and tips about underlying concepts and graphic design practices that will benefit students as they enter the job market.

The projects in this book reflect a range of different types of Photoshop jobs, from creating a magazine ad to correcting menu images to building a Web page. When you finish the eight projects in this book (and the accompanying Portfolio Builder exercises), you will have a substantial body of work that should impress any potential employer.

The eight Photoshop CS6 projects are described briefly here; more detail is provided in the full table of contents (beginning on Page viii).

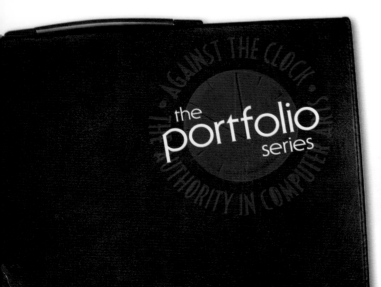

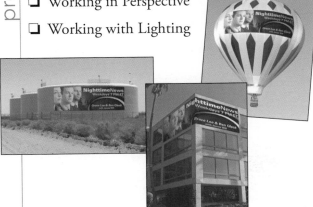

Our goal in this book is to familiarize you with the majority of the Photoshop tool set so you can be more productive and more marketable in your career as a graphic designer.

It is important to keep in mind that Photoshop is an extremely versatile and powerful application. The sheer volume of available tools, panels, and features can seem intimidating when you first look at the software interface. Most of these tools, however, are fairly simple to use with a bit of background information and a little practice.

Wherever necessary, we explain the underlying concepts and terms that are required for understanding the software. We're confident that these projects provide the practice you need to be able to create sophisticated artwork by the end of the very first project.

CONTENTS

Contents

Contents

Contents

PREREQUISITES

The Professional Portfolio Series is based on the assumption that you have a basic understanding of how to use your computer. You should know how to use your mouse to point and click, as well as how to drag items around the screen. You should be able to resize and arrange windows on your desktop to maximize your available space. You should know how to access drop-down menus, and understand how check boxes and radio buttons work. It also doesn't hurt to have a good understanding of how your operating system organizes files and folders, and how to navigate your way around them. If you're familiar with these fundamental skills, then you know all that's necessary to use *The Professional Portfolio Series*.

RESOURCE FILES

All of the files you need to complete the projects in this book — except, of course, the Photoshop application files — are on the Student Files Web page at www.againsttheclock.com. See the inside back cover of this book for access information.

Each archive (ZIP) file is named according to the related project (e.g., **PS6_RF_Project1.zip**). At the beginning of each project, you must download the archive file for that project and expand that archive to access the resource files that you need to complete the exercises. Detailed instructions for this process are included in the Interface chapter.

Files required for the related Portfolio Builder exercises at the end of each project are also available on the Student Files page; these archives are also named by project (e.g., **PS6_PB_Project1.zip**).

ATC FONTS

You must download and install the ATC fonts from the Student Files Web page to ensure that your exercises and projects will work as described in the book. Specific instructions for installing fonts are provided in the documentation that came with your computer. You should replace older (pre-2004) ATC fonts with the ones on the Student Files Web page.

SYSTEM REQUIREMENTS

The Professional Portfolio Series was designed to work on both Macintosh or Windows computers; where differences exist from one platform to another, we include specific instructions relative to each platform. One issue that remains different from Macintosh to Windows is the use of different modifier keys (Control, Shift, etc.) to accomplish the same task. When we present key commands, we follow the Macintosh/Windows format — Macintosh keys are listed first, then a slash, followed by the Windows key commands.

Minimum System Requirements for Adobe Photoshop CS6:

Windows

- Intel® Pentium® 4 or AMD Athlon® 64 processor
- Microsoft® Windows® XP* with Service Pack 3 or Windows 7 with Service Pack 1 (Note: 3D features and some GPU-enabled features are not supported on Windows XP.)
- 1GB of RAM
- 1GB of available hard-disk space for installation; additional free space required during installation
- 1024×768 display (1280×800 recommended) with 16-bit color and 512MB of VRAM
- OpenGL 2.0–capable system
- DVD-ROM drive

Mac OS

- Multicore Intel processor with 64-bit support
- Mac OS X v10.6.8 or v10.7
- 1GB of RAM
- 2GB of available hard-disk space for installation; additional free space required during installation (cannot install on a volume that uses a case-sensitive file system)
- 1024×768 (1280×800 recommended) resolution display with 16-bit color and 512MB of VRAM
- OpenGL 2.0–capable system
- DVD-ROM drive

Broadband Internet connection and registration are required for software activation, validation of subscriptions, and access to online services.

Adobe Photoshop is the industry-standard application for working with pixels — both manipulating existing ones and creating new ones. Many Photoshop experts specialize in certain types of work. Photo retouching, artistic painting, image compositing, and color correction are only a few types of work you can create with Photoshop. Our goal in this book is to teach you how to use the available tools to succeed with different types of jobs that you might encounter in your professional career.

Although not intended as a layout-design application, you can use Photoshop to combine type, graphics, and images into a finished design; many people create advertisements, book covers, and other projects entirely in Photoshop. Others argue that Photoshop should never be used for layout design; Adobe InDesign is the preferred page-layout application. We do not advocate doing *all* or even *most* layout composite work in Photoshop, but because many people use the application to create composite designs, we feel the projects in this book portray a realistic workflow.

The simple exercises in this introduction are designed to let you explore the Photoshop user interface. Whether you are new to the application or upgrading from a previous version, we highly recommend following these steps to click around and become familiar with the basic workspace. When you begin Project 1, you will be better prepared to jump right in and start pushing pixels.

EXPLORE THE PHOTOSHOP INTERFACE

The first time you launch Photoshop, you will see the default user interface (UI) settings as defined by Adobe. When you relaunch after you or another user has quit, the workspace defaults to the last-used settings — including open panels and the position of those panels on your screen. We designed the following exercise so you can explore different ways of controlling panels in the Photoshop user interface.

1. **Create a new empty folder named WIP (Work in Progress) on any writable disk (where you plan to save your work).**

2. **Download the PS6_RF_Interface.zip archive from the Student Files Web page.**

3. **Macintosh users: Place the ZIP archive in your WIP folder, then double-click the file icon to expand it.**

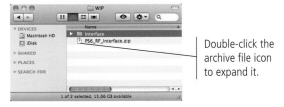

Double-click the archive file icon to expand it.

Windows users: Double-click the ZIP archive file to open it. Click the folder inside the archive and drag it into your primary WIP folder.

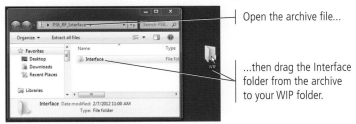

Open the archive file...

...then drag the Interface folder from the archive to your WIP folder.

The resulting **Interface** folder contains all the files you need to complete the exercises in this introduction.

4. Macintosh users: While pressing Command-Option-Shift, start Photoshop. Click Yes when asked if you want to delete Settings files.

Windows users: Choose Adobe Photoshop CS6 in the Start menu, and then immediately press Control-Alt-Shift. Click Yes when asked if you want to delete the Settings files.

This step resets Photoshop to the preference settings that are defined by Adobe as the application defaults. This helps to ensure that your application functions in the same way as what we show in our screen shots.

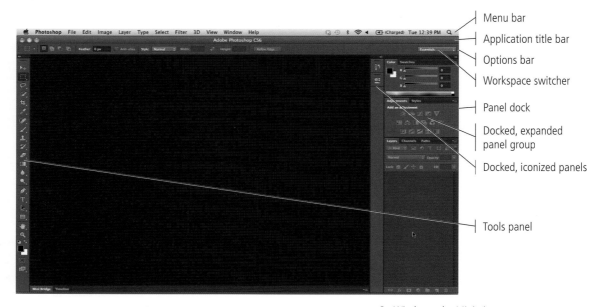

Menu bar
Application title bar
Options bar
Workspace switcher
Panel dock
Docked, expanded panel group
Docked, iconized panels
Tools panel

On Windows, the Minimize, Restore, and Close buttons appear on the right end of the Menu bar.

Menu bar
Options bar

In general, the Macintosh and Windows workspaces are virtually identical, with a few primary exceptions:

- On Macintosh, the application's title bar appears below the Menu bar; the Close, Minimize, and Restore buttons appear on the left side of the title bar, and the Menu bar is not part of the Application frame.

- On Windows, the Close, Minimize, and Restore buttons appear at the right end of the Menu bar, which is part of the overall Application frame.

Also, Macintosh users have two extra menus (consistent with the Macintosh operating system structure). The Apple menu provides access to system-specific commands. The Photoshop menu follows the Macintosh system-standard format for all applications; this menu controls basic application operations such as About, Hide, Preferences, and Quit.

Finally, remember that on Macintosh systems, the Preferences dialog box is accessed in the Photoshop menu; Windows users access the Preferences dialog box from the Edit menu.

Note:

*Many menu commands and options in Photoshop are **toggles**, which means they are either on or off; when an option is checked, it is toggled on (visible or active). You can toggle an active option off by choosing the checked menu command, or toggle an inactive option on by choosing the unchecked menu command.*

Understanding the Application Frame

On Windows, each running application is contained within its own frame; all elements of the application — including the Menu bar, panels, tools, and open documents — are contained within the Application frame.

Adobe also offers the Application frame to Macintosh users as an option for controlling the workspace. When the Application frame is active, the entire workspace exists in a self-contained area that can be moved around the screen. All elements of the workspace (excluding the Menu bar) move when you move the Application frame.

The Application frame is active by default, but you can toggle it off by choosing Window>Application Frame. If the menu option is checked, the Application frame is active; if the menu option is not checked, it is inactive.

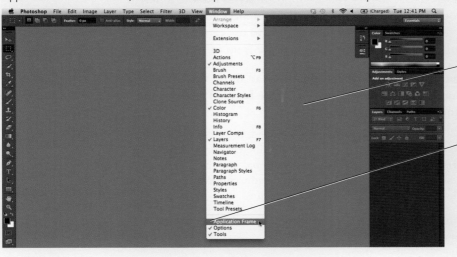

When the Application frame is not active, the desktop is visible behind the workspace elements.

When the Application frame is not active, the option is unchecked in the Window menu.

5. **Macintosh users: Choose Photoshop>Preferences>Interface.**
   Windows users: Choose Edit>Preferences>Interface.

   Preferences customize the way many of the program's tools and options function. When you open the Preferences dialog box, the active pane is the one you choose in the Preferences submenu. Once open, however, you can access any of the Preference categories by clicking a different option in the left pane; the right side of the dialog box displays options related to the active category.

   If you have used a previous version of Photoshop, you might have already noticed the rather dark appearance of the panels and interface background. In CS6, the application uses a darker "theme" as the default. You can change this color in the Interface pane of the Preferences dialog box.

Note:

*As you work your way through this book, you will learn not only what you can do with these different collections of Preferences, but also **why** and **when** you might want to adjust them.*

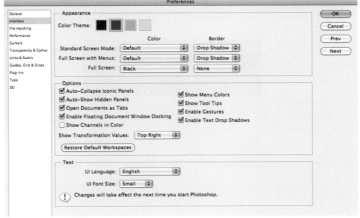

6. **Click OK to dismiss the Preferences dialog box, then continue to the next exercise.**

EXPLORE THE ARRANGEMENT OF PHOTOSHOP PANELS

As you gain experience and familiarity with Photoshop, you will develop personal artistic and working styles. You will also find that different types of jobs often require different but specific sets of tools. Adobe recognizes this wide range of needs and preferences among users; Photoshop includes a number of options for arranging and managing the numerous panels so you can customize and personalize the workspace to suit your specific needs.

We designed the following exercise to give you an opportunity to explore different ways of controlling Photoshop panels. Because workspace preferences are largely a matter of personal taste, the projects in this book instruct you to use certain tools and panels, but where you place those elements within the interface is up to you.

1. **With Photoshop open, Control/right-click the title bar above the left column of docked panel icons. Choose Auto-Collapse Iconic Panels in the contextual menu to toggle on that option.**

    As we explained in the Getting Started section, when commands are different for the Macintosh and Windows operating systems, we include the different commands in the Macintosh/Windows format. In this case, Macintosh users who do not have right-click mouse capability can press the Control key and click to access the contextual menu. You do not have to press Control *and* right-click to access the menus.

    (If you're using a Macintosh and don't have a mouse with right-click capability, we highly recommend that you purchase one.)

    Control/right-clicking a dock title bar opens the dock contextual menu, where you can change the default panel behavior. If you toggle on the Auto-Collapse Iconic Panels option (which is inactive by default), a panel will collapse as soon as you click away from it.

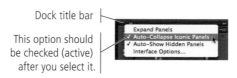

Dock title bar

This option should be checked (active) after you select it.

2. **In the left column of the panel dock, hover your mouse cursor over the top button until you see the name of the related panel ("History") in a tool tip.**

3. **Click the History button to expand that panel.**

    The expanded panel is still referred to as a **panel group** even though the History panel is the only panel in the group.

Panel group drop zone

Clicking a panel button expands that panel to the left of the button.

Click here to manually collapse the panel back into the dock.

Dock column title bar

Hover your mouse cursor over a button to see a tool tip that identifies the panel.

4. **Click away from the expanded panel, anywhere in the workspace.**

    Because the Auto-Collapse Iconic Panels option is toggled on (from Step 1), the History panel collapses as soon as you click away from the panel.

Note:

All panels can be toggled on and off using the Window menu.

If you choose a panel that is open but iconized, the panel expands to the left of its icon.

If you choose a panel that is open in an expanded group, that panel comes to the front of the group.

If you choose a panel that isn't currently open, it opens in the same position as when it was last closed.

Note:

*Collapsed panels are referred to as **iconized** or **iconic**.*

Note:

The Auto-Collapse Iconic Panels option is also available in the User Interface pane of the Preferences dialog box, which you can open directly from the dock contextual menu.

Note:

When you expand an iconized panel that is part of a group, the entire group expands; the button you clicked is the active panel in the expanded group.

5. Click the History panel button to re-expand the panel. Control/right-click the expanded panel group's drop zone and choose Close from the contextual menu.

The panel group's contextual menu is the only way to close a docked panel. You can choose Close to close only the active panel, or close an entire panel group by choosing Close Tab Group from the contextual menu.

Control/right-click the panel group drop zone to access that panel group's contextual menu.

6. Repeat Step 5 to close the Properties panel.

Closing the remaining group removes the entire second dock column.

7. In the remaining dock column, Control/right-click the drop zone of the Color panel group and choose Close Tab Group from the contextual menu.

When you close a docked group, other panel groups in the same column expand to fill the available space.

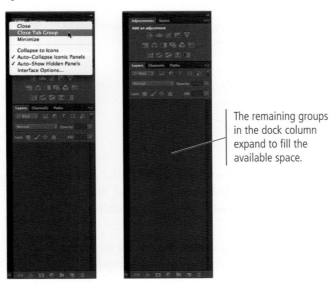

The remaining groups in the dock column expand to fill the available space.

8. Click the Layers panel tab and drag left, away from the panel dock.

A panel that is not docked is called a **floating panel**. You can iconize floating panels (or panel groups) by double-clicking the title bar of the floating panel group.

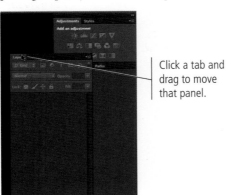
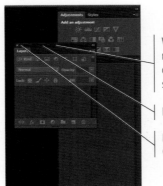

Click a tab and drag to move that panel.

When you release the mouse button, the dragged panel "floats" separate from the dock.

Floating panel title bar

Panel (group) Close button

9. **Click the Layers panel tab (in the floating panel group). Drag between the two existing docked panel groups until a blue line appears, then release the mouse button.**

To move a single panel to a new location, click the panel tab and drag. To move an entire panel group, click the panel group drop zone and drag. If you are moving panels to another position in the dock, the blue highlight indicates where the panel (group) will be placed when you release the mouse button.

The blue highlight shows where the panel will be placed if you release the mouse button.

When you release the mouse button, the Layers panel becomes part of a separate panel group.

10. **Control/right-click the drop zone behind the Adjustments/Styles panel group, and choose Minimize from the contextual menu.**

When a group is minimized, only the panel tabs are visible. Clicking a tab in a collapsed panel group expands that group and makes the selected panel active.

Minimizing a panel group collapses it to show only the panel tabs.

11. **Move the cursor over the line between the Layers and Channels/Paths panel groups. When the cursor becomes a double-headed arrow, click and drag down until the Layers panel occupies approximately half of the available dock column space.**

You can drag the bottom edge of a docked panel group to vertically expand or shrink the panel; other panels in the same column expand or contract to fit the available space.

When the cursor becomes a double-headed arrow, click and drag the line between panel groups to change the height of a panel.

Other panels in the same dock column resize accordingly.

12. **Double-click the title bar above the column of docked panels to collapse those panels to icons.**

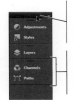

Double-clicking the dock title bar collapses an expanded column (or vice versa).

Buttons that are grouped together in the dock represent a panel group.

13. **Move the cursor over the left edge of the dock column. When the cursor becomes a double-headed arrow, click and drag right.**

If you only see the icons, you can also drag the dock edge to the left to reveal the panel names. This can be particularly useful until you are more familiar with the application and the icons used to symbolize the different panels.

Click here and drag right to hide the panel names.

Note:

Dragging the left edge of a dock column changes the width of all panels in that dock column. This works for both iconized and expanded columns.

14. **On the left side of the workspace, double-click the Tools panel title bar.**

The Tools panel can't be expanded, but it can be displayed as either one or two columns; double-clicking the Tools panel title bar toggles between the two modes.

The one- or two-column format is a purely personal choice. The one-column layout takes up less horizontal space on the screen, which can be useful if you have a small monitor. The two-column format fits in a smaller vertical space, which can be especially useful if you have a widescreen monitor.

Double-click the Tools panel title bar to toggle between the one-column and two-column layouts.

Note:

Throughout this book, our screen shots show the Tools panel in the one-column format. Feel free to work with the panel in two columns if you prefer.

Note:

The Tools panel can also be floated by clicking its title bar and dragging away from the edge of the screen. To re-dock the floating Tools panel, simply click the title bar and drag back to the left edge of the screen; when the blue line highlights the edge of the workspace, releasing the mouse button puts the Tools panel back into the dock.

15. **Continue to the next exercise.**

In the Tools panel, tools with a small white mark in the lower-right corner have **nested tools**.

This arrow means the tool has other nested tools.

A tool tip shows the name of the tool.

If you hover your mouse over a tool, a **tool tip** shows the name of the tool, as well as the associated keyboard shortcut for that tool if one exists. (If you don't see tool tips, check the Show Tool Tips option in the General pane of the Preferences dialog box.)

You can access nested tools by clicking the primary tool and holding down the mouse button, or by Control/right-clicking the primary tool to open the menu of nested options.

If a tool has a defined shortcut, pressing that key activates the associated tool. Most nested tools have the same shortcut as the default tool. By default, you have to press Shift plus the shortcut key to access the nested variations; for example, press Shift-M to toggle between the Rectangular and Elliptical Marquee tools. You can change this behavior in the General pane of the Preferences dialog box by unchecking the Use Shift Key for Tool Switch option. When this option is off, you can simply press the shortcut key multiple times to cycle through the variations.

Not all nested tools can be accessed with a shortcut. In the marquee tools, for example, the shortcut toggles only between the rectangular and elliptical variations.

Finally, if you press and hold a tool's keyboard shortcut, you can temporarily call the appropriate tool (called **spring-loaded keys**); after releasing the shortcut key, you return to the tool you were using previously. For example, you might use this technique to switch temporarily from the Brush tool to the Eraser tool while painting.

The following chart offers a quick reference of nested tools, as well as the shortcut for each tool (if any). Nested tools are shown indented and in italics.

Move tool (V)

Rectangular Marquee tool (M)
   Elliptical Marquee tool (M)
   Single Row Marquee tool
   Single Column Marquee tool

Lasso tool (L)
   Polygonal Lasso tool (L)
   Magnetic Lasso tool (L)

Quick Selection tool (W)
   Magic Wand tool (W)

Crop tool (C)
   Perspective Crop tool (C)
   Slice tool (C)
   Slice Select tool (C)

Eyedropper tool (I)
   3D Material Eyedropper tool (I)
   Color Sampler tool (I)
   Ruler tool (I)
   Note tool (I)
   Count tool (I)

Spot Healing Brush tool (J)
   Healing Brush tool (J)
   Patch tool (J)
   Content Aware Move tool (J)
   Red Eye tool (J)

Brush tool (B)
   Pencil tool (B)
   Color Replacement tool (B)
   Mixer Brush tool (B)

Clone Stamp tool (S)
   Pattern Stamp tool (S)

History Brush tool (Y)
   Art History Brush tool (Y)

Eraser tool (E)
   Background Eraser tool (E)
   Magic Eraser tool (E)

Gradient tool (G)
   Paint Bucket tool (G)
   3D Material Drop tool (G)

Blur tool
   Sharpen tool
   Smudge tool

Dodge tool (O)
   Burn tool (O)
   Sponge tool (O)

Pen tool (P)
   Freeform Pen tool (P)
   Add Anchor Point tool
   Delete Anchor Point tool
   Convert Point tool

Horizontal Type tool (T)
   Vertical Type tool (T)
   Horizontal Type Mask tool (T)
   Vertical Type Mask tool (T)

Path Selection tool (A)
   Direct Selection tool (A)

Rectangle tool (U)
   Rounded Rectangle tool (U)
   Ellipse tool (U)
   Polygon tool (U)
   Line tool (U)
   Custom Shape tool (U)

Hand tool (H)
   Rotate View tool (R)

Zoom tool (Z)

CREATE A SAVED WORKSPACE

You have extensive control over the appearance of your Photoshop workspace — you can choose what panels are visible, where they appear, and even the size of individual panels or panel groups. Over time you will develop personal preferences — the Layers panel always appears at the top, for example — based on your work habits and project needs. Rather than re-establishing every workspace element each time you return to Photoshop, you can save your custom workspace settings so they can be recalled with a single click.

1. **Click the Workspace switcher in the Options bar and choose New Workspace.**

   The Workspace switcher is labeled Essentials (the default workspace) by default.

   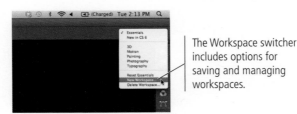

   The Workspace switcher includes options for saving and managing workspaces.

2. **In the New Workspace dialog box, type Portfolio and then click Save.**

   You didn't define custom keyboard shortcuts or menus, so those two options are not relevant in this exercise.

3. **Open the Window menu and choose Workspace>Essentials (Default).**

   Saved workspaces can be accessed in the Window>Workspace submenu as well as the Workspace switcher on the Options bar.

   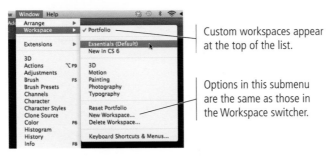

   Custom workspaces appear at the top of the list.

   Options in this submenu are the same as those in the Workspace switcher.

   Calling a saved workspace restores the last-used state of the workspace. You made a number of changes since calling the Essentials workspace at the beginning of the previous exercise, so calling the Essentials workspace restores the last state of that workspace — in essence, nothing changes from the saved Portfolio workspace.

   The only apparent difference is the active workspace name.

Note:

Because workspace preferences are largely a matter of personal taste, the projects in this book instruct you regarding which panels to use, but not where to place those elements within the interface.

Note:

If a menu option is greyed out, it is not available for the active selection.

Note:

The Delete Workspace option opens a dialog box where you can choose a specific user-defined workspace to delete. You can't delete the default workspaces that come with the application.

4. **Open the Workspace switcher and choose Reset Essentials (or choose Window>Workspace>Reset Essentials).**

Remember, saved workspaces remember the last-used state; calling a workspace again restores the panels exactly as they were the last time you used that workspace. For example, if you close a panel that is part of a saved workspace, the closed panel will not be reopened the next time you call the same workspace. To restore the saved state of the workspace, including opening closed panels or repositioning moved ones, you have to use the Reset option.

Note:

If you change anything and quit the application, those changes are remembered even when Photoshop is relaunched.

5. **Continue to the next exercise.**

Customizing Keyboard Shortcuts and Menus

People use Photoshop for many different reasons; some use only a limited set of tools to complete specific projects. Photoshop allows you to define the available menu options and the keyboard shortcuts that are associated with menu commands, panel menus, and tools.

At the bottom of the Edit menu, two options (Keyboard Shortcuts and Menus) open different tabs of the same dialog box. (If you don't see the Keyboard Shortcuts or Menus options in the Edit menu, choose Show all Menu Items to reveal the hidden commands.) Once you have defined custom menus or shortcuts, you can save your choices as a set so you can access the same custom choices again without having to redo the work.

Click here to access existing saved sets. Save the changes to the current set. Save the changes as a new set. Delete the selected set.

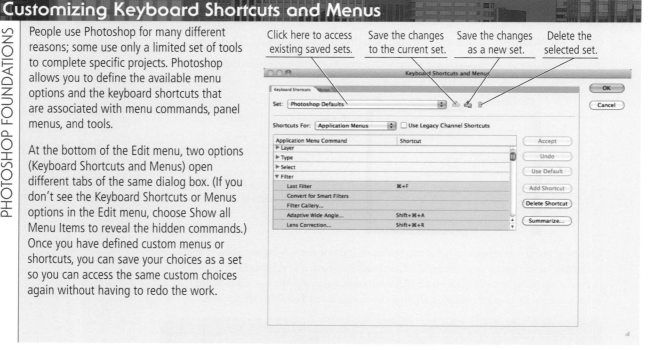

EXPLORE THE PHOTOSHOP DOCUMENT VIEWS

There is much more to using Photoshop than arranging the workspace. What you do with those panels — and even which panels you need — depends on the type of work you are doing in a particular file. In this exercise, you open a Photoshop file and explore interface elements that will be important as you begin creating digital artwork.

Note:

Press Command/ Control-O to access the Open dialog box.

1. **In Photoshop, choose File>Open.**

2. **Navigate to your WIP>Interface folder and select bryce2.jpg in the list of available files.**

   The Open dialog box is a system-standard navigation dialog. This is one area of significant difference between Macintosh and Windows users.

3. **Press Shift, and then click bryce3.jpg in the list of files.**

   Pressing Shift allows you to select multiple contiguous (consecutive) files in the list.

4. Click Open.

Photoshop files appear in a **document window**.

Each open document is represented by a separate tab.

The active file tab is lighter than other tabs.

The **document tabs** show the file name, view percentage, color space, and current viewing mode.

View Percentage field

Use this menu to show different document information, such as file size (default), profile, dimensions, etc.

5. Click the bryce2.jpg tab to make that document active.

6. Highlight the current value in the View Percentage field (in the bottom-left corner of the document window) and type 40.

Different people prefer larger or smaller view percentages, depending on a number of factors (eyesight, monitor size, and so on). As you complete the projects in this book, you will see our screen shots zoom in or out as necessary to show you the most relevant part of a particular file. In most cases we do not tell you what specific view percentage to use for a particular exercise, unless it is specifically required for the work being done.

Note:

Macintosh users: If you turn off the Application frame, opening multiple files creates a document window that has a separate title bar showing the name of the active file.

Click the tab to activate a specific file in the document window.

Changing the view percentage of the file does not affect the size of the document window.

7. Choose View>Fit On Screen.

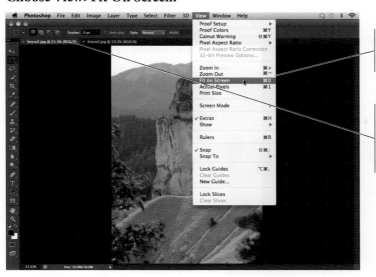

These five options affect the view percentage of a file.

The Fit On Screen command automatically calculates view percentage based on the size of the document window.

8. Click the Zoom tool in the Tools panel. In the Options bar, click the Actual Pixels button.

The Options bar appears by default at the top of the workspace below the Menu bar. It is context sensitive, which means it provides different options depending on which tool is active.

When the Zoom tool is active, the Actual Pixels button (the same as the Actual Pixels command in the View menu) changes the image view to 100%.

Note:

You can toggle the Options bar on or off by choosing Window>Options.

Note:

Dragging with the Zoom tool enlarges the selected area to fill the document window.

If Resize Windows to Fit is checked, zooming in a floating window affects the size of the actual document window.

If Zoom All Windows is checked, zooming in one window affects the view percentage of all open files.

Scrubby Zoom enables dynamic image zooming depending on the direction you drag in the document window.

The Options bar shows options related to the active tool.

Zoom tool

9. Press Option/Alt, and then click anywhere in the document window.

One final reminder: we list differing commands in the Macintosh/Windows format. On Macintosh, you need to press the Option key; on Windows, press the Alt key. (We will not repeat this explanation every time different commands are required for the different operating systems.)

Clicking with the Zoom tool enlarges the view percentage in specific, predefined percentage steps. Pressing Option/Alt while clicking with the Zoom tool reduces the view percentage in the reverse sequence of the same percentages.

Option/Alt-clicking with the Zoom tool reduces the view percent in the predefined sequence of percentages.

When the Zoom tool is active, pressing Option/Alt changes the cursor to the Zoom Out icon.

Note:

You can zoom a document between approximately 0.098% and 3200%. We say approximately because the actual smallest size is dependent on the original image size; you can zoom out far enough to "show" the image as a single tiny square, regardless of what percentage of the image that represents.

10. Click the Hand tool (near the bottom of the Tools panel). Click in the document window, hold down the mouse button, and drag around.

The Hand tool is a very easy and convenient option for changing the area of an image that is currently visible in the document window.

If Scroll All Windows is checked, dragging in one window affects the visible area of all open files.

These four buttons duplicate the same options in the View menu.

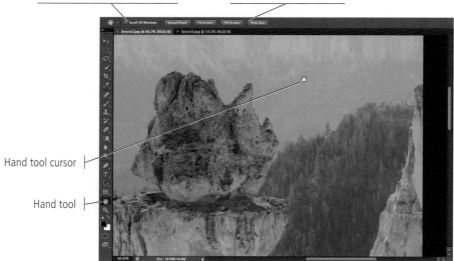

Hand tool cursor

Hand tool

Note:

You can press the Spacebar to access the Hand tool when another tool is active.

11. Click the bryce3.jpg tab to make that document active.

12. **In the Tools panel, choose the Rotate View tool (nested under the Hand tool). Click in the document window and drag right to turn the document clockwise.**

The Rotate View tool turns an image without permanently altering the orientation of the file; the actual image data remains unchanged. This tool allows you to more easily work on objects or elements that are not oriented horizontally (for example, working with text that appears on an angle in the final image).

If you are unable to rotate the image view, your graphics processor does not support OpenGL — a hardware/software combination that makes it possible to work with complex graphics operations. If your computer does not support OpenGL, you will not be able to use a number of Photoshop CS6 features (including the Rotate View tool).

Type a specific angle in this field to rotate the image view.

Click and drag around this icon to rotate the image view.

Clicking Reset View restores the original image orientation.

If Rotate All Windows is checked, dragging in one window affects the view angle of all open files.

Rotate View tool cursor

Rotate View tool

The red arrow of the compass indicates the image's original North.

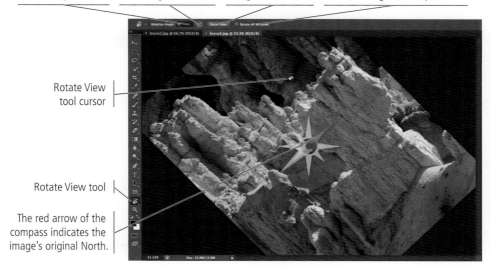

13. **In the Options bar, click the Reset View button.**

As we said, the Rotate View tool is **non-destructive** (i.e., it does not permanently affect the pixels in the image). You can easily use the tool's options to define a specific view angle or to restore an image to its original orientation.

Resetting the view restores the image's original orientation.

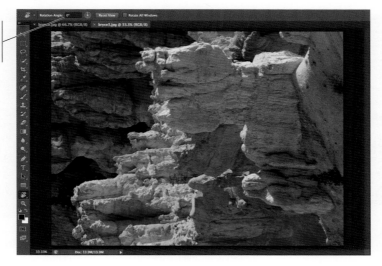

14. **Continue to the next exercise.**

EXPLORE THE ARRANGEMENT OF MULTIPLE DOCUMENTS

You will often need to work with more than one Photoshop file at once. Photoshop incorporates a number of options for arranging multiple documents. We designed the following simple exercise so you can explore these options.

1. **With bryce2.jpg and bryce3.jpg open, choose File>Open.**

   The Open dialog box defaults to the last-used location, so you should not have to navigate back to the WIP>Interface folder.

2. **Click bryce1.jpg in the list to select that file.**

3. **Press Command/Control and click bryce4.jpg to add that file to the active selection.**

   Pressing Command/Control allows you to select and open non-contiguous files.

Note:

All open files are listed at the bottom of the Window menu.

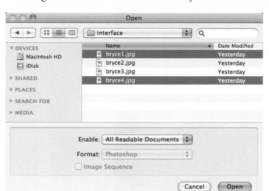

4. **Click Open to open both selected files.**

5. **With bryce4.jpg active, choose Window>Arrange>Float in Window.**

   You can also separate all open files by choosing Window>Arrange>Float All In Windows.

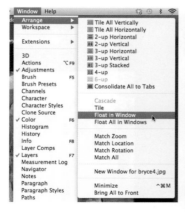

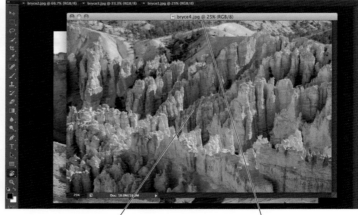

Floating a document separates the file into its own document window.

The title bar of the separate document window shows the same information that was in the document tab.

6. **Choose Window>Arrange>4-up.**

   The defined arrangements provide a number of options for tiling multiple open files within the available workspace. These arrangements manage all open files, including those in floating windows.

   The options' icons suggest the result of each command. The active file remains active; this is indicated by the brighter text in the active document's tab.

Note:

If more files are open than what a specific arrangement indicates, the extra files will be consolidated as tabs into the window with the active file.

7. **Choose Window>Arrange>Consolidate All to Tabs.**

   This command restores all documents — floating or not— into a single tabbed document window.

8. **At the bottom of the Tools panel, click the Change Screen Mode button.**

   Photoshop has three different **screen modes**, which change the way the document window displays on the screen. The default mode, which you saw when you opened these three files, is called Standard Screen mode.

9. **Choose Full Screen Mode with Menu Bar from the Change Screen Mode menu.**

In Full Screen Mode with Menu Bar, the document window fills the entire workspace.

In Full Screen Mode with Menu Bar, the document tabs are hidden behind the Menu bar.

10. **Click the Change Screen Mode button in the Tools panel and choose Full Screen Mode. Read the resulting warning dialog box, and then click Full Screen.**

Move your mouse cursor to the left edge of the screen to temporarily show the Tools panel.

In Full Screen Mode, the Menu bar, title bar, and all panels are hidden.

Move your mouse cursor to the right edge of the screen to temporarily show docked panels.

PHOTOSHOP FOUNDATIONS

Most Photoshop projects require some amount of zooming in and out to various view percentages, as well as navigating around the document within its window. As we show you how to complete different stages of the workflow, we usually won't tell you when to change your view percentage because that's largely a matter of personal preference. However, you should understand the different options for navigating around a Photoshop file so you can easily and efficiently get to what you want, when you want to get there.

View Percentage Field

You can type a specific percentage in the View Percentage field in the bottom-left corner of the document window.

View Menu

The View menu also provides options for changing the view percentage, including the associated keyboard shortcuts. (The Zoom In and Zoom Out options step through the same predefined view percentages that the Zoom tool uses.)

Zoom In	Command/Control-plus (+)
Zoom Out	Command/Control-minus (-)
Fit On Screen	Command/Control-0 (zero)
Actual Pixels (100%)	Command/Control-1

Zoom Tool

You can click with the **Zoom tool** to increase the view percentage in specific, predefined intervals. Pressing Option/Alt with the Zoom tool allows you to zoom out in the same predefined percentages. If you drag a marquee with the Zoom tool, you can zoom into a specific location; the area surrounded by the marquee fills the available space in the document window.

When the Zoom tool is active, you can also activate the Scrubby Zoom option in the Options bar. This allows you to click and drag left to reduce the view percentage, or drag right to increase the view percentage; in this case, the tool does not follow predefined stepped percentages.

Hand Tool

Whatever your view percentage, you can use the **Hand tool** to drag the file around in the document window. The Hand tool changes only what is visible in the window; it has no effect on the actual pixels in the image.

Mouse Scroll Wheel

If your mouse has a scroll wheel, rolling the scroll wheel up or down moves the image up or down within the document window. If you press Command/Control and scroll the wheel, you can move the image left (scroll up) or right (scroll down) within the document window. You can also press Option/Alt and scroll the wheel up to zoom in or scroll the wheel down to zoom out.

(In the General pane of the Preferences dialog box, the Zoom with Scroll Wheel option is unchecked by default. If you check this option, scrolling up or down with no modifier key zooms in or out and does not move the image within the document window.)

Navigator Panel

The **Navigator panel** is another method of adjusting how close your viewpoint is and what part of the page you're currently viewing (if you're zoomed in close enough so you can see only a portion of the page). The Navigator panel shows a thumbnail of the active file; a red rectangle represents exactly how much of the document shows in the document window.

The red rectangle shows the area of the file that is visible in the document window.

Drag the red rectangle to change the visible portion of the file.

Use the slider and field at the bottom of the panel to change the view percentage.

11. Press the Escape key to return to Standard Screen mode.

12. Click the Close button on the bryce4.jpg tab.

When multiple files are open, clicking the Close button on a document tab closes only that file.

13. **Macintosh: Click the Close button in the top-left corner of the Application frame.**

Closing the Macintosh Application frame closes all open files, but does *not* quit the application.

On Macintosh, closing the Application frame closes all files open in that frame.

Windows: Click the Close button on each document tab to close the files.

Clicking the Close button on the Windows Menu bar closes all open files *and* quits the application. To close open files *without* quitting, you have to manually close each file.

Click the Close buttons on each document tab to close the open files.

Clicking the Menu bar Close button closes all open files, and also quits the application.

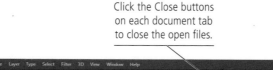

The Undo command (Edit>Undo or Command/Control-Z) only steps back to the last one action you completed; after you use the Undo command, it toggles to Redo. You can also use the Step Backward command (Edit>Step Backward or Command-Option-Z/Control-Alt-Z) to move back in the history one step at a time, or use the History panel (Window>History) to navigate back to earlier stages of your work.

Every action you take is recorded as a state in the History panel. You can click any state to return to that particular point in the document progression. You can also delete specific states or create a new document from a particular state using the buttons at the bottom of the panel.

By default, the History panel stores the last 20 states; older states are automatically deleted. You can change that setting in the Performance pane of the Preferences dialog box. Keep in mind, however, that storing a larger number of states will increase the memory that is required to work with a specific file.

Keep the following in mind when using the History panel:

- The default snapshot shows the image state when it was first opened.

- The oldest state is at the top of the list; the most recent state appears at the bottom.

- The History State slider identifies the active state.

- You can save any particular state as a snapshot to prevent it from being deleted when that state is no longer within the number of states that can be stored.

- The history is only stored as long as the file is open; when you close a file, the history (including snapshots) is not saved.

- When you select a specific state, the states below it are dimmed so you can see which changes will be discarded if you go back to a particular history state.

- Selecting a state and then changing the image eliminates all states that come after it.

- Deleting a state deletes that state and those that came after it. If you choose Allow Non-Linear History in the History Options dialog box (accessed in the History panel Options menu), deleting a state deletes only that state.

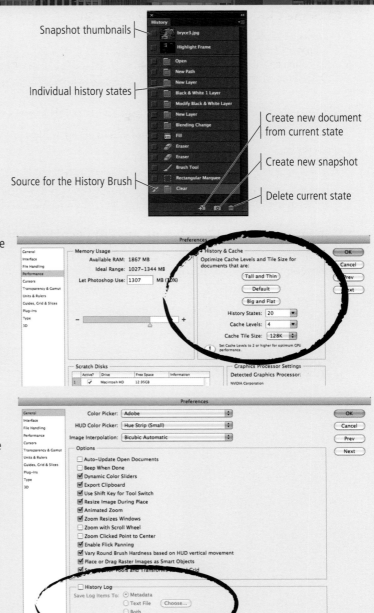

Snapshot thumbnails

Individual history states

Source for the History Brush

Create new document from current state

Create new snapshot

Delete current state

If you need to keep a record of a file's history even after you close the file, you can activate the History Log option in the General pane of the Preferences dialog box. When this option is checked, you can save the history log as metadata, in a text file, or both. You can also determine the level of detail that will be recorded in the history log.

- Sessions Only records each time you launch or quit and each time you open and close individual files.

- Concise adds the text that appears in the History panel to the Sessions information.

- Detailed gives you a complete history of all changes made to files.

Composite Movie Ad

Tantamount Studios, one of the largest film production companies in Hollywood, is developing a new movie called "Aftermath." You have been hired to develop an advertisement that will be used to announce the movie in several different trade magazines.

This project incorporates the following skills:

❑ Creating a single composite ad from multiple supplied images

❑ Compositing multiple photographs, using various techniques to silhouette the focal object in each image

❑ Incorporating vector graphics as rasterized layers and Smart Object layers

❑ Scaling and aligning different objects in relation to the page and to each other

❑ Managing individual layout elements using layers and layer groups

❑ Saving multiple versions of a file to meet different output requirements

client comments

Here's a basic synopsis of the movie:

A massive hurricane, unlike anything ever seen on the West Coast of the United States, takes aim at San Francisco. The category 6 hurricane sparks tidal waves, fires, floods — the resulting destruction dwarfs even the earthquake and fire of 1906. The movie follows the storm survivors through the process of rebuilding, both personally and politically.

This movie is going to be one of our summer blockbusters, and we're throwing a lot of resources behind it. We'll be putting the same ad in multiple magazines, and they all use different software to create the magazine layouts. We need the ad to work for all of our placements, regardless of what software is being used by the magazine publishers.

art director comments

The client loved the initial concept sketch I submitted last week, so we're ready to start building the files. I've had the photographer prepare the images we need, and the client has provided the studio and rating logo files. They also sent me the first two magazines' specs:

Magazine 1

–   Bleed size: 8.75 × 11.25"

–   Trim size: 8.5 × 11"

–   Live area: 8 × 10.5"

–   Files should be submitted as native layout files or layered TIFF

Magazine 2

–   Sizes are the same as Magazine 1

–   Files should be submitted as flattened TIFF or PDF

project objectives

To complete this project, you will:

❑   Resize a raster image to change resolution

❑   Composite multiple images into a single background file

❑   Incorporate both raster and vector elements into the same design

❑   Transform and arrange individual layers to create a cohesive design

❑   Create layer groups to easily manage related layer content

❑   Use selection techniques to isolate images from their backgrounds

❑   Save two different types of TIFF files for different ad requirements

Stage 1 Compositing Images and Artwork

Technically speaking, **compositing** is the process of combining any two or more objects (images, text, illustrations, etc.) into an overall design. When we talk about compositing in Photoshop, we're typically referring to the process of combining multiple images into a single cohesive image. Image compositing might be as simple as placing two images into different areas of a background file; or it could be as complex as placing a person into a group photo, carefully clipping out the individual's background, and adjusting the shadows to match the lighting in the group.

Types of Images

There are two primary types of digital artwork: vector graphics and raster images.

Vector graphics are composed of mathematical descriptions of a series of lines and shapes. Vector graphics are **resolution independent**; they can be freely enlarged or reduced, and they are automatically output at the resolution of the output device. The shapes that you create in Adobe InDesign, or in drawing applications such as Adobe Illustrator, are vector graphics.

Raster images, such as photographs or files created in Adobe Photoshop, are made up of a grid of independent pixels (rasters or bits) in rows and columns (called a **bitmap**). Raster files are **resolution dependent** — their resolution is fixed, determined when you scan, photograph, or otherwise create the file. You can typically reduce raster images, but you cannot enlarge them without losing image quality.

Line art is a type of raster image that is made up entirely of 100% solid areas; the pixels in a line-art image have only two options: they can be all black or all white. Examples of line art are UPC bar codes or pen-and-ink drawings.

Screen Ruling

The ad that you will be building in this project is intended to be placed in print magazines, so you have to build the new file with the appropriate settings for commercial printing. When reproducing a photograph on a printing press, the image must be converted into a set of printable dots that fool the eye into believing it sees continuous tones. Prior to image-editing software, pictures that were being prepared for printing on a press were photographed through a screen to create a grid of halftone dots. The result of this conversion is a halftone image; the dots used to simulate continuous tone are called **halftone dots**. Light tones in a photograph are represented as small halftone dots; dark tones become large halftone dots.

The screens used to create the halftone images had a finite number of available dots in a horizontal or vertical inch. That number was the **screen ruling**, or **lines per inch (lpi)** of the halftone. A screen ruling of 133 lpi means that in a square inch there are 133 × 133 (17,689) possible locations for a halftone dot. If the screen ruling is decreased, there are fewer total halftone dots, producing a grainier image; if the screen ruling is increased, there are more halftone dots, producing a clearer image.

Line screen is a finite number based on a combination of the intended output device and paper. You can't randomly select a line screen. Ask your printer what line screen will be used before you begin creating your images.

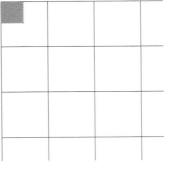
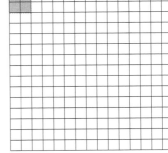

72 ppi   300 ppi

Each white square represents a pixel. The highlighted area shows the pixel information used to generate a halftone dot. If an image only has 72 pixels per inch, the output device has to generate four halftone dots per pixel, resulting in poor printed quality.

If you can't find out ahead of time, or if you're unsure, follow these general guidelines:

- Newspaper or newsprint: 85–100 lpi

- Magazine or general commercial printing: 133–150 lpi

- Premium-quality-paper jobs (such as art books or annual reports): 150–175 lpi; some specialty jobs might use 200 lpi or more

Image Resolution

When a printer creates halftone dots, it calculates the average value of a group of pixels in the raster image and generates a spot of appropriate size. A raster image's resolution — measured in **pixels per inch (ppi)** — determines the quantity of pixel data the printer can read. Regardless of their source — camera, scanner, or files created in Photoshop — images need to have sufficient resolution so the output device can generate enough halftone dots to create the appearance of continuous tone. In the images to the right, the same raster image is reproduced at 300 ppi (top) and 72 ppi (bottom); notice the obvious degradation in quality in the 72-ppi version.

Ideally, the printer will have four pixels for each halftone dot created. The relationship between pixels and halftone dots defines the rule of resolution for raster-based images — the resolution of a raster image (ppi) should be two times the screen ruling (lpi) that will be used for printing.

For line art, the general rule is to scan the image at the same resolution as the output device. Many laser printers and digital presses image at 600–1200 dots per inch (dpi); imagesetters used to make printing plates for a commercial press typically output at much higher resolution, possibly 2400 dpi or more.

OPEN A FILE FROM ADOBE BRIDGE

Adobe Bridge is a stand-alone application that ships and installs along with Photoshop. This asset-management tool enables you to navigate, browse, and manage files anywhere on your system. If you have the entire Adobe Creative Suite, Bridge can also help stream-line the workflow as you flip from one application to another to complete a project.

1. **Download PS6_RF_Project1.zip from the Student Files Web page.**

2. **Expand the ZIP archive in your WIP folder (Macintosh) or copy the archive contents into your WIP folder (Windows).**

   This results in a folder named **Movie**, which contains all of the files you need for this project. You should also use this folder to save the files you create in this project.

   If necessary, refer to Page 1 of the Interface chapter for specific information on expanding or accessing the required resource files.

3. **In Photoshop, open the Mini Bridge panel.**

   If you are working from the default Essentials workspace, the Mini Bridge panel is docked at the bottom of the document window (grouped with the Timeline panel).

   If the Mini Bridge panel is not currently visible, you can open it by choosing Window>Extensions>Mini Bridge.

Note:

Adobe Bridge is a complete stand-alone application. However, this is a book about Photoshop, not Bridge. We're simply introducing you to the Bridge interface and showing you how to use Bridge to navigate and access files. We encourage you to read the Bridge documentation (accessed in the Help menu when you are in the Bridge application).

4. **If you see a Launch Bridge or Reconnect button in the panel, click it to launch the separate Bridge application.**

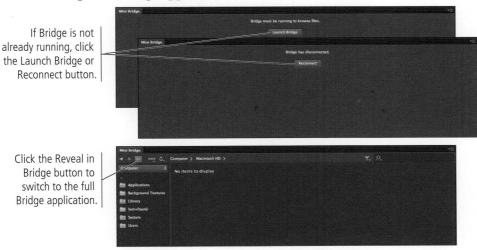

If Bridge is not already running, click the Launch Bridge or Reconnect button.

Click the Reveal in Bridge button to switch to the full Bridge application.

5. **Click the Reveal in Bridge button below the Mini Bridge panel tab.**

6. **In Bridge, use the Folders panel to navigate to your WIP>Movie folder.**

   Bridge is primarily a file manager, so you can think of it as a media browser. If some panels aren't visible, you can access them in the Bridge Window menu.

7. **Click the bricks.jpg thumbnail in the Content panel to select it.**

8. **If you don't see the Metadata panel, choose Window>Metadata. Review the File Properties of the selected image.**

   The most important information in File Properties is the resolution and color mode. This image was photographed at 72 ppi in the RGB color mode. (We explain more about color modes in Project 3: Menu Image Correction.)

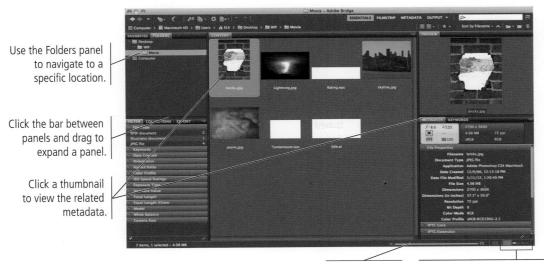

Use the Folders panel to navigate to a specific location.

Click the bar between panels and drag to expand a panel.

Click a thumbnail to view the related metadata.

Drag the slider to change the thumbnail size.

Change the Content panel view to (from left) thumbnail, details, or list view.

9. **Double-click the bricks.jpg thumbnail to open that file in Photoshop.**

   In this case, Bridge is an alternative to the File>Open method for opening files in Photoshop. The Bridge method can be useful because it provides more information than Photoshop's Open dialog box.

10. **If the rulers are not visible on the top and left edges, choose View>Rulers.**

   As you can see in the rulers, this image has a very large physical size. As you saw in the image metadata (in Bridge), however, the current image is only 72 ppi; for commercial printing, you need at least 300 ppi. You can use the principle of **effective resolution** to change the file to a high enough resolution for printing.

Note:

We are intentionally overlooking issues of color space for the sake of this project. You will learn about color spaces and color management in Project 3: Menu Image Correction.

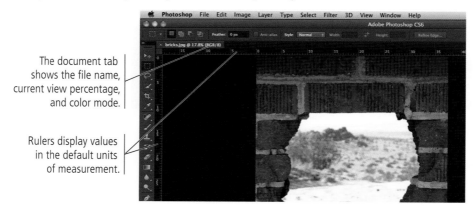

The document tab shows the file name, current view percentage, and color mode.

Rulers display values in the default units of measurement.

Note:

Although designers trained in traditional (non-digital) methods are sometimes comfortable talking about picas or ciceros, most people use inches as the standard unit of measurement in the U.S.

You can change the default unit of measurement in the Units & Rulers pane of the Preferences dialog box. Double-clicking either ruler opens the appropriate pane of the Preferences dialog box.

11. **Choose File>Save As. If necessary, navigate to your WIP>Movie folder as the target location. Change the file name (in the Save As field) to aftermath.**

   Since this is a basic image file with only one layer (so far), most of the other options in the Save As dialog box are grayed out (not available).

12. **Choose Photoshop in the Format menu and then click Save.**

   You can save a Photoshop file in a number of different formats, all of which have specific capabilities, limitations, and purposes. While you are still working on a file, it's best to keep it as a native Photoshop (PSD) file. When you choose a different format, the correct extension is automatically added to the file name.

Files saved in the native Photoshop format display a ".psd" extension.

Note:

Also called "native", the PSD format is the most flexible format to use while building files in Photoshop.

13. **Continue to the next exercise.**

You can control a number of options related to saving files in the File Handling pane of the Preferences dialog box.

Image Previews. You can use this menu to always or never include image thumbnails in the saved file. If you choose Ask When Saving in this menu, the Save As dialog box includes an option to include the image preview/thumbnail.

On Macintosh, you have two additional options: Icon and Windows Thumbnail. You can check the Icon option to show the image thumbnail in the Open dialog box and Finder (instead of the default Photoshop file icon). Although Macintosh can almost always read Windows information, Windows sometimes has trouble with certain Macintosh data — specifically, file thumbnails; you can check the Windows Thumbnail option to include a thumbnail that will be visible in the Windows Open dialog box.

Append File Extension. On Macintosh, you can use this menu to always or never include the file extension in the saved file. If the Ask When Saving option is selected in this menu, the Save As dialog box includes options to append the file extension (in lower case or not). On Windows, file extensions are always added to saved files; this preference menu has only two options: Use Upper Case and Use Lower Case.

Macintosh

Windows

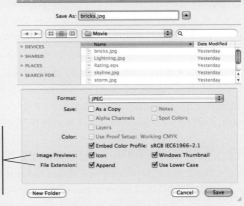

If Ask When Saving is selected in the File Handling preferences, the Save As dialog box presents options to include Image Previews and File Extension.

Save As to Original Folder. When this option is checked, choosing File>Save As automatically defaults to the location where the original file is located.

Save in Background. In Photoshop CS6, the Save process occurs by default in the background — in other words, you can continue working even while a file is being saved. In previous versions, you could not interact with the application while a file was being saved. Especially when you work with large files, this can be a significant time saver because you don't have to sit and wait the several minutes it might take to save a very large file. (The only thing you can't do while a file is being saved is use the Save As command; if you try, you will see a warning advising you to wait until the background save is complete.)

When a file is being saved in the background, the completed percentage appears in the document tab.

Automatically Save Recovery Information Every... This new feature in Photoshop CS6 means that your work is being saved in a temporary file, every 10 minutes by default; if something happens — an application crash or power outage, for example — you will be able to restore your work back to the last auto-saved version. In other words, the most you will lose is 10 minutes' work!

Every raster image has a defined, specific resolution that is established when the image is created. If you scan an image to be 3″ high by 3″ wide at 150 ppi, that image has 450 pixels in each vertical column and 450 pixels in each horizontal row. Simply resizing the image stretches or compresses those pixels into a different physical space, but does not add or remove pixel information. If you resize the 3 × 3″ image to 6 × 6″ (200% of the original), the 450 pixels in each column or row are forced to extend across 6″ instead of 3″, causing a marked loss of quality.

The **effective resolution** of an image is the resolution calculated after any scaling is taken into account. This number is equally important as the original image resolution — and perhaps moreso. The effective resolution can be calculated with a fairly simple equation:

Original resolution ÷ (% magnification ÷ 100) = Effective resolution

If a 300-ppi image is magnified 150%, the effective resolution is:

300 ppi ÷ 1.5 = 200 ppi

In other words, the more you enlarge a raster image, the lower its effective resolution becomes. In general, you can make an image 10% or 15% larger without significant adverse effects; the more you enlarge an image, however, the worse the results. Even Photoshop, which offers very sophisticated formulas (called "algorithms") for sizing images, cannot guarantee perfect results.

Effective resolution can be a very important consideration when working with client-supplied images, especially those that come from consumer-level digital cameras. Many of those devices capture images with a specific number of pixels rather than a number of pixels per inch (ppi). In this exercise, you will explore the effective resolution of an image to see if it can be used for a full-page printed magazine ad.

1. **With aftermath.psd open, choose Image>Image Size.**

   The Image Size dialog box shows the number of pixels in the image, as well as the image dimensions and current resolution. You can change any value in this dialog box, but you should understand what those changes mean before you do so.

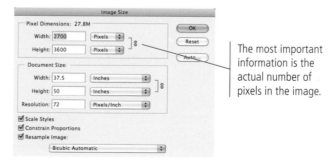

The most important information is the actual number of pixels in the image.

2. **Check the Resample Image option at the bottom of the dialog box.**

   The options in this dialog box remember the last-used choices. The Resample option might already be checked in your dialog box.

   Resampling means maintaining the existing resolution in the new image dimensions; in other words, you are either adding or deleting pixels to the existing image. When this option is turned on, you can change the dimensions of an image without affecting the resolution, or you can change the resolution of an image (useful for removing excess resolution or **downsampling**) without affecting the image size.

3. **Change the Resolution field to 300 pixels/inch.**

When you change the resolution with resampling turned on, you do not change the file's physical size. To achieve 300-ppi resolution at the new size, Photoshop needs to add a huge number of pixels to the image. You can see at the top of the dialog box that this change would increase the total number of pixels from 2700 × 3600 to 11250 × 15000.

You can also see that changing the resolution of an image without affecting its physical dimensions would have a significant impact on the file size. Changing the resolution to 300 ppi at the current size would increase the file size to nearly 483 megabytes.

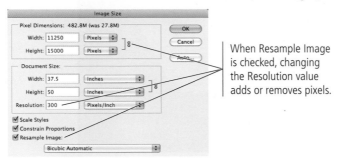

When Resample Image is checked, changing the Resolution value adds or removes pixels.

4. **Press Option/Alt and click the Reset button to restore the original image dimensions in the dialog box.**

In many Photoshop dialog boxes, pressing the Option/Alt key changes the Cancel button to Reset. You can click the Reset button to restore the original values that existed when you opened the dialog box.

Pressing Option/Alt changes the Cancel button to Reset.

5. **Uncheck the Resample Image option at the bottom of the dialog box.**

6. **Change the Resolution field to 300 pixels/inch.**

Resizing *without* resampling basically means distributing the same number of pixels over a different amount of physical space. When you resize an image without resampling, you do not change the number of pixels in the image. (In fact, those fields in the dialog box become simple text; the fields are unavailable and you cannot change the number of pixels in the image.)

You can see how changing one of the linked fields (Resolution) directly affects the other linked fields (Width and Height). By resizing the image to be 300 ppi — enough for commercial print quality — you now have an image that is 9″ × 12″.

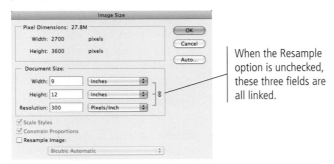

When the Resample option is unchecked, these three fields are all linked.

7. **Click OK to apply the change and return to the document window.**

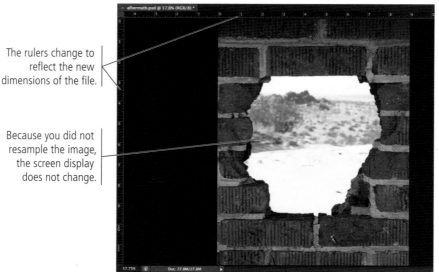

The rulers change to reflect the new dimensions of the file.

Because you did not resample the image, the screen display does not change.

8. **Save the file and continue to the next exercise.**

Because you have already saved this working file with a new name, you can simply choose File>Save, or press Command/Control-S to save without opening a dialog box. If you want to change the file name, you can always choose File>Save As.

More on Resolution and Resampling

PHOTOSHOP FOUNDATIONS

Discarding Pixels

Higher resolution means larger file sizes, which translates to longer processing time for printing or longer download time over the Internet. When you scale an image to a smaller size, simply resizing can produce files with far greater effective resolution than you need. Resampling allows you to reduce the physical size of an image without increasing the resolution, resulting in a smaller file size.

The caveat here is that once you discard (delete) pixels, they are gone. If you later try to re-enlarge the smaller image, you will not achieve the same quality as the original (before it was reduced). You should always save reduced images as copies instead of overwriting the originals.

Resampling

In general, you should always scan images to the size you will use in your final job. If you absolutely must resize a digital image, you can use resampling to achieve better results than simply changing the image size. Photoshop offers five types of resampling algorithms to generate extra pixel data (when increasing the image size) or to determine which pixels to discard (when reducing the image size).

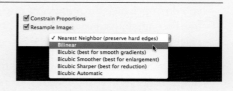

- **Nearest Neighbor** is a low-quality but quick method. Nearest neighbor interpolates new pixel information based on only one of the squares in the grid of pixels, usually resulting in an image with a blocky appearance.
- **Bilinear** is a medium-quality resampling method. Bilinear resampling averages adjacent pixels to create new information.
- **Bicubic** creates the most accurate pixel information for continuous-tone images; it also takes the longest

to process and produces a softer image. To understand how this option works, think of a square bisected both horizontally and vertically — bicubic resampling averages the value of all four of those squares (pixels) to interpolate the new information.

- **Bicubic Smoother** is useful for enlarging images with smoother results than basic bicubic resampling.
- **Bicubic Sharper** is useful for reducing the size of an image and maintaining sharp detail.

CROP THE CANVAS AND PLACE RULER GUIDES

The final step in preparing the workspace is defining the live area of the page. **Trim size** is the actual size of a page once it has been cut out of the press sheet. According to your client, the magazine has a trim size of 8.5″ × 11″.

Any elements that print right to the edge of a page (called **bleeding**) must actually extend beyond the defined trim size. The **bleed allowance** is the amount of extra space that should be included for these bleed objects; most applications require at least 1/8″ bleed allowance on any bleed edge.

Because of inherent variation in the mechanical printing and trimming processes, most magazines also define a safe or **live area**; all important design elements (especially text) should stay within this live area. The live area for this project is 8 × 10.5″.

Note:

You should familiarize yourself with the most common fraction-to-decimal equivalents:

1/8 = 0.125

1/4 = 0.25

3/8 = 0.375

1/2 = 0.5

5/8 = 0.625

3/4 = 0.75

7/8 = 0.875

1. **With aftermath.psd open, choose the Crop tool in the Tools panel.**

    When you choose the Crop tool, a crop marquee appears around the edges of the image. The marquee has eight handles, which you can drag to change the size of the cropped area.

Set Additional Crop Options

Crop tool

Marquee handles allow you to resize the crop area before finalizing the crop.

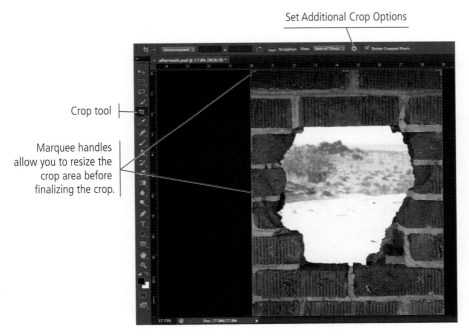

Note:

You can press the Escape key to cancel the crop marquee and return to the uncropped image.

Note:

You can rotate a crop marquee by placing the cursor slightly away from a corner handle.

2. **In the Options bar, make sure Unconstrained is selected in the left menu, and check the Delete Cropped Pixels option.**

    The menu on the left end of the Options bar can be used to define a specific aspect ratio for the cropped area (see Page 35).

    If the Delete Cropped Pixels option is checked, areas outside the cropped areas are permanently removed from all layers in the file. If this option is not checked, cropped pixels remain in the file, but exist outside the edges of the file canvas. The Background layer, if one exists, is converted to a regular layer (you'll learn more about Background layers later in this project).

    This is an important distinction — by maintaining cropped pixels, you can later transform or reposition layers to reveal different parts of the layer within the newly cropped canvas size.

3. **Click the right-center handle of the crop marquee and drag left until the cursor feedback shows W: 8.750 in.**

When you drag certain elements in the document window, live cursor feedback (also called "heads-up display") shows information about the tranformation. When dragging a side crop marquee handle, for example, the feedback shows the new width of the area.

You might need to zoom into at least 66.7% view percentage to achieve the exact dimensions needed for this project.

Note:

If rulers are not still visible, choose View>Rulers or press Command/Control-R.

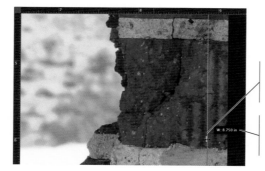

Click and drag the marquee handle to resize the marquee area.

Use the cursor feedback to find the appropriate measurement.

4. **Repeat Step 3 with the bottom-center handle until feedback shows the area of H: 11.250 in.**

Remember, the defined trim size for this ad is 8.5″ × 11″. Anything that runs to the page edge has to incorporate a 0.125″ bleed allowance, so the actual canvas size must be large enough to accommodate the bleed allowance on all edges:

[Width]   8.5″ + 0.125″ + 0.125″ = 8.75

[Height]   11″ + 0.125″ + 0.125″ = 11.25

The Crop Tools in Depth

When the Crop tool is selected, the Options bar can be used to define a number of settings related to the cropped area.

The left menu includes a number of common aspect ratios as presets. If you choose one of these options, the crop marquee is constrained to the aspect ratio defined in the preset. It's important to note that these presets do not define the actual size of the resulting crop, only the aspect ratio.

You can also choose the **Size and Resolution** option to define custom settings for the result of a crop. For example, if you define the width and height of a crop area as 9″ × 9″ at 300 ppi, when you click and drag to draw, the crop area will be restricted to the same proportions defined in the Width and Height fields (in this example, 1:1).

When you finalize the crop, the resulting image will be resized to be 9″ × 9″, regardless of the actual size of the crop marquee. This presents a problem if you remember the principles of resolution.

Enlarging a 3″ × 3″ area (for example) to 9″ × 9″ means the application needs to create enough pixels to fill in the 6 extra inches — at 300 ppi, Photoshop needs to create ("interpolate") more than 1800 pixels per linear inch. Although Photoshop can slightly enlarge images with reasonable success, such a significant amount of new data will not result in good quality. As a general rule, you should avoid enlarging raster images, and certainly no more than about 10%.

The crop area is constrained to the aspect ratio of the defined width and height.

The resulting cropped image is the actual size defined in the Crop Image Size & Resolution dialog box.

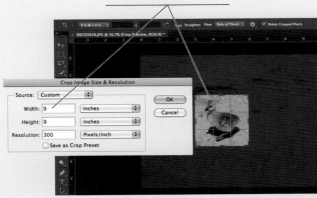

You can use the **View menu** to show a variety of overlays within the crop area; these follow basic design principles, such as the Rule of Thirds and the Golden Spiral.

You can also use the commands in this menu to turn the overlay on or off. If you choose Auto Show Overlay, the selected overlay only appears when you drag the marquee handles or click inside the marquee area to move the image inside the crop area.

You can also click the **Set Additional Crop Options** button to access a variety of crop-related choices.

- If you check the **Use Classic Mode** option, the crop marquee reverts to the same appearance and behavior as in previous versions of Photoshop.

- When **Auto Center Preview** is checked, the crop area will always be centered inthe document window; the image dynamically moves in the document window as you resize the crop area.

- When **Show Cropped Area** is checked, the area outside the crop marquee remains visible in the document window until you finalize the crop.

- When **Enable Crop Shield** is checked, areas outside the crop marquee are partially obscured by a semi-transparent solid color. You can use the related options to change the color and opacity of the shielded area.

When the Crop tool is selected, you can click the **Straighten** button in the Options bar and then draw a line in the image to define what should be a straight line in the resulting image. The image behind the crop marquee rotates to show what will remain in the cropped canvas; the line you drew is adjusted to be perfectly horizontal or vertical.

Click the Straighten button, then draw a line representing what you want to be "straight" in the cropped image.

The image is rotated behind the crop marquee to be "straight" based on the line you drew.

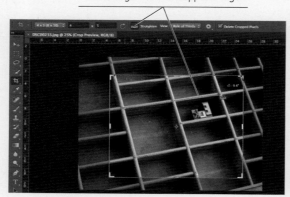

The **Perspective Crop tool** (nested under the Crop tool) can be used to draw a non-rectangular crop area. To define the area you want to keep, simply click to place the four corners of the area, then drag the corners in any direction as necessary. When you finalize the crop, the image inside the crop area is straightened to a front-on viewing angle. You should use this option with care, however, because it can badly distort an image.

In this first example, we used the actual lines in the photograph to draw the perspective crop marquee. After finalizing the crop, the type case appears to be perfectly straight rather than the original viewing angle at which it was photographed.

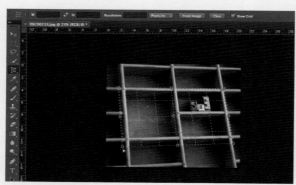
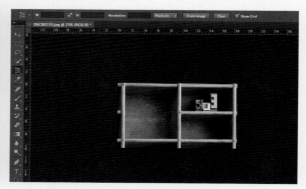

In this second example, we used the Perspective Crop tool to try to adjust the photograph of an historic hop kiln. You can see the obvious distortion in the resulting image.

5. **Click inside the crop area and drag to reposition the image so it is approximately centered in the crop area.**

When you change the size of the marquee, the area outside the marquee is "shielded" by a darkened overlay so you can get an idea of what will remain after you finalize the crop.

You can drag the image inside the crop area to change the portion that will remain in the cropped image. By default, the crop area remains centered in the document window; instead, the image moves behind the crop area.

Note:

You can also use the Arrow keys on your keyboard to "nudge" the image in a specific direction.

You can click inside the crop area to drag the area without changing its size.

By default, the crop marquee remains centered in the document window.

Areas outside the crop marquee are darkened.

The image moves behind the marquee to show which section will be inside the cropped area.

Note:

It might be helpful to toggle off the Snap feature (View>Snap), which causes certain file elements to act as magnets when you move a marquee or drag a selection.

6. **Press Return/Enter to finalize the crop.**

7. **Choose the Move tool, and then open the Info panel (Window>Info).**

As we explained in the Interface chapter, the panels you see depend on what was done the last time you (or someone else) used the Photoshop application. Because workspace arrangement is such a personal preference, we tell you what panels you need to use but we don't tell you where to put them.

Note:

Remember: panels can always be accessed in the Window menu.

8. **Click the horizontal page ruler at the top of the page and drag down to create a guide positioned at the 1/8″ (0.125″) mark.**

If you watch the vertical ruler, you can see a marker indicating the position of the cursor. In addition to the live cursor feedback, the Info panel also shows the precise numeric position of the guide you are dragging.

Here again, it helps to zoom in to a higher view percentage if you want to precisely place guides. We found it necessary to use at least 66.7% view before the Info panel reflected exactly the 0.125″ position. If you zoom in, you can press the Spacebar to temporarily access the Hand tool to reposition the image so you can see the top-left corner.

Note:

If rulers are not visble, choose View>Rulers or press Command/ Control-R.

Note:

The X coordinate refers to an object's horizontal position and Y refers to the vertical position.

Click and drag from the horizontal ruler to add a horizontal guide.

The blue line indicates the location of the guide you're dragging.

Watch the ruler or cursor feedback to see the location of the guide you're dragging.

The Info panel shows the exact Y location of the guide you're dragging.

9. **Click the vertical ruler at the left and drag right to place a guide at the 0.125″ mark.**

   Watch the marker on the horizontal ruler to judge the guide's position.

   Drag from the
   vertical ruler to add
   a vertical guide.

   The cursor feedback and
   Info panel show the
   exact X location of the
   guide you're dragging.

   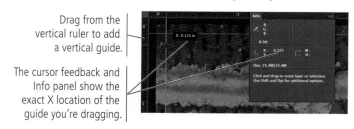

Note:

Use the Move tool to reposition placed guides. Remove individual guides by dragging them back onto the ruler.

If you try to reposition a guide and can't, choose View>Lock Guides. If this option is checked, guides are locked; you can't move them until you toggle this option off.

10. **Choose View>New Guide. In the resulting dialog box, choose the Vertical option and type 8.625 in the field and click OK.**

    You don't need to type the unit of measurement because the default unit for this file is already inches. Photoshop automatically assumes the value you type is in the default unit of measurement.

    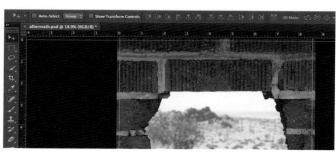

11. **Choose View>New Guide again. Choose the Horizontal option and type 11.125 in the field. Click OK.**

    At this point you should have four guides – two vertical and two horizontal, each 1/8″ from the file edges. These mark the trim size of your final 8.5 × 11″ file.

    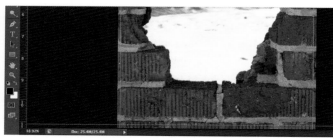

Note:

Press Option/Alt and click a guide to change it from vertical to horizontal (or vice versa). The guide rotates around the point where you click, which can be useful if you need to find a corner based on the position of an existing guide.

12. **In the top-left corner of the document window, click the zero-point crosshairs and drag to the top-left intersection of the guides.**

    You can reposition the zero point to the top-left corner of the bleed allowance by double-clicking the zero-point crosshairs.

    Zero-point crosshairs

    Drag to here to change the
    0/0 point of the rulers. This
    new zero point will be the
    origin for measurements
    you make in this file.

    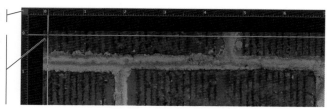

13. **Drag new guides 0.25″ inside each trim guide to mark the live area of the page.**

These guides mark the defined live area of the ad (8 × 10.5″). This is how we determined where to put these guides:

[Width]   8.5″ − 8.0″ = 0.5 ÷ 2 = 0.25″

[Height]   11″ − 10.5″ = 0.5″ ÷ 2 = 0.25″

Notice that this step says "drag new guides". It is important to realize that the View>New Guide dialog box always positions guides from the original document zero-point (top-left corner); If you use that method, you would have to place the guides 0.375″ from each edge of the file — 0.125″ for the existing bleed guide plus 0.25″ for the live area.

The live cursor feedback is also subject to this limitation. When you drag guides, the feedback always shows measurements based on the original zero point. The Info panel, however, correctly shows measurements based on the repositioned zero point.

Cursor feedback shows measurements based on the original zero point.

The Info panel shows measurements based on the repositioned zero point.

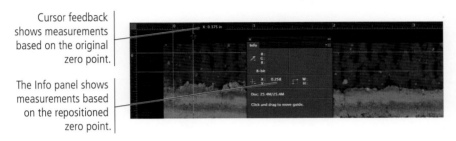

14. **Click the View menu and make sure a checkmark appears to the left of Lock Guides. If no checkmark is there, choose Lock Guides to toggle on that option.**

After you carefully position specific guides, it's a good idea to lock them so you don't accidentally move or delete them later. If you need to move a guide at any point, simply choose View>Lock Guides to toggle off the option temporarily.

The outside guides mark the trim edge.

The inside guides mark the live area.

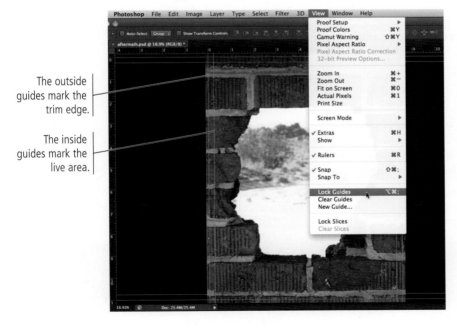

Note:

You can press Command/ Control-; to toggle the visibility of page guides.

15. **Save the file and continue to the next exercise.**

DRAG A FILE TO COMPOSITE IMAGES

Compositing multiple images in Photoshop is a fairly simple process — or at least, it starts out that way. There are, of course, a number of technical and aesthetic issues that you must resolve when you combine multiple images in a single design.

1. **With aftermath.psd open, use the Mini Bridge panel to navigate back to the Bridge application.**

2. **Click the storm.jpg thumbnail, then review the metadata for that file.**

    This image is only 180 ppi, but it has a physical size much larger than the defined ad size. The principle of effective resolution might make this image usable in the composite ad.

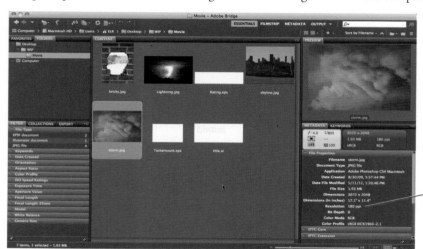

The storm.jpg image is 180 ppi.

3. **Double-click the storm.jpg thumbnail to open that file in Photoshop.**

4. **Open the Window>Arrange menu and choose 2-up (Vertical) to show both open files at one time.**

    As you saw in the Interface chapter, these options are useful for arranging and viewing multiple open files within your workspace.

5. **Choose the Move tool in the Tools panel.**

6. **Click in the storm.jpg image window and drag into the aftermath.psd image window, then release the mouse button.**

    Basic compositing can be as simple as dragging a selection from one file to another. If no active selection appears in the source document, this action moves the entire active layer from the source document.

Move tool

The outline shows the shape of the layer you're dragging from one document to another.

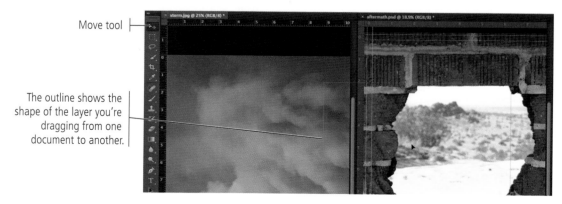

7. **Click the Close button on the storm.jpg document tab to close that file.**

   After closing the storm file, the aftermath.psd document window expands to fill the available space.

   If you remember from the Bridge metadata, the storm image was 17.1″ × 11.4″ at 180 ppi. Photoshop cannot maintain multiple resolutions in a single file. When you move the image content into the aftermath file, it adopts the resolution of the target file (in this case, 300 ppi). The concept of effective resolution transforms the storm image/layer to approximately 10.25″ × 6.825″ at 300 ppi.

8. **Open the Layers panel (Window>Layers).**

   The original aftermath.psd file had only one layer — Background. Before editing, every scan and digital photograph has this characteristic. When you copy or drag content from one file into another, it is automatically placed on a new layer with the default name "Layer *n*", where "n" is a sequential number.

When a file contains more than one layer, the document tab shows the name of the active layer.

A new layer (Layer 1) is automatically added to contain the contents that you dragged from the storm.jpg file.

The Background layer contains the original bricks file content.

9. **Choose File>Save, and read the resulting message.**

   Because this is the first time you have saved the file after adding new layers, you should see the Photoshop Format Options dialog box, with the Maximize Compatibility check box already activated. It's a good idea to leave this check box selected so your files will be compatible with other CS6 applications and other versions of Photoshop.

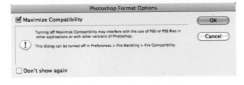

Note:

If you don't see this warning, check the File Handling pane of the Preferences dialog box. You can set the Maximize PSD and PSB File Compatibility menu to Always, Never, or Ask.

10. **Make sure the Maximize Compatibility check box is selected and click OK.**

11. **Continue to the next exercise.**

OPEN FILES WITH MINI BRIDGE

Mini Bridge provides access to certain file-management operations of the full Bridge application, from a panel directly within Photoshop.

1. **With** `aftermath.psd` **open, choose View>Fit on Screen to show the entire image centered in the document window.**

2. **If necessary, open the Mini Bridge panel.**

3. **In the Mini Bridge panel, click the arrow to the right of Computer to open the list of available folders. Use these arrows to navigate to the location of your WIP>Movie folder.**

   Once you find the Movie folder, the images in the folder appear in the primary area of the panel.

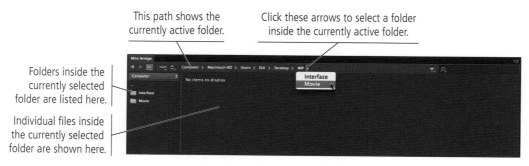

This path shows the currently active folder.

Click these arrows to select a folder inside the currently active folder.

Folders inside the currently selected folder are listed here.

Individual files inside the currently selected folder are shown here.

4. **Scroll through the thumbnails (if necessary), and double-click the** `skyline.jpg` **image thumbnail to open that file.**

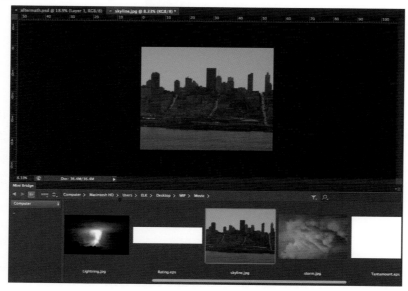

Note:

As in the full Bridge application, double-clicking a file in the Mini Bridge panel opens that file in a separate document window.

5. **Open the Image Size dialog box (Image>Image Size). Make sure the Resample Image option is not checked and change the Resolution field to 300 ppi. Click OK to return to the document window.**

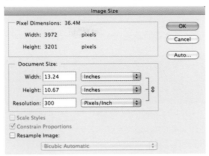

6. **Choose the Rectangular Marquee tool in the Tools panel and review the options in the Options bar.**

By default, dragging with a marquee tool creates a new selection. You can use the buttons on the left end of the Options bar to add to the current selection, subtract from the current selection, or intersect with the current selection.

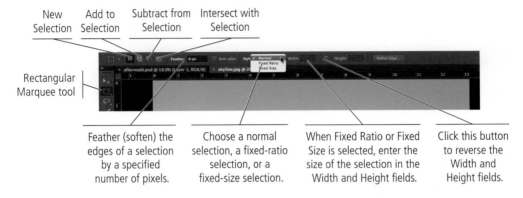

New Selection

Add to Selection

Subtract from Selection

Intersect with Selection

Rectangular Marquee tool

Feather (soften) the edges of a selection by a specified number of pixels.

Choose a normal selection, a fixed-ratio selection, or a fixed-size selection.

When Fixed Ratio or Fixed Size is selected, enter the size of the selection in the Width and Height fields.

Click this button to reverse the Width and Height fields.

7. **Choose the New Selection option in the Options bar. Click outside of the top-left corner, drag down past the bottom edge of the image, and drag right to create a selection area that is 8.5″ wide.**

You can't select an area larger than the current canvas, so the top, left, and bottom edges of the selection snap to the canvas edges. The live cursor feedback, as well as the mark on the horizontal ruler, help to determine the selection area's width.

Note:

The edges of this image will be hidden by the bricks, so you don't need the full 8.75″ width of the overall ad.

Note:

Press Shift while dragging a new marquee to constrain the selection to a square (using the Rectangular Marquee tool) or circle (using the Elliptical Marquee tool).

Selection marquee

Rectangular Marquee tool cursor

8. **Click inside the selection marquee and drag it to the approximate center of the image.**

   You can move a selection marquee by clicking inside the selected area with the Marquee tool and dragging to the desired area of the image.

   The live cursor feedback shows how far you have moved the area.

The Marquee tool is still active.

"Marching ants" identify the selected area.

Click inside the selection marquee and drag to reposition it.

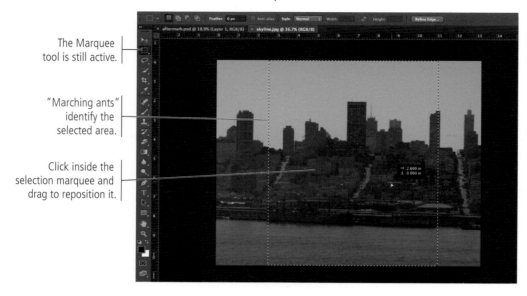

Note:

If you want to move a marquee, make sure the Marquee tool is still selected. If the Move tool is active, clicking inside the marquee and dragging will actually move the contents within the selection area.

9. **In the Options bar, choose the Subtract from Selection option.**

10. **Click near the waterline at the left edge of the existing selection, drag down past the bottom edge of the image, and right past the right edge of the existing selection.**

Note:

Press Shift to add to the current selection or press Option/Alt to subtract from the current selection.

Subtract from Selection is active.

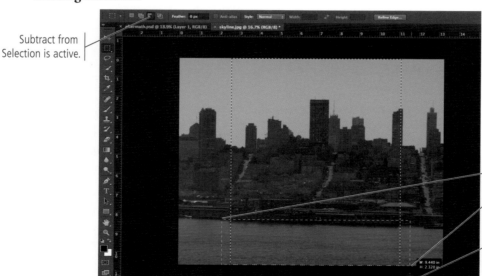

Click here...

...and drag to here.

The cursor shows a minus sign because you are subtracting from the existing selection.

You only want the city to appear in the ad, so you don't need the water area of this image. When you release the mouse button, the selection is the area of the first marquee, minus the area of the second marquee. (This two-step process isn't particularly necessary in this case, but you should know how to add to and subtract from selections.)

11. **Choose Edit>Copy.**

    The standard Cut, Copy, and Paste options are available in Photoshop, just as they are in most applications. Whatever you have selected will be copied to the Clipboard, and whatever is in the Clipboard will be pasted.

12. **Click the Close button on the skyline.jpg document tab to close the file. When asked, click Don't Save.**

    Although the city would have adopted the resolution of the composite file, you manually resized the image so you could see the appropriate measurements for making your selection. You don't need to save this change.

13. **With the aftermath.psd file active, choose Edit>Paste.**

    The copied selection is pasted in the center of the document window. Because you used the Fit on Screen option at the beginning of this exercise, the pasted image is centered in the document. Another new layer is automatically created to store the pasted content.

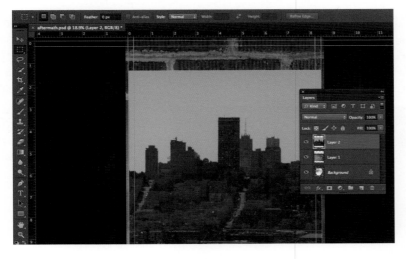

14. **Save the file and continue to the next exercise.**

PLACE A FILE FROM MINI BRIDGE

In addition to opening new files, you can also use the Mini Bridge panel to place content directly into an open file. This removes a few steps from the process of compositing multiple images.

1. **With aftermath.psd open, choose View>Fit on Screen.**

2. **In the Mini Bridge panel, navigate to the WIP>Movie folder if necessary.**

3. **Click the Lightning.jpg thumbnail in the panel and drag it to the aftermath.psd document window.**

   The placed file appears with bounding box handles and crossed diagonal lines. The placement isn't final until you press Return/Enter; if you press the Escape key, the file will not be placed.

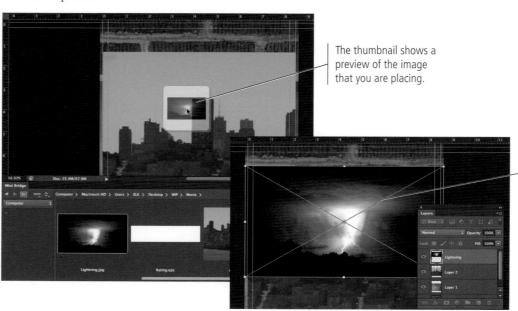

The thumbnail shows a preview of the image that you are placing.

Crossed diagonal lines and bounding box handles indicate that the placement is not yet final.

4. **Press Return/Enter to finalize the placement.**

   After you finalize the placement, the bounding box handles and crossed diagonal lines disappear. In the Layers panel, the placed file has its own layer (just as the copied layers do). This layer, however, is automatically named, based on the name of the placed file.

   The layer's thumbnail indicates that this layer is a **Smart Object** — it is linked to the file that you placed. Changes in the original file will also be reflected in the file where the original is placed. (You will work extensively with Smart Objects in Project 2: African Wildlife Map)

Note:

You can place either raster or vector files as Smart Objects. If you place a raster file as a Smart Object, double-clicking the thumbnail opens the placed raster file in another Photoshop window.

The layer adopts the name of the placed file.

This icon identifies a Smart Object layer.

5. Control/right-click the Smart Object layer name and choose Rasterize Layer.

You don't need to maintain a link to the original file, so this step converts the Smart Object layer to a regular layer.

Control/right-click the layer name to access the contextual menu for that layer.

The Lightning layer is now a regular layer.

6. Save the file and continue to the next exercise.

RASTERIZE A VECTOR FILE

As you learned earlier, vector graphics are based on a series of mathematical descriptions that tell the computer processor where to draw lines. Logos and title treatments — such as the ones you will use in this project — are commonly created as vector graphics. Although Photoshop is typically a "paint" (pixel-based) application, you can also open and work with vector graphics created in illustration programs like Adobe Illustrator.

1. With aftermath.psd open, choose File>Open and navigate to your WIP>Movie folder.

2. Select title.ai in the list of files and then click Open.

This is an Adobe Illustrator file of the movie title text treatment. The Format menu defaults to Photoshop PDF because Illustrator uses PDF as its underlying file structure.

When you open a vector file (Illustrator, EPS, or PDF) in Photoshop, it is rasterized (converted to a raster graphic). The Import PDF dialog box allows you to determine exactly what and how to rasterize the file. The default values in this box are defined by the contents of the file you're opening.

The Crop To options determine the size of the opened file. Depending on how the file was created, some of these values might be the same as others:

- **Bounding Box** is the outermost edges of the artwork in the file.
- **Media Box** is the size of the paper as defined in the file.
- **Crop Box** is the size of the page including printer's marks.
- **Bleed Box** is the trim size plus any defined bleed allowance.
- **Trim Box** is the trim size as defined in the file.
- **Art Box** is the area of the page as defined in the file.

3. **Highlight the Width field and type 8, and make sure the Resolution field is set to 300 pixels/inch.**

You know the live area of the ad you're building is 8″ wide, so you can import this file at a size small enough to fit into that space. Because the Constrain Proportions option is checked by default, the height changes proportionally to match the new width.

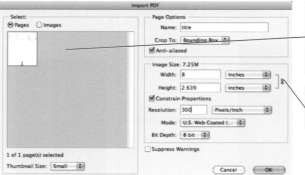

If you're opening a multi-page PDF or an Illustrator file with more than one artboard, this window shows previews of each "page" in the file.

When this chain icon appears, the width and height are constrained.

4. **Click OK.**

The title treatment file opens in Photoshop. The checkered area behind the text indicates that the background is transparent. If you look at the Layers panel, you will see that Layer 1 isn't locked; because it's transparent, it is not considered a background layer.

5. **Choose Select>All.**

This command creates a marquee for the entire canvas.

The gray-and-white checked pattern identifies areas of transparency in the layer content.

Using the Select>All command surrounds the entire canvas in a selection marquee.

6. **Choose Edit>Copy, then click the Close button on the title document tab to close that file. Click Don't Save when asked.**

7. **With the aftermath.psd file active, choose Edit>Paste.**

Note:

Command/Control-clicking a layer thumbnail results in a selection around the contents of that layer.

8. **Save aftermath.psd and continue to the next exercise.**

PLACE MULTIPLE EPS GRAPHICS

Vector graphics offer several advantages over raster images, including sharper edges and free scaling without deteriorating image quality. To take advantage of these benefits, you might want to maintain vector files as vector objects instead of rasterizing them. Photoshop CS6 gives you the option to do exactly that — maintaining vector information and raster information in the same file.

1. **With aftermath.psd open, open the Mini Bridge panel (Window> Extensions>Mini Bridge) if the panel is not already open.**

2. **Click the Rating.eps thumbnail to select it.**

3. **Press Command/Control and then click the Tantamount.eps file to add it to the active selection.**

    These vector graphics were created in Adobe Illustrator and saved as EPS files. (The EPS format supports both raster and vector information, however, so don't assume that an EPS file always contains only vector information.)

4. **Click either of the selected thumbnails and drag into the aftermath.psd image window to place both files.**

    Unlike opening or placing a native Illustrator file, there are no further options when you place an EPS file.

Note:

If you place a native Illustrator file from the Mini Bridge panel, you can define the Crop To area for the placement, but you can't access any of the other options that are available when you open an Illustrator file.

The cursor icon shows how many files are being placed.

Press Command/Control to select non-contiguous files in the panel.

After releasing the mouse button, the first selected file appears with crossed diagonal lines (not yet finalized).

5. **Press Return/Enter to finalize the placement of the first file.**

After finalizing, the first file no longer shows the bounding box handles.

The second file automatically appears, ready to be finalized.

Note:

If you have the entire Adobe Creative Suite, Smart Objects provide extremely tight integration between Adobe Photoshop and Adobe Illustrator. You can take advantage of the sophisticated vector-editing features in Adobe Illustrator, and then place those files into Photoshop without losing the ability to edit the vector information.

6. **Press Return/Enter again to finalize the placement of the second file.**

The two placed files are stored on layers named based on the placed file names.

The placed files are Smart Object layers.

7. **Save the file and continue to the next stage of the project.**

Right now, you have a fairly incomprehensible mess of four raster images and three vector objects all piled on top of one another. You will start to make sense of these files in the next stage.

Stage 2 Managing Layers

Your ad file now has most of the necessary pieces, but it's still not an actual design — just a pile of images. When you composite images into a cohesive design, you almost certainly need to manipulate and transform some of the layers to make all of the pieces work together.

Photoshop includes a number of options for managing layers: naming layers for easier recognition, creating layer groups so multiple layers can be manipulated at once, moving layers around on the canvas, transforming layers both destructively and non-destructively, controlling individual layer visibility, and arranging the top-to-bottom stacking order of layers to determine exactly what is visible. You will use all of these options in this stage of the project.

NAME LAYERS AND LAYER GROUPS

It's always a good idea to name your layers because it makes managing the file much easier — especially when you work with files that include dozens of layers. Even with only four unnamed layers in this file (counting the Background layer), it would be tedious to have to toggle each layer on to find the one you want.

1. **With aftermath.psd open, review the Layers panel.**

2. **Click the eye icons to hide all but Layer 1.**

   Toggling layer visibility is an easy way to see only what you want to see at any given stage in a project.

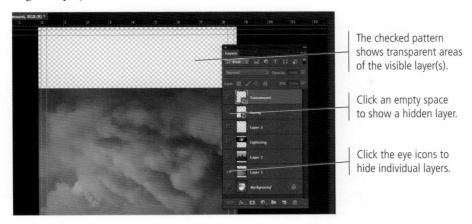

The checked pattern shows transparent areas of the visible layer(s).

Click an empty space to show a hidden layer.

Click the eye icons to hide individual layers.

Note:

To show or hide a series of contiguous layers, click the visibility icon (or empty space) for the first layer you want to affect, hold down the mouse button, and drag down to the last layer you want to show or hide.

Note:

You can Option/Alt-click a layer's visibility icon to hide all other layers in the file.

3. **Double-click the Layer 1 layer name, and then type Storm.**

   You can rename any layer by simply double-clicking the name and typing.

Double-click the layer name to access it.

Press Return/Enter after typing to finalize the new name.

4. **Click the eye icon to hide the renamed Storm layer, and then click the empty space to the left of Layer 2 to show only that layer.**

5. **Double-click the Layer 2 name and then type Skyline to rename the layer.**

6. **Repeat Steps 4–5 to rename Layer 3 as Title.**

7. **Click the spaces on the left side of the Layers panel (where the eye icons were) to show all hidden layers.**

8. **In the Layers panel, click the Tantamount layer to select it.**

9. **Press Shift and click the Rating layer to select that layer as well.**

   Since the Tantamount layer was already selected, the Rating layer should now be a second selected (highlighted) layer.

Note:

Press Shift and click to select contiguous layers in the Layers panel.

Press Command/Control and click to select non-contiguous layers in the Layers panel.

10. Click the button in the top-right corner of the panel to open the Layers panel Options menu. Choose New Group from Layers.

This option creates a group that automatically contains the selected layers. You can also create an empty group by choosing New Group (this option is available even when no layer is selected) or by clicking the New Group button at the bottom of the panel.

Click here to open the panel Options menu.

Two layers are selected.

New Group button

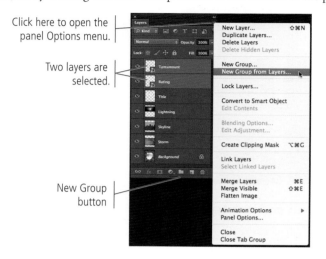

Note:

You can create a group from selected layers by dragging the selected layers onto the New Group button at the bottom of the panel. In this case, the new group is automatically named "Group N" (N is a placeholder for a sequential number); of course, you can rename a layer group just as easily as you can rename a layer.

11. In the New Group from Layers dialog box, type Logos in the Name field and click OK.

As with any other layer, you should name groups based on what they contain so you can easily identify them later.

Note:

You can create up to ten levels of nested layer groups, or groups inside of other groups.

12. Click the arrow to the left of the Logos group name to expand the layer group.

You have to expand the layer group to be able to access and edit individual layers in the group. If you select the entire layer group, you can move all layers within the group at the same time. Layers in the group maintain their position relative to one another.

Note:

You can click the eye icon for a layer folder to hide the entire layer group (and all layers inside the folder).

13. Save the file and continue to the next exercise.

MOVE AND TRANSFORM SMART OBJECT LAYERS

Photoshop makes scaling, rotating, and other transformations fairly easy to implement, but it is important to realize the potential impact of your transformations.

1. **With `aftermath.psd` open, click the Tantamount layer (in the Logos folder) in the Layers panel to select only that layer.**

2. **Choose the Move tool in the Tools panel.**

   As the name suggests, the Move tool is used to move a selection around on the canvas. You can select a specific area, and then click and drag to move only the selection on the active layer. If there is no active selection area, you can click and drag to move the contents of the entire active layer.

3. **In the Options bar, make sure the Auto-Select option is not checked.**

   When Auto-Select is checked, you can click in the image window and drag to move the contents of the layer containing the pixels where you click; you do not need to first select the layer in the Layers panel before moving the layer content. This is very useful in some cases, as you will see later in this project. However, the Auto-Select option is *not* very useful when the contents of multiple layers are stacked on top of each other (as is the case in your file as it exists now).

   Note:

   Deselect all layers by clicking in the empty area at the bottom of the Layers panel.

4. **Click in the image window and drag until the Tantamount layer content snaps to the bottom-right live-area guides.**

   If you toggled off the Snap feature when you used the Crop tool, you should turn it back on now by choosing View>Snap.

This option should not be checked.

Move tool

With no marching ants in the image window, select the layer you want to move, then click and drag in the document window to move the layer's contents.

5. **Click the Rating layer in the Layers panel to select that layer.**

6. **Click in the image window and drag until the Rating layer content snaps to the bottom-left live-area guides.**

7. **With the Rating layer still active, choose Edit>Free Transform.**

   When you use the transform options, bounding box handles surround the selection.

Note:

You can also use the Edit>Transform submenu to apply specific transformations to a layer or selection.

8. **Press Shift, click the top-right bounding box handle, and then drag down and left until the layer content is approximately two-thirds the original size.**

The selection (in this case, the entire Rating layer) dynamically changes as you scale the layer. Pressing Shift while you drag a handle constrains the image proportions as you resize it. When you release the mouse button, the handles remain in place until you finalize ("commit") the transformation.

The live cursor feedback shows the new dimensions of the transformed selection.

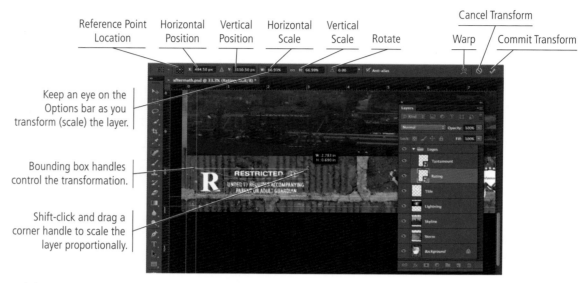

Keep an eye on the Options bar as you transform (scale) the layer.

Bounding box handles control the transformation.

Shift-click and drag a corner handle to scale the layer proportionally.

Reference Point Location · Horizontal Position · Vertical Position · Horizontal Scale · Vertical Scale · Rotate · Warp · Cancel Transform · Commit Transform

While you're manually transforming a layer or selection, the Options bar shows the specifics. You can also type into these fields to apply specific numeric transformations.

9. **Press Return/Enter to finalize the transformation.**

After finalizing the transformation, the bounding-box handles disappear.

10. **With the Rating layer still active, press Command/Control-T to enter Free Transform mode again and look at the Options bar.**

Because the rating layer is a Smart Object layer, the W and H fields still show the scaling percentage based on the original.

The W and H fields still show the scaling you applied in Step 8.

11. **In the Options bar, choose the bottom-left reference point location.**

The selected reference point defines the point around which transformations are made. By selecting the bottom-left point, for example, the bottom-left corner of the active selection will remain in place when you scale the selection in the next steps; the top-right corner will move based on the scaling you define.

12. **Click the Link icon between the W and H fields to constrain proportions during the transformation.**

13. **Type 50 in the Options bar W field.**

The bottom-left reference point is selected.

Click the Lock icon to constrain the height and width proportionally.

14. **Click the Commit Transform button on the Options bar (or press Return/Enter) to finalize the transformation.**

15. **Collapse the layer group by clicking the arrow at the left of the group name.**

Note:

If you press Return/ Enter, you have to press it two times to finalize the transormation. The first time you press it, you apply the change to the active field; the second time, you finalize the transformation and exit Free Transform mode.

16. **Save the file and continue to the next exercise.**

 ## TRANSFORM A REGULAR LAYER

Smart Object layers enable non-destructive transformations, which means those transformations can be changed or undone without affecting the quality of the layer content. Transforming a regular layer, on the other hand, is destructive and permanent.

1. **With aftermath.psd open, hide all but the Storm layer. Click the Storm layer in the Layers panel to select it.**

2. **Choose Edit>Transform>Flip Horizontal.**

The Transform submenu commands affect only the selected layer.

3. Press Command/Control-T to enter Free Transform mode.

Some handles might not be visible within the boundaries of the document window. If necessary, zoom out so you can see all eight handles of the layer content.

The edge of the bounding box shows that some parts of the layer do not fit within the current file dimensions.

4. In the Options bar, choose the center reference point if it is not already selected.

5. Click the Link icon between the W and H fields to constrain the proportions.

6. Place the cursor over the W field label to access the scrubby slider for that field.

The center reference point is selected.   Click the Link icon to constrain proportions.

Place the cursor over a field label to access the "scrubby slider" for that field.

Note:

When you see the scrubby slider cursor, you can drag right to increase or drag left to decrease the value in the related field.

7. Click and drag left until the W field shows 90%.

8. **Press Return/Enter to finalize the transformation.**

9. **With the Storm layer still active, press Command/Control-T to re-enter Free Transform mode.**

   Once you commit the transformation on a regular layer, the transformation is final. Looking at the Options bar now, you can see that it shows the layer at 100% instead of the 90% from Step 7.

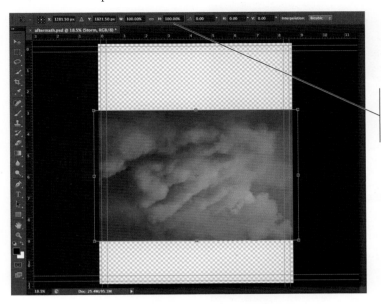

Re-entering Free Transform mode shows that the regular layer is again 100%, even after scaling.

10. **Press Esc to exit Free Transform mode without changing anything.**

11. **Save the file and continue to the next exercise.**

TRANSFORM THE BACKGROUND LAYER

Your file currently has a number of layers, most of which were created by pasting or placing external files into the original file. Because every photograph and scan (and some images that you create from scratch in Photoshop) begins with a default locked Background layer, it is important to understand the special characteristics of that layer:

- You can't apply layer transformations, styles, or masks to the Background layer.

- You can't move the contents of the Background layer around in the document.

- If you delete pixels from the Background layer, the removed pixels will automatically be filled with the current background color.

- The Background layer cannot include transparent pixels, which are necessary for underlying layers to be visible.

- The Background layer is always the bottom layer in the stacking order; you can't add or move layers lower than the Background layer.

In the final composite file for this project, you need to flip the bricks image from top to bottom, remove the desert area from the hole in the bricks, and place the other photographs to appear through the hole in the wall. For any of these options to work properly, you need to convert the default Background layer to a regular layer.

Note:

If you transform a Smart Object layer, the scale percentage is maintained even after you finalize the change (unlike scaling a regular layer, where the layer re-calibrates so the new size is considered 100% once you finalize the scaling).

Note:

If you crop an image that includes a Background layer, the Background layer is automatically converted to a regular layer if the Delete Cropped Pixels option is not checked.

1. **With `aftermath.psd` open, hide the Storm layer and then show the Background layer.**

2. **Click the Background layer to select it and then choose Edit>Transform.**

   The Transform submenu commands are not available for the locked Background layer.

Note:

Although the Background layer exists by default in many files, it is not a required component.

Many commands are not available because the Background layer is locked.

3. **With the Background layer still selected, choose Image>Image Rotation> Flip Canvas Vertical.**

   To affect the locked background layer, you have to flip the actual canvas.

4. **Show the Logos layer group.**

   Because you flipped the canvas, the Tantamount and Ratings layers are also flipped upside-down. Rotating or flipping the entire canvas affects all layers in the file; this is obviously not what you want to do.

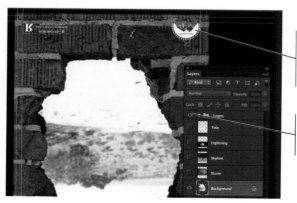

Because you flipped the canvas, the logos are now upside-down.

Showing the layer group shows all layers in that group.

5. **Choose Edit>Undo to restore the canvas to its original orientation.**

   The Undo command affects the last action you performed. Showing or hiding a layer is not considered an "action," so the Undo command simply un-flips the canvas. As you can see, though, the Logos group is again hidden, as it was when you flipped the canvas in Step 3.

6. **In the Layers panel, double-click the Background layer.**

7. **In the resulting New Layer dialog box, type `Bricks` in the Name field, then click OK.**

   Renaming the Background layer automatically unlocks and converts it to a regular layer.

Note:

The Undo menu command changes to reflect the action that will be affected. In this case, the actual command is Edit>Undo Flip Canvas Vertical.

The renamed Bricks layer is no longer locked. It is now a regular layer.

8. **With the Bricks layer selected in the panel, choose Edit>Transform>Flip Vertical.**

   Because the layer is no longer locked, you can now access and apply the transform commands that affect only the selected layer.

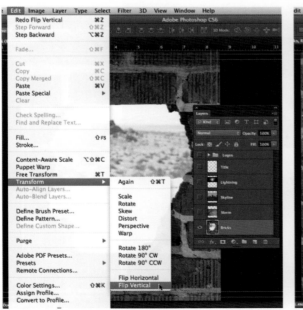
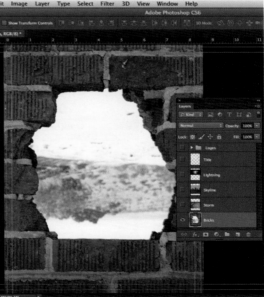

9. **Show all layers in the file.**

10. **Save the file and continue to the next stage of the project.**

Stage 3 Creating Complex Selections

At this stage of the project, you still have a few issues to resolve: some of the images are still randomly stacked on top of one another, and some images have areas that are hiding other images (the blue sky in the Skyline layer, for example). In this stage, you start fixing these problems.

Virtually any Photoshop project involves making some kind of selection. Making selections is so important, in fact, that there are no fewer than nine tools dedicated specifically to this goal, as well as a whole Select menu and a few other options for making and refining selections.

In an earlier lesson you learned how to use the Rectangular Marquee tool to draw simple selections. In the next series of exercises, you use several other selection methods to isolate pixels from their backgrounds (called **silhouetting**).

MAKE A FEATHERED SELECTION

1. **With aftermath.psd open, hide all but the Lightning layer. Click the Lightning layer to make it active.**

2. **Select the Lasso tool in the Tools panel.**

3. **Drag a rough shape around the lightning in the photo.**

   The lasso tools allow you to make irregular selections — in other words, selections that aren't just rectangular or elliptical. When you release the mouse button, the end point automatically connects to the beginning point of the selection.

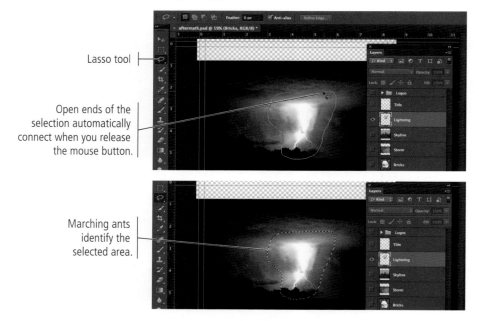

Lasso tool

Open ends of the selection automatically connect when you release the mouse button.

Marching ants identify the selected area.

4. **With the marching ants active, choose Select>Modify>Feather.**

   Feathering means to soften the edge of a selection so the image blends into the background instead of showing a sharp line around the edge. The Smooth, Expand, and Contract options in the Select>Modify submenu are self-explanatory; the Border option creates a specific number of pixels around the active selection (like the stroke/border that surrounds a shape in an illustration program).

Note:

*You could also create a feathered selection by typing in the Feather field of the Options bar **before** drawing the selection marquee.*

5. **In the resulting dialog box, type 35 in the Feather Radius field. Click OK to return to the image window.**

The Feather Radius defines the distance from solid to transparent. In the image window, there's no apparent difference in the selection because the marching ants can't show shades of a selection.

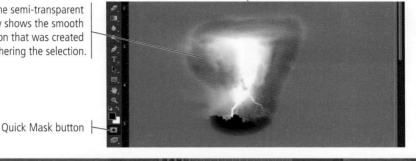

6. **Click the Quick Mask button at the bottom of the Tools panel to toggle into Quick Mask mode.**

This mode creates a temporary red overlay (called an Alpha channel) that shows the graded selection. By default, the overlay is semi-transparent, which allows you to see the underlying image.

The semi-transparent overlay shows the smooth transition that was created by feathering the selection.

Quick Mask button

The Lasso Tools

PHOTOSHOP FOUNDATIONS

The basic **Lasso tool** works like a pencil, following the path where you drag the mouse.

The **Polygonal Lasso tool** creates selections with straight lines, anchoring a line each time you click the mouse. To close a selection area, you must click the first point in the selection.

The **Magnetic Lasso tool** snaps to edges of high contrast; you can use the Options bar to control the way Photoshop detects the edges of an image. **Width** is the distance away from the edge the cursor can be and still detect the edge; if you set this value higher, you can move the cursor farther from the edge. **Contrast** is how different the foreground can be from the background and still be detected; if there is a very sharp distinction between the foreground and background (as in the case of the white quill against the blue background in these sample images), you can set this value higher. **Frequency** is the number of points that will be created to make the selection; setting this number higher creates finer selections, while setting it lower creates smoother edges.

It isn't uncommon for a mouse to unexpectedly jump when you don't want it to — which can be particularly troublesome if you're drawing a selection with the Polygonal or Magnetic Lasso tools. If you aren't happy with your Polygonal or Magnetic Lasso selection, press Escape to clear the selection and then try again.

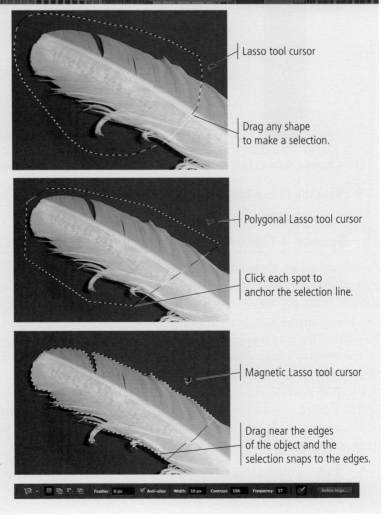

Lasso tool cursor

Drag any shape to make a selection.

Polygonal Lasso tool cursor

Click each spot to anchor the selection line.

Magnetic Lasso tool cursor

Drag near the edges of the object and the selection snaps to the edges.

7. **Click the Quick Mask button at the bottom of the Tools panel to toggle off the Quick Mask.**

8. **Choose Select>Inverse.**

   You want to remove the area around the lightning, so you have to select everything *other than* what you originally selected — in other words, the inverse of the previous selection.

Marching ants surround the image edge and the original selection.

The area between the two marquees is the current selection.

Note:

Press Command/Control-Shift-I to invert the active selection.

9. **With the Lightning layer selected in the Layers panel, press Delete/Backspace.**

   Selection marquees are not particular to a specific layer. You have to make sure the correct layer is active before you use the selection to perform some action.

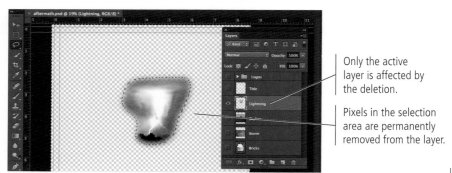

Only the active layer is affected by the deletion.

Pixels in the selection area are permanently removed from the layer.

10. **Choose Select>Deselect to turn off the active selection (marching ants).**

11. **Save the file and continue to the next exercise.**

Note:

Pressing Command/Control-D deselects the active selection.

SELECT A COLOR RANGE AND CREATE A LAYER MASK

As we said earlier, there are many selection options in Photoshop CS6, each with its own advantages and disadvantages. You have already used the marquee tools and lasso tools to select general areas of images.

Many images have both hard and soft edges, and/or very fine detail that needs to be isolated from its background (think of a model's blowing hair overlapping the title on the cover of a magazine). In this type of image, other tools can be used to create a very detailed selection based on the color in the image.

Rather than simply deleting pixels, as you did for the lightning image, another option for isolating an object with a path is to create a **layer mask** that hides unwanted pixels. Areas outside the mask are hidden but not deleted, so you can later edit the mask to change the visible part of the image.

1. **With aftermath.psd open, hide all but the Skyline layer. Click the Skyline layer to make it active.**

2. **Choose the Magic Wand tool (under the Quick Selection tool). In the Options bar, make sure the New Selection button is active and set the Tolerance field to 32.**

The Magic Wand tool is an easy way to select large areas of solid color. The first four options in the Options bar are the same as those for the Marquee tools (New Selection, Add to Selection, Subtract from Selection, and Intersect with Selection).

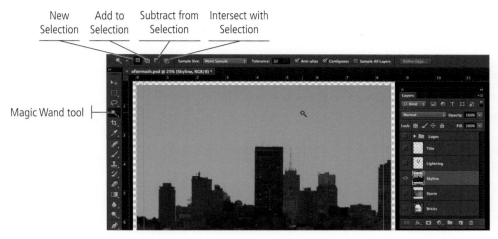

New Selection   Add to Selection   Subtract from Selection   Intersect with Selection

Magic Wand tool

Tolerance is the degree of variation between the color you click and the colors Photoshop will select; higher tolerance values select a larger range based on the color you click. If you're trying to select a very mottled background (for example), you should increase the tolerance; be careful, however, because increasing the tolerance might select too large a range of colors if parts of the foreground object fall within the tolerance range.

The **Anti-alias** check box, selected by default, allows edges to blend more smoothly into the background, preventing a jagged, stair-stepped appearance.

When **Contiguous** is selected, the Magic Wand tool only selects adjacent areas of the color; unchecking this option allows you to select all pixels within the color tolerance, even if some pixels are non-contiguous (for example, inside the shape of the letter Q).

By default, selections relate to the active layer only. You can check **Sample All Layers** to make a selection of all layers in the file.

The **Refine Edge** button opens a dialog box where you can use a number of tools to fine-tune the selection edge.

Note:

Anti-aliasing is the process of blending shades of pixels to create the illusion of sharp lines in a raster image.

3. **Click anywhere in the blue sky area of the image.**

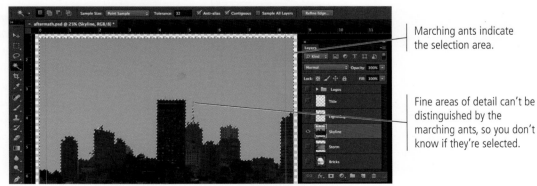

Marching ants indicate the selection area.

Fine areas of detail can't be distinguished by the marching ants, so you don't know if they're selected.

4. **Choose Select>Deselect to turn off the current selection.**

Although you could keep adding to the selection with the Magic Wand tool, the marching ants can't really show the fine detail.

5. **Choose Select>Color Range.**

6. **Make sure the Localized Color Clusters option is unchecked.**

7. **Choose White Matte in the Selection Preview menu (if it is not already).**

    By changing the Selection Preview, you can more easily determine exactly what is selected. You can preview color range selections in the image window as:

    - **None** shows the normal image in the document window.
    - **Grayscale** shows the entire image in shades of gray; selected areas are solid white and unselected areas are solid black.
    - **Black Matte** shows unselected areas in solid black; selected areas appear in color.
    - **White Matte** shows unselected areas in solid white; selected areas appear in color.
    - **Quick Mask** adds a partially transparent overlay to unselected areas.

8. **Set the Fuzziness value to 25 and click anywhere in the blue sky (in the document window).**

    Fuzziness is similar to the Tolerance setting for the Magic Wand tool. Higher Fuzziness values allow you to select more variation from the color you click.

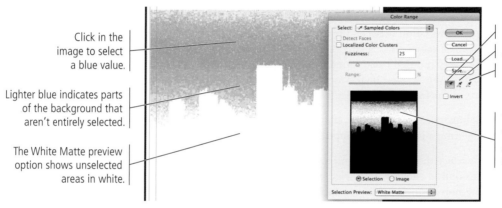

Click in the image to select a blue value.

Lighter blue indicates parts of the background that aren't entirely selected.

The White Matte preview option shows unselected areas in white.

Eyedropper tool
Add to Sample
Subtract from Sample

The low Fuzziness value doesn't select a large enough range of blues.

9. **Change the Fuzziness value to 80 and watch the effect on the dialog box preview.**

    Changing the Fuzziness value expands (higher numbers) or contracts (lower numbers) the selection. Be careful, though, since higher fuzziness values can eliminate fine lines and detail.

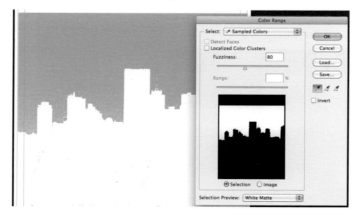

Selecting Localized Color Clusters

The **Localized Color Clusters** option in the Color Range dialog box can be used to select specific areas of a selected color. When this option is checked, the Range slider defines how far away (in physical distance) a color can be located from the point you click and still be included in the selection.

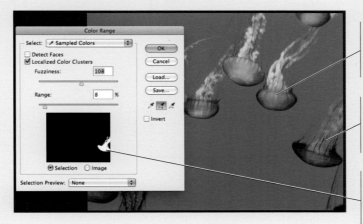

The same colors in other jellyfish are not selected because they are outside the reduced Range value.

We used a number of clicks with different Fuzziness values to sample the colors in this jellyfish.

Using Localized Color Clusters and a reduced Range value, we were able to isolate this jellyfish from its school.

Selection Presets

The Select menu at the top of the dialog box includes several presets for isolating specific ranges of primary colors (Reds, Yellows, Greens, Cyans, Blues, or Magentas), or specific ranges of color (highlights, midtones, or shadows).

If you select the **Skin Tones** preset, you can then activate the Detect Faces option at the top of the dialog box. By adjusting the Fuzziness slider, you can use this dialog box to make reasonably good selections of people's skin.

As you can see in this example, however, no automatic option is a perfect substitute when subjective decision-making is required. The tones in the rolling pin's reflection are very close to the color of skin, so they are included in the selection. This automatic selection method is still a good starting point, though, for making the complex selection of only a person's (or people's) skin.

Choose a preset from this menu.

When you choose the Skin Tones preset, you can also activate the Detect Faces option.

Some colors are close to skin tones, but are are not skin. You will have to manually edit the mask to correct these areas.

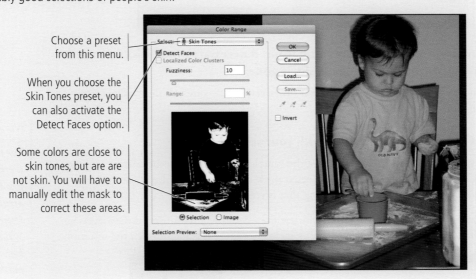

10. **In the Color Range dialog box, click the Add to Sample eyedropper.**
In the document window, click where parts of the blue sky are not shown in
full strength.

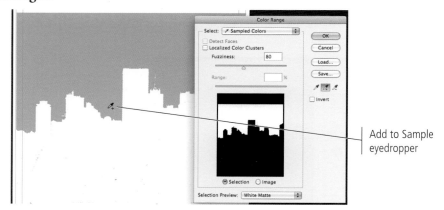

Add to Sample
eyedropper

11. **Check the Invert box in the Color Range dialog box.**

Because your goal is to isolate the city and not the sky, it helps to look at what you want
to keep instead of what you want to remove.

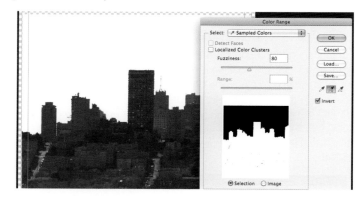

Note:

*When the Color Range
dialog box is open, you
can press Command/
Control to switch
between the Selection
and Image previews
within the dialog box.*

12. **Continue adding to (or subtracting from, if necessary) your selection until**
you are satisfied that all the blue sky is gone.

You can also adjust the Fuzziness slider if necessary, but be sure you don't adjust it too
far to include areas of the city.

13. **Click OK when you're satisfied with your selection.**

When you return to the image window, the marching ants indicate the current selection.
In the Color Range dialog box, you selected the blue and inverted the selection — in
other words, your selection is everything that isn't blue.

If you zoom out to see the entire file, you see the marching ants surround the canvas as
well as the blue sky. Since the transparent area is not blue, it is included in the selection.

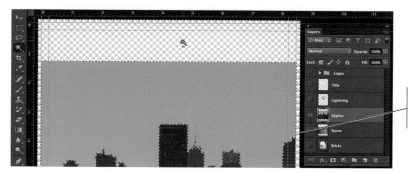

Marching ants
surround the
image edge.

Note:

*For the purposes of this
exercise, don't worry if
you have small unselected
areas in the sky area. In
Project 2: African
Wildlife Map, you will
learn how to paint on a
mask to clean up specific
areas such as the artifacts
you might see in your sky.*

14. **Choose the Magic Wand tool in the Tools panel and choose the Subtract from Selection option on the Options bar.**

15. **Click anywhere in the transparent area (the gray-and-white checkerboard) to remove that area from the selection.**

16. **In the Layers panel, click the Add Layer Mask button.**

A **layer mask** is a map of areas that will be visible in the selected layer. The mask you just created is a raster-based pixel mask, based on the active selection when you created the mask. This is a non-destructive way to hide certain elements of a layer without permanently deleting pixels; you can edit or disable the layer mask at any time.

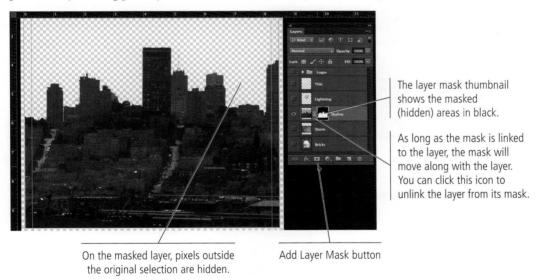

The layer mask thumbnail shows the masked (hidden) areas in black.

As long as the mask is linked to the layer, the mask will move along with the layer. You can click this icon to unlink the layer from its mask.

On the masked layer, pixels outside the original selection are hidden.

Add Layer Mask button

17. **Control/right-click the mask thumbnail and choose Disable Layer Mask from the contextual menu.**

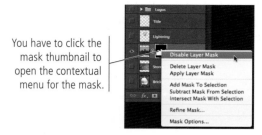

You have to click the mask thumbnail to open the contextual menu for the mask.

When you disable the mask, the background pixels are again visible. This is one of the advantages of using masks — the background pixels are not permanently removed, they are simply hidden.

When the mask is disabled, the masked pixels are visible.

A red X indicates that the mask is disabled.

18. **Control/right-click the mask thumbnail and choose Apply Layer Mask from the contextual menu.**

This option applies the mask to the attached layer, permanently removing the masked pixels from the layer.

Note:

Creating selections, reversing them, and then deleting the pixels surrounding an object is a common method for creating silhouettes — but not necessarily the best method. Masks protect the original pixels while providing exactly the same result.

The masked pixels are permanently removed from the layer.

The mask is removed from the layer.

19. **Choose Edit>Undo to restore the layer mask.**

As you saw in the previous step, applying a mask permanently removes the masked pixels. This essentially defeats the purpose of a mask, so you are restoring it in this step.

20. **Control/right-click the mask thumbnail and choose Enable Layer Mask from the contextual menu.**

21. **Save the file and continue to the next exercise.**

MAKE AND REFINE A QUICK SELECTION

As you just saw, you can make selections based on the color in an image. This technique is useful when you want to select large areas of solid color, or in photos with significant contrast between the foreground and background. When the area you want to select has a complex edge, refining the selection edge can produce very detailed results.

1. **With aftermath.psd open, hide all but the Bricks layer. Click the Bricks layer to select it as the active layer.**

2. **Choose the Quick Selection tool (nested under the Magic Wand tool).**

3. **In the Options bar, make sure the Sample All Layers option is not checked.**

   You only want to select the area in the bricks layer (the hole in the wall), so you do not want to make a selection based on the content of other layers in the file.

4. **Click at the top area of the hole in the wall and drag down to the bottom edge of the hole.**

   The Quick Selection tool essentially allows you to "paint" a selection. As you drag, the selection expands and automatically finds the edges in the image.

Note:

If you stop dragging and then click in a nearby area, the selection grows to include the new area.

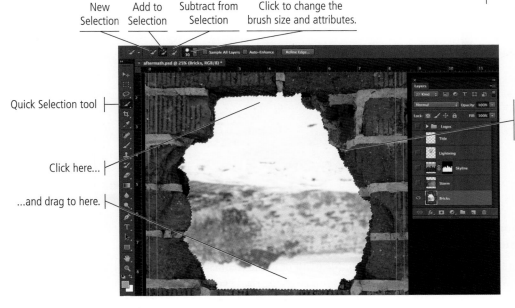

5. **Click the Refine Edge button in the Options bar.**

6. **Click the View button. Choose the On White option from the menu if it is not already selected.**

   The preview options allow you to change the way your image appears in the document window while you refine the edges within the dialog box.

   - **Marching Ants** shows the basic standard selection.
   - **Overlay** shows the unselected areas with a Quick Mask overlay.
   - **On Black** shows the selection in color against a black background.
   - **On White** shows the selection in color against a white background.
   - **Black & White** shows the selected area in white and the unselected area in black.
   - **On Layers** shows only the selected area; unselected areas are hidden.
   - **Reveal Layer** shows the entire layer, with no visual indication of the selection.

7. Experiment with the adjustments until you're satisfied with the selection edge.

You want to include a small amount of darkness around the edge so that, when you invert the selection to remove the hole in the wall, there is no light halo effect left by the selection edge. We used the Shift Edge slider to slightly expand the selection edge.

- **Radius** is the number of pixels around the edge that are affected. Higher radius values (up to 250 pixels) improve the edge in areas of fine detail.

- **Smooth** reduces the number of points that make up your selection and, as the name suggests, makes a smoother edge. You can set smoothness from 0 (very detailed selection) to 100 (very smooth selection).

- **Feather** softens the selection edge, resulting in a transition that does not have a hard edge (in other words, blends into the background). You can feather the selection up to 250 pixels.

- **Contrast** is the degree of variation allowed in the selection edge. Higher Contrast values (up to 100%) mean sharper selection edges.

- **Shift Edge** shrinks or grows the selection edge by the defined percentage (from −100% to 100%).

- **Decontaminate Colors** can be checked to remove a certain percentage of color from the edge of a selection.

Note:

It might help to work with a closer view while you refine edges. You can use the Zoom and Hand tools in the Refine Edge dialog box to change the image view behind the open dialog box.

The On White preview shows the selected area on a white background.

The dark edge should be easily visible using the On White preview.

8. At the bottom of the dialog box, choose the Layer Mask option in the Output To menu.

This menu can be used to create a new layer or file (with or without a mask) from the selection. You want to mask the existing layer, so you are using the Layer Mask option.

9. Click OK to accept your refined selection.

The resulting layer mask hides areas that were not selected.

10. **Click the mask thumbnail in the Layers panel to select only the mask, and then open the Properties panel (Window>Properties).**

As you know, you want to remove the hole in the wall and not the wall. You selected the area in the hole to create the mask, but you now need to invert the mask.

Like the Options bar, the Properties panel is contextual. Different options are available in the panel depending on what is selected in the Layers panel.

When a layer mask is selected, you can manipulate a variety of properties related to the selected mask. (You will use different aspects of the Properties panel in later projects.)

11. **In the Properties panel, click the Invert button.**

This button reverses the mask, so now only the bricks are visible.

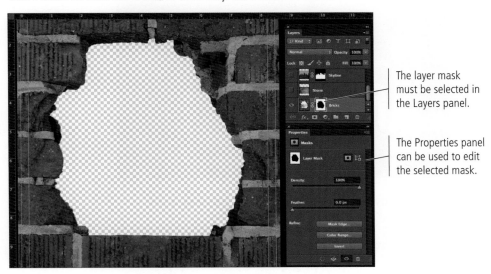

The layer mask must be selected in the Layers panel.

The Properties panel can be used to edit the selected mask.

12. **Save the file and continue to the next exercise.**

 ## ARRANGE LAYER POSITION AND STACKING ORDER

The ad is almost final, but a few pieces are still not quite in position. You already know you can use the Move tool to move the contents of a layer around on the canvas. You can move a layer to any position in the **stacking order** (the top-to-bottom position of a layer) by simply dragging it to a new position in the Layers panel.

1. **With aftermath.psd open, make all layers visible.**

2. **Click the Bricks layer in the Layers panel and drag up. When a heavy bar appears below the Title layer, release the mouse button.**

The heavy line indicates where the layer will be positioned when you release the mouse button.

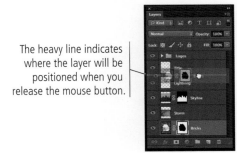

Note:

Press Command/ Control-[(left bracket) to move a layer down in the stacking order.

Press Command/ Control-] (right bracket) to move a layer up in the stacking order.

Be careful: If the border appears around a layer group, releasing the mouse button would place the dragged layer inside of the group.

3. **With the Move tool active, check the Auto-Select option in the Options bar. Open the attached menu (to the right of the Auto-Select check box) and choose Layer.**

When Layer is selected in the Auto-Select menu, only the relevant layer will move even if it is part of a layer group. If you want all layers in a group containing the selected layer to move, you can choose Group in the menu.

4. **In the document window, click any pixel in the storm image, and drag until the image fills the top of the hole in the bricks.**

Make sure you click an area where no pixels from another layer are visible. (Because the layer mask on the Bricks layer hides the inner pixels, you can click within the mask shape to select the underlying layers.)

Check the Auto-Select option and choose Layer in the menu.

Click any pixel in the storm image and drag to move that layer's content.

Be careful to not click an area where a different layer is visible.

You don't have to first select a specific layer to move that layer's content.

5. **In the document window, click any pixel in the city image and drag until you are happy with the position of the layer content.**

6. **In the Layers panel, click the Lightning layer and drag it below the Skyline layer.**

7. **In the document window, click any pixel of the lightning image and drag to position the layer content so the lightning appears to strike one of the buildings.**

8. **In the document window, click any pixel in the title treatment and drag down so the title appears in the bottom half of the canvas.**

Your layers should appear in the same order as shown in the following image, with the Logos layer group at the top of the layer stack.

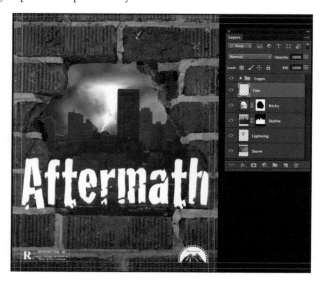

Note:

When the Move tool is active, you can move the selected object or layer 1 pixel by pressing the Arrow keys. Pressing Shift with any of the Arrow keys moves the selected object/layer by 10 pixels.

9. **Save the file and continue to the final stage of the project.**

PHOTOSHOP FOUNDATIONS

When you work with complex files, you might find yourself with dozens — or even hundreds — of layers. Descriptive names can help you navigate through the layers, but you still have to scroll through the panel to find what you need.

Layer filtering, available at the top of the Layers panel, allows you to narrow down the panel to only layers that meet certain criteria — making it much easier to locate a specific layer.

When **Kind** is selected in the menu, you can use the associated buttons to show only certain types of layers (adjustment layers, smart objects, etc.).

Click this switch to turn filtering on and off.

Only layers that meet the defined filtering criteria appear in the panel.

When **Name** is selected, you can type in the attached field to find layers with names that include the text you enter in the field. The defined text string does not need to be at the beginning of the layer name; for example, typing "ti" would return both Rating and Title layers in the file for this project.

When **Effect** is selected, you can use the secondary menu to find only layers with a specified effect (applied using the Layer>Layer Style submenu).

Use this menu to filter layers by kind, name, effect, mode, attribute, or color.

Filter for:

Smart objects

Shape layers

Type layers

Adjustment layers

Pixel layers

When **Attributes** is selected, you can choose from a number of layer attributes — visible, linked, clipped, etc.

When **Mode** is selected, you can use the secondary menu to find only layers to which a certain blending mode has been assigned.

When **Color** is selected, you can choose any of the built-in colors from the secondary menu. (These colors, which appear around the layer's visibility icon, can be assigned to individual layers in each layer's contextual menu.)

Stage 4 Saving Photoshop Files for Print

At the beginning of the project, you saved this file in Photoshop's native format (PSD). However, many Photoshop projects require saving the completed file in at least one other format. Many artists prefer to leave all files in the PSD format since there is only one file to track. Others prefer to send only flattened TIFF files of their artwork because the individual elements can't be changed. Ultimately, the format (or formats, if the file is being used in multiple places) you use will depend on where and how the file is being placed.

Many Photoshop projects are pieces of a larger composition; the overall project defines the format you need to use when you save a complete project. The ad you just created, for example, will be placed in magazine layouts, which will be built in a page-layout application such as Adobe InDesign or QuarkXPress. Although the current versions of both industry-standard page-layout applications can support native layered PSD files, older versions can't import those native files. If a magazine is being designed in QuarkXPress 4, for example (and some still are), you can't place a layered PSD file into that layout. As the Photoshop artist, you have to save your work in a format that is compatible with the magazine layout.

As you know, the ad you created will be placed in multiple magazines, and different publishers have provided different file requirements. You need to save two different versions of the ad to meet those requirements.

SAVE A LAYERED TIFF FILE

Some software that can't use native PSD files can use layered TIFF files, which allow you to maintain as much of the native information as possible in the resulting file.

1. **With aftermath.psd open, choose File>Save As.**

2. **If necessary, navigate to your WIP>Movie folder as the target location.**

   The Save As dialog box defaults to the last-used location. If you continued the entire way through this project without stopping, you won't have to navigate.

3. **In the Save As field, type _layered at the end of the current file name (before the .psd extension).**

Common File Formats

Photoshop, with the extension PSD, is the native format.

Photoshop EPS can maintain vector and raster information in the same file, and can maintain spot-color channels.

JPEG is a lossy compressed file format that does not support transparency.

Large Document Format, using the extension PSB, is used for images larger than 2 GB (the limit for PSD files); this format supports all Photoshop features including transparency and layers.

Photoshop PDF can contain all required font and image information in a single file, which can be compressed to reduce file size.

Photoshop 2.0 saves a flattened file that can be opened in Photoshop 2.0; all layer information is discarded.

Photoshop Raw supports CMYK, RGB, and grayscale images with alpha channels, and multichannel and LAB images without alpha channels; this format does not support layers.

PNG is a raster-based format that supports both continuous-tone color and transparency. It is sometimes used for print applications, but is more commonly used in digital publishing (specifically, Web design).

TIFF is a raster-based image format that supports layers, alpha channels, and file compression.

4. **Click the Format menu and choose TIFF.**

5. **Make sure the Layers check box is selected in the lower half of the dialog box.**

   Because this file contains layers, this option is probably checked by default. If your file contained alpha channels, annotations, or spot colors, those check boxes would also be available. The As a Copy check box can be used if you want to save multiple versions of the same file with different options (which you will do in the next exercise).

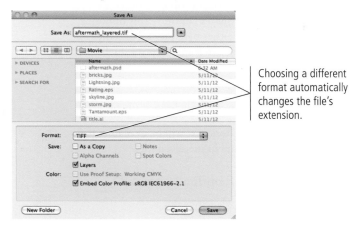

Choosing a different format automatically changes the file's extension.

6. **Leave the remaining options at their default values and click Save.**

7. **In the resulting TIFF Options dialog box, make sure the None image compression option is selected.**

   TIFF files can be compressed (made smaller) using one of three methods:

   - **None** (as the name implies) applies no compression to the file. This option is safe if file size is not an issue, but digital file transmission often requires files to be smaller than a full-page, multi-layered Photoshop file.

   - **LZW** (Lempel-Ziv-Welch) compression is **lossless**, which means all file data is maintained in the compressed file.

   - **ZIP** compression is also lossless, but is not supported by all desktop-publishing software (especially older versions).

   - **JPEG** is a **lossy** compression scheme, which means some data will be thrown away to reduce the file size. If you choose JPEG compression, the Quality options determine how much data can be discarded. Maximum quality means less data is thrown out and the file is larger. Minimum quality discards the most data and results in a smaller file size.

8. **Leave the Pixel Order radio button at the default value, and choose the Byte Order option for your operating system.**

Pixel Order determines how channel data is encoded. The Interleaved (RGBRGB) option is the default; Per Channel (RRGGBB) is called "planar" order.

Byte Order determines which platform can use the file, although this is somewhat deceptive. On older versions of most desktop-publishing software, Macintosh systems can read the PC byte order but Windows couldn't read the Macintosh byte order — which is why even the Macintosh system defaults to the IBM PC option. This option is becoming obsolete because most newer software can read either byte order. Nonetheless, some experts argue that choosing the order for your system can improve print quality, especially on desktop output devices.

Save Image Pyramid creates a tiered file with multiple resolution versions; this isn't widely used or supported by other applications, so you can typically leave it unchecked.

If your file contains transparency, the Save Transparency check box will be available. If you don't choose this option, transparent areas will be white in the saved file.

9. **In the Layer Compression area, make sure the RLE option is selected.**

These three options explain — right in the dialog box — what they do.

10. **Click OK to save the file.**

Photoshop warns you that including layers will increase the file size.

11. **Click OK to dismiss the warning and save the file.**

12. **Continue to the next exercise.**

Note:

If you don't see the warning, it's possible that someone checked the Don't Show Again check box. If you want to make sure that you see all warnings and messages, click Reset All Warning Dialogs in the General pane of the Preferences dialog box.

SAVE A FLATTENED TIFF FILE

Magazines using older page-layout applications need files that no longer maintain the layer information — called **flattened** files. You can flatten a file's layers manually using the Layers panel Options menu, or simply flatten the file during the Save As process.

1. **With `aftermath_layered.tif` open in Photoshop, choose File>Save As.**

If you continued directly from the previous exercise, this is the version you just saved. If you quit before you began this exercise, make sure you open the TIFF version and not the PSD version from your WIP>Movie folder.

Assuming that you started this exercise with the TIFF file from the previous exercise, the format and file name extension already reflect the TIFF options.

Note:

You can manually flatten a file by choosing Layer>Flatten Image.

2. **Uncheck the Layers check box.**

The As a Copy box is now selected by default. A warning shows that the file must be saved as a copy when the Layers option is unchecked. This is basically a failsafe built into Photoshop that prevents you from overwriting your layered file with a flattened version.

Note:

Older desktop-publishing software doesn't always support compressed TIFF files. When saving for those workflows, you might have to save the file without compression, regardless of the resulting file size.

3. **In the Save As field, highlight the words "layered copy" and type flat.**

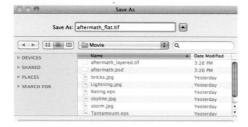

4. **Click Save. In the resulting TIFF Options dialog box, make sure the None compression option is selected and the Byte Order is set to IBM PC. At the bottom of the dialog box, make sure the Discard Layers and Save a Copy option is checked.**

5. **Click OK to save the second version of the file.**

6. **When the save is complete, choose File>Close. Click Don't Save when asked.**

fill in the blank

1. _____ is likely to cause degradation of a raster image when it's reproduced on a printing press.

2. A _____ is a linked file that you placed into another Photoshop document.

3. The _____ is context sensitive, providing access to different functions depending on what tool is active.

4. The _____ is the final size of a printed page.

5. The _____ tool is used to draw irregular-shaped selection marquees.

6. The _____ tool is used to select areas of similar color by clicking and dragging in the image window.

7. The _____ tool can be used to drag layer contents to another position within the image, or into another open document.

8. When selecting color ranges, the _____ value determines how much of the current color range falls into the selection.

9. A _____ can be used to non-destructively hide certain areas of a layer.

10. _____ is a lossy compression method that is best used when large file size might be a problem.

short answer

1. Briefly describe the difference between raster images and vector graphics.

2. Briefly explain three separate methods for isolating an image from its background.

3. Briefly explain the concept of a layer mask.

Portfolio Builder Project

Use what you learned in this project to complete the following freeform exercise.
Carefully read the art director and client comments, then create your design to meet the needs of the project.
Use the space below to sketch ideas; when finished, write a brief explanation of the reasoning behind your design.

art director comments

Tantamount Studios is pleased with your work on the *Aftermath* ad, and they would like to hire you again to create the ad concept and final files for another movie that they're releasing early next year.

To complete this project, you should:

❏ Download the **PS6_PB_Project1.zip** archive from the Student Files Web page to access the client-supplied title artwork and rating placeholder file.

❏ Find appropriate background and foreground images for the movie theme (see the client's comments at right).

❏ Incorporate the title artwork, logos, and rating placeholder that the client provided.

❏ Composite the different elements into a single completed file; save both a layered version and a flattened version.

client comments

The movie is titled *Above and Beyond*. Although the story is fictionalized, it will focus on the men who led the first U.S. Airborne unit (the 501st), which suffered more than 2000 casualties in the European theater of World War II.

We don't have any other images in mind, but the final ad should reflect the time period (the 1940s) of the movie. The 501st Airborne was trained to parachute into battle, so you should probably incorporate some kind of parachute image.

This movie is a joint venture between Sun and Tantamount, so both logos need to be included in the new ad. It isn't rated yet, so please use the "This Movie Is Not Yet Rated" artwork as a placeholder.

Create this ad big enough to fit on an 8.5 × 11" page, but keep the live area an inch inside the trim so the ad can be used in different-sized magazines.

project justification

_____

_____

_____

_____

_____

_____

_____

_____

_____

_____

_____

_____

_____

_____

Making selections is one of the most basic, and most important, skills that you will learn in Photoshop. Selections are so important that Photoshop dedicates an entire menu to the process.

As you created the movie ad in this project, you used a number of skills and techniques that you will apply in many (if not all) projects you build in Photoshop. You learned a number of ways to make both simple and complex selections — and you will learn additional methods in later projects. You also learned how to work with multiple layers, which will be an important part of virtually every Photoshop project you create, both in this book and throughout your career.

Composite images by dragging from one document to another

Transform a regular layer

Composite images by copying and pasting

Incorporate vector graphics into a raster image

Move layer content around on the canvas

Composite images by placing from Mini Bridge

Transform a Smart Object layer

Make a basic selection with a Marquee tool

Create a feathered selection to blend one layer into another

Create a silhouette using the Select Color Range utility

Create a silhouette using the Quick Selection tool

Refine a selection using the Refine Edges utility

Use a layer mask to hide pixels on a layer

African Wildlife Map

Your client, the Global Wildlife Fund (GWF), is a not-for-profit organization dedicated to preserving wildlife resources around the world. Every year GWF does a direct-mail fundraising drive, offering premiums for certain levels of membership donations. This year they want to offer a series of limited-edition art prints. Anyone who donates at least $100 will be allowed to pick one of the prints; people who donate over $1000 will receive the entire set of six prints. Your job is to create the first piece in the series as a sample.

This project incorporates the following skills:

❏ Using a small, low-resolution image as a drawing template

❏ Creating complex, scalable vector shape layers

❏ Compositing images as Smart Objects

❏ Creating and modifying selections and layer masks

❏ Applying filters and effects to create artistic effects

❏ Developing custom artistic backgrounds

This is our 25th anniversary, and we want our fundraising drive to set records. In the past, we've sent out address labels, note pads, and even beanie animals as incentives for donating. This year we want to commission a series of paintings that we could reproduce as limited-edition prints for people who contribute a certain amount of money.

We're a not-for-profit organization, and we try to keep most of our finances dedicated to conservation activities. A colleague suggested that we might be able to find someone who can do what we want with Photoshop, and probably do it much faster and for far less money than a traditional artist.

Here's what we have in mind: we thought each piece in the series could be the shape of a different continent with various indigenous animals inside each continent. (We're going to skip Antarctica.) You can start with Africa, because we've already gathered up a collection of images for that poster. We'd rather not have to pay for stock images when we already have so many of our own images in-house.

I downloaded a comp image with a map of Africa that we can use to get the shape right, and then we can incorporate their photos into the map outline. I think the ideal size for the final piece is 10 × 12″.

Photoshop is ideal for this type of job; there are dozens of filters for making photographs look like artwork. You're going to have to be creative with the background; Africa is surrounded by water, and we don't want to give them a plain, flat blue background.

To complete this project, you will:

❑ Create a compound shape layer using variations of the Pen tool

❑ Composite and work with multiple images as Smart Objects

❑ Modify selections to create soft-edge layer masks

❑ Use the brush tools to refine a layer mask

❑ Create a clipping mask from a vector shape layer

❑ Apply artistic filters using the Filter Gallery

❑ Define a custom gradient

❑ Use patterns and filters to create a custom artistic background

❑ Print a desktop proof

Stage 1 **Working with Vector Shape Layers**

Any project that you build in Photoshop — especially an oversize project like this map — requires some amount of zooming in and out to various view percentages, as well as navigating around the document within its window. As we show you how to complete different stages of the workflow, we usually won't tell you when to change your view percentage because that's largely a matter of personal preference. Nonetheless, you should understand the different options for navigating around a Photoshop file so you can easily and efficiently get to what you want, when you want to get there.

To review information from the Interface chapter, keep in mind that you have a number of options for navigating around a document:

- Click with the Hand tool to drag the image around in the document window.

- Click with the Zoom tool to zoom in; Option/Alt-click to zoom out.

- Use the View Percentage field in the bottom-left corner of the document window.

- Use the options in the View menu (or the corresponding keyboard shortcuts).

- Use the Navigator panel.

> **Note:**
>
> *As you complete the exercises in this project, use any of these methods to zoom in or out on different areas of the file.*

REVIEW AND RESAMPLE THE EXISTING SOURCE IMAGE

This project — like many others you will build throughout your career — starts with an existing image, which you will open and use as the basis for the rest of the project. Whenever you start with an existing file, it's best to evaluate what you already have before you make any changes.

1. **Download PS6_RF_Project2.zip from the Student Files Web page.**

2. **Expand the ZIP archive in your WIP folder (Macintosh) or copy the archive contents into your WIP folder (Windows).**

   This results in a folder named **Africa**, which contains the files you need for this project. You should also use this folder to save the files you create in this project.

3. **In Photoshop, choose File>Open. Navigate to the file africa.jpg in the WIP>Africa folder and click Open.**

4. **Make sure your image displays at 100% and the rulers are visible, and then choose Image>Image Size.**

   The africa.jpg file is slightly less than 3″ wide by 3″ high, with a resolution of 300 dpi. In Project 1: Composite Movie Ad, you learned that commercial printing typically requires 300 dpi, so this image would be considered "print quality" at its current size; however, you need to build the final artwork at 10 × 12″ — nearly 4 times the current size.

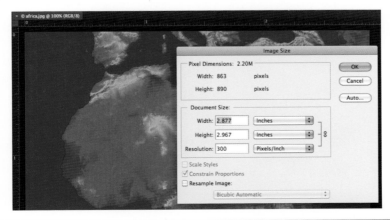

5. **Check the Resample Image option at the bottom of the dialog box.**

6. **Highlight the Height field and type 12.**

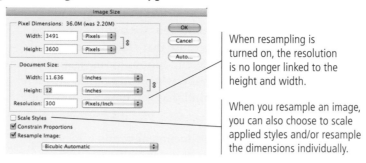

When resampling is turned on, the resolution is no longer linked to the height and width.

When you resample an image, you can also choose to scale applied styles and/or resample the dimensions individually.

7. **Click OK to return to the document window.**

   The map image, which was originally crisp and clear, is now blurry and pixelated. You no longer have clean lines to use as the basis for the map outline.

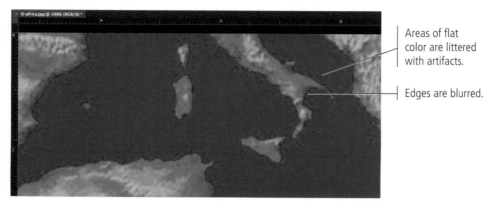

Areas of flat color are littered with artifacts.

Edges are blurred.

You can also see the effect of more pixels on file size — more pixels at larger sizes means much larger (potentially huge) file sizes.

8. **Choose Edit>Undo Image Size to return the file to its original size.**

   The Photoshop Undo command is a single-action toggle; after you use the command, it becomes Redo for the same action. To move back through more than one action, you must use the Step Backward command or the History panel.

9. **Choose View>Rulers to toggle them off.**

10. **Save the file as a Photoshop file named `africa_working.psd` in your WIP>Africa folder, and then continue to the next exercise.**

Note:

Press Command/Control-Z to undo the previous action.

Press Command-Option-Z/Control-Alt-Z to step backward one action at a time through the file history.

CREATE A VECTOR-BASED SHAPE LAYER

If you completed Project 1: Composite Movie Ad, you learned that one of the disadvantages of raster images is that their size and resolution are fixed at the time they are created. Photoshop is very powerful, but it simply can't create enough pixels to generate a high-quality 12″ image from a 4″ image.

Vector graphics, on the other hand, are based on mathematically defined lines and points instead of pixels. When you output a vector file, the output device calculates the relative position of the lines and points necessary to create the final version at whatever size you need. Because of this, vectors can be resized as large as you need without any loss of quality.

To work around the problem of low resolution in the original map image, you're going to create a vector shape layer using the original map as a guide.

1. **With africa_working.psd open, choose the Freeform Pen tool (nested under the Pen tool) in the Tools panel.**

   The Pen tool can be used to create precise vector paths called Bézier curves, defined by the position of anchor points and the length and angle of handles that are connected to those anchor points. You can use the regular Pen tool to place individual anchor points and drag handles, precisely controlling the shape of the resulting paths (see Photoshop Foundations: Understanding Anchor Points and Handles on Page 90).

   For this project, your ultimate goal is an artistic rendering — which means you don't have to precisely match the individual points and curves of the continental shape. Rather than individually creating every anchor point and precisely pulling every curve, you can use the Freeform Pen tool to draw as you would with a pencil.

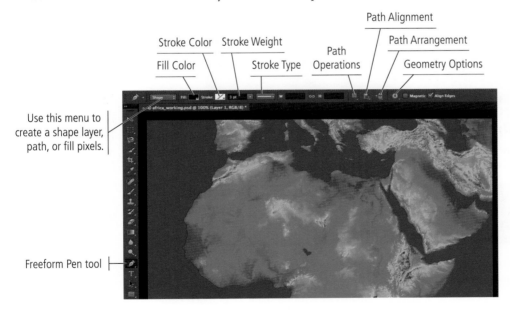

2. **In the Options bar, choose the Shape option in the left menu.**

   The Pen tools can be used to create shape layers or paths. Shape layers are vector-based, which means they have mathematically defined edges and can be filled with colors or pixel-based images. Paths are also vector-based, but they do not create their own layers and cannot be directly filled; instead, paths are most commonly used to isolate certain portions of an image.

3. **Click the Fill color swatch to open the pop-up Swatches panel. Click a color swatch that will be easily visible against the background map image.**

You can define the separate fill and stroke colors of a vector shape layer, just as you might do for an object you create in Adobe Illustrator or InDesign.

Clicking the Fill or Stroke color swatch opens a pop-up panel, where you can select a specific swatch to use as the attribute's color. Four buttons at the top of the panel change the attribute to (from left) None, Solid, a Gradient, or a Pattern. You can also click the Color Picker button to define any color that is not already in the Swatches panel.

Note:

We selected a light blue, which will stand out well against the background image.

Click the swatch to open the pop-up Swatches panel.

Use "None"
Use a solid color
Use a gradient
Use a pattern

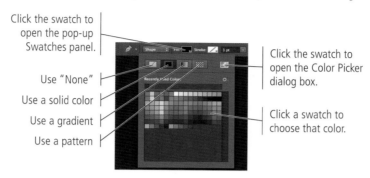

Click the swatch to open the Color Picker dialog box.

Click a swatch to choose that color.

4. **In the Options bar, click the Geometry Options button to access the options for the Freeform Pen tool.**

5. **Set the Curve Fit field to 2 px and press Return/Enter to close the options dialog box.**

This field remembers the last-used value; 2 px is the application default value, but this setting might have been changed by another user.

Note:

The Path Operations menu defaults to New Layer. However, it retains the last-used selection as long as the same tool remains active. If you switch to a different tool, the path operation reverts back to the New Layer option.

6. **Click the Path Operations button and review the options.**

These options define how a new path will interact with any existing paths. (Illustrator and InDesign users might recognize these as options from the Pathfinder panel.)

By default, every new shape you draw is created as a New Layer. The other options allow new shapes to interact with existing shapes on the selected shape layer.

- **Combine Shapes** adds new shapes to an already selected shape layer. Each path's shape is maintained as a separate vector path.

- **Subtract Front Shape** removes the area of secondary shapes from existing shapes.

- **Intersect Shape Areas** results in a shape that is only the area where a new shape overlaps an existing shape.

- **Exclude Overlapping Shapes** is similar to Subtract; overlapping areas are removed from the existing shape, but non-overlapping areas of the new shape are filled with the shape color.

- The **Merge Shape Components** option results in a single (possibly compound) shape. Any overlapping paths are combined into one shape/path.

7. **Zoom in to Madagascar (the island east of the main African continent).**

8. **With the Freeform Pen tool still active, click near the top of Madagascar to establish the starting point, hold down the mouse button, and then drag to trace the outside edge of the island.**

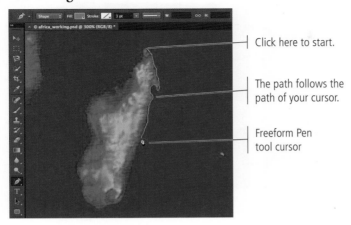

Click here to start.

The path follows the path of your cursor.

Freeform Pen tool cursor

9. **Release the mouse button about halfway down the east side of the island.**

When you release the mouse button, the shape you drew fills with the defined Fill color. This happens even when you draw a shape that isn't a closed path.

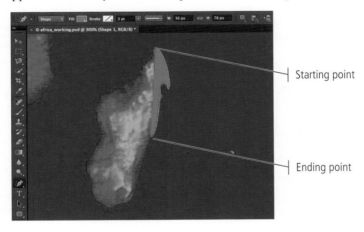

Starting point

Ending point

Note:

When you draw by holding down a button (mouse button or the button on a graphics tablet/pen) it is not uncommon for the line to "jump" where you don't want it to jump. If this happens, press Esc to remove your selection or path and start drawing again.

10. **Place the mouse cursor over the point where you stopped dragging.**

When the Pen tool cursor is over the end of an open path, the small slash in the icon indicates that you can click to continue drawing the same path.

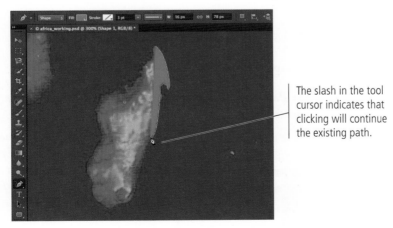

The slash in the tool cursor indicates that clicking will continue the existing path.

11. **Click over the open end point and continue tracing the outline of the island.**

When you return to the original starting point, a small circle in the tool cursor indicates that you are closing the shape. If you release the mouse button when you see the circle, the entire island shape will fill with the shape color.

The tool cursor shows that releasing the mouse button here will close the shape.

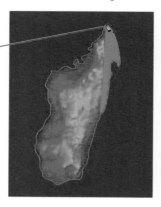
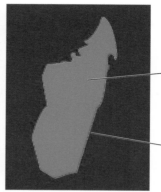

Releasing the mouse button fills the entire shape with the color you selected in the Color Picker.

The resulting path can be edited with the Direct Selection tool (nested under the Path Selection tool).

12. **Look at the Layers panel.**

When you draw with a Pen tool in Shape Layer mode, the resulting vector shape exists on its own layer.

The vector shape layer's icon identifies the shape's fill color.

Note:

The underlying map image is simply a guide for you to create the necessary vector shapes. Your shapes do not need to be perfect — although they should be close.

13. **Save the file and continue to the next exercise. If you get a warning about maximizing capability, click OK.**

ADD TO AN EXISTING SHAPE LAYER

The Freeform Pen tool is very useful for drawing custom vector shapes, whether you're tracing a map or drawing original freeform art. When using this tool, however, you must hold down the mouse button the entire time you draw (unless you have a graphics tablet).

In the case of this artwork, you have a better option because you don't need to precisely match the shape of the continent. The Freeform Pen tool has a Magnetic mode that snaps to edges of high-contrast pixel values in the image. Using this method will make it far easier to complete the outline you need.

1. **With africa_working.psd open, zoom out so you can see the entire image.**

2. **Make sure the shape layer is selected in the Layers panel.**

3. **With the Freeform Pen tool active, click the Path Operations button in the Options bar and choose Combine Shapes in the menu.**

You want to create a single shape layer with all the land masses, so you must make sure each new disconnected shape is added to the previous shapes.

Note:

An object that is made up of multiple, separate pieces is called **a compound path.** *Compound paths can also be used to remove inner areas from a shape, such as the interior of the letter A or the number 9.*

4. **Check the Magnetic option in the Options bar, then click the Geometry Options button.**

You can still define the Curve Fit option when drawing in Magnetic mode. You can also use this panel to control the magnetic behavior:

- **Width** determines how far from an edge you have to drag (1–256 pixels) for Photoshop to still find the edge.
- **Contrast** determines how much variation (1–100%) must exist between pixels for Photoshop to define an edge.
- **Frequency** determines the rate at which Photoshop places anchor points. Higher values (up to 100) create anchor points faster than lower values (down to 0).

5. **Set the Width to 40, the Contrast to 20%, and the Frequency to 25.**

This image has very high contrast between the land and the water, so you can use a lower contrast value and still find the edges.

Note:

The Pen Pressure option only applies if you have a pressure-sensitive graphics tablet. When this option is turned on, higher pressure decreases the Width tolerance.

6. **Click at the northeast point of Somalia to place the first anchor point, release the mouse button, and then drag around the shape of the African continent.**

You don't have to hold down the mouse button when you draw with the Freeform Pen tool in Magnetic mode. Although you can click specific points while you draw to manually place anchor points along the way, Photoshop automatically draws the path and points as necessary to create the shape.

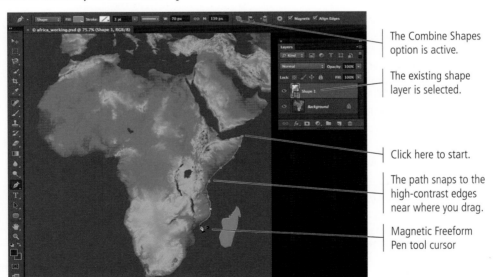

The Combine Shapes option is active.

The existing shape layer is selected.

Click here to start.

The path snaps to the high-contrast edges near where you drag.

Magnetic Freeform Pen tool cursor

An **anchor point** marks the end of a line **segment**, and the point **handles** determine the shape of that segment. That's the basic definition of a vector, but there is a bit more to it than that. (The Photoshop Help files refer to handles as direction lines, and distinguishes different types of points with different names. Our aim here is to explain the overall concept of vector paths, so we use the generic industry-standard terms. For more information on Adobe's terminology, refer to the Photoshop CS6 Help files.)

Each segment in a path has two anchor points and two associated handles. We first clicked to create Point A and dragged (without releasing the mouse button) to create Handle A1. We then clicked and dragged to create Point B and Handle B1; Handle B2 is automatically created as a reflection of B1 (Point B is a **symmetrical point**).

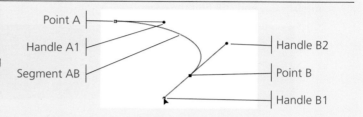

This image shows the result of dragging Handle B1 to the left instead of to the right when we created the initial curve. Notice the difference in the curve here, compared to the curve above. When you drag a handle, the connecting segment arcs away from the direction of the handle you drag.

It's important to understand that every line segment is connected to two handles. In this example, Handle A1 and Handle B2 determine the shape of Segment AB. Dragging either handle affects the shape of the connected segment.

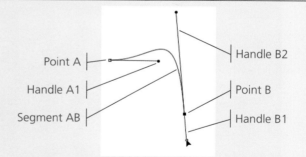

Clicking and dragging a point creates a symmetrical (smooth) point; both handles start out at equal length, directly opposite one another. Changing the angle of one handle of a symmetrical point also changes the opposing handle of that point. In the example here, repositioning Handle B1 also moves Handle B2, which affects the shape of Segment AB. (You can, however, change the length of one handle without affecting the length of the other handle.)

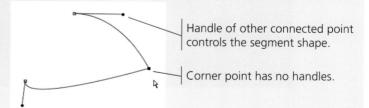

You can create corner points by simply clicking with the Pen tool instead of clicking and dragging. Corner points do not have their own handles; the connected segments are controlled by the handles of the other associated points.

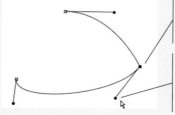

Handle of other connected point controls the segment shape.

Corner point has no handles.

You can convert a symmetrical point into a corner point by clicking the point with the Convert Point tool [⌐] (nested under the Pen tool). You can also add a handle to only one side of an anchor point by Option/Alt-clicking a point with the Convert Point tool and dragging.

Option/Alt-click this point with the Convert Point tool and drag to create only one handle.

This handle controls the connected segment; the handle is not reflected on the other side of the point.

7. **When you get to the point where Africa meets the Arabian Peninsula, drag across the Suez Canal. Photoshop will find and recognize the edge where Africa meets the Red Sea.**

8. **Drag around to the original starting point and click to close the shape.**

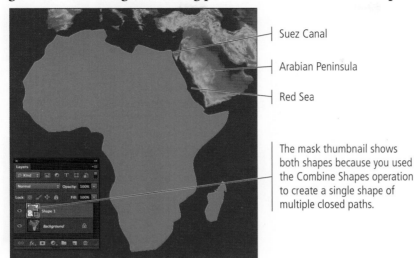

Suez Canal

Arabian Peninsula

Red Sea

The mask thumbnail shows both shapes because you used the Combine Shapes operation to create a single shape of multiple closed paths.

Note:

Even if the cursor is not directly over the open endpoint, you can double-click with the Freeform Pen tool in Magnetic mode to close the shape.

9. **Save the file and continue to the next exercise.**

CONTROL AND EDIT A SHAPE LAYER

When you outlined the shape of Africa, the Magnetic mode of the Freeform Pen tool made the work much easier than manually tracing the shape — but the path is not perfectly matched to the original. In this case, the result is acceptable because you don't need precision to achieve your ultimate goal.

In many cases, however, the path you first draw will be a good starting point, but will need some (if not significant) refinement before you can call it complete. You will probably need to edit at least one or two points or segments, move existing points, or even add or delete points before your path exactly matches the shape you're outlining. As you complete this exercise, we show you how to correct the path in our screen shots. You should follow the general directions to correct the path that you drew in the previous exercise as necessary.

1. **In the open africa_working.psd file, zoom in to the southern part of Europe at the top of the image.**

2. **Choose the Freeform Pen tool (if necessary). In the Options bar, choose New Layer in the Path Operations menu and activate the Magnetic option.**

   Remember, this menu retains the last-used setting as long as the same tool remains active. If you continued directly from the previous exercise, Combine Shapes would still be selected. We are including these steps to show you what to do if you accidentally create new layers for subsequent shapes — a very easy mistake to make — instead of combining all the shapes into a single layer.

Understanding Path Operations

When you first choose one of the vector drawing tools — Pen, Freeform Pen, or one of the Shape tools — the Path Operations menu defaults to **New Layer**. When this option is active, every new path will be created on a separate layer.

Combining Shapes

Combine Shapes creates the new path on the existing (selected) shape layer.

Subtract Front Shape creates the new path on the existing (selected layer), and removes overlapping areas of the new shape from the existing shape.

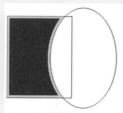

Intersect Shape Areas results in the shape of only overlapping areas in the existing and new shapes.

Exclude Overlapping Areas removes overlapping areas between the existing and new shapes.

Merging Shapes

It is important to note that with the four options explained above, the result is the appearance of a single shape, but the original paths of each shape are maintained. You can still select and manipulate each component path independently.

To make the interaction of overlapping shapes permanent, you can select the paths you want to affect and choose **Merge Shape Components**. This results in a single shape that is the combination of any selected paths; unselected paths are not affected.

The actual result of this command depends on the interaction of the selected paths. In the example to the right, the top shape had been created with the Exclude Overlapping Areas operation.

After applying the Merge Shape Components operation, anchor points were added where the original paths intersected. The original component shapes no longer exist. You can see this in the bottom image, where we used the Direct Selection tool to move the individual anchor points that were created by merging the shapes.

3. **Click to anchor the path where Italy meets the top edge of the image, then drag around Italy to create the path.**

When you drag around the tip of the "boot," the area is too narrow for Photoshop to accurately create the outline.

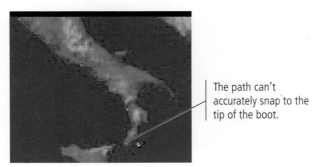

The path can't accurately snap to the tip of the boot.

4. **Drag back to the tip of the boot and click to manually place an anchor point, and then continue dragging around the outline. Anywhere the path doesn't accurately snap to the edge, click to manually create a point.**

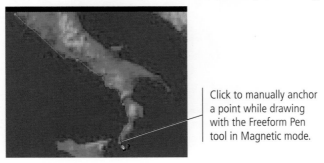

Click to manually anchor a point while drawing with the Freeform Pen tool in Magnetic mode.

5. **Click over the original starting point to close the shape.**

When you close the shape, you can probably see that it needs some help.

6. Use the following information to fine-tune your outline of Italy.

This is one place where we can't give you specific instructions because everyone's path will be a bit different. Keep the following points in mind as you refine your shape:

Use the Add Anchor Point tool to add a point to a path.

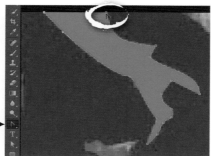

Use the Convert Anchor Point tool to change a smooth point to a corner point (or vice versa).

Note:

Manually clicking while using the Freeform Pen tool in Magnetic mode is a good way to make sharp turns along thin areas, which you will see shortly.

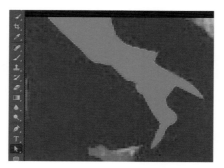

Use the Direct Selection tool to select and edit individual anchor points and their handles.

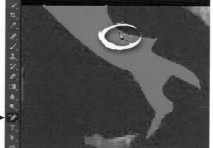

Use the Delete Anchor Point tool to delete a point from the path.

This is our final result:

7. Look at the Layers panel.

Because you chose the New Layer path operation before creating Italy's shape, this exercise resulted in a new shape layer — Shape 2.

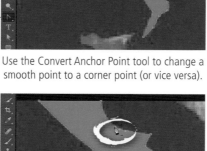

8. With the Shape 2 layer selected in the Layers panel, Shift-click Shape 1 to select both layers.

9. **Open the Layers panel Options menu and choose Merge Shapes.**

This command combines the shapes on all selected layers into a single shape layer — basically the same as using the Combine Shapes path operation. The new combined layer adopts the name of the highest layer in the previous selection.

Note:

Don't confuse this Merge option with the Merge Shape Components option in the Path Operations menu. The Merge Shapes option in the Layers panel actually combines the various shapes into a single layer, but maintains all of the existing paths.

10. **Save the file and continue to the next exercise.**

Selecting and Modifying Paths

PHOTOSHOP FOUNDATIONS

When you draw vector paths, you can use the Path Selection tool to select and move specific paths on a layer.

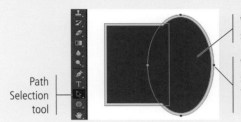

Path Selection tool

We clicked the oval to select only that path.

When a path is selected, you can see the anchor points that make up that path.

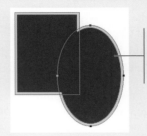

Click and drag with the Path Selection tool to move the selected path.

When the Path Selection tool is active, you can use the W and H fields to modify the width and height (respectively) of the selected shape. It is important to note, however, that multiple paths on the same layer are all affected by the change.

In the example to the right, you can see that only the oval is selected. By changing the W field (making the shape wider), you are actually affecting the width of both shapes on the layer and not just the selected oval. If you want to manipulate the shape of individual paths, you should create each shape on a separate layer.

Changing the width or height of a shape affects the entire layer, not just the selected path.

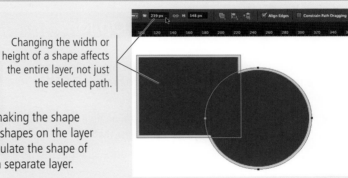

The same concept is true of changing the fill or stroke attributes. Any changes you make to the fill color, or to the stroke color, weight, or type apply to *all* paths on the selected layer.

You can also select a specific shape to change the path operation that applies to it. In the example to the right, the rectangle was created first and then the oval was created with the Combine Shapes path operation. We then used the Path Selection tool to select the oval, and chose the Subtract Front Shape operation. Unless you merge the paths into a single shape, you can always select an individual path and change the way it interacts with underlying shapes.

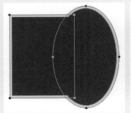
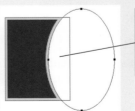

Changing the path operation of the selected path changes the way it interacts with the bottom path.

Because the path operations affect underlying shapes, you should also understand the concept of **stacking order**. When you create multiple shapes on the same shape layer, they exist from bottom to top in the order in which you create them — the first shape is on the bottom, then the next shape, and so on until the last shape created is at the top of the stack. You can use the **Path Arrangement** menu to control the stacking order of selected paths on the same shape layer.

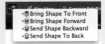

SUBTRACT FROM A SHAPE LAYER

You now have a single shape layer consisting of three different shapes. The final step of creating the continent shape layer is to outline the remaining land areas, and then remove the areas of large bodies of water from the shape.

1. **With africa_working.psd open, use what you have learned about drawing shape layers to add the remaining land areas to the existing shape layer. Use the following guidelines as you create the shapes:**

   - Make sure the shape layer is selected in the Layers panel and use the Combine Shapes path operation.

   - Make sure all the points that touch the image edges are corner points, with no extraneous points on the segments that touch the image edge.

   - **Remember:** The Path Operations menu retains the last-used selection as long as you are still using the same tool. You can continue combining (for example) as many new shapes as you like until you switch to a different tool — say, the Direct Selection tool to modify a specific anchor point.

   - Include the larger islands in the Mediterranean Sea (Sicily, Corsica, Sardinia, Crete, and Cyprus).

   - For now, don't worry about tracing the Black and Caspian Seas above the Arabian Peninsula. You will remove those in the next few steps.

   When you have finished drawing the outlines, you're almost done — except that you covered two large seas and at least five major lakes within the African continent. You will fix that problem next.

2. Choose the Path Selection tool in the Tools panel, then click away from all the shapes to deselect all paths in the active shape.

The Path Selection tool is used to select and modify entire paths. The Direct Selection tool is used to select and modify individual anchor points or segments on a specific path.

If any path in the existing shape is still selected when you choose a new path operation, the selected operation would affect the selected paths in the existing shape. To avoid this potential problem, you are first deselecting the path.

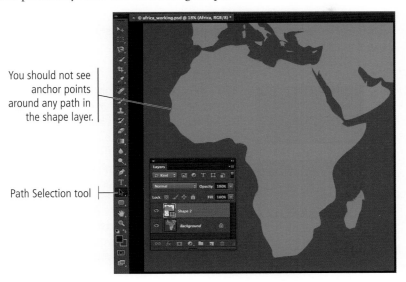

You should not see anchor points around any path in the shape layer.

Path Selection tool

3. In the Layers panel, change the shape layer's opacity to 50%.

You can change the opacity of any layer, including a shape layer. By reducing the layer opacity, you can see the underlying layers enough to trace the seas and lakes.

Note: If you had to merge multiple shape layers after Step 1, your shape layer might have a different number than what you see in our screen shot. Just be sure you select the shape layer in your file before completing the following steps.

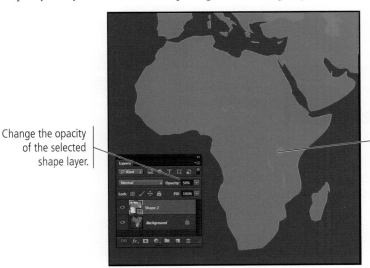

Change the opacity of the selected shape layer.

The shape fill is now semi-transparent, allowing you to see and trace the seas and lakes.

4. With the Freeform Pen tool active (with or without Magnetic mode), choose the Subtract Front Shape path operation.

This option removes the area of a new shape from the existing shape; non-overlapping areas are not filled with the shape color.

For the Pen tool, you can check the Rubber Band option in the Geometry Options menu to show a preview of the path curve as you move the cursor.

When the Rubber Band option is active, you can see a preview of the curve that will be created when you click to place an anchor point.

The basic shape tools — Rectangle, Rounded Rectangle, Ellipse, Polygon, and Line — have most of the same basic options as the Pen and Freeform Pen tool. You can use them to create a vector path or a shape layer with a defined fill and stroke. The geometry options relate to the specific type of shape you create with a specific tool.

Rectangle and Ellipse Tools

When the **Unconstrained** option is selected, you can simply click and drag to create a rectangle of any size.

Rectangle tool

If you choose the **Square** option (or Circle for the Ellipse tool), the shape you draw will be constrained to equal width and height (1:1 aspect ratio).

Ellipse tool

You can use the **Fixed Size** option to create a shape at a specific width and height. When you click in the canvas, you see a preview of the shape that will be created; you can drag around the canvas to determine where you want to place the shape when you release the mouse button.

You can also use the **Proportional** option to define the aspect ratio of the shape you will create. When you click and drag, the shape is constrained to the proportions you define.

If you choose the **From Center** option, the center of the shape you create will be placed where you first click.

Rounded Rectangle Tool

Most of the options for this tool are the same as for the regular Rectangle tool. In the Options bar, however, you can use the Radius field to define the appearance of the shape's corners.

Rounded Rectangle tool

To understand the concept of corner radius, think of an imaginary circle placed at the corners of a rectangle. The two sides are connected with one-fourth of a circle, which has a radius equal to the amount of the rounding.

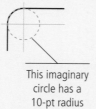

This imaginary circle has a 10-pt radius

Polygon Tool

When you draw with the Polygon tool, you can define the number of sides in the related field on the Options bar. In the Geometry Options menu, you can define a specific Radius, or the length of each side of the polygon. If the Smooth Corners option is checked, corners on the shape are rounded.

Polygon tool

If you check the Star option, you can define the distance at which each side is indented from the outside edges of the shape. The number of sides defines the number of points on the resulting star shape. If you check the Smooth Indents option, the insets of the star will have rounded corners.

Line Tool

When you draw with the Line tool, you can use the Geometry Options menu to add arrowheads to the start and/or end of the line. The Width and Length fields define those attributes of the arrowheads, as a percentage of the line weight; the Concavity field defines the arrowheads' inset as a percentage of its length.

Line tool

Custom Shape Tool

The Custom Shape tool makes it easy to create custom vector shapes from one of several defined libraries. You can open the Shape panel in the Options bar to access the built-in libraries of shapes.

Geometry options for the Custom Shape tool are the same as for the Rectangle and Ellipse tools.

5. **Using the same techniques you used to create the existing shape layer, trace the outline of the Caspian Sea.**

The Black Sea is still obscured. It is visible because the shape layer is semi-transparent.

Because you subtracted this area from the shape layer, the background image is now fully visible.

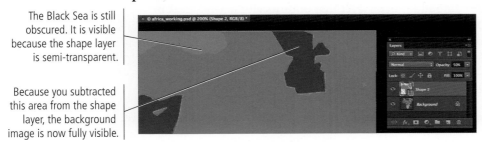

6. **Continue removing the areas of any large bodies of water from the shape layer. Make sure you exclude the larger African lakes identified in the following image:**

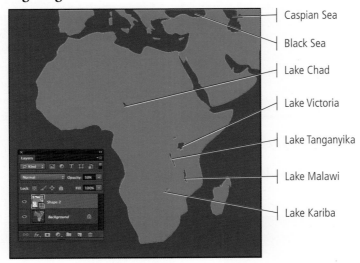

Caspian Sea

Black Sea

Lake Chad

Lake Victoria

Lake Tanganyika

Lake Malawi

Lake Kariba

7. **In the Layers panel, double-click the shape layer's name to highlight it, then type Africa to rename the layer.**

8. **Save the file and continue to the next exercise.**

RESAMPLE THE SHAPE LAYER AND CHANGE THE CANVAS SIZE

You now have a complete compound shape layer that outlines all the land areas in the original image. The file, however, is still only about 4″ wide. Before you add the animal images, you need to convert the file to the appropriate size so the placed animal pictures are not resampled when you enlarge the image.

1. **With africa_working.psd open, choose Image>Image Size.**

2. **In the Image Size dialog box, make sure the Resample Image option is active.**

3. **Change the Height field to 12 [inches] and click OK.**

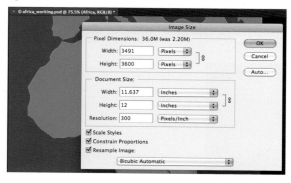

Note:

You're adding a sizeable amount of information to this file, so the resampling process might take a few minutes. Depending on the power and speed of your computer, you might see a progress bar as the image size is remapped.

4. **Zoom in so you can clearly see the shape layer edges.**

5. **In the Layers panel, click away from the shape layer to turn off the vector path in the document window.**

The vector edge of the shape layer is still just as sharp as it was when you created it at the original size.

The background image is still badly pixelated, just as it was when you resized it earlier.

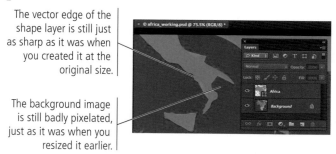

Note:

Clicking the empty area at the bottom of the Layers panel is the best option to deselect the shape layer.

6. **Change your view to fit the entire image in the document window.**

7. **Choose Image>Canvas Size.**

When you resampled the image to 12″ high, you might have noticed that the width was proportionally changed to 11.636″. That's slightly larger than the 10″ you want, so you need to crop the image to the correct dimensions.

In Project 1: Composite Movie Ad, you used the Crop tool to crop a file to a specific size. If you know the exact size you need, you can change the size of the canvas to change the size of an image.

The Anchor area shows the reference point around which the canvas will be enlarged or cropped. If the center point is selected, for example, reducing the width by 1″ would remove 0.5″ from the left and right edges of the image.

8. **Change the Width field to 10 [inches] and click OK.**

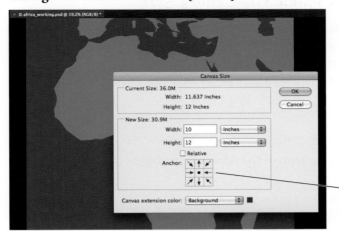

Note:

If you activate the Relative check box, you can define how much you want to add or subtract instead of defining a specific height and width. For example, you can reduce the height by 1" by typing −1 in the height field.

The inward-pointing arrows show that space will be removed from the left and right of the image.

When you reduce a canvas size, you're warned that elements outside the new dimensions will be clipped (removed).

Note:

If you are enlarging the canvas, you can use the Canvas Extension Color option to define the color that will be used in the new area outside the existing image size.

9. **Click Proceed to crop the canvas to 10″ wide.**

10. **In the Layers panel, click the Africa shape layer to select it and reveal the path.**

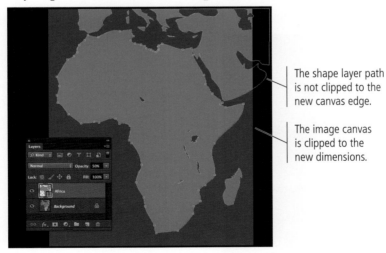

The shape layer path is not clipped to the new canvas edge.

The image canvas is clipped to the new dimensions.

11. **Save the file and continue to the next exercise.**

ADD COLOR AND TEXTURE TO THE SHAPE LAYER

Aside from their usefulness as scalable vector paths, shape layers can be filled with solid colors (as yours is now), with styles or patterns (which you will add in this exercise), or even with other images (which you will do later).

Most of the shape layer in this file is going to be filled with pictures of animals, but some areas will remain visible. Adding a texture to the whole shape layer will create an effective background in areas where the animal pictures don't completely fill in the shape layer.

1. **With africa_working.psd open, click the eye icon of the Africa shape layer to hide that layer.**

   You're going to pull a color from the placed image to use as the layer's fill color. To do that, you must be able to see the underlying layer.

2. **In the Layers panel, double-click the layer thumbnail of the (hidden) shape layer.**

   Clicking the thumbnail of a shape layer opens the Color Picker dialog box, where you can choose a color to apply using three different techniques:

   • Numerically define a color in any of the available color modes.

   • Click in the Color Picker window.

   • Move the cursor over the image window to access the Eyedropper tool, then click in the image window and sample a color from the image.

3. **Click the eyedropper cursor in one of the gold areas of the image.**

   We sampled a color in the lower left part of the main African continent.

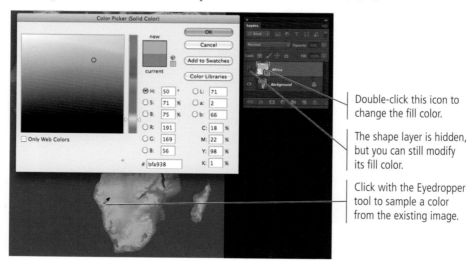

Double-click this icon to change the fill color.

The shape layer is hidden, but you can still modify its fill color.

Click with the Eyedropper tool to sample a color from the existing image.

4. **Click OK to close the Color Picker.**

   The shape layer fill changes as soon as you choose a color in the Color Picker dialog box; however, you can't see this effect while the layer is hidden.

5. **Show the Africa layer, and change its opacity back to 100%.**

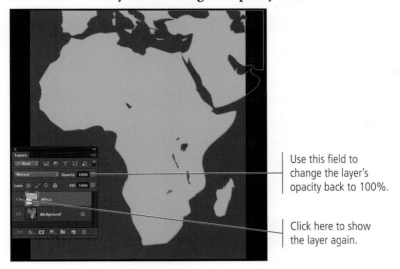

Use this field to change the layer's opacity back to 100%.

Click here to show the layer again.

6. **Choose Window>Styles to open the Styles panel.**

This panel shows the predefined styles that can be applied to a shape layer. The icons give you an idea of what the styles do, but these small squares can be cryptic.

7. **Click the arrow in the top-right corner of the Styles panel and choose Large List from the Options menu.**

We prefer the list view because the style names provide a better idea of what the styles do. The Large List option displays a bigger style thumbnail than the Small List view.

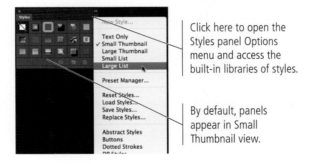

Click here to open the Styles panel Options menu and access the built-in libraries of styles.

By default, panels appear in Small Thumbnail view.

8. **Open the Styles panel Options menu again and choose Textures near the bottom of the list.**

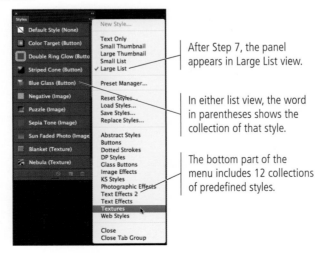

After Step 7, the panel appears in Large List view.

In either list view, the word in parentheses shows the collection of that style.

The bottom part of the menu includes 12 collections of predefined styles.

9. **Click OK to replace the current set with the Textures set.**

When you call a new set of styles, Photoshop asks if you want to replace the current set or append the new set to the existing set(s).

If you select Append, the new styles will be added to the existing ones. This can result in a very long list, which makes it difficult to find what you want. By replacing the current set, you will only see the styles in the texture set. This does not delete the previous styles, it only removes them from the panel; you can recall the previous styles by choosing Reset Styles in the panel Options menu.

10. **Make sure the shape layer is selected in the Layers panel and then click Ancient Stone in the Styles panel to apply the style to the shape layer.**

A **style** is simply a saved group of effects that can be applied with a single click. You can create your own styles using the Layer Effects dialog box (which you will do in Project 4: City Promotion Cards).

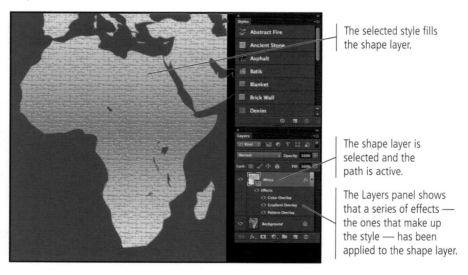

The selected style fills the shape layer.

The shape layer is selected and the path is active.

The Layers panel shows that a series of effects — the ones that make up the style — has been applied to the shape layer.

11. **In the Layers panel, click the arrow to the right of the fx icon of the Africa layer.**

This collapses the list of applied effects, which helps keep the Layers panel easier to manage.

Click here to collapse or expand the list of applied effects.

12. **Save the file and continue to the next stage of the project.**

Understanding the Paths Panel

If you use the Pen tool in Paths mode, the vector path that you create is stored in the Paths panel rather than attached to a specific layer.

When you first create a path, it is stored as the work path. If you use the Combine Shapes geometry option, drawing another shape adds to the current work path, which is stored temporarily until you deselect the path.

If you want to be able to access a path later in your work, you can save the work path with a user-defined name. Saved paths are stored in the Paths panel until you intentionally delete them.

Path mode

The work path is only temporary.

Click here to open the panel Options menu.

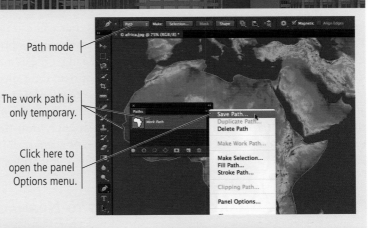

If you click a saved path name in the panel, the path becomes visible in the document window. You can then use the vector drawing and editing tools to edit the path.

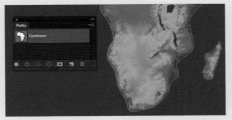

Click a saved path to select it and reveal the path in the document window.

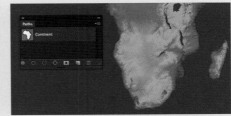

Click the empty area of the panel to deselect the active path and hide it in the document window.

In the Paths panel options menu, you can choose **Make Selection** to make a marching-ants selection based on the path shape. You can use the resulting dialog box to define the details of the selection.

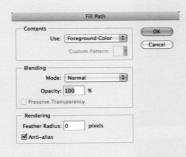

If you choose **Fill Path** in the Options menu, you can use the resulting dialog box to determine how the fill will be created. You can choose the color or pattern, the blending mode and opacity, and whether to feather the edge of the resulting fill so it blends smoothly into underlying layers.

If you choose the **Stroke Path** option, you must also choose which tool will create the stroke; the applied stroke will have the last-used settings for the selected tool. In other words, you have to define the tool options (brush size, hardness, etc.) that you want before using this option.

The Fill Path and Stroke Path options add the resulting pixels to the currently active layer — an important distinction from the Shape Layer option, which automatically creates a new layer when you begin drawing the vector path. It is also important to remember that, although the path remains a vector path, color that is applied to the fill or stroke of the path is raster or pixel-based; it does not have the same scalability as a vector shape layer.

If you choose the **Clipping Path** option, the selected path will become a clipping path, which is essentially a vector mask that defines the visible area of an image if the file is placed into a page-layout application such as Adobe InDesign. (The white area in the path thumbnail defines what areas will be visible in the image.)

Buttons across the bottom of the Paths panel provide quick access to many of the features explained here. They are, from left:

- Fill Path with Foreground Color
- Stroke Path with Brush
- Load Path as a Selection
- Make Work Path from Selection
- Add Layer Mask
- Create New Path
- Delete Path

Stage 2 Compositing with Smart Objects

Your client provided a number of animal pictures that you can use in the finished artwork. In Project 1: Composite Movie Ad, you learned several basic methods for compositing files into another file — copying and pasting (or dragging), and placing a file as a Smart Object. Your ultimate goal determines which of these methods is most appropriate for a specific job.

When you apply tranformations or filters to a regular layer, the pixels on the layer are permanently affected (unless you undo the filter or step back through the History panel). Smart Objects are layers that preserve source content, which means you can apply **non-destructive** edits to the layer. Those transformations do not alter the actual image data of a smart object; you can restore the original image content, or make changes to the transformations that you apply, without negatively affecting quality.

 ## COMPARE SMART OBJECT LAYERS TO NORMAL LAYERS

In this stage of the project, you will apply layer masks and filters to the client's animal pictures. However, you don't want to modify the actual photo files, and you need to be able to change the filter settings if the client doesn't like the initial results. In this exercise, you will place two of the animal images as Smart Object layers and paste two of the animal images as regular layers, so we can point out the differences between the two types of layers.

1. **With africa_working.psd open, choose File>Place.**

   The File>Place command has the same effect as dragging a thumbnail from the Mini Bridge panel into an open image.

2. **Navigate to addax.tif in your WIP>Africa folder, click Place, and then press Return/Enter to finalize the placement in the document window.**

Note:

In addition to placing files as Smart Objects, you can also open a file as a Smart Object in the File menu.

When you place a file, it shows diagonal lines before the placement is finalized.

After finalizing the placement, the layer is added to the file.

The layer icon shows that the placed file is a Smart Object layer.

3. **Repeat Steps 1–2 to place `lion.tif` into your working file.**

   Unfortunately, you cannot select more than one file at a time in the Place dialog box.

4. **Choose File>Open. Select `giraffe.jpg` and `gorilla.tif` and click Open.**

5. **Make the africa_working file the active one, then choose Window>Arrange> 3-Up Stacked to show all three documents at once within the workspace.**

6. **Choose the Move tool in the Tools panel.**

7. **Click the Giraffe window to activate that file, and then drag the giraffe image into your working map file. Close the giraffe file.**

8. **Repeat Step 7 for the gorilla file.**

9. **Fit the entire working file into the document window, and then review the Layers panel.**

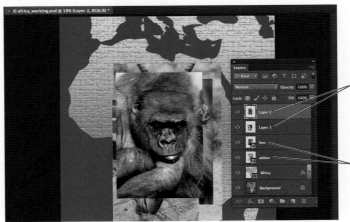

The giraffe layer (Layer 1) and gorilla layer (Layer 2) are regular Photoshop layers. They are not linked to external files.

The lion and addax layers are Smart Object layers; the layer names are defined by the names of the files you placed.

10. **Rename the two regular layers to reflect which animals reside on those layers.**

    Remember, to rename a layer, simply double-click the layer name in the Layers panel and then type the new name.

11. **Save the file and continue to the next exercise.**

Note:

In a later exercise, you will explore the different ways in which Photoshop manages masks for regular layers compared to Smart Object layers.

You need a bit of background about channels to understand what's happening in the Quick Mask you will use in the next exercise. (You will use channels extensively in later projects.)

Every image has one channel for each component color. An RGB image has three channels: Red, Green, and Blue; a CMYK image has four channels: Cyan, Magenta, Yellow, and Black. Each channel contains the information for the amount of that component color in any given pixel.

An RGB image has three channels, one for each additive primary.

In RGB images, the three additive primaries can have a value of 0 (none of that color) to 255 (full intensity of that color). Combining a value of 255 for each primary results in white; a value of 0 for each primary results in black.

In CMYK images, the three subtractive primaries plus black are combined in percentages from 0 (none of that color) to 100 (full intensity of that color) to create the range of printable colors. Channels in a CMYK image represent the printing plates or separations required to output the job.

A CMYK image has four channels, one for each subtractive primary plus one for black.

When you work in Quick Mask mode, an extra Alpha channel is created to temporarily store the selection area. An Alpha channel functions like a regular channel, in that it has the same range of possible values (0–255 in an RGB image, 0–100 in a CMYK image). However, the Alpha value determines the degree of transparency of a pixel. In other words, a 50% value in the Alpha channel means that area of the image will be 50% transparent.

The Quick Mask channel stores the degree of transparency based on the current selection.

The semi-transparent red overlay shows areas being masked (i.e., the areas outside the current selection).

Alpha channels allow you to design with degrees of transparency. You can blend one image into another, blend one layer into another, or blend an entire image into a background in a page-layout application.

You can change the appearance of masks by double-clicking the Quick Mask button in the Tools panel, or double-clicking the Quick Mask thumbnail in the Channels panel.

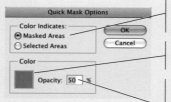

Change the mask to overlay the masked area instead of the selected area.

Click here to change the color of the mask in the image window.

Quick Masks are useful when you need to work with a temporary selection or if you are still defining the exact selection area. As long as you stay in Quick Mask mode, the temporary Alpha channel remains in the Channels panel (listed in italics as "Quick Mask"). If you return to Standard mode, the Quick Mask disappears from the window and the panel.

Use this option to make the mask more or less transparent. (This setting only affects the appearance of the mask in Photoshop.)

Once you have created a complex selection, you can save it as a permanent Alpha channel by dragging the Quick Mask channel onto the New Channel button at the bottom of the Channels panel. This adds a channel named "Quick Mask copy" (not in italics), which will be a permanent part of the file even if you exit Quick Mask mode.

Permanent Alpha channel

Temporary Quick Mask channel

New Channel button

WORK WITH FEATHERED SELECTIONS IN QUICK MASK MODE

In the Interface chapter, we said that making selections is so important that Photoshop has an entire menu dedicated to that task. In Project 1: Composite Movie Ad, you learned several methods for creating selections. To complete the map in this project, you will expand on those skills to create soft-edge layer masks that help blend the animals into the background.

1. **With `africa_working.psd` open, hide all the layers except the lion. Click the lion layer in the Layers panel to select that layer.**

2. **Choose the Elliptical Marquee tool (nested under the Rectangular Marquee tool) in the Tools panel.**

3. **Press Option/Alt, then click the middle of the lion's nose and drag out to create a selection with the center point where you first clicked.**

   Pressing Option/Alt places the center of the selection marquee at the point where you click; when you drag out, the marquee is created around that point.

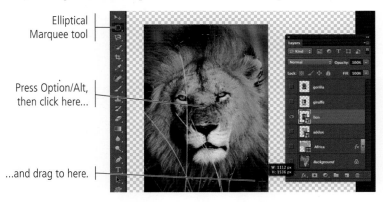

Elliptical Marquee tool

Press Option/Alt, then click here...

...and drag to here.

Note:

If you choose Transform Selection in the Select menu, the selection marquee shows bounding box handles, which you can use to transform the marquee just as you would transform a layer.

4. **Choose Select>Modify>Feather. In the Feather Selection dialog box, type 25 in the Feather Radius field, then click OK.**

Note:

When a marquee is visible and a Marquee tool is active, you can click inside the marquee area and drag to reposition the selection area in the image.

5. **Click the Quick Mask button at the bottom of the Tools panel to toggle into Quick Mask mode.**

   This mode creates a temporary Alpha channel that shows the feathered selection.

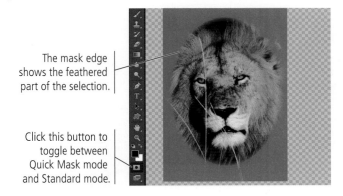

The mask edge shows the feathered part of the selection.

Click this button to toggle between Quick Mask mode and Standard mode.

6. **Click the Quick Mask button at the bottom of the Tools panel to toggle off the Quick Mask.**

   If you don't turn off the Quick Mask mode, Step 7 will create an empty layer mask.

7. **In the Layers panel, click the Add Layer Mask button.**

   A layer mask is basically an Alpha channel connected to a specific layer.

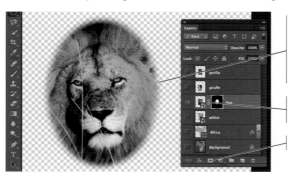

The feathered-selection-turned-layer-mask allows the lion image to blend into the background instead of ending abruptly.

The layer mask is linked to the selected layer.

Add Layer Mask button

Note:

Alternatively, you could Command/Control-click the Quick Mask in the Channels panel to show the marching ants, and then click the Add Layer Mask button in the Layers panel.

8. **Hide the lion layer and show the gorilla layer. Click the gorilla layer in the Layers panel to make that the active layer.**

9. **Choose the Elliptical Marquee tool in the Tools panel. In the Options bar, type 25 px in the Feather field.**

10. **Press Option/Alt, then click the middle of the gorilla's nose and drag out to create a selection with the center point where you first clicked.**

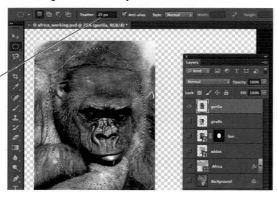

Use this field to define the feather radius of the selection you draw.

11. **Click the Add Layer Mask button in the Layers panel.**

   By changing the Feather option for the marquee tools, you draw a selection that is already feathered without requiring the secondery stap of opening a dialog box (as you did in Step 4). Keep in mind, however, that if you draw a feathered selection (using the tool option setting), you can't undo the feather without also undoing the selection area.

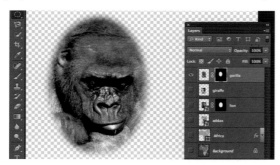

Note:

When a masked layer is selected in the Layers panel, the layer mask appears in the Channels panel as a temporary Alpha channel.

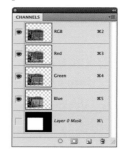

   Even though one of these layers is a Smart Object and one is a regular layer, the result is basically the same. Both layers show the appropriate layer mask in the Layers panel.

12. **Hide the gorilla layer, save the file, and continue to the next exercise.**

APPLY A LAYER MASK TO A SMART OBJECT LAYER

In the previous exercise, you created a feathered layer mask for a Smart Object layer; you added the layer mask within the main africa_working Layers panel, so the layer mask did not affect the original file. Depending on the project you're building, you might want to create a layer mask once and have it affect all instances of that Smart Object. In this case, you should edit the actual Smart Object file instead of affecting only a single placed instance.

1. **In africa_working.psd, show only the addax layer.**

Double-click this thumbnail to open the Smart Object file.

2. **Double-click the addax layer thumbnail to open the Smart Object file in its own window. If you see a warning message, click OK.**

   This message tells you that you must save the Smart Object with the same name for the changes to reflect in the africa_working file. You can't use the Save As function to save the file with a different name or in a different location.

Note:

If you don't see this message, you can open the General pane of the Preferences dialog box and click the Reset All Warning Dialogs button.

   The addax file opens separately, appearing by default as a separate tab at the top of the document window.

The addax image is a flat image, which means it has only a Background layer that is locked.

3. **Using the Rectangular Marquee tool, create a 25-pixel feathered selection around the addax's head.**

4. **In the Layers panel, double-click the Background layer to see your options.**

   In the Layers panel, the Add Layer Mask option is not available because the file has only one layer — Background. You can't apply a layer mask to the Background layer of a file, so you first have to convert the Background layer to a regular layer.

5. **In the New Layer dialog box, leave the options at their default values and click OK.**

   The former Background layer is now a regular unlocked layer named Layer 0. You could have renamed it, but that is unnecessary for this exercise.

6. **With the feathered selection still active, click the Add Layer Mask button at the bottom of the Layers panel.**

7. **Choose File>Save (or press Command/Control-S).**

   The TIFF Options dialog box appears because your file now has new layer information. Even though the file has only one layer, that layer is partially transparent.

Note:

This technique wouldn't work if you placed a JPEG file as a Smart Object. To save a JPEG file with layer information, you must save the file as a copy — and you would see a related warning if you tried to do so. Saving as a copy means saving under a different file name, which would defeat the purpose and function of Smart Objects.

8. **Leave the TIFF options at their default values and click OK. If you see a warning about including layers, click OK again.**

9. **Close the addax.tif file.**

When you look at the africa_working file, you can see that the layer mask has been applied to the addax image, but the Layers panel doesn't show the layer mask thumbnail. That's because the mask is applied in the Smart Object, not in the main file.

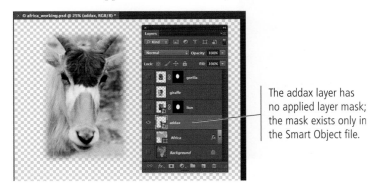

The addax layer has no applied layer mask; the mask exists only in the Smart Object file.

10. **Save the file, then continue to the next exercise.**

 EDIT A LAYER MASK

Creating a layer mask from a selection is easy enough, and it's sometimes sufficient for a particular job (as was the case for the lion). In other cases, however, you might want to create a mask that is beyond what you can easily accomplish with the basic selection tools. If necessary, you can paint directly on a layer mask to achieve virtually any effect — such as a mask that better outlines the addax and its long, curved horns.

1. **With africa_working.psd open, double-click the addax layer thumbnail to open the Smart Object file. Click OK in the message about saving the Smart Object file.**

2. **In the Layers panel, click the layer mask thumbnail to select it.**

These corner icons indicate that the base layer is selected.

Clicking the layer mask thumbnail selects the mask so you can edit it.

3. **In the Channels panel (Window>Channels), make sure the Layer 0 Mask channel is visible.**

Layer masks are not visible by default; you have to turn them on in the Channels panel to see them. This isn't strictly necessary, since you can paint a mask without seeing it, but it is easier (at least when you're first learning) to be able to see what you're painting. By painting on a layer mask, you're not really "painting" anything; instead, you're actually "painting" the visibility of the associated layer.

Making the mask channel visible allows you to see the red overlay in the image.

4. **Double-click the Layer 0 Mask channel thumbnail. Change the Opacity value to 100% in the Layer Mask Display Options dialog box, then click OK.**

Remember, this change only affects the transparency of the mask, not the degree of transparency applied to the layer. By setting the mask opacity to 100%, you know that anything solid red will be hidden and anything with no red will be visible.

5. **Choose the Brush tool in the Tools panel, and then click the Default Foreground and Background Colors button at the bottom of the Tools panel.**

If you look at the layer mask thumbnail for the layer, you can see it's just a black-and-white shape. White areas of the thumbnail show which parts of the layer are visible in the main document; the black parts of the mask hide the associated areas of the layer. This is an important distinction: painting with black on a layer mask hides those areas; painting with white on a layer mask reveals those areas.

Note:

Painting with black on a layer mask hides those areas; painting with white on a layer mask reveals those areas.

Brush tool

Click here to return the foreground to black and the background to white.

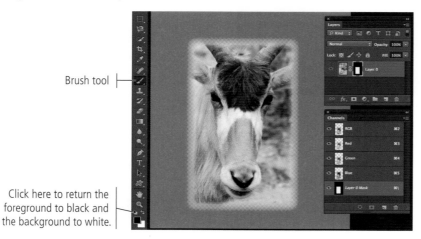

6. **In the Options bar, open the Brush Preset picker to access the tool options.**

This panel shows the different brushes that are included with Photoshop. The default brush set includes a number of specific-diameter hard- and soft-edge brushes, as well as some artistic options. A number below a brush icon shows the size of the brush; if you click a specific brush in the panel, the same number displays in the Size field.

7. **Change the Size value to 200 px and the Hardness value to 0%.**

Click here to access the Brush Preset picker.

Note:

You will use brushes extensively in Project 7: House Painting; for now, you only need to know how to select a brush and how to paint with it.

8. **Click once to the right of the addax's face.**

The Brush tool paints with whatever is defined as the foreground color, which is black in this case. Because you're using a soft-edge brush, the place where you click blends from solid black to nothing — resulting in a soft edge to the brush stroke (or dot in this case).

Even though you're painting with black, the stroke appears as red because that's the defined mask color.

The Brush tool cursor reflects the size of the brush you're using.

A soft-edge brush adds a feathered edge to what you paint.

Remember, you're painting on the layer mask.

9. **Using the brush, click and drag to paint the entire area to the right of the animal's head.**

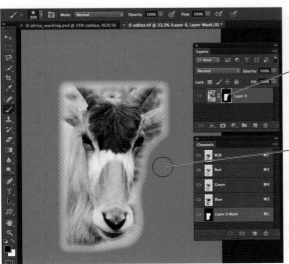

The layer mask thumbnail reflects the area you painted black.

Paint in this area to refine the mask around the animal's head.

10. **Click the Switch Foreground and Background Colors button near the bottom of the Tools panel.**

11. **Paint over the area where the tip of the right ear should be.**

    Because you're now painting with white, you're basically removing area from the mask. You can also use the Eraser tool on a mask. Be careful, though, because erasing an area of the mask when the foreground color is white has the same effect as painting with black — "erasing" on the mask actually adds to the mask.

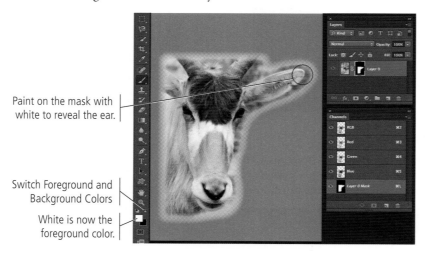

    Paint on the mask with white to reveal the ear.

    Switch Foreground and Background Colors

    White is now the foreground color.

Note:

You can change the Brush tool cursor in the Cursors pane of the Preferences dialog box. Standard shows only the tool icon; Precise shows a crosshair icon; Normal shows the solid-area brush size; Full Size expands the normal brush to include the feathered area. You can also choose to show a crosshair icon in the center of the brush area.

12. **Continue refining the mask to make both horns and ears visible, until you're satisfied with the result.**

    You should have no hard edges around the outside of the image.

    Remember, switching the foreground and background colors allows you to add or remove areas of the mask without changing tools.

13. **Save the addax file and close it.**

    Remember, you're working in a Smart Object file, so don't choose Save As or save the file with a different name. Once the process has updated, the Smart Object layer in the africa_working file shows the results of the refined layer mask.

Note:

You can create a layer mask from scratch by adding the mask with nothing selected, and then painting and erasing as necessary to mask the areas you want to hide. You can even use a black-to-white gradient on a layer mask to create unique effects in a non-specific shape.

14. **Save the map file and continue to the next exercise.**

Accessing Brush Libraries

PHOTOSHOP FOUNDATIONS

In the first part of this project, you learned how to access additional sets of built-in styles. You can use the same basic technique to access any of the built-in brush libraries from the Brush Preset picker Options menu. If you call a brush library from the menu, you have the choice of appending the brushes to the current set or replacing the current set with the new library (just as you do with built-in style libraries).

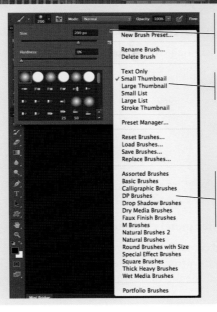

Click here to access the Brush Preset picker Options menu.

Change the view of the brushes in the panel.

A number of different basic and artistic brushes can be accessed in these built-in libraries.

 ## USE THE PROPERTIES PANEL

In the previous exercises, you learned how to create a feathered selection and a layer mask based on that selection. You also learned how to use black and white to paint directly on a layer mask. These same techniques work for both normal layers and Smart Object layers. The Properties panel provides another option for creating and managing layer masks. This panel consolidates mask-related options from multiple locations in a single, convenient interface.

1. **With** `africa_working.psd` **open, hide the addax layer and show the giraffe layer. Click the giraffe layer to select it.**

2. **Choose the Lasso tool in the Tools panel. Drag to create a selection roughly matching the shape of the giraffe's head.**

Note:

If your Layers and Channels panels are grouped, you will need to switch back to the Layers panel after completing the last exercise.

3. Click the Add Layer Mask button at the bottom of the Layers panel.

4. Open the Properties panel (Window>Properties).

The Properties panel contains different options for different types of selections. When a mask is available for the active layer, the panel shows options related to that mask. You can use the buttons at the top of the panel to select the mask on the active layer, or add a new vector mask.

The Density slider changes the opacity of the overall mask. If you reduce the density to 80%, for example, underlying layers will be 20% visible through the mask. (Don't confuse this with the opacity of an alpha channel, which only affects the appearance of the mask on screen.)

5. In the Properties panel, drag the Feather slider until the field shows 25 px.

When you feather a selection and then make a layer mask from that selection, the feathering becomes a permanent part of the mask (unless you manually paint the mask to remove the feathering).

The Properties panel allows you to adjust the feathering of a hard-edge mask, and then later change or even remove the feathering if necessary, without painting on the mask.

Click here to add a vector mask.

Click here to select the mask on the active layer.

6. Choose the Brush tool from the Tools panel.

7. In the Options bar, open the Brush Preset picker. At the top of the panel, use the slider to change the Size to 100 px, and set the Hardness to 100%.

Note:

The Mask Edge and Color Range buttons in the Properties panel open the Refine Mask and [Select] Color Range dialog boxes (respectively). You used both of these dialog boxes to complete Project 1: Composite Movie Ad.

8. **If necessary, click the Switch Foreground and Background Colors button to make the foreground color black. Paint around the edges of the giraffe's horns.**

The mask should closely follow the shape of the horns. If you paint over part of a horn (or anything else you want to keep), simply change the foreground color to white and paint to remove that area from the mask.

Although you are painting with a hard-edge brush, the result is a soft edge because the mask is feathered in the Properties panel.

Note:

Press X to switch the current foreground and background colors. This is very useful to remember when you are painting on a mask, because you can reset the default (black and white) colors and switch them as necessary depending on what you want to accomplish.

Note:

You can use the bracket keys to enlarge (]) or reduce ([) the brush size.

Vector Masks vs. Pixel Masks

PHOTOSHOP FOUNDATIONS

Clicking the **Add a Vector Mask** button creates a vector-based mask from the active path (either the current work path or a saved path that is selected in the Paths panel).

You can use the Properties panel to feather the mask edges and adjust the density, but the Refine options are not available for a vector mask; refining a vector mask is performed using the Path Selection tool, Direct Selection tool, and Pen tool.

The Layers panel shows the vector mask thumbnail, and the Paths panel shows a vector mask path that is only visible in the panel when the layer is selected. Nothing is added to the Channels panel because channels are only raster-based.

Clicking the **Add a Pixel Mask** button adds a pixel-based mask in the shape of the current selection. This requires the marching-ants selection, and not an active path.

For a pixel-based mask, you can refine the mask edges using the Mask Edge and Color Range buttons. Clicking the Invert button swaps the black-to-white value of pixels in the mask, reversing the visible areas of the masked layer.

A pixel mask is added to the active layer and to the Channels panel, but nothing is added to the Paths panel.

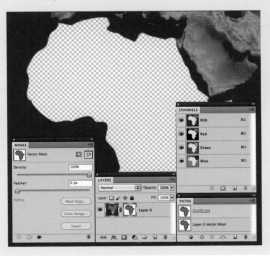

9. **In the Properties panel, change the Feather value to 0 px.**

   Remember, you were painting with a hard-edge brush, so the edges where you painted have a hard edge. Because the Properties panel allows you to change the Feather value, you can easily turn feathering on or off to monitor your progress.

10. **Change the Feather value back to 25 px.**

11. **Save the file and continue to the next exercise.**

 ## CONVERT REGULAR LAYERS TO SMART OBJECTS

Your file currently has two layers that you simply copied into the map file. You need to change these layers to Smart Objects before you apply filters. You can convert a regular layer to a Smart Object layer (or vice versa) easily, but it is important to know what to expect before you start converting in either direction.

1. **With africa_working.psd open, Control/right-click the giraffe layer name in the Layers panel.**

   When you Control/right-click a layer name, you see a contextual menu of options that are specific to the selected layer. Different options are available when you Control/right-click the layer thumbnail icons.

2. **Choose Convert to Smart Object in the menu.**

> **Note:**
>
> *Depending on the size of the file and the speed of your computer, this conversion might take a while; a Progress bar might show a Merging Layers message.*

Remember, you copied the giraffe image into the map file, so it was not originally placed as a Smart Object. When the process is complete, the Layers panel shows that the giraffe layer is now a Smart Object.

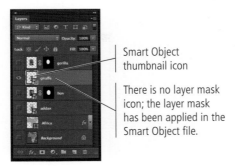

Smart Object
thumbnail icon

There is no layer mask
icon; the layer mask
has been applied in the
Smart Object file.

3. **Double-click the giraffe Smart Object thumbnail to open the file; click OK if you see a warning message.**

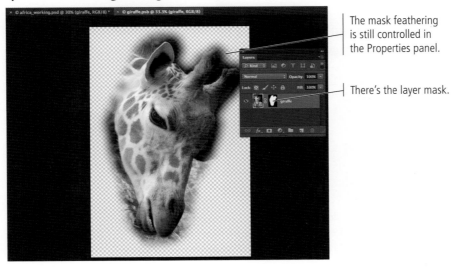

The mask feathering
is still controlled in
the Properties panel.

There's the layer mask.

4. **Close the giraffe file.**

5. **In the map file, repeat this process to convert the gorilla layer to a Smart Object.**

6. **Look closely at the thumbnail of the gorilla layer.**

You might notice that nothing is visible in the thumbnail. That's because the layer was hidden when you converted it to a Smart Object.

7. **Double-click the gorilla layer thumbnail to open that file.**

   Although the layer in the main file became visible when you converted it to a Smart Object, the layer inside the Smart Object file is hidden.

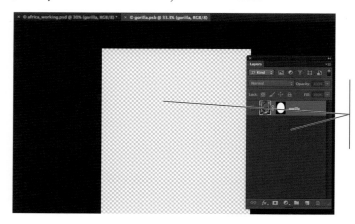

The masked gorilla layer is there, but the layer is hidden because it was hidden when you created the Smart Object in Step 5.

8. **Show the gorilla layer, save the gorilla file, and then close it.**

In the main file, the gorilla is now visible because that Smart Object layer is visible and the appropriate layer is now visible within the Smart Object file.

   Each of the four Smart Objects has a layer mask. However, one of the layer masks (for the lion) is applied within the map file instead of within the Smart Object file. For the sake of uniformity (and to show you how to do it), you're going to move that layer mask into the Smart Object file.

9. **Show the lion layer. Control/right-click the lion layer and choose Convert to Smart Object from the contextual menu.**

   Although the layer is already a Smart Object, you must complete this step to move the existing layer mask from the map file into the Smart Object file.

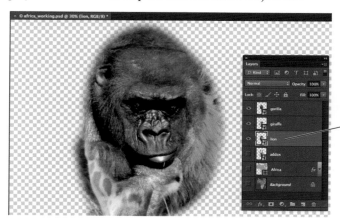

By converting the layer to a Smart Object, the layer mask is removed from the map file layer and placed inside the Smart Object file.

10. **Double-click the lion Smart Object thumbnail to open that file.**

    The file contains the original Smart Object, as well as the layer mask you created. The more Smart Objects you have (including nested ones), the larger your file size. To avoid unnecessary bloating, you can eliminate the nested Smart Object.

11. **In the Layers panel, Control/right-click the area to the right of the layer name for the lion layer. Choose Rasterize Layer from the contextual menu.**

    The layer mask from the map file has been moved to this Smart Object file.

    The Smart Object file has a nested Smart Object.

    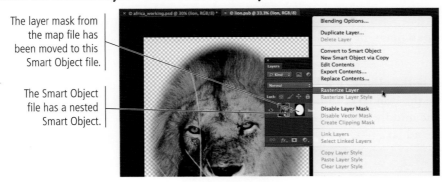

    Rasterizing the Smart Object basically removes the link to any external file, making the Smart Object a part of the file in which it has been placed.

    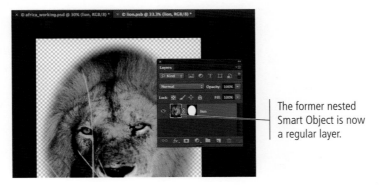

    The former nested Smart Object is now a regular layer.

12. **Save the lion file and close it.**

    Other than the missing layer mask thumbnail, there is no apparent change in the map. By completing the last few steps, you reduced the complexity of the file you're building — a good thing since you're going to add more layers later.

13. **Save the africa_working file and continue to the next exercise.**

Rasterizing Smart Objects with Masks

If you rasterize a Smart Object file that has a layer mask, the layer mask in the Smart Object will be applied before the file becomes a part of the master file.

In the image to the right, the gorilla Smart Object had a layer mask in the placed file before the Smart Object was rasterized. Rasterizing the gorilla layer converts the Smart Object layer to a regular layer, but the layer mask from the placed file is no longer available or editable.

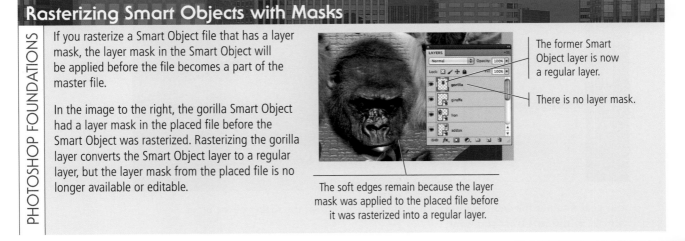

The former Smart Object layer is now a regular layer.

There is no layer mask.

The soft edges remain because the layer mask was applied to the placed file before it was rasterized into a regular layer.

You now have four masked animals and the shape of the map, but your client wants the animal pictures to appear *inside* the map shape. You can accomplish this task by using the map shape as a clipping mask. It's relatively easy to create a clipping mask from any layer. As with Smart Objects, however, you should know what to expect when you create a clipping mask. Specifically, you should understand how the different layers will behave and interact with one another.

1. **With africa_working.psd open, fit the file into the document window and make all layers visible.**

2. **Using the Move tool, drag the giraffe to fill the bottom portion of the African continent. Move the lion layer into the top-left area, move the addax so its ear extends into the middle east, and move the gorilla into the space between the lion and the addax.**

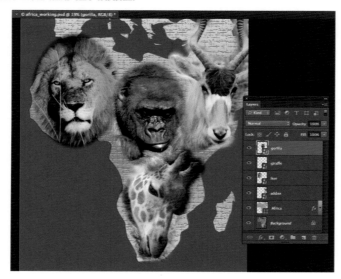

Note:

Remember, if the Auto-Select option is checked in the Options bar, you can simply click pixels of the layer you want to move without first selecting the layer.

3. **Control/right-click the gorilla layer and choose Create Clipping Mask from the contextual menu.**

A clipping mask is another way to show only certain areas of a layer; in this case, using the shape of one layer (giraffe) to show parts of the layer above it (gorilla). Because very little area of the gorilla layer is inside the area of the giraffe layer, most of the gorilla is now hidden.

The gorilla layer is indented and linked to the giraffe layer.

The only visible area is where the gorilla overlaps the giraffe.

Your goal is to put the animals inside the map shape, not inside the shapes of the other animals, so this isn't what you want.

4. **Control/right-click the gorilla layer and choose Release Clipping Mask from the contextual menu.**

   As with layer masks, clipping masks do not permanently modify the pixels in the layer, so you can always hide or remove clipping masks without damaging the masked images.

Note:

Remember, to access the contextual menu for a specific layer, you have to Control/right-click in the area to the right of the layer name.

5. **Shift-click to select all four animal layers. Control/right-click any of the selected layers and choose Create Clipping Mask from the contextual menu.**

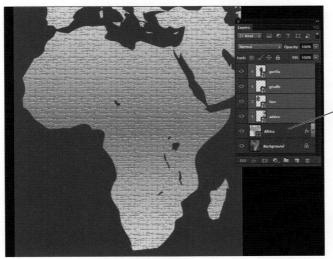

When multiple layers are selected, all the selected layers are clipped by the next-lowest layer.

   This highlights a problem that occurs when working with a shape layer filled with a pattern (this shape layer is filled with the Ancient Stone pattern/style). This style includes overlays, which technically overlay the animal layers you placed inside the clipping mask. In other words, the pattern overlay completely obscures the animal layers.

   If you don't need or want to maintain the layer style, you can simply clear the layer style using the layer's contextual menu. In this case, however, you want to keep the style but prevent it from overlaying the clipped animal images, so you need to use a different technique.

6. **In the Layers panel, click the *fx* button to expand the list of effects for the Africa layer.**

7. **Click the Africa layer in the Layers panel to select it, and then choose Layer>Layer Style>Create Layers.**

   This command converts each applied effect to a separate layer, all of which are clipped by the original shape layer; only the area within the shape layer is visible.

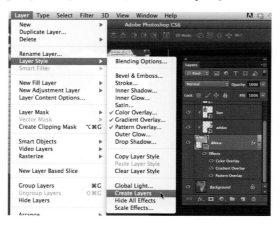

8. **When you see a warning that some effects cannot be reproduced with layers, click OK.**

   This warning is very common, but we prefer to let the conversion happen and review the results before we make a final design decision. If you're not satisfied with the result, you can always undo the conversion and try again.

9. **Review the image and the Layers panel.**

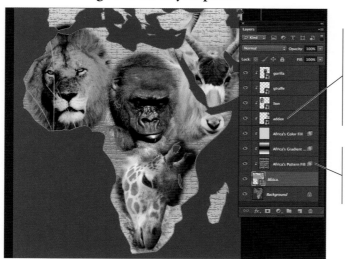

The animals are still clipped by the shape layer, and they are positioned higher in the layer stacking order than the fill layers created from the effects.

The effects layers are now individual layers, which are also clipped by the shape layer.

Note:

Now that you can see how the animals appear within the continent shape, it's easier to see where changes might be necessary.

Note:

The client supplied several other animal photos (in the WIP> Africa folder). Feel free to add more animals to your artwork if you want to experiment further with masking techniques.

10. **Use the Move tool to reposition the animal layers as necessary to fill the continent as much as possible.**

11. **Save the file and continue to the next stage of the project.**

Stage 3 Using Filters and Adjustments

Your client originally wanted a traditional painter to create this job, but decided instead on a digital version to save time and money. The advantage of using Photoshop is that you can easily create an art-like version of existing files using the built-in filters. You can make images look like pencil sketches, paintings, or any of dozens of other options. You can even compound multiple filters to create unique effects that would require extreme skill in traditional art techniques such as oil painting.

Photoshop ships with more than 100 filters divided into 13 categories; some of these are functional while others are purely decorative. You will use some of the art filters in this project and experiment with some of the functional filters in later projects.

APPLY NON-DESTRUCTIVE FILTERS TO SMART OBJECTS

Because the animals are placed into the map file as Smart Objects, any filters that you choose to apply do not affect the placed file data. In other words, they are non-destructive. This means you can later change the filter settings, add additional filters, or even delete a filter effect without damaging the placed file.

1. **With africa_working.psd open, select the giraffe layer in the Layers panel.**

   Filters apply to the selected layer, not to the entire file.

2. **Choose Filter>Oil Paint.**

3. **Use the View Percentage field in the bottom-left corner of the dialog box to show the image at 50% (or higher, if you have the screen space).**

   Zooming in on the preview gives you a better idea of the potential result.

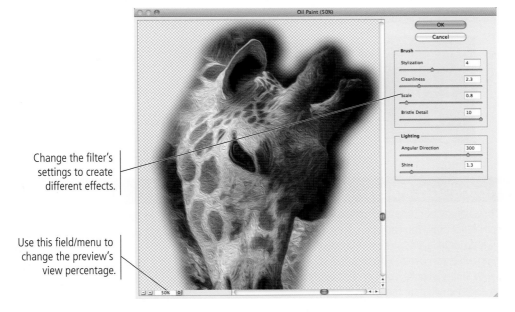

Change the filter's settings to create different effects.

Use this field/menu to change the preview's view percentage.

4. **Experiment with the different filter settings until you are pleased with the result.**

   The Oil Paint filter does exactly what you might expect — it creates the effect of an actual oil painting from a photograph.

   When you change the filter settings, the preview window dynamically changes to show the new options.

   Note:

   It's a good idea to look at your changes at 100% at least once to get a better idea of what you're applying.

5. **Click OK to apply the filter to the giraffe layer.**

   In the Layers panel, a new icon appears in the giraffe layer, and a Smart Filters layer appears indented below it.

Click this button to collapse (hide) the Smart Filters options in the panel.

Click any of these eye icons to temporarily turn off the filter.

Double-click the filter name to re-open the Filter Gallery and make changes.

6. **Press Option/Alt, then click the Smart Filter listing under the giraffe layer and drag it to the gorilla layer.**

   This copies the applied filters, using the exact same settings, to the target layer.

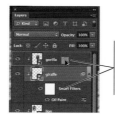

Press Option/Alt, then drag the Filter Gallery item to the gorilla layer to copy the applied effects.

More About Photoshop Filters

Filters can be used for a variety of purposes, from purely aesthetic to technically functional. You can apply filters to specific selections, individual layers, or even individual channels depending on what you need to accomplish. If you combine filters with Smart Objects, you can also apply nondestructive filters and then change the settings or turn off the filters to experiment with different results.

In addition to the options in the Filter Gallery, a wide range of other filters can be accessed in the various Filter submenus. You will use a number of these in other projects throughout this book, but we encourage you to explore the various settings. Any filter that includes an ellipsis (...) in the menu command opens a secondary dialog box, where you can control the filter's specific settings.

Keep the following points in mind when you use filters:

- Filters can be applied to the entire selected layer or to an active selection.
- Some filters work only on RGB images; if you are in a different color mode, some or all filter options — including the Filter Gallery — will be unavailable.
- All filters can be applied to 8-bit images; available filter options are limited for 16-bit and 32-bit images (see Project 3: Menu Image Correction).
- If you don't have enough available RAM to process a filter effect, you might get an error message.

7. **In the Layers panel, click the arrow button to the right of the gorilla layer.**

Applied smart effects, filters, and styles are listed under the layer name. You can collapse or expand the listings by clicking this button.

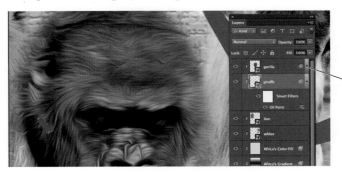

Click these arrows to hide or show the Smart Filters information.

8. **Repeat Step 6 to apply the same filters to the lion and addax layers.**

Feel free to modify the filter settings as appropriate until you are satisfied with the result for each layer.

9. **In the Layers panel, collapse the Smart Filter information for each animal layer.**

10. **Save the file and continue to the next exercise.**

 ## APPLY DESTRUCTIVE FILTERS TO REGULAR LAYERS

The previous exercise highlighted the benefits of applying non-destructive filters to Smart Objects. If you're working with regular layers, however, filters are destructive; they can't be edited or removed (although they can be undone).

1. **With africa_working.psd open, select the Africa's Pattern Fill layer.**

Remember, this layer was created when you converted the shape layer's applied effects to layers. It is currently clipped by the shape layer.

2. **Choose Filter>Filter Gallery.**

If the Filter menu includes the Filter Gallery at the top of the list, that top command applies the last-used filter gallery settings to the selected layer. To open the actual Filter Gallery dialog box, you have to choose the Filter Gallery command that appears at the third spot in the menu.

This command applies the last-used filter without opening the Filter Gallery dialog box.

This command opens the Filter Gallery dialog box with the last-used settings applied.

3. **In the middle pane of the dialog box, expand the Distort collection of filters and click the Glass thumbnail.**

The left side of the Filter Gallery dialog box shows a preview of the applied filter(s). As with the Oil Paint filter, you can use the menu and field in the bottom-left corner to change the view percentage of the preview.

In the middle column of the dialog box, the available filters are broken into six categories; inside each folder, thumbnails show a small preview of each filter.

The top half of the right side of the dialog box shows settings that are specific to the selected filter (from the middle column).

The bottom half of the right side shows the filters that are applied to the selected layer.

Note:

The filter might not be obvious in the image window, especially if you're viewing the file at a low view percentage (we're using 33% in these screen shots). We recommend previewing at a higher percentage in the Filter Gallery.

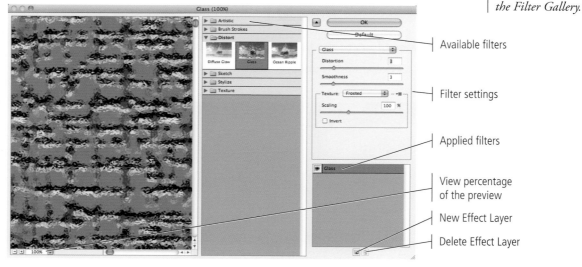

— Available filters

— Filter settings

— Applied filters

— View percentage of the preview

— New Effect Layer

— Delete Effect Layer

4. **Adjust the filter options until you are satisfied with the result, then click OK to apply the filter.**

In the image, the pattern behind the animals is now much softer and less defined. Filtering the pattern layer helps you achieve the goal of a "painting" effect.

The regular layer shows no Smart Filter; filters applied to regular layers are destructive and permanent.

Note:

Filters are applied from the bottom up; when you want to create a unique effect, experiment with multiple filters, as well as the order in which they are applied.

5. **Select the Africa layer and choose Filter>Stylize>Diffuse.**

Rather than leaving the sharp, defined edges of the vector shape layer, you are going to use the Diffuse filter to help blend the edges into the other areas of the image.

Functional filters such as Diffuse are not applied in the Filter Gallery; instead, each filter has its own dialog box. However, before you can access the Diffuse dialog box, you have to rasterize the shape layer.

6. **Read the resulting warning message.**

   You can't apply filters to vector shape layers. Photoshop automatically warns you that the layer will be rasterized, which means you will no longer be able to edit the path that created the shape. Depending on your goals, you might want to duplicate the shape layer and hide a copy before you rasterize the shape layer to apply the filter.

7. **Click OK in the warning message to rasterize the shape layer.**

8. **While the Diffuse dialog box is open, use the keyboard shortcuts to zoom in on the image in the document window. Use the scroll bars to drag the image until you see an edge of the shape layer.**

   The Diffuse dialog box can apply four different types of diffusion:
   - **Normal** diffusion scatters pixels randomly.
   - **Darken Only** replaces light pixels with dark ones.
   - **Lighten Only** replaces dark pixels with light ones.
   - **Anisotropic** scatters pixels where there is the least difference in color.

   You can use the keyboard shortcuts to change the view percentage of a file even when a dialog box is open. You can also scroll a document if you have scroll-wheel capabilities on your mouse.

Note:

Webster's dictionary defines diffuse as "to pour, spread out, or disperse in every direction; spread or scatter wildly." The Photoshop Diffuse filter reflects the second half of that definition, scattering the pixels in the selected layer.

9. **Move the mouse cursor over an edge of the African continent in the document window. Click an edge of the former shape layer to change the preview area of the dialog box.**

   When you see the edges, you can see the effect of the diffusion. (If the shape layer had more than just flat color, you would see the effect right away.) The diffused pixels allow the layer edges to blend into the background instead of ending at an abrupt, sharp edge.

Note:

You can also click and drag in the preview area of the dialog box to change the visible area in only the preview.

With the dialog box open, clicking in the image changes the visible area in preview window.

When the dialog box is open, you can use the scroll bars to change the visible part of the image.

10. **Leave the mode set to Normal and click OK.**

11. **Save the file and continue to the next stage of the project.**

Fading Effects

The Fade option (Edit>Fade) changes the opacity and blending mode of the last-used filter, painting tool, or color adjustment; you can also fade the effects of using the Liquify filter, and Brush Strokes filters. The following example shows the result of fading the Emboss filter that was applied in the left image.

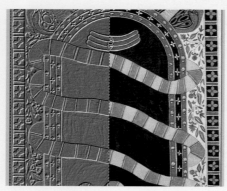
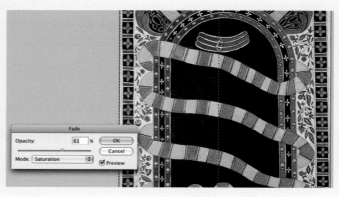

Stage 4 Creating an Artistic Background

Since the background image (the original map) is badly deteriorated from resampling, you're going to use several built-in Photoshop tools to create a custom artistic background. Doing so gives you an advantage: you can create any effect you want instead of using the flat blue color in the existing background image. In this series of exercises, you combine Photoshop's filters with a custom gradient and a pattern fill, and then liquify the background to create a watery background to use in place of the low-resolution map image.

 USE THE EYEDROPPER TOOL

In Photoshop, there is almost always more than one way to complete a task. In this exercise, you use the Eyedropper tool to change the Foreground and Background colors by sampling from the original map image.

1. **With africa_working.psd open, zoom out to show the entire image in the document window.**

2. **Using the Layers panel, hide all but the background layer.**

   You can hide multiple layers by clicking and dragging over the eye icons of each layer that you want to hide.

   Click here and drag down over the layer eye icons to hide multiple layers.

   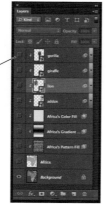

   Note:

   Hiding the Africa layer effectively hides all the layers clipped by the hidden layer.

   You can also Option/Alt click the layer you want to be visible; this hides all other layers in the file.

3. **Choose the Eyedropper tool in the Tools panel.**

4. **In the Options bar, choose 5 by 5 Average in the Sample Size menu and choose All Layers in the Sample menu. Make sure the Show Sampling Ring option is checked.**

The default eyedropper option — Point Sample — selects the color of the single pixel where you click. Using one of the average values avoids the possibility of sampling an errant artifact color because the tool finds the average color in a range of adjacent pixels.

By default, the sample will be selected from All [visible] Layers. You can choose Current Layer in the Sample menu to choose a color from only the active layer.

5. **Move the cursor over a blue area in the visible image and click to change the foreground color.**

When you click with the Eyedropper tool, the sampling ring shows the previous foreground color on the bottom and the current sample color on the top half.

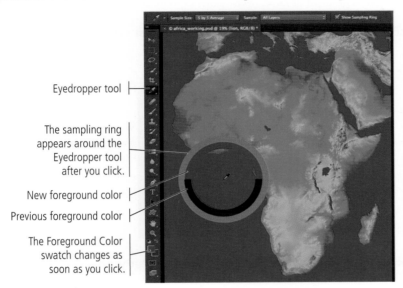

Eyedropper tool

The sampling ring appears around the Eyedropper tool after you click.

New foreground color

Previous foreground color

The Foreground Color swatch changes as soon as you click.

Note:

While you hold down the mouse button, you can drag around the image to find the color you want. The sampling ring previews what color will be selected if you release the mouse button.

6. **Move the cursor over a darker green area of the image. Option/Alt-click to change the background color.**

Pressing Option/Alt while you click with the Eyedropper tool changes the Background color. In this case, the sampling ring shows the previous background color on the bottom and the current selection on the top.

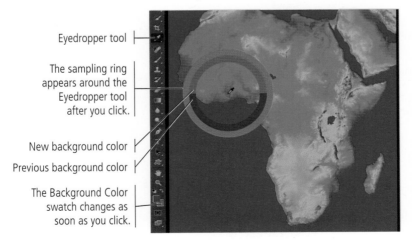

Eyedropper tool

The sampling ring appears around the Eyedropper tool after you click.

New background color

Previous background color

The Background Color swatch changes as soon as you click.

7. **Save the file and continue to the next exercise.**

CREATE A CUSTOM GRADIENT

A **gradient** (sometimes called a blend) is a fill that creates a smooth transition from one color to another or across a range of multiple colors. Photoshop can create several different kinds of gradients (linear, radial, etc.) from one color to another, and you can access a number of built-in gradients. You can also create your own custom gradients, which you will do in this exercise.

1. **With `africa_working.psd` open, choose the Gradient tool in the Tools panel.**

2. **In the Options bar, click the arrow to the right of the gradient sample bar to show the Gradient Picker panel.**

   The Gradient Picker panel shows a set of predefined gradients, including black-to-white, foreground-to-transparent, foreground-to-background, and several other common options. You can also access additional gradient libraries in the panel Options menu.

3. **Open the Gradient Picker panel Options menu and choose Small List view.**

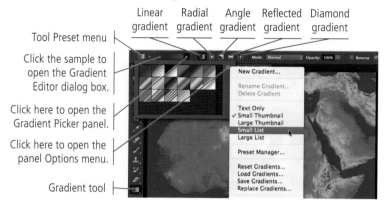

4. **Open the Gradient Picker panel again (if necessary) and choose Foreground to Background from the list of gradients. Press Return/Enter to close the Gradient Picker panel.**

5. **Click the gradient sample in the Options bar to open the Gradient Editor dialog box.**

   You can use this dialog box to edit existing gradients or create new ones.

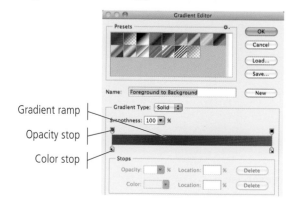

6. **Click the right color stop below the gradient ramp. Drag left until the Location field shows 25%.**

Click a stop to select it.

Click the swatch to open the Color Picker for the selected stop.

Open this menu to set the stop color to the active Foreground or Background color.

Click below the ramp to add a new stop.

Verify the stop position as you drag it across the ramp.

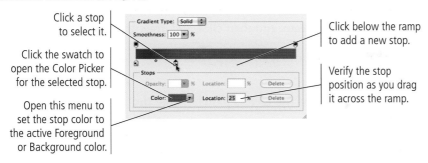

Note:

As soon as you click the color stop, the name changes to Custom because you're defining a custom gradient.

7. **Click the left color stop to select it, then release the mouse button. Press Option/Alt, then click the left stop again and drag to the right end of the ramp.**

This adds a new stop with the same settings as the one you selected before Option/Alt-dragging. If you do non click and release *before* pressing Option/Alt, you will move the existing stop rather than copying ("cloning") it.

Select this stop, then Option/Alt-drag to copy it.

Drag the copy to the right end of the ramp.

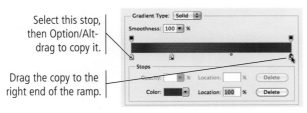

Note:

You can simply click below the gradient ramp to add a new stop at the location where you click. The new stop adopts a color as necessary, based on the existing gradient.

8. **Repeat Step 7 to create a third blue stop at a location of 50%.**

9. **Repeat Step 7 for the green stop at 25%, and drag the cloned stop right until the location of the new stop is 75%.**

Select this stop, then Option/Alt-drag to copy it.

Drag the copy to a location of 75%.

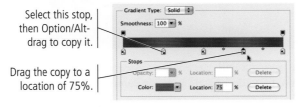

Note:

Drag a stop off the gradient ramp to remove it from the gradient.

Note:

Double-click a specific color stop to open the Color Picker where you can change the color of that stop.

10. **Type `Ocean Blues` in the Name field and click the New button.**

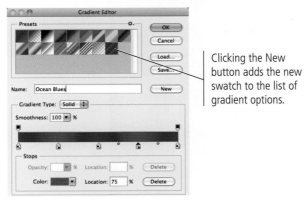

Clicking the New button adds the new swatch to the list of gradient options.

11. **Click OK to close the dialog box.**

12. **Save the file and continue to the next exercise.**

CREATE A GRADIENT FILL LAYER

Once you define the gradient you want, applying it is fairly easy: add a layer (if necessary), select the type of gradient you want to create, and then click and drag.

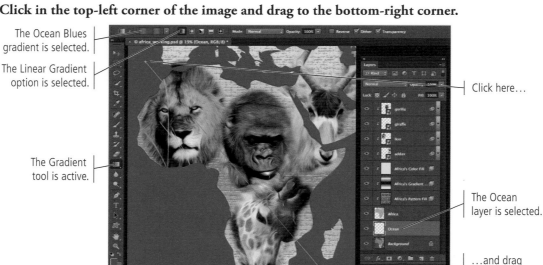

1. **With africa_working.psd open, show all layers, and then click the Background layer to select it.**

2. **Click the New Layer button at the bottom of the Layers panel. Name the new layer Ocean.**

   When you add a new layer, it is automatically added directly above the selected layer.

3. **Make sure the Gradient tool is selected. In the Options bar, make sure the Ocean Blues gradient is selected and the Linear gradient option is active.**

4. **Click in the top-left corner of the image and drag to the bottom-right corner.**

Note:

If you added a new layer between any of the layers in the Shape Layer clipping mask set, the new layer would become the basis of the clipping path for any layers above it.

The Ocean Blues gradient is selected.

The Linear Gradient option is selected.

The Gradient tool is active.

Click here...

The Ocean layer is selected.

...and drag to here.

When you release the mouse button, the layer fills with the gradient. Areas before and after the line drawn with the Gradient tool fill with the start and stop colors of the gradient (in this case, they're both the blue color).

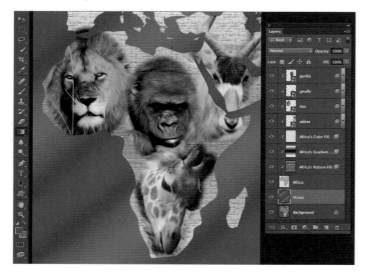

5. **Save the file and continue to the next exercise.**

CREATE A PATTERN FILL LAYER

The gradient layer is a good start for your art background, but it needs some
texture to look more like a painting. A pattern fill will create the texture you need.

1. **With africa_working.psd open, create a new layer named Waves above
   the Ocean layer.**

2. **Choose the Paint Bucket tool (nested under the Gradient tool) and review
   the Options bar.**

    When you click with the Paint Bucket tool, it fills areas of similar color (like the Magic
    Wand tool you used to make selections in Project 1: Composite Movie Ad). You can
    define the Paint Bucket tool tolerance in the Options bar, just as you did for the Magic
    Wand tool.

3. **Choose Pattern in the left menu of the Options bar, and then open the
   Pattern panel.**

4. **In the Pattern panel Options menu, choose Small List to see the names of
   the various patterns.**

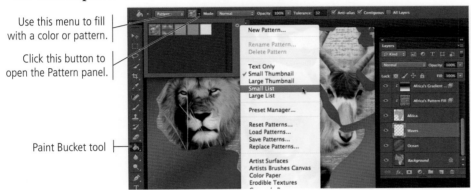

5. **Choose Artist Surfaces in the Options menu to show that set of patterns.**

6. **When you see a warning that the patterns will replace the current set, click OK.**

7. **Scroll through the list and click Oil Pastel on Canvas.**

Click here and drag to extend the height of the panel.

8. **Place the cursor anywhere in the image window and click.**

Because there is nothing on the currently selected layer, every pixel in the layer is within the tool's tolerance — the entire layer fills with the pattern.

9. **Save the file and continue.**

 ADJUST LAYER ORDER AND BLENDING MODE

The pattern fill layer is currently on top of the gradient layer. You need to reverse that order, and then blend the two layers together to create the textured, colored ocean background.

1. **With africa_working.psd open, drag the Waves layer below the Ocean layer in the Layers panel.**

Now the gradient obscures the pattern, which isn't right either. To blend the two layers together, you have to change the top layer's blending mode.

2. **Select the Ocean layer, and then click the Blending Mode menu at the top of the Layers panel.**

   Photoshop provides access to 27 different layer blending modes (the default is Normal, or no blending applied).

3. **Choose Overlay in the Blending Mode menu.**

   The texture of the pattern is now visible behind the gradient. The pattern is very obvious, however, which doesn't lend well to the "painting" effect you're trying to create.

Use this menu to change the blending mode.

4. **Select the Waves layer, then choose Filter>Filter Gallery.**

5. **In the Filter Gallery window, open the Distort folder and apply the Ocean Ripple filter. In the right side of the dialog box, change the filter settings to:**

   Ripple Size = 3, Ripple Magnitude = 9

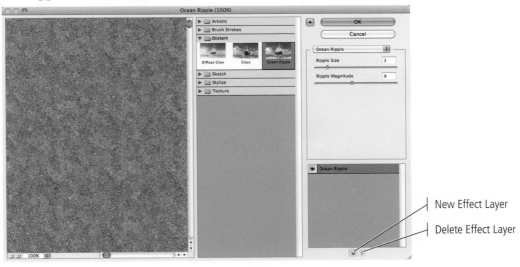

New Effect Layer

Delete Effect Layer

6. **Click the New Effect Layer button.**

   You can apply multiple filters to the same layer by clicking the New Effect Layer button. If more than one filter is applied, you can drag the filters in this pane to reorder the filters — which can have a significant impact on the overall effect. You can temporarily disable a specific filter by clicking the eye icon, or permanently remove a filter by selecting it in the list and then clicking the Delete Effect Layer button.

7. **With the top effect layer selected, open the Artistic folder and apply the Smudge Stick filter. In the right side of the dialog box, change the filter settings to:**

   Settings: Stroke Length = 2, Highlight Area = 7, Intensity = 10

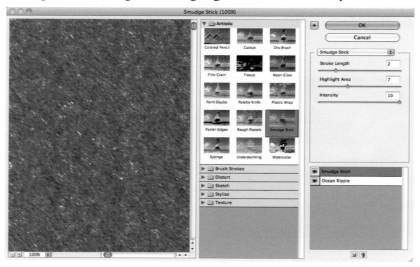

8. **Click OK to close the Filter Gallery.**

   The pattern is now less obvious, and the filters have added a more random texture.

9. **With the Waves layer selected, choose Filter>Blur>Blur.**

   This filter does not have a dialog box interface; it simply blurs the pixels in the selected layer. If you want more control over the blur, you must use one of the more sophisticated blur filters (see Project 4: City Promotion Cards).

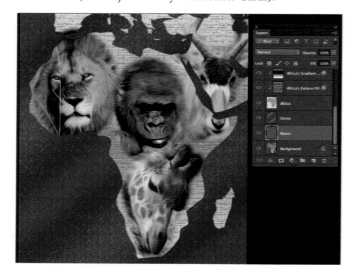

Note:

The result of the Blur filter might not be apparent unless you're viewing the image at 100% magnification.

10. **Save the file and continue to the next exercise.**

PHOTOSHOP FOUNDATIONS

When working with blending modes, think of the top layer as the "blend" layer and the next lowest layer as the "base".

- **Normal** is the default mode (no blending applied).
- **Dissolve** results in a random scattering of pixels of both the blend and base colors.
- **Darken** returns the darker of the blend or base color. Base pixels that are lighter than the blend color are replaced; base pixels that are darker than the blend color remain unchanged.
- **Multiply** multiplies (hence the name) the base color by the blend color, resulting in a darker color. Multiplying any color with black produces black; multiplying any color with white leaves the color unchanged (think of math — any number times 0 equals 0).
- **Color Burn** darkens the base color by increasing the contrast. Blend colors darker than 50% significantly darken the base color by increasing saturation and reducing brightness; blending with white has no effect.
- **Linear Burn** darkens the base color similar to Color Burn; using Linear Burn, the brightness is reduced about twice as much for blend colors in the mid-tone range.
- **Darker Color** compares the channel values of the blend and base colors, resulting in the lower value.
- **Lighten** returns whichever is the lighter color (base or blend). Base pixels that are darker than the blend color are replaced; base pixels that are lighter than the blend color remain unchanged.
- **Screen** is basically the inverse of Multiply, always returning a lighter color. Screening with black has no effect; screening with white produces white.
- **Color Dodge** brightens the base color. Blend colors lighter than 50% significantly increase brightness; blending with black has no effect.
- **Linear Dodge (Add)** is similar to Color Dodge, but creates smoother transitions from areas of high brightness to areas of low brightness.
- **Lighter Color** compares channel values of the blend and base colors, resulting in the higher value.
- **Overlay** multiplies or screens the blend color to preserve the original lightness or darkness of the base.
- **Soft Light** darkens or lightens base colors depending on the blend color. Blend colors lighter than 50% lighten the base color (as if dodged); blend colors darker than 50% darken the base color (as if burned).

- **Hard Light** combines the Multiply and Screen modes. Blend colors darker than 50% are multiplied, and blend colors lighter than 50% are screened.
- **Vivid Light** combines the Color Dodge and Color Burn modes. Blend colors lighter than 50% lighten the base by decreasing contrast; blend colors darker than 50% darken the base by increasing contrast.
- **Linear Light** combines the Linear Dodge and Linear Burn modes. If the blend color is lighter than 50%, the result is lightened by increasing the base brightness. If the blend color is darker than 50%, the result is darkened by decreasing the base brightness.
- **Pin Light** preserves the brightest and darkest areas of the blend color; blend colors in the mid-tone range have little (if any) effect.
- **Hard Mix** pushes all pixels in the resulting blend to either all or nothing. The base and blend values of each pixel in each channel are added together (e.g., R 45 [blend] + R 230 [base] = R 275). Pixels with totals over 255 are shown at 255; pixels with a total lower than 255 are dropped to 0.
- **Difference** inverts base color values according to the brightness value in the blend layer. Lower brightness values in the blend layer have less of an effect on the result; blending with black has no effect.
- **Exclusion** is very similar to Difference, except that mid-tone values in the base color are completely desaturated.
- **Subtract** removes the blend color from the base color.
- **Divide** looks at the color information in each channel and divides the blend color from the base color.
- **Hue** results in a color with the luminance and saturation of the base color and the hue of the blend color.
- **Saturation** results in a color with the luminance and hue of the base color and the saturation of the blend color.
- **Color** results in a color with the luminance of the base color and the hue and saturation of the blend color.
- **Luminosity** results in a color with the hue and saturation of the base color and the luminance of the blend color (basically the opposite of the Color mode).

LIQUIFY A LAYER

You're nearly done, but the background layers still have a strong patterned feel — which makes sense, since you created them with a pattern fill. In this exercise, you use the Liquify filter to push around the background layer pixels in a freeform style to create a unique, non-patterned background.

1. **With africa_working.psd open, Shift-click the Ocean and Waves layers to select both.**

2. **Control/right click either of the selected layers and choose Merge Layers from the contextual menu.**

   When you merge selected layers, the resulting single layer adopts the name of the selected layer that was highest in the stacking order.

Note:

You can also choose Merge Layers from the Layers panel Options menu.

3. **With the resulting Ocean layer still selected, choose Filter>Liquify.**

   The Liquify filter has its own interface and tools. Depending on which tool you select, different options become available in the right side of the dialog box.

4. **Click the Forward Warp tool in the top-left corner.**

5. **Check the Advanced Mode box in the right side of the dialog box, then review the available options.**

   For any of the distortion tools, you have to define a brush size, density (feathering around the edges), and pressure. Some tools also allow you to define the brush rate (how fast distortions are made); using the Turbulence tool, you can set the Turbulent Jitter (how tightly pixels are scrambled by the effect).

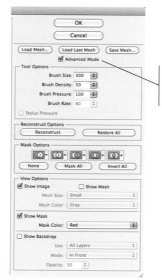

Turn on Advanced mode to see all available options.

Understanding the Liquify Filter

Tools in the Liquify filter distort the brush area when you drag; the distortion is concentrated at the center of the brush area, and the effect intensifies as you hold down the mouse button or repeatedly drag over an area. (The **Hand** and **Zoom tools** have the same function here as in the main Photoshop interface.)

A. The **Forward Warp tool** pushes pixels as you drag.

B. The **Reconstruct tool** restores distorted pixels.

C. The **Twirl Clockwise tool** rotates pixels clockwise as you hold down the mouse button or drag. Press Option/Alt to twirl pixels counterclockwise.

D. The **Pucker tool** moves pixels toward the center of the brush, creating a zoomed-out effect if you simply hold down the mouse button without dragging.

E. The **Bloat tool** moves pixels away from the center of the brush, creating a zoomed-in effect.

F. The **Push Left tool** moves pixels left when you drag up, and right when you drag down. You can also drag clockwise around an object to increase its size, or drag counterclockwise to decrease its size.

G. The **Freeze Mask tool** protects areas where you paint.

H. The **Thaw Mask tool** removes the protection created by the Freeze Mask tool.

Reconstructing Pixels

When you manipulate pixels in the Liquify dialog box, you can press Command/Control-Z to undo your last brush stroke in the dialog box. Clicking the **Restore All** button has the same effect as using the Undo keyboard shortcut.

You can also use the **Reconstruct** button to affect the last-applied stroke. Rather than undoing the entire stroke, you can use the resulting Revert Reconstruction dialog box to lessen the effect by a specific percentage.

Using Masks in the Liquify Filter

You can freeze areas in the Liquify preview to protect them from distortion with a mask that looks and behaves like Quick Mask mode in the main interface. You can also use the Mask options to freeze areas based on existing selections, transparent areas, or layer masks in the original image.

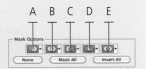

A. **Replace Selection** creates a new mask from the selection, transparency, or mask.

B. **Add to Selection** adds the selection, transparency, or mask to the currently thawed area.

C. **Subtract from Selection** adds the selection, transparency, or mask to the currently frozen area.

D. **Intersect with Selection** creates a mask with areas that are frozen in the preview, and in the selection, transparency, or mask from the original image.

E. **Invert Selection** inverts the mask in the preview image within the boundaries of the selection, transparency, or mask from the original image.

You can click the **None** button to thaw all masked areas; click the **Mask All** button to mask the entire image; or click the **Invert All** button to reverse the current mask.

Changing the Filter View

The **Show Image** option, active by default, shows the active layer in the filter's preview area. If you check the **Show Mesh** option, the preview also shows a grid that defaults to small, gray lines. You can use the Mesh Size and Mesh Color menus to change the appearance of the grid.

When the **Show Mask** option is checked, any mask you paint with the Freeze Mask tool appears in the filter's preview area. You can use the Mask Color menu to change the color of the visible mask.

When the **Show Backdrop** option is checked you can include other layers in the filter's preview area. The Use menu, which defaults to All Layers, also lists individual layers in the file so that you can show only a certain layer in the preview. You can use the Mode and Opacity menus to change the way extra layer(s) appear in the preview.

6. **Use the View Percentage menu to make the entire layer visible in the dialog box preview area.**

7. **Using the Forward Warp tool, select a large brush size, medium density, and high pressure.**

8. **Drag in the preview where the green blends into the blue, starting at the left side and dragging to the right.**

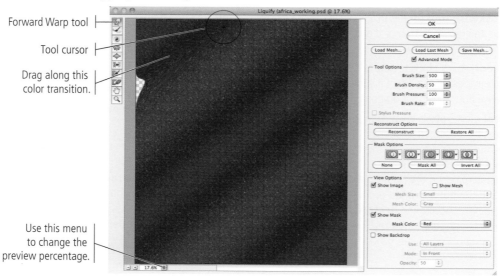

Forward Warp tool

Tool cursor

Drag along this color transition.

Use this menu to change the preview percentage.

9. **Click near where the pushed layer edge appears, then drag down and left to push the color back into the now-transparent area.**

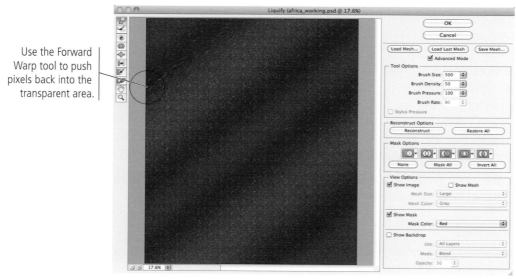

Use the Forward Warp tool to push pixels back into the transparent area.

10. **Continue pushing pixels along the gradient lines, and then experiment with some of the other tools. Our solution, shown here, made heavy use of the Turbulence and Twirl Clockwise tools to push the pixels around.**

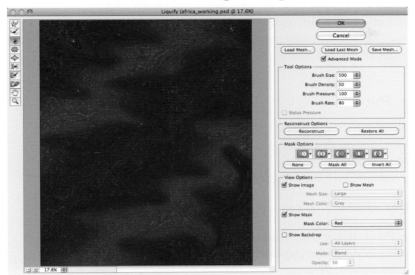

Note:

If necessary, you can press Command/Control-Z to undo your last brush stroke in the Liquify dialog box.

11. **Click OK to return to the image.**

Depending on the size of the layer you are liquifying, the process might take a while to complete; be patient.

12. **Choose File>Save As. Save the file as a native Photoshop file named `africa_final.psd` in your WIP>Africa folder.**

13. **Continue to the final stage of the project.**

Stage 5 Outputting Files

The last stage of most jobs — after the client has approved the work — is printing a proof. A printed proof is basically the output provider's roadmap of how the final job should look. As more processes move to all-digital workflows, a printed proof is not always required — especially if you're submitting files digitally. But some output providers still require a printed proof, and you might want to print samples of your work at various stages of development.

PRINT THE COMPOSITE PROOF

To output this file at 100%, you need a sheet at least tabloid size (11 × 17"). If you don't have that option, you can use the Photoshop Print dialog box to fit the job onto letter-size paper. Keep in mind, however, that many of the effects that you created with filters will lose some of their impact when you reduce the file to fit onto a letter-size page.

1. **With africa_final.psd open, choose File>Print.**

2. **In the Printer menu of the Print dialog box, choose the printer you're using (preferably one that can print tabloid-size paper).**

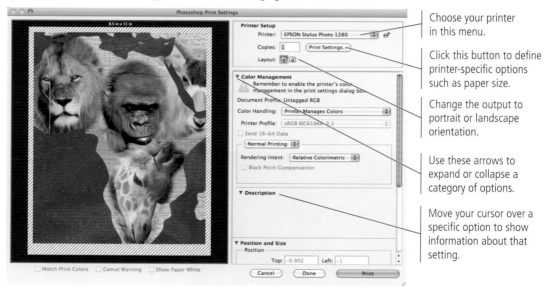

Choose your printer in this menu.

Click this button to define printer-specific options such as paper size.

Change the output to portrait or landscape orientation.

Use these arrows to expand or collapse a category of options.

Move your cursor over a specific option to show information about that setting.

3. **If you have a tabloid-size printer, click the Print Settings button. Choose Tabloid/US B in the Paper Size menu, and then click Save to return to the Print dialog box.**

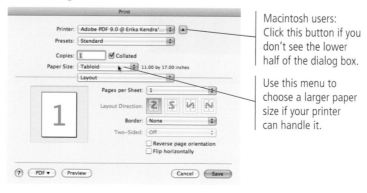

Macintosh users: Click this button if you don't see the lower half of the dialog box.

Use this menu to choose a larger paper size if your printer can handle it.

Print Output Options

Use the following as a guide to help you decide which options to include in your output:

Color Management options

(Color management is explained in detail in Project 3: Menu Image Correction.)

- Color Handling determines whether color management is applied by the printer or by Photoshop.
- Printer Profile defines the known color characteristics of the output device you are using.
- Normal Printing simply prints the file to your printer, using no defined output profile for color management.
  - Rendering Intent defines how colors are shifted to fit inside the printer's output capabilities.
  - Black Point Compression adjusts for differences in the black point (the darkest possible black area) between the file and the output device.
- Hard Proofing simulates the color output properties of another printer, based on the defined profile in the Proof Setup menu.
  - Simulate Paper Color applies the absolute colorimetric rendering intent to simulate the appearance of color on the actual paper that would be used on the defined output device (for example, newsprint on a web press).
  - Simulate Black Ink simulates the brightness of dark colors as they would appear on the defined output device. If this option is not checked, dark colors are simply printed as dark as possible on the actual printer you are using.

Position and Size Options

- **Position** defines the location of the output on the paper. It is centered by default; you can use the Top and Left fields to position the output at a specific distance from the paper corner. You can also click in the preview area and drag to reposition the image on the paper.
- **Scale** defaults to 100%, creating a full-size print; the **Height** and **Width** fields define the size of the image being printed. If you change the Scale field, the Height and Width fields reflect the proportional size. You can also define a specific size in the Height and Width fields; in this case, the Scale field is adjusted accordingly.
- If you check **Scale to Fit Media**, the image is automatically scaled to fit inside the printable area on the selected paper size.
- **Print Resolution** defines the resolution that will be sent to the output device. Remember the principle of effective resolution; if you print a 300-ppi image at 200%, the printer has only 150 ppi to work with.
- If you check **Print Selected Area**, handles appear in the preview area. You can drag those handles to define the image area that will be output.

Printing Marks

- **Corner Crop Marks** adds crop marks to show the edges of the image (where it should be cut).
- **Center Crop Marks** adds a crop mark at the center of each edge of the image.
- **Registration Marks** adds bulls-eye targets and star targets that are used to align color separations on a printing press. (Calibration bars and star target registration marks require a PostScript printer.)
- **Description** adds description text (from the File>File Info dialog box) outside the trim area in 9-pt Helvetica.
- **Labels** adds the file name above the image.

Functions

- **Emulsion Down** reverses the image on the output. This option is primarily used for output to a filmsetter or imagesetter.
- **Negative** inverts the color values of the entire output. This option is typically used if you are outputting directly to film, which will then be used to image a photo-sensitive printing plate (a slowly disappearing workflow).
- The **Background** option allows you to add a background color that will print outside the image area.
- The **Border** option adds a black border around an image. You can define a specific width (in points) for the border.
- The **Bleed** option moves crop marks inside the image by a specific measurement.

PostScript Options

(If your printer is not PostScript compatible, the PostScript options will not be available.)

- **Calibration Bars** adds swatches of black in 10% increments (starting at 0% and ending at 100%).
- The **Interpolation** option can help reduce the jagged appearance of low-resolution images by automatically resampling up when you print. This option is only available on PostScript Level 2 or 3 printers.
- The **Include Vector Data** option sends vector information in the output stream for a PostScript printer, so the vector data can be output at the highest possible resolution of the output device.

4. **Regardless of the paper you are printing on, choose the Portrait layout option (below the number of copies).**

   Ideally, you should always print proofs at 100%. If this is not possible, however, you can print a sample content proof by scaling the page to fit the available paper size.

5. **Review the options in the scrolling pane below the Print Setup options.**

   Different types of output jobs require different settings. If you are simply printing a desktop proof, as in this project, you can leave most of these options at their default values.

6. **If you do not have a tabloid-size printer, check Scale to Fit Media in the Position and Size options.**

   As a general rule, proofs should be printed at 100% of the actual file size. The proof you are creating in this project is for your own records, so you can scale it to a smaller size if you don't have tabloid printing capability.

   Alternatively, you can use the Print Selected Area option to output different portions of the image onto separate sheets, and then manually assemble the multiple sheets into a single page.

Note:

If you submit a scaled proof with a print job, make sure you note the scale percentage prominently on the proof.

When Print Selected Area is checked, use these handles to determine what area to print.

Click and drag in the preview area to change the position of the image on the paper.

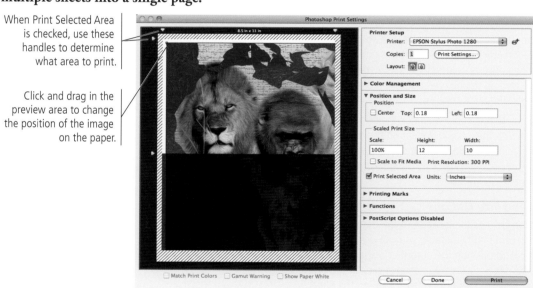

7. **Click Print to output the file.**

8. **When the output process is complete, close the file.**

1. You can toggle on _____ to see the feathered areas of a soft-edge mask.

2. The _____ tool is used to create vector-based shapes and paths.

3. _____ control the shape of a curve between two anchor points.

4. In RGB mode, a _____ value of each color channel results in black.

5. The _____ tool can be used to fill areas with solid colors or patterns.

6. A _____ is a smooth transition from one color to another.

7. A _____ is a resolution-independent, vector-based layer that can be filled with a solid color or pattern.

8. The _____ command is used to show only areas of one layer that fall within the area of the underlying layer.

9. In the Liquify filter, the _____ tool can be used to protect specific areas from being liquified.

10. The _____ allows you to experiment with different filters and filter settings, and compound multiple filters to create unique artistic effects.

1. Briefly describe the concept of resampling, and how it relates to effective resolution.

2. Briefly describe the advantages and disadvantages of placing files as Smart Objects.

3. Briefly explain the concept of alpha channels.

Portfolio Builder Project

Use what you learned in this project to complete the following freeform exercise.
Carefully read the art director and client comments, then create your design to meet the needs of the project.
Use the space below to sketch ideas; when finished, write a brief explanation of the reasoning behind your design.

art director comments

The Global Wildlife Fund is very happy with your work on the Africa poster. They would like you to create at least two more of the pieces in the series. If you only have time for two, use North America and Asia.

To complete this project, you should:

❏ Search the Internet for maps you can use as templates to create the continent shapes.

❏ Download the **PS6_PB_Project2.zip** archive from the Student Files Web page to access the client-supplied animal photos.

❏ Save the animal images in the TIFF format if you want to place them as Smart Objects.

❏ Create each piece with styles similar to the ones you used in the Africa map.

❏ Create each poster at 10 × 12″ for the final size.

client comments

Remember, this is a series of pieces that make up an entire collection, so each piece should be similar. We really like the style you created in the first version, and we want the other pieces to have a similar feel. Use the same style as the Africa artwork for each of the other pieces.

One thing we do want is a similar-but-different background for each piece. Of course they're all water, but the water isn't exactly the same around the entire globe. Make sure there's some variation from one background to the next — maybe a slightly different color or a different pattern.

We sent some images you can use — we know there aren't enough for most of the continents, so please find other images as necessary to fill out each continent. Just make sure the animals you put into each continent actually live in those areas. Keep in mind, we'd like to avoid a huge stock-image bill.

Our campaign kicks off in a little less than two months; can you complete the work in two weeks?

project justification

Project Summary

This project extended many of the concepts you learned in Project 1: Composite Movie Ad, adding new options for compositing multiple images into a single cohesive piece of artwork. Smart Objects, which played a major role in this project, are one of the most significant advances in image compositing technology. They allow you to apply effects and filters without affecting or damaging the original image data. You also learned how to create and edit soft-edge layer masks to smooth the transitions between layer edges, and you learned how to manage those layer masks in regular layers and Smart Objects.

This project also introduced some of the creative tools that can turn photos and flat colors into painting-like artwork. You learned to use the Filter Gallery — with its many options, custom gradients, gradient and pattern fill layers, and blending modes — and the Liquify filter. You will use these options many times in your career as you complete different types of projects in Photoshop.

Create a compound vector shape layer using a low-resolution image as a template

Add a pattern and fill color to the vector shape layer

Composite multiple images using Smart Objects

Create a clipping mask to place images into the vector shape layer

Use soft-edge layer masks to blend one image into another

Apply filters to images to create a "painting" effect

Use gradients and patterns to create a custom background

Liquify pixels to create unique effects

Menu Image Correction

Your client is the owner of The Chateau, a five-star gourmet restaurant that has been operating in northern Los Angeles County for over five decades. The restaurant changes its menu frequently, so they currently use a chalkboard menu, presented on an easel at each table when guests are seated. The owner recently received a number of comments about the chalkboard menu being difficult to read, so he decided to create printed menus with the standard offerings and use the chalkboard to display the chef's daily specials.

This project incorporates the following skills:

❑ Repairing damaged images

❑ Understanding the relationship between tonal range and contrast

❑ Correcting image lighting and exposure problems

❑ Understanding how gray balance affects overall image color

❑ Correcting minor and severe image color problems

❑ Preparing corrected images for printing

❑ Combining exposures into an HDR image

Project Meeting

client comments

The Chateau is a unique destination restaurant that consistently wins awards from local and national food and wine reviewers. The restaurant was first opened in 1952 by Paul and Gina Roseman as a rest stop and diner for travelers along the Sierra Highway. While the restaurant remains in the family, it has evolved from home-style comfort food to more exotic fare such as wild game with a French twist.

The history of the restaurant is important to us. We have a Roseman family portrait — my great-grandparents — that we'd like to include on the back of the menu. The picture is a bit grainy and has some damage, though, and we'd like you to clean it up as much as possible. We also want to include a picture of the current executive chef, who is Paul and Gina's great-grandniece, in the same section. The only picture we have of her is very dark though, and we're hoping you can make it look better.

In addition, we've taken several pictures of different meals that Suzanne created. We want you to make sure they will look as good as possible when printed. You're the expert, so we trust that you know what needs to be done.

art director comments

Digital images come from a wide variety of sources: scanned photographs and digital cameras are the two most common, as is the case for the client's images for this project. Some images can be used as is, or at least with only minor correction. Realistically, most professional photographers reshoot an image until they have one that doesn't need your help.

Unfortunately, however, not every project involves a professional photographer. Consumer-level cameras have come down in price and gone up in quality to the point where many non-professionals shoot their own photos without proper skill or knowledge. That means many of those images require a bit of help — and some require a lot.

Even when a professional photographer is involved, not every image comes from a perfectly lit studio. Location shots — where a subject is photographed in a "real-world" setting — can't always be captured perfectly. Those images usually need work as well. Fortunately, Photoshop provides a powerful toolset for solving most image problems, or at least improving the worst of them.

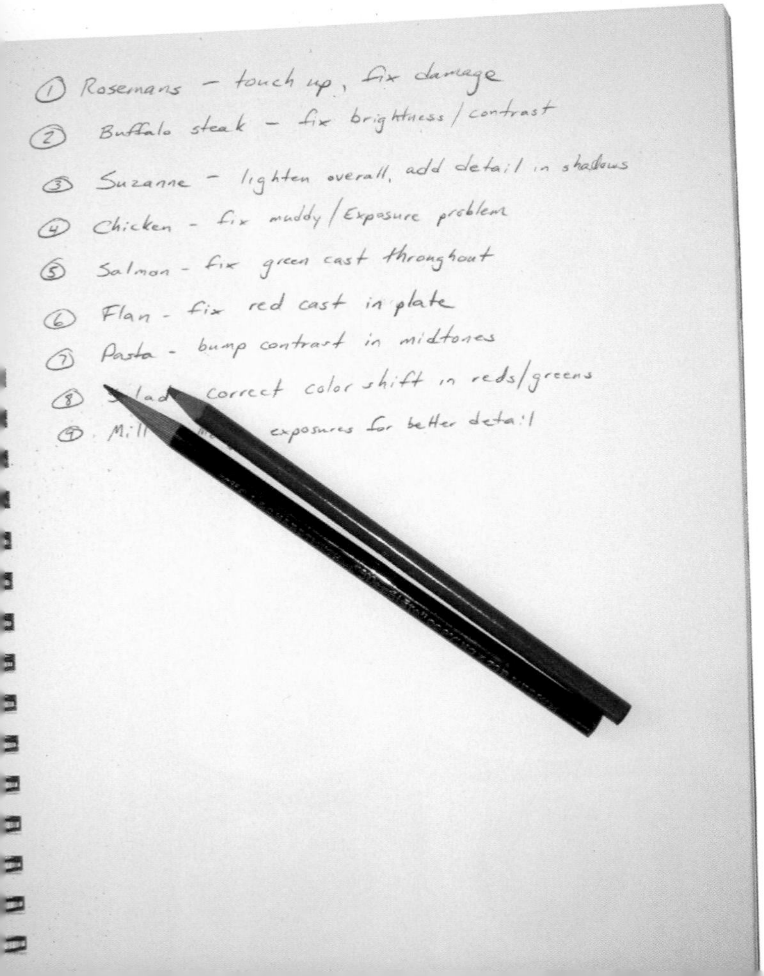

Handwritten notes:

1. Rosemans — touch up, fix damage
2. Buffalo steak — fix brightness/contrast
3. Suzanne — lighten overall, add detail in shadows
4. Chicken — fix muddy/Exposure problem
5. Salmon — fix green cast throughout
6. Flan — fix red cast in plate
7. Pasta — bump contrast in midtones
8. _lad_ correct color shift in reds/greens
9. Mill_ exposures for better detail

project objectives

To complete this project, you will:

❏ Remove grain with blur and sharpen techniques

❏ Heal severe scratches

❏ Clone out major damage

❏ Correct minor problems with the Brightness/Contrast adjustment

❏ Correct tonal range with the Levels adjustment

❏ Correct lighting problems with the Exposure adjustment

❏ Correct overall color problems with the Color Balance adjustment

❏ Correct precise color values with the Curves adjustment

❏ Correct an RGB image to CMYK gamut limits

❏ Embed color profile information in a file

❏ Combine multiple exposures with the Merge to HDR Pro utility

Stage 1 Retouching Damaged Images

Image repair is the process of fixing scratches, removing dust, making tears disappear, and generally putting broken or damaged pictures back together again. **Retouching**, on the other hand, is the technique of changing an image by adding something that wasn't there or removing something that was there. Damage can come from a wide range of sources: creases, scratches from any number of abrasive objects, water spots, and tape marks to name just a few. Other image problems such as photographic grain are a natural part of photographs (especially old ones), and dust is common (if not inevitable) whenever photographs are scanned.

There are many different ways to approach image repairs. As you complete the exercises in this stage of the project, you will use several tools — from basic to complex — to clean up damage in the client's family portrait from the early 1940s.

 ## REMOVE GRAIN WITH BLUR AND SHARPEN TECHNIQUES

Photographic film is made up of microscopic grains of light-sensitive material. These grains capture the image information, which is eventually processed into a print or transparency. While not usually apparent in a standard photographic print, the grain in a photograph can become pronounced when scanned with a high-resolution scanner. Enlarging an image during scanning further enhances any grain that already exists.

When grain is evident in a digital image, the grain pattern can destroy fine detail and create a mottled appearance in areas of solid color or subtle tone variation. Slower-rated film typically has the smallest and least-evident grain, while faster film can produce significant graininess.

Sharpening and blurring techniques are the best methods for removing photographic grain. The techniques you use in this exercise work for any image with grain. Older images — such as the one your client wants to use — almost always have obvious grain problems that can be fixed to some degree; antique images can be fixed only just so much. The techniques you learn in this project produce very good results if you need to remove grain from modern scanned images.

1. Download **PS6_RF_Project3.zip** from the Student Files Web page.

2. Expand the ZIP archive in your WIP folder (Macintosh) or copy the archive contents into your WIP folder (Windows).

   This results in a folder named **Menu**, which contains the files you need for this project. You should also use this folder to save the files you create in this project.

3. Open the file **rosemans.jpg** from your WIP>Menu folder.

Obvious glue marks remain from the original mounting.

Scratches mar several areas of the image.

A sharp crease cuts into the Rosemans' daughter.

The corner has been torn off.

4. Choose View>Actual Pixels to view the image at 100%.

Grain is most obvious in large areas of solid (or nearly solid) color.

Grain in lighter areas can produce a sickly appearance in a person's face.

The Noise Filters

Noise is defined as random pixels that stand out from the surrounding pixels, either hurting the overall appearance of the image (as in the case of visible grains in an old photograph) or helping to prevent printing problems (as in the case of a gradient that extends across a large area). Photoshop includes several filters (Filters>Noise) that can add or remove noise.

The **Add Noise filter** applies random pixels to the image. Uniform distributes color values of noise between 0 and the defined amount. Gaussian distributes color values of noise along a bell-shaped curve. Monochromatic adds random pixels without affecting the colors in the image.

The **Despeckle** filter detects the edges in an image and blurs everything except those edges.

The **Dust & Scratches filter** reduces noise by comparing the contrast of pixels within the defined radius; pixels outside the defined threshold are adjusted.

The **Median filter** reduces noise by blending the brightness of pixels within a selection. The filter compares the brightness of pixels within the defined radius, and replaces pixels that differ too much from surrounding pixels with the median brightness value of the compared pixels.

The **Reduce Noise** filter provides far greater control over different aspects of noise correction. In Basic mode, you can remove luminance noise and color noise in the composite image.

In Advanced mode, you can remove noise from individual color channels. (**Luminance noise**, also called grayscale noise, makes an image appear grainy; **color noise** usually appears as color artifacts in the image.)

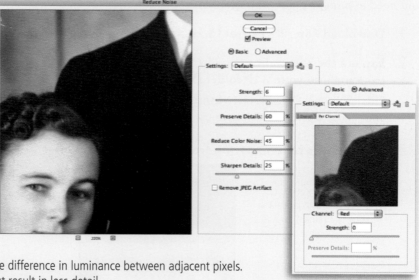

- **Strength** controls the amount of luminance noise reduction.

- **Preserve Details** controls how carefully the filter compares the difference in luminance between adjacent pixels. Lower values remove more noise but result in less detail.

- **Reduce Color Noise** removes random color pixels from the image.

- **Sharpen Details** sharpens the image. Because the noise reduction process inherently blurs the image, this option applies the same kind of sharpening that is available in the Photoshop Sharpen filters.

- **Remove JPEG Artifacts** removes artifacts and halos caused by saving an image with a low JPEG quality setting (in other words, using a high lossy compression scheme).

5. **Choose Filter>Blur>Gaussian Blur.**

   All Photoshop blur filters work in essentially the same way: they average the brightness values of contiguous pixels to soften the image.

6. **Make sure Preview is checked and change the Radius field to 1.5 pixels.**

   The **Radius** field defines (in pixels) the amount of blurring that will be applied. Photoshop uses this value to average the brightness of a pixel with that of surrounding pixels. A radius value near 1 can soften an image and remove most photographic grain.

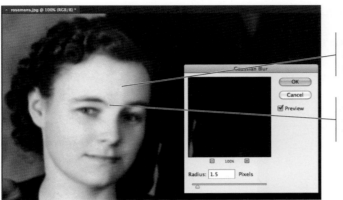

A small amount of Gaussian blur removes most of the photographic grain.

Areas of fine detail are also slightly blurred by the Gaussian Blur filter.

7. **Click OK to apply the Gaussian Blur to the image.**

   To remove the photographic grain, you had to blur the entire image; this means that areas of fine detail were also blurred. You can use a second technique — unsharp masking — to restore some of the lost edge detail.

The Blur Filters

PHOTOSHOP FOUNDATIONS

The Filter>Blur menu includes a number of choices for applying corrective or artistic blurs to an image or selection.

Field Blur, **Iris Blur**, and **Tilt-Shift** open a special Blur Gallery interface. You will use this option in Project 4: City Promotion Cards.

Average finds the average color of an image or selection, and then fills the image or selection with that color to create a smooth appearance.

Blur and **Blur More** smooth transitions by averaging the pixels next to the hard edges of defined lines and shaded areas. When you apply these filters, you have no additional control: Blur is roughly equivalent to a 0.3-pixel radius blur, and Blur More uses approximately a 0.7-pixel radius.

Box Blur averages the color value of neighboring pixels. You can adjust the size of the area used to calculate the average value; a larger radius value results in more blurring.

Gaussian Blur blurs the selection by a specific amount.

Lens Blur adds blur to an image to create the effect of a narrower depth of field so some objects in the image remain in focus, while others areas are blurred.

Motion Blur includes an option for changing the blur angle, as well as a Distance value that defines the number of pixels to blur.

Radial Blur either spins the pixel around the center point of the image, or zooms the pixel around the center point based on the Amount setting. The farther a pixel is from the center point, the more the pixel is blurred. You can drag in the Blur Center window to move the center point of the blur.

Shape Blur uses a specific shape (**kernel**) to create the blur. Radius determines the size of the kernel; the larger the kernel, the greater the blur.

Smart Blur allows you to blur tones closely related in value without affecting edge quality. Threshold determines how closely pixels must be related in tone before being blurred. You can also specify a Quality level, and change the Mode setting. Using Edge Only mode, edges are outlined in white and the image is forced to black. Using Overlay Edges mode, the color image is blurred and edges are outlined in white.

Surface Blur blurs an image while trying to preserve edges. The Radius option specifies the size of the blur in whole numbers. The Threshold option controls how much the tonal values of neighboring pixels must differ before being blurred.

8. **Choose Filter>Sharpen>Unsharp Mask and make sure the Preview check box is active in the dialog box.**

Unsharp masking sharpens an image by increasing contrast along the edges in an image. **Amount** determines how much the contrast in edges will increase; typically, 150–200% creates good results in high-resolution images. **Radius** determines how many pixels will be included in the edge comparison; higher radius values result in more pronounced edge effects. **Threshold** defines the difference that is required for Photoshop to identify an edge. A threshold of 15 means that colors must be more than 15 levels different; using a higher Threshold protects the smooth tones in the faces, while still allowing detail in the faces (the eyes, for example) to be sharpened.

9. **Change the Amount to 150%, the Radius to 3.0 pixels, and the Threshold to 15 levels.**

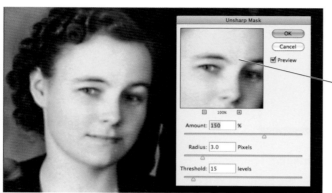

Drag here or click in the document window to change the visible area in the preview window.

10. **Click OK to apply the Unsharp Mask filter.**

11. **Choose File>Save As. Save the file as a native Photoshop file named** `rosemans_working.psd` **in your WIP>Menu folder. Continue to the next exercise.**

Remember, you have to choose File>Save As to save the file with a different name or format.

Note:

Using Gaussian Blur and Unsharp Masking in tandem is a common technique for cleaning up grainy images.

Note:

The degree of sharpening applied to an image is often a matter of personal choice; however, oversharpening an image produces a halo effect around the edges.

Note:

The Sharpen, Sharpen More, and Sharpen Edges filters apply sharpening with no user control.

The Smart Sharpen Filter

The Smart Sharpen filter allows you to control the amount of sharpening that occurs in shadow and highlight areas.

Remove defines the algorithm used to sharpen the image. Gaussian Blur is the method used by the Unsharp Mask filter. Lens Blur detects edges and detail, and provides finer detail and fewer halos. Motion Blur tries to reduce the effects of blur due to movement at a defined angle.

The **More Accurate** check box processes the file more slowly for a more accurate blur removal.

In Advanced mode, you can use the Shadow and Highlight tabs to adjust sharpening of only those areas.

Fade Amount adjusts the amount of sharpening.

Tonal Width controls the range of tones that will be modified. Smaller values restrict the adjustments to only darker regions for shadows and only lighter regions for highlights.

Radius defines the size of the area around each pixel used to determine whether a pixel is in the shadows or highlights.

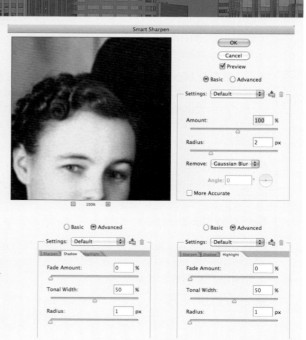

HEAL SEVERE SCRATCHES

The blur and sharpen routine from the previous exercise improved the client's image — the obvious grain is gone. Even though the edges are slightly less sharp than the original scan, they are sharp enough to produce good results when the image is printed. If you're working with images that aren't 70 years old, you will be able to produce far sharper edges using these same techniques.

There are still a number of problems in the image that require intervention. Photoshop includes several tools for changing the pixels in an image — from painting with a brush to nudging selections on a layer to using repair tools specifically designed for adjusting pixels based on other pixels in the image.

The **Spot Healing Brush tool** allows you to remove imperfections by blending the surrounding pixels. The **Healing Brush tool** has a similar function, except you can define the source pixels that will be used to heal a specific area. The **Patch tool** allows you to repair a selected area with pixels from another area of the image by dragging the selection area.

Note:

Throughout this project, you are going to clean up blemishes on images and make other adjustments that require looking at very small areas. It can be very helpful to clean your monitor so you don't mistake on-screen dust and smudges with flaws in the images you are adjusting.

1. **With** `rosemans_working.psd` **open, view the image at 100%. Set up the document window so you can see the lower half of the image.**

2. **Select the Spot Healing Brush tool in the Tools panel.**

3. **In the Options bar, open the Brush Preset picker and choose a 20-pixel hard-edge brush. Choose the Proximity Match radio button.**

Click this button to open the Brush Preset picker, where you can change the brush settings.

Use a 20-pixel hard-edge brush.

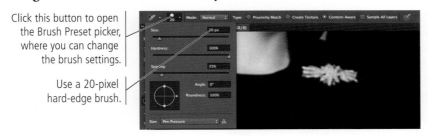

The **Proximity Match** method uses the pixels around the edge of the selection to find an image area to use as a patch for the selected area. The **Create Texture** method uses all the pixels in the selection to create a texture for repairing the area. **Content Aware** mode attempts to match the detail in surrounding areas while healing pixels (this method does not work well for areas with hard edges or sharp contrast). If you select **Sample All Layers**, the tool pulls pixel data from all visible layers.

Note:

You will work extensively with brushes and brush settings in Project 7: House Painting.

4. **Place the cursor over the small white spot in the bottom-left corner of the image. Click immediately over the white spot to heal it.**

The Spot Healing Brush tool shows the size of the selected brush.

5. **Using the same technique, remove the remaining white spots from the dark areas of the Rosemans' clothing.**

6. **Choose the Healing Brush tool (nested under the Spot Healing Brush tool).**

7. **In the Options bar, open the Brush Preset picker. Choose a small brush size that's slightly larger than the white spot on the girl's chin (we used 9 pixels).**

   When using the Healing Brush tool, the Mode menu determines the blending mode used to heal an area. The default option (Normal) samples the source color and transparency to blend the new pixels smoothly into the area being healed. The Replace mode preserves texture in the healed area when you use a soft-edge brush.

Use a brush size just large enough to cover the blemish.

Healing Brush tool

Note:

Multiple, Screen, Darken, Lighten, Color, and Luminosity modes have the same function as the blending modes for specific layers and brushes (refer to Project 2: African Wildlife Map for an explanation of each blending mode).

8. **Place the cursor directly below the spot you want to heal. Press Option/Alt and click to define the healing source.**

   Pressing Option/Alt with the Healing Brush tool changes the cursor icon to a crosshair, which you can click to select the source of the brush (the pixels that will be used to heal the spot where you next click).

Note:

You can use the bracket keys to enlarge (]) or reduce ([) the Healing Brush tool brush size.

Pressing Option/Alt allows you to define the source pixels that will be used to heal the next spot you click.

Aligning the Healing Source

PHOTOSHOP FOUNDATIONS

When you work with the Healing Brush and Clone Stamp tools, you have the option to align the source to the cursor. If the Align option is turned off, the source starting point will be relative to the image. If the Align option is turned on, the source starting point will be relative to the cursor. The following images illustrate this idea.

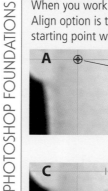

A We first Option/Alt-clicked at the guide intersection to define the healing source.

B The crosshair shows the source of the healing.

This circle shows the cursor location where we clicked with the Healing Brush tool.

C When the Aligned option is turned **on**, the source moves relative to the tool cursor.

Clicking farther to the right moves the source the same distance from its defined origin.

D When the Aligned option is turned **off**, the source remains in the same position even when the Healing Brush tool is clicked farther to the right.

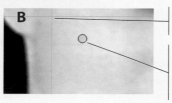

9. **Place the cursor over the blemish on the girl's chin and click.**

Unlike the Spot Healing Brush tool, the Healing Brush tool allows you to define the source of the healing. By choosing nearby pixels as the healing source, the blemish on the girl's chin disappears, and that spot blends nicely into the surrounding pixels.

The Healing Brush tool blends colors from the source pixels (which you defined in Step 8) with colors in the area where you click. You can also change the source from Sampled (the pixels you defined by Option/Alt-clicking) to Pattern, which uses pixels from a defined pattern to heal the area. The Pattern option is a good choice for creating artistic effects, rather than healing blemishes in an existing photo.

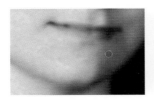 

After clicking, the spot is healed using the source pixels.

Note:

Using the Sample menu in the Options bar, you can sample source pixels from the current layer, from all layers including and below the current layer, or from all visible layers.

Note:

It might help to zoom in when you want to heal small areas such as this spot on the girl's chin. We are working at 200% in these screen shots.

10. **Save the file and continue to the next exercise.**

CLONE OUT MAJOR DAMAGE

The client's image has definitely been improved by removing the grain and healing the small blemishes, but four major areas of damage still need to be fixed. These larger areas require more control over the healing process, which the Clone Stamp tool provides.

The Clone Stamp tool paints one part of an image over another part, which is useful for duplicating objects or removing defects in an image. As with the Healing Brush tool, you can define the source that will be cloned when you click with the tool; the difference is that whole pixels are copied, not just their color values.

1. **With the file rosemans_working.psd open, zoom into the bottom-left corner (where the crease marks the image) and select the Clone Stamp tool.**

2. **In the Brush Preset picker (in the Options bar), choose a soft-edge brush large enough to cover the crease.**

When you are using the Clone Stamp tool, the Options bar combines brush options (brush size, blending mode, opacity, and flow) with healing options (alignment and sample source, which you used in the previous exercise).

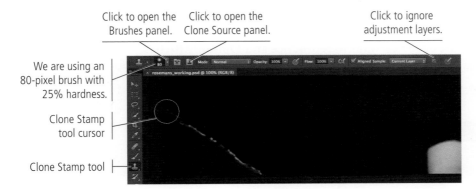

Click to open the Brushes panel.

Click to open the Clone Source panel.

Click to ignore adjustment layers.

We are using an 80-pixel brush with 25% hardness.

Clone Stamp tool cursor

Clone Stamp tool

3. **In the Options bar, make sure the Aligned Sample option is turned on (checked).**

In this case, you want the cloning source to remain relative to the cursor, even if you stop and start several times. If you clone a large area relative to the same source origin (in other words, with the Align option turned off), you could end up with an unwanted pattern in the area you clone.

4. **Place the cursor directly above and to the right of the crease. Option/Alt-click to define the cloning source.**

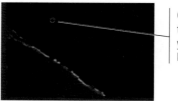

Option/Alt-click to define the cloning source, just as you did with the Healing Brush tool.

Note:

When using the Clone Stamp tool, hard-edge brushes can result in harsh lines where you clone pixels; soft-edge brushes can help prevent harsh lines from appearing.

5. **Click over an area of the crease and drag to clone out the crease.**

As you drag, notice that the source crosshairs move in relation to the Clone Stamp cursor. Because you turned on the Aligned Sample option in Step 3, you can stop and restart cloning, and the source will retain the same relative position to the tool cursor.

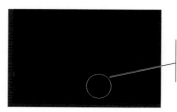

Drag with the Clone Stamp tool until the crease is no longer visible.

Note:

You can use the bracket keys to enlarge (]) or reduce ([) the Clone Stamp brush size.

6. **Use the same process to fill in the torn area in the bottom-right corner of the image.**

7. **Zoom into the scratch on the man's left shoulder.**

Cloning out damage in areas of solid color is fairly simple. This area presents a more difficult problem since the area you need to fix has an edge that must be maintained.

Note:

When you are cloning — especially large areas — it's usually a good idea to clone in small strokes or even single clicks. This method can help you avoid cloning in patterns or "railroad tracks" that do as much damage as good. When cloning large areas, it's also a good idea to frequently resample the clone source to avoid cloning the same pixels into a new noticeable pattern.

8. **In the Brush Preset picker, select a brush that just barely covers the edge of the man's jacket, and turn off the Aligned Sample option.**

To prevent cloning a hard edge, we used a 30-pixel brush with a 50% Hardness value.

9. **Place the cursor over the edge you want to reproduce and Option/Alt-click to define the source.**

Because the Aligned Sample option is turned off, each successive click uses the same source point.

Turn off the Aligned Sample option.

Option/Alt-click to define the clone source.

10. **Place the cursor over the scratched pixels on the man's shoulder.**

As you move the Clone Stamp tool cursor, the source pixels move along with the tool cursor to give you a preview of what will happen when you click.

11. **Click without dragging when the cloned pixels appear to align properly with the area behind the scratch.**

Clicking without dragging clones a 30-pixel area. Because the brush we chose has 50% hardness, the center (where the shoulder edge is) is clear, but the outside parts of the brush are feathered into the surrounding area.

Note:

If you're not happy with the result of a clone, simply undo the action (Command/Control-Z, or using the History panel) and try again. Cloning — especially edges — often takes more than one try to achieve the desired result.

12. **Move the cursor slightly to the left, again centering the cursor preview over the would-be edge, and click without dragging.**

With the Aligned Sample option turned off, you can click again to clone pixels from the same source.

13. **Repeat this process as necessary to clone out the remaining scratch along the man's shoulder.**

We clicked two more times to completely remove the scratch along the shoulder line.

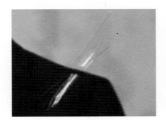

14. **Choose the Lasso tool in the Tools panel. Draw a marquee around the scratches in the background, above the man's shoulder.**

Be careful to avoid the man's shoulder in the selection area.

Avoid the edge in your selection.

15. **Choose Edit>Fill. Choose Content-Aware in the Use menu and click OK.**

Photoshop evaluates the image and determines what should be created inside the selection area. The fill might take a few seconds to process, so be patient.

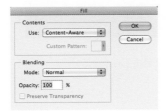

16. Choose Select>Deselect to turn off the selection marquee.

Content-Aware Fill works very well on areas of subtle shading, such as the backdrop in this image, or other areas where you do not need to maintain fine detail or edges in the selected area. If you try to use this option on a sharp edge, however, the Content-Aware Fill results are unpredictable. Other tools, such as the Clone Stamp tool, work better for retouching distinct edges.

Note:

Press Command/ Control-D to turn off a selection marquee.

17. Use the same method as in Steps 14–15 to remove the scratches from the man's coat, and the scratches and glue residue on the left side of the photo.

At the ends of the image, it's okay to drag outside the edge of the canvas; Photoshop identifies the edge and snaps the selection edge to the canvas edge.

18. Choose File>Save As and choose TIFF in the Format menu. Change the file name to rosemans_fixed.tif and save it with the default TIFF options in your WIP>Menu folder.

19. Close the file and continue to the next stage of the project.

The Clone Source Panel in Depth

The Clone Source panel (Window>Clone Source) allows you to store up to five sources for the Clone Stamp or Healing Brush tool. These sources can be from any layer of any open image, which allows you to create unique blended effects by combining pixels from multiple layers or multiple files.

Store and access up to five sources from any layer of any open image.

Transform the offset, size, and angle of the clone source.

The Show Overlay options allow you to show (at the defined opacity) the source pixels on top of the area where you are cloning. For example, let's say you want to clone the gorilla into the giraffe photo. You would first define a clone source in the gorilla image, and then make the giraffe image active.

With the Show Overlay option checked, placing the Clone Stamp cursor over the giraffe image shows the gorilla on top of the giraffe. When you click in the giraffe image with the Clone Stamp tool, that area of the gorilla image will be cloned into the giraffe image; the overlay allows you to preview the areas of the source that will be cloned into the giraffe image.

If the Auto Hide option is checked, the overlay is only visible when the mouse button is not clicked. The Invert option reverses the overlay into a negative representation of the source image. You can also change the blending mode of the overlay from the default Normal to Darken, Lighten, or Difference.

We defined a clone source here.

Using the overlay, you can see the Clone Stamp cursor in relation to the clone source. Clicking will clone this spot from the gorilla image into the giraffe image.

We defined a clone source here.

When the Clipped option is checked, the clone source appears only within the tool cursor area.

Stage 2 Correcting Lighting Problems

Before you start correcting problems with lighting and color, you should understand the different parts of an image, as well as the terms used to describe these areas.

- **Highlights** are defined as the lightest areas of the image that include detail. Direct sources of light such as a light bulb or reflected sunlight on water are called **specular highlights**; they should not be considered the highlights of an image.

- **Shadows** are the darkest areas of the image that still contain some detail; areas of solid black are not considered shadow tones.

- The shades between the highlights and shadows are the **midtones** (or **gamma**) of the image.

Contrast and saturation play an integral role in reproducing high-quality images. **Contrast** refers to the tonal variation within an image; an image primarily composed of highlights and shadows is a high-contrast image, while an image with more detail in the midtones is a low-contrast image.

Contrast is closely linked to **saturation**, which refers to the intensity of a color or its variation away from gray. The saturation of individual colors in an image, and the correct saturation of different colors in relation to one another, affects the overall contrast of the image. If an image is under- or oversaturated, the contrast suffers — detail is lost and colors appear either muted or too bright.

Note:

Image adjustments can be applied directly to the image pixels or as non-destructive adjustment layers using the Adjustments panel. In this project, you edit the actual image pixels; you use the adjustment layer method in Project 6: Advertising Samples.

CORRECT PROBLEMS WITH BRIGHTNESS/CONTRAST

Depending on the image, several tools are available for correcting problems related to images that are either too dark or too light. The most basic adjustment option — Brightness/Contrast — can fix images that need overall adjustment to brightness, contrast, or both. If an image requires more sophisticated adjustment, you should use one of the other adjustment options.

1. **Open the file buffalo.jpg from your WIP>Menu folder.**

   This image has an overall dark feel, probably caused by poor lighting or underexposure. The Brightness/Contrast adjustment can correct this problem.

2. **Choose Image>Adjustments>Brightness/Contrast and make sure the Preview option is checked.**

3. **Drag the Brightness slider to +35.**

   Increasing the overall brightness creates an immediate improvement in this image, although some areas of detail are still muddy.

4. Drag the Contrast slider to +10.

Increasing the contrast brings out more detail in the food texture, which is the focal point of the image (pay particular attention to the meat).

5. Click OK to apply the change.

6. Save the file in your WIP>Menu folder as a TIFF file named `buffalo_fixed.tif` using the default TIFF options.

7. Close the file and continue to the next exercise.

CORRECT CONTRAST AND TONAL RANGE WITH LEVELS

The **tonal range** of an image is the amount of variation between the lightest highlight and the darkest shadow in a particular image. A grayscale image can contain 256 possible shades of gray. Each channel of a color image can also contain 256 possible shades of gray. To achieve the best contrast in an image, the tonal range of the image should include as many levels of gray as are available.

While the Brightness/Contrast option is a good choice for making basic adjustments, the Levels adjustment is the best approach for enhancing image detail throughout the entire tonal range. Using Levels, adjusting contrast is a three-step process:

- Determine the image's highlight areas (the lightest areas that contain detail).

- Determine the image's shadow areas (the darkest areas that contain detail).

- Adjust the gamma (the contrast in midtones of an image) to determine the proportion of darker tones to lighter tones.

1. Open the file `chef.jpg` from the WIP>Menu folder.

2. **Display the Histogram panel (Window>Histogram), and then choose Expanded View from the panel Options menu.**

The Histogram panel can help you identify problems that need to be corrected. When you first display the panel, it probably appears in Compact view, which shows only the graphs for the individual color channels and the composite image.

3. **In the Histogram panel, change the Channel menu to RGB.**

The histogram — the chart that shows the distribution of tones — can display a single graph for the entire composite image (all channels combined) or for individual channels.

In Expanded view, the panel shows the distribution of pixels from the darkest to the lightest portion of the image, for the entire image or for individual color channels.

If you see a warning icon, click it to reset the cache.

Choose from this menu to view and modify the histogram for individual channels.

These shadow values are pushing out of the histogram "container," which shows that there is a problem in the shadow tones.

The empty space at the left of the histogram indicates that some tones in the available range are not being used.

Histogram Statistics

The Histogram panel (Window>Histogram) shows the distribution of pixels — or more accurately the tonal values of those pixels — from the darkest to the lightest portions of an image, for the entire image or for individual color channels. The Histogram panel can help identify problems that need to be corrected. In Expanded view, you can see more information about how pixels are distributed in the image (from shadows on the left to highlights on the right).

- The **Mean** value is an average point of the brightness values. A Mean of 128 usually identifies a well-balanced image. Images with a Mean of 170 to 255 are light; images with a Mean lower than 90 are very dark.

- The **Standard Deviation** (Std Dev) value represents how widely the brightness values vary.

- The **Median** value shows the middle value in the range of color values.

- The **Pixels** value displays the total number of pixels used for the graphic displayed on the histogram.

- The **Level** statistic displays the intensity level of the pixels below the mouse cursor.

- **Count** shows the number of pixels in the area below the cursor.

- Values displayed as a **Percentile** represent the percentage of pixels **below or to the left** of the cursor location. Zero represents the left edge of the image and 100% is the right edge.

- The **Cache Level** is determined by the Performance preferences and is related to the Cache Refresh icon (and Warning icon). The larger your cache, the more you can do before the image and the disk cache don't match. On the other hand, a larger cache requires more RAM for the application to run smoothly.

4. **If you see one, click the Warning icon in the upper-right corner of the Histogram panel to reset the cache.**

   Every time you zoom in or out of an image, Photoshop stores the results of the display in a **cache** (a drive location that keeps track of what you're doing). The image you're looking at on the histogram often doesn't match the results on the drive. The Warning icon shows there's a problem; clicking the icon resets the image and rereads the cache.

Note:

If you see the Warning icon in the Histogram panel, click the icon to match the disk cache with what's happening in the live image.

5. **Choose Image>Adjustments>Levels and make sure Preview is checked.**

   The Levels dialog box shows a histogram like the one shown in the Histogram panel.

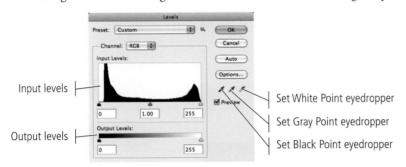

The Levels dialog box has two sets of sliders to control input levels and output levels. Each set has a black slider for adjusting the shadows in an image and a white slider to adjust highlights. The Input Levels slider also has a gray triangle in the center of the slider bar for adjusting gamma or midtones.

The Input sliders in the Levels dialog box correspond to the tonal range of the image. Any pixels that exist to the left of the Input Shadow slider are reproduced as solid black, and they have no detail; any pixels that exist to the right of the Input Highlight slider are reproduced as pure white.

Identifying Shadows and Highlights

When you move the Shadow and Highlight sliders in the Levels dialog box, you change the **black point** and **white point** of the image — the points at which pixels become black or white. The goal is to find highlight and shadow points that maintain detail. Choosing a point that has no detail causes the area to turn totally white (highlight) or black (shadow) with no detail reproduced. In some images, it can be difficult to visually identify the black and white points in an image; in these cases you can use the Levels dialog box to help you find those areas.

If you press Option/Alt while dragging the Input Shadow or Input Highlight slider, the image turns entirely white or black (respectively). As you drag, the first pixels that become visible are the darkest shadow and the lightest highlight.

Once you identify the highlight and shadow points in the image, select the White Point eyedropper and click the highlight, and then select the Black Point eyedropper and click the shadow to define those two areas of the image.

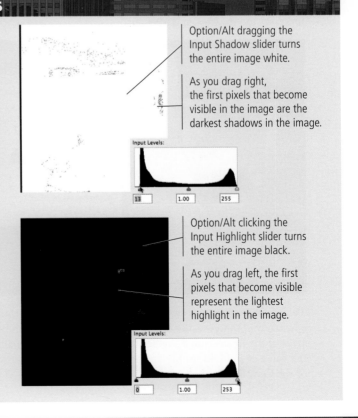

Option/Alt dragging the Input Shadow slider turns the entire image white.

As you drag right, the first pixels that become visible in the image are the darkest shadows in the image.

Option/Alt clicking the Input Highlight slider turns the entire image black.

As you drag left, the first pixels that become visible represent the lightest highlight in the image.

6. Move the Input Shadow slider to the right until it touches the left edge of the curve.

This simple adjustment extends the colors in the image to take advantage of all 256 possible tones. This adjustment has a small effect on the shadow area of the image, but the majority of the colors in the image are still clustered near the shadow point (as you can see by the spike in the histogram).

Choose from this menu to view and modify the histogram for an individual channel.

The white space at the left of the histogram indicates that some of the tones in the available range are not being used.

Dragging the Shadow Input slider to the left edge of the histogram extends the shadows into the full tonal range.

7. Move the Input Gamma slider to the left until the middle box below the slider shows approximately 1.75.

The Input Gamma slider controls the proportion of darker tones to lighter tones in the midtones of an image. If you increase gamma, you increase the proportion of lighter grays in the image; this effectively increases contrast in lighter shades and lightens the entire image. If you decrease gamma, you extend the tonal range of darker shades; this allows those areas of the image to be reproduced with a larger range of shades, which increases the contrast in darker shades.

Note:

You can change input and output levels by moving the sliders, entering actual values in the boxes below the slider sets, or by using the eyedroppers to select the brightest and darkest points in the image.

Dragging the Gamma Input slider extends the range between the midtone and the highlights, creating greater contrast and showing more detail throughout the image.

To decrease contrast in an image, you can adjust the Output sliders. This method effectively compresses the range of possible tones that can be reproduced, forcing all areas of the image into a smaller tonal range. Areas originally set to 0 are reproduced at the value of the Output Shadow slider; areas originally set to 255 are output at the value of the Output Highlight slider.

8. **Click OK to close the Levels dialog box.**

9. **Save the file in your WIP>Menu folder as a TIFF file named `chef_fixed.tif`.**

10. **Close the file and then continue to the next exercise.**

The Gradient Map Adjustment

The **Gradient Map adjustment** (Image>Adjustments>Gradient Map) enables you to create interesting artistic effects by mapping the tones of an image to the shades in a defined gradient.

In the Gradient Map dialog box, you can apply any defined gradient by clicking the arrow to the right of the gradient sample and choosing from the pop-up menu, or you can edit the selected gradient by clicking the sample gradient ramp. The **Dither** option adds random noise to the effect. If you check the **Reverse** option, image highlights map to the left end of the gradient, and image shadows map to the right end of the gradient, effectively reversing the gradient map.

The composite histogram of an RGB image starts at the darkest point and ends at the lightest point with 256 total possible tonal values. If you think of the gradient as having 256 steps from one end to the other, then you can see how the shades of the selected gradient map to the tones of the original image.

CORRECT LIGHTING PROBLEMS WITH THE EXPOSURE ADJUSTMENT

Many images are either over- or underexposed when photographed. If an image is under-exposed, it appears dark and lacks detail in the shadows. If an image is overexposed, it appears too light and lacks detail in the highlights. You can use the Exposure adjustment to correct exposure — and thus, the overall detail and contrast in the image.

Keep in mind, however, that Photoshop cannot create information that doesn't exist. If you have an underexposed image with no detail in the shadow areas, Photoshop cannot generate that detail for you. Some problems are simply beyond fixing.

The Exposure dialog box is designed to make tonal adjustments to 32- and 64-bit HDR (high dynamic range) images, but it also works with 8-bit and 16-bit images. The Exposure adjustment works by performing calculations in a linear color space (gamma 1.0) rather than the image's current color space.

Note:

HDR refers to high-density range (32- or 64-bit) images.

1. **Open chicken.jpg from your WIP>Menu folder.**

2. **Choose Image>Adjustments>Exposure and make sure Preview is checked.**

White Point eyedropper
Gray Point eyedropper
Black Point eyedropper

3. **Click the White Point eyedropper, and then click the white area on the top edge of the plate.**

The eyedroppers in the Exposure dialog box adjust the image's luminance (or the degree of lightness, from white to black). By adjusting the luminance only, you can change the lightness of the image without affecting the color.

Note:

The White Point and Gray Point eyedroppers affect the Exposure value. The Black Point eyedropper affects the Offset value.

- Clicking with the Black Point eyedropper shifts the point you click to black (0 luminance).

- Clicking with the White Point eyedropper shifts the point you click to white (100 luminance).

- Clicking with the Gray Point eyedropper shifts the point you click to gray (50 luminance).

Click here with the White Point eyedropper to define the white area of the image.

Clicking with the White Point eyedropper changes the Exposure setting.

4. **Drag the Gamma Correction slider left to extend the midtone range, which increases contrast and brings out detail in the image. (We used a setting of 1.25.)**

The Gamma slider adjusts the image midtones. Dragging the slider left lightens the image, improving contrast and detail in the midtones and highlights. Dragging the slider right darkens the image, extending the range and increasing detail in the shadows.

Extending the Gamma Correction value into the shadow range brings out more detail in the midtones.

5. **Click the Offset slider and drag very slightly left to add detail back into the midtones and shadows.**

The Offset slider lightens (dragged to the right) or darkens (dragged to the left) the shadows and midtones of the image. The white point (highlight) remains unaffected, but all other pixels are affected.

Decreasing the Offset value adds detail back into the shadows.

6. **Click OK to finalize the adjustment.**

7. **Save the file as a TIFF file named `chicken_fixed.tif` in your WIP>Menu folder.**

8. **Close the file and continue to the next stage of the project.**

Stage 3   Correcting Color Problems

You can't accurately reproduce color without a basic understanding of color theory, so we present a very basic introduction in this project. Be aware that there are entire, weighty books written about color science; we're providing the condensed version of what you absolutely must know to work effectively with files in any color mode.

Before starting to color-correct an image, you should understand how different colors interact with one another. There are two primary color models — RGB and CMYK — used to output digital images. (Other models such as LAB and HSB have their own purposes in color conversion and correction, but they are not typically output models.)

Additive vs. Subtractive Color

The most important thing to remember about color theory is that color is light, and light is color. You can easily prove this by walking through your house at midnight; you will notice that what little you can see appears as dark shadows. Without light, you can't see — and without light, there is no color.

The **additive color** model (RGB) is based on the idea that all colors can be reproduced by combining pure red, green, and blue light in varying intensities. These three colors are considered the **additive primaries**. Combining any two additive primaries at full strength produces one of the **additive secondaries** — red and blue light combine to produce magenta, red and green combine to produce yellow, and blue and green combine to produce cyan. Although usually considered a "color," black is the absence of light (and, therefore, of color). White is the sum of all colors, produced when all three additive primaries are combined at full strength.

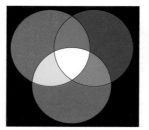 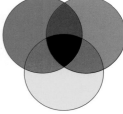

Additive color model   *Subtractive color model*

Reproducing color on paper requires **subtractive color theory**, which is essentially the inverse of additive color. Instead of adding red, green, and blue light to create the range of colors, subtractive color begins with a white surface that reflects red, green, and blue light at equal and full strength. To reflect (reproduce) a specific color, you add pigments that subtract or absorb only certain wavelengths from the white light. To reflect only red, for example, the surface must subtract (or absorb) the green and blue light.

Remember that the additive primary colors (red, green, and blue) combine to create the additive secondaries (cyan, magenta, and yellow). Those additive secondaries are also called the **subtractive primaries**, because each subtracts one-third of the light spectrum and reflects the other two-thirds:

- Cyan absorbs red light, reflecting only blue and green light.

- Magenta absorbs green light, reflecting only red and blue light.

- Yellow absorbs blue light, reflecting only red and green light.

A combination of two subtractive primaries, then, absorbs two-thirds of the light spectrum and reflects only one-third. As an example, a combination of yellow and magenta absorbs both blue and green light, reflecting only red.

Color printing is a practical application of subtractive color theory. The pigments in the cyan, magenta, yellow, and black (CMYK) inks are combined to absorb different wavelengths of light. By combining different amounts of the subtractive primaries, it's possible to produce a large range (or gamut) of colors.

Note:

Additive color theory is practically applied when a reproduction method uses light to reproduce color. A computer monitor is black when turned off. When the power is turned on, light in the monitor illuminates at different intensities to create the range of colors you see.

Many vague and technical-sounding terms are mentioned when discussing color. Is hue the same as color? The same as value? As tone? What's the difference between lightness and brightness? What is chroma? And where does saturation fit in?

This problem has resulted in several attempts to normalize color communication. A number of systems have been developed to define color according to specific criteria, including Hue, Saturation, and Brightness (HSB); Hue, Saturation, and Lightness (HSL); Hue, Saturation, and Value (HSV); and Lightness, Chroma, and Hue (LCH). Each of these models or systems plots color on a three-dimensional diagram, based on the elements of human color perception — hue, colorfulness, and brightness.

Hue is what most people think of as color — red, green, purple, and so on. Hue is defined according to a color's position on a color wheel, beginning from red (0°) and traveling counterclockwise around the wheel.

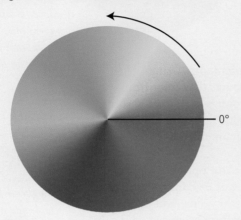

Chroma is similar to saturation, but chroma factors in a reference white. In any viewing situation, colors appear less vivid as the light source dims. The process of chromatic adaptation, however, allows the human visual system to adjust to changes in light and still differentiate colors according to the relative saturation.

Brightness is the amount of light reflected off an object. As an element of color reproduction, brightness is typically judged by comparing the color to the lightest nearby object (such as an unprinted area of white paper).

Lightness is the amount of white or black added to the pure color. Lightness (also called "luminance" or "value") is the relative brightness based purely on the black-white value of a color. A lightness value of 0 means there is no addition of white or black. Lightness of +100 is pure white; lightness of −100 is pure black.

Saturation (also called "intensity") refers to the color's difference from neutral gray. Highly saturated colors are more vivid than those with low saturation. Saturation is plotted from the center of the color wheel. Color at the center is neutral gray and has a saturation value of 0; color at the edge of the wheel is the most intense value of the corresponding hue and has a saturation value of 100.

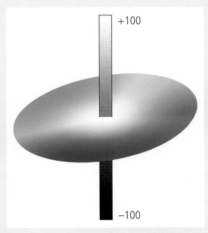

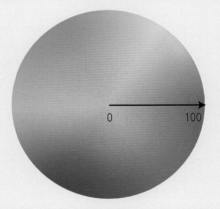

All hues are affected equally by changes in lightness.

If you bisect the color wheel with a straight line, the line creates a saturation axis for two complementary colors. A color is dulled by the introduction of its complement. Red, for example, is neutralized by the addition of cyan (blue and green). Near the center of the axis, the result is neutral gray.

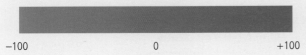

−100   0   +100

Although the RGB and CMYK models handle color in different ways, these two color models are definitely linked. RGB colors are directly inverse (opposite) to CMY colors, referring to the position of each color on a color wheel. The relationship between primary colors is the basis for all color correction.

Referencing a basic color wheel can help you understand how RGB colors relate to CMY colors. If you center an equilateral triangle over the color wheel, the points of the triangle touch either the RGB primaries or the CMY primaries. Adding together two points of the triangle results in the color between the two points. Red and blue combine to form magenta, yellow and cyan combine to form green, and so on.

Opposite colors on the color wheel are called **color complements**. Using subtractive color theory, a color's complement absorbs or subtracts that color from visible white light. For example, cyan is opposite red on the color wheel; cyan absorbs red light and reflects green and blue. If you know green and blue light combine to create cyan, you can begin to understand how the two theories are related.

How does all this apply to color correction?

If you want to add a specific color to an image, you have three options: add the color, add equal parts of its constituent colors, or remove some of its complement color. For example, to add red to an image, you can add red, add yellow and magenta, or remove cyan. Conversely, this means that to remove a color from an image, you can remove the color itself, remove equal parts of its constituents, or add its complement. To remove cyan from an image, for example, you can remove cyan, remove blue and green, or add red.

Make sure you understand the relationships between complementary colors:

- To add red, add yellow and magenta or remove cyan.

- To add blue, add cyan and magenta or remove yellow.

- To add green, add cyan and yellow or remove magenta.

- To remove cyan, remove blue and green or add red.

- To remove yellow, remove green and red or add blue.

- To remove magenta, remove blue and red or add green.

Understanding Gray Balance

Understanding the concept of neutral gray is also fundamental to effective color correction. Once you correct the contrast (tonal range) of an image, many of the remaining problems can be at least partially (if not entirely) corrected by correcting the **gray balance**, or the component elements of neutral grays within an image.

In the RGB color model, equal parts of red, green, and blue light combine to create a shade of gray that is equal to the percentage of each component — R=0 G=0 B=0 creates pure black, while R=255 G=255 B=255 creates pure white. To correct an image in RGB mode, you should evaluate and correct the neutral grays so they contain equal percentages of the three primary colors.

Using the CMYK color model, equal percentages of cyan, magenta, and yellow theoretically combine to produce an equal shade of gray — C=0 M=0 Y=0 creates pure white, while C=100 M=100 Y=100 theoretically creates pure black. In practice,

Note:

Because white is a combination of all colors of light, white paper should theoretically reflect equal percentages of all light wavelengths. However, different papers absorb or reflect varying percentages of some wavelengths, thus defining the paper's apparent color. The paper's color affects the appearance of inks printed on that paper.

Note:

It might seem easiest to simply add or subtract the color in question, but a better result might be achieved by adding one color and subtracting another. For example, if an image needs less blue, simply removing cyan can cause reds to appear pink or cyan to appear green. Adding magenta and yellow to balance the existing cyan creates a better result than simply removing cyan.

Note:

An important point to remember is that any color correction requires compromise. If you add or remove a color to correct a certain area, you also affect other areas of the image.

however, the impurities of ink pigments — specifically cyan — do not live up to this theory. When you print an area of equal parts cyan, magenta, and yellow, the result is a muddy brown because the cyan pigments are impure. To compensate for the impurities of cyan, neutral grays must be adjusted to contain equal parts of magenta and yellow, and a slightly higher percentage of cyan.

CORRECT COLOR CAST WITH THE COLOR BALANCE ADJUSTMENT

Color cast is the result of improper gray balance, when one channel is significantly stronger or weaker than the others. An image with improper gray balance has an overall predominance of one color, which is most visible in the highlight areas. The image that you will correct in this exercise has a strong green cast that needs to be removed.

1. **Open the file salmon.jpg from your WIP>Menu folder.**

2. **Display the Info panel (Window>Info).**

3. **If you don't see both RGB and CMYK color modes in the Info panel, choose Panel Options in the Info panel Options menu. Use the Info Panel Options dialog box to choose Actual Color for the First Color Readout and CMYK Color for the Second Color Readout, then click OK.**

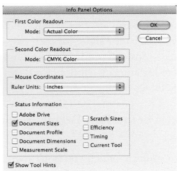

Note:

This exercise relies purely on numbers to correct gray balance. To see an accurate preview of image color on screen, you should calibrate your monitor and create a monitor profile that you can load into Photoshop.

4. **Choose the Color Sampler tool (nested under the Eyedropper tool).**

5. **In the Options bar, choose 3 by 3 Average in the Sample Size menu.**

   Instead of correcting based on individual pixel values, you can average a group of contiguous pixels as the sample value. Doing so prevents accidentally correcting an image based on a single anomalous pixel (a dust spot, for example).

Use this menu to define the sample size.

Color Sampler tool

Color Sampler tool cursor

The Info panel shows color values for the current cursor location, in both RGB and CMYK modes.

6. **Click the cursor on the lower-left plate lip to place a color sample.**

7. **Click to add a second sample point to the top-right plate lip.**

   The two samples show a strong predominance of green; the numbers in the Info panel reflect the visible color cast in the image.

Sample points are numbered in order of creation.

This is the color sample that we placed in Step 6.

The Info panel shows the values associated with each of the sample points you created.

8. **Choose Image>Adjustments>Color Balance.**

   Color Balance is a basic correction tool that can effectively remove overall color cast. The Color Balance dialog box presents a separate slider for each pair of complementary colors. You can adjust the highlights, shadows, or midtones of an image by selecting the appropriate radio button; the Preserve Luminosity check box ensures that only the colors shift, leaving the tonal balance of the image unchanged.

9. **Click the Highlights radio button in the Tone Balance section at the bottom of the Color Balance dialog box.**

   The focal point of this image is green spinach, which you don't want to affect. Instead, you need to remove the green cast from the highlight, where it is most obvious.

10. **Drag the Magenta/Green slider left until the middle field shows –10.**

    Remember, adding a color's complement is one method for neutralizing that color. Increasing magenta in the highlight areas neutralizes the green color cast.

The values after the "/" show the result of the changes; these will become the actual sample values if you click OK.

Changing the color balance brings the three values much closer to equal (called "in balance").

These fields correspond to the three color sliders. The middle field shows the Magenta/Green adjustment.

11. **Click OK to apply the adjustment.**

12. **Save the file in your WIP>Menu folder as a TIFF file named salmon_fixed.tif.**

13. **Close the file and continue to the next exercise.**

CORRECT GRAY BALANCE WITH CURVES

The Curves adjustment is the most powerful color-correction tool in Photoshop. If you understand the ideas behind curves, you can use this tool to remove color cast, enhance overall contrast, and even modify color values in individual channels.

The diagram in the Curves dialog box is the heart of the Curves adjustment. When you open the Curves dialog box, a straight diagonal line in the graph represents the existing color in the image.

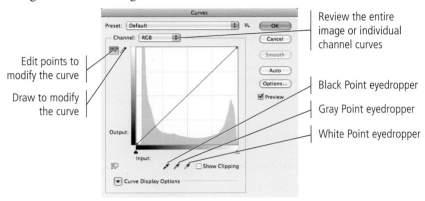

Edit points to modify the curve

Draw to modify the curve

Review the entire image or individual channel curves

Black Point eyedropper

Gray Point eyedropper

White Point eyedropper

The horizontal axis represents the input color value, and the vertical axis represents the output color value. The upper-right point is the maximum value for that color mode (255 for RGB images and 100 for CMYK images). The bottom-left corner of the curves grid is the zero point.

The color mode of the image determines the direction of the input and output scales. In both CMYK and RGB, 0 means "none of that color." However, remember the difference between the two different color modes:

- The additive RGB color model starts at black and adds values of each channel to produce different colors, so 0, 0, 0 in RGB equals black.

- The subtractive CMYK model starts with white (paper) and adds percentages of each ink (channel) to produce different colors, so 0, 0, 0, 0 in CMYK equals white.

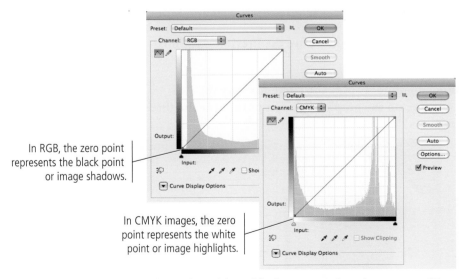

In RGB, the zero point represents the black point or image shadows.

In CMYK images, the zero point represents the white point or image highlights.

Note:

Remember, the additive colors (RGB) at full strength combine to create pure white, while the subtractive colors (CMYK) at full strength combine to create pure black.

Every curve is automatically anchored by a black point and a white point. (For RGB, the black point is at the bottom left and the white point is at the top right.) You can add points along the curve by simply clicking the curve. You can also move any point on the curve by clicking and dragging.

When you move points on the curve of an image (whether for the whole image or for an individual channel), you are telling Photoshop to, "Map every pixel that was [this] input value to [that] output value." In other words, using the following image as an example, a pixel that was 128 (the input value) will now be 114 (the output value). Because curves are just that — curves, and not individual points — adjusting one point on a curve changes the shape of the curve as necessary.

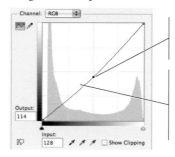

This point changes the input value of 128 to an output value of 114.

On either side of the adjusted point, the curve is adjusted to smoothly meet the other points on the curve (in this case, the black and white points).

1. **Open the file flan.jpg from the WIP>Menu folder.**

2. **Using the Color Sampler tool, place a sample point on the left plate lip.**

   This image has a strong red cast that needs to be neutralized. You can correct cast by removing the cast color or adding the other two primaries; the goal is equal (or nearly equal) parts of red, green, and blue in the neutral areas such as the plate lip.

The sample shows a strong red cast in what should be neutral areas.

   In the Info panel, the sample values show that the red channel has a value of 231, the green channel has a value of 210, and the blue channel has a value of 207. To fix the cast in this image, you will use the middle of these values (the green channel) as the target and adjust the other two curves.

3. **Choose Image>Adjustments>Curves and make sure the Preview option is checked in the Curves dialog box.**

4. **Choose Red in the Channel menu to display the curve for only the Red channel, and then click the line on the graph to place a point near the three-quarter grid intersection.**

Click here to add a point to the curve.

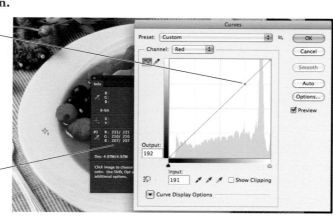

Numbers before the slash are the original values. Numbers after the slash are the values that result from your changes in the Curves dialog box.

5. **With the new point selected on the curve, type the original Red value in the Input field (ours is 231).**

6. **Type the target value in the Output field (ours is the Green value of 210).**

The number after the slash shows that the Red value for this sample will be equal to the Green value when you click OK.

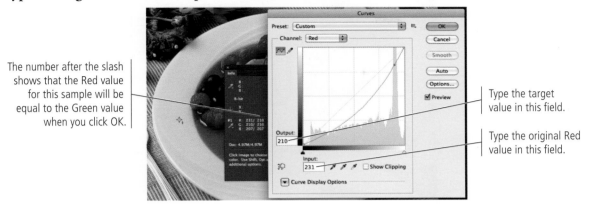

Type the target value in this field.

Type the original Red value in this field.

7. **In the Channel menu, choose the other channel that you need to adjust based on your sample values (ours is Blue). Add a point to the curve, and then adjust the input value to match your target output value (the original Green value, in our example). Using our sample point, we adjusted the 207 Input value to a 210 Output value.**

You can add the point anywhere along the curve; when you change the Input and Output values, the point automatically moves to that location along the curve.

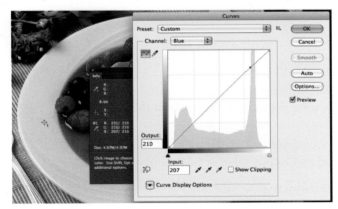

8. **Click OK to apply the changes and close the Curves dialog box.**

You can see how simply correcting gray balance has a significant impact on the image:

9. **Save the file in your WIP>Menu folder as a TIFF file named flan_fixed.tif.**

10. **Close the file and continue to the next exercise.**

Adjusting Curves On-Screen

The On-Image Adjustment tool in the Curves dialog box allows you to make curve adjustments by interacting directly with the image (behind the dialog box).

When the On-Image Adjustment tool is active, clicking in the image places a point on the curve based on the pixel data where you clicked; you can then drag up or down within the image area to move that point of the curve (in other words, to change the output value of the selected input value).

You can add 14 points on a curve, and delete points by pressing Command/Control-delete.

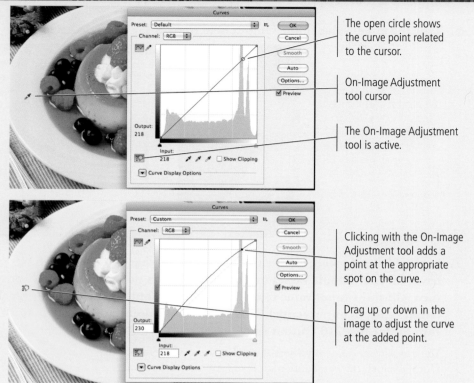

The open circle shows the curve point related to the cursor.

On-Image Adjustment tool cursor

The On-Image Adjustment tool is active.

Clicking with the On-Image Adjustment tool adds a point at the appropriate spot on the curve.

Drag up or down in the image to adjust the curve at the added point.

 ## CORRECT CONTRAST WITH CURVES

Remember, contrast is essentially the difference between the values in an image. By adjusting the points on the curve, you increase the tonal range between those points — which means you also increase the contrast in that same range.

In the following image, Point A has an Input value of 167 and an Output value of 182. Point B has an Input value of 87 and an Output value of 62. Mathematically:

- Original tonal range (Input values): 167 to 87 = 80 available tones

- New tonal range (Output values): 182 to 62 = 120 available tones

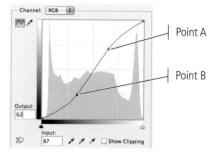

Point A

Point B

By making these two curve adjustments, we significantly increased the tonal range available for the image's midtones, which means we also significantly increased the contrast in the midtones. A steeper curve indicates increased tonal range and increased contrast. Notice, however, that the curves before Point B and after Point A are much shallower than the original curves, which means this change also significantly reduces the contrast in the shadow and highlight areas.

Points to Remember about Curves

Curves are very powerful tools, and they can be intimidating. To simplify the process and make it less daunting, keep these points in mind:

- Aim for neutral grays.

- You can adjust the curve for an entire image, or you can adjust the individual curves for each channel of the image.

- The horizontal tone scale shows the Input value, and the vertical tone scale shows the Output value.

- Changes made to one area of a curve affect all other areas of the image.

- The steeper the curve, the greater the contrast.

- Increasing contrast in one area inherently decreases contrast in other areas.

Curve Display Options

PHOTOSHOP FOUNDATIONS

The Curve Display options allow you to control what is visible in the graph. (If you can't see the Curve Display options, click the button to the left of the heading.)

The Show Amount Of radio buttons reverse the input and output tone scales. Light is the default setting for RGB images; Pigment/Ink % is the default setting for CMYK images.

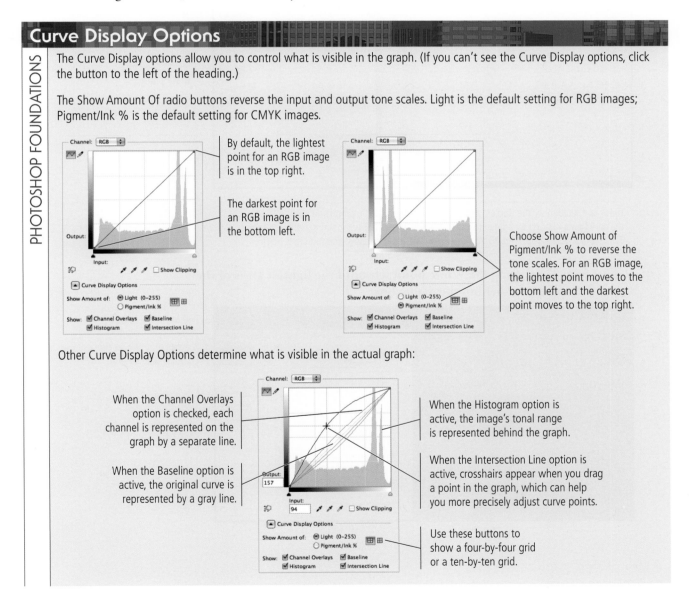

By default, the lightest point for an RGB image is in the top right.

The darkest point for an RGB image is in the bottom left.

Choose Show Amount of Pigment/Ink % to reverse the tone scales. For an RGB image, the lightest point moves to the bottom left and the darkest point moves to the top right.

Other Curve Display Options determine what is visible in the actual graph:

When the Channel Overlays option is checked, each channel is represented on the graph by a separate line.

When the Baseline option is active, the original curve is represented by a gray line.

When the Histogram option is active, the image's tonal range is represented behind the graph.

When the Intersection Line option is active, crosshairs appear when you drag a point in the graph, which can help you more precisely adjust curve points.

Use these buttons to show a four-by-four grid or a ten-by-ten grid.

1. **Open the file `pasta.jpg` from the WIP>Menu folder.**

2. **Choose Image>Adjustments>Curves and make sure Preview is checked.**

3. **Activate the Show Clipping option, click the black point on the bottom-left corner of the graph, and then drag until some pixels start to appear in the image (behind the dialog box).**

   We dragged the Input Black point just past the point where the histogram shows the darkest shadows in the image. (You performed this same action in the Levels dialog box when you adjusted the Input Shadow slider.) The Input and Output fields show that any pixels with an Input value of 13 will be output as 0; in other words, anything with an Input value lower than 13 will be clipped to solid black.

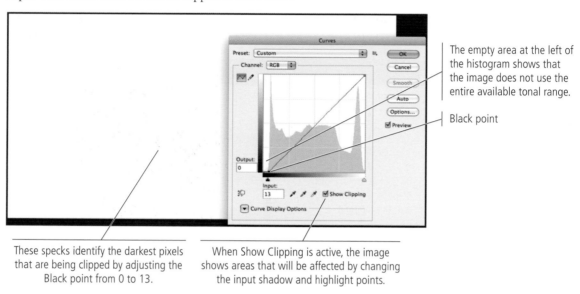

The empty area at the left of the histogram shows that the image does not use the entire available tonal range.

Black point

These specks identify the darkest pixels that are being clipped by adjusting the Black point from 0 to 13.

When Show Clipping is active, the image shows areas that will be affected by changing the input shadow and highlight points.

4. **Repeat Step 3, dragging the White point left until the lightest areas of the image start to appear behind the dialog box.**

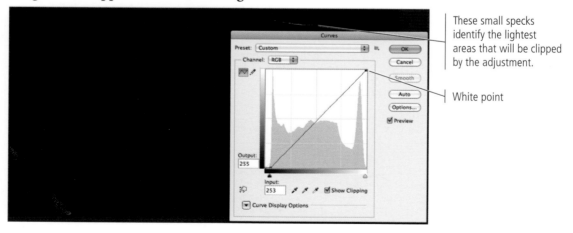

These small specks identify the lightest areas that will be clipped by the adjustment.

White point

5. Turn off the Show Clipping option so you can see the actual image behind the dialog box.

Even this small change improved the image, but the midtones — especially in the pasta, which is the focal area of the image — need some additional contrast. To accomplish that change, you need to steepen the curve in the middle of the graph.

Note:

Contrast adjustments can have a major impact on color as well as on sharpness. Take particular note of the green basil leaves; no direct color adjustment was done to these two images, but the leaves are noticeably greener and brighter after you adjust the curves.

6. Click the curve to create a point at the quartertone gridline and drag it slightly to the right.

We adjusted the curve point from an Input value of 81 to an Output value of 62.

Three-quartertone gridlines

Quartertone gridlines

7. Click the curve at the three-quartertone gridline and drag the point to the left.

We adjusted the 175 Input value to a 190 Output value.

The adjusted points steepen the curve, increasing contrast between the two points.

8. **Click OK to apply the changes and close the dialog box.**

   Adjusting the contrast with curves improved the detail in the image and enhanced the overall image color.

9. **Save the file in your WIP>Menu folder as a TIFF file named `pasta_fixed.tif`.**

10. **Close the file and continue to the next stage of the project.**

Automatic Color Correction

Clicking Options in the right side of the Curves dialog box opens the Auto Color Correction Options dialog box. These settings will apply if you click the Auto button in the Levels or Curves dialog box, or if you choose one of the automatic adjustments in the Image>Adjustments menu (Auto Tone, Auto Contrast, or Auto Color). The Algorithms options determine how Photoshop will adjust the image's tonal range.

- **Enhance Monochromatic Contrast** is applied if you choose Auto Contrast. This option clips all channels identically, preserving overall color while making highlights appear lighter and shadows darker.

- **Enhance Per Channel Contrast** is applied if you choose Auto Levels. This option maximizes the tonal range in each channel by moving the darkest shadow to 0 (or 100 for CMYK images) and the lightest highlight to 255 (or 0 for CMYK images). The overall color relationship is not maintained, which might result in color cast in the adjusted image.

- **Find Dark & Light Colors** is applied if you choose Auto Color. This option uses the average lightest and darkest pixels to maximize contrast and minimize clipping. **Snap Neutral Midtones** also relates to the Auto Color adjustment; this option finds an average neutral color in an image, and then adjusts midtone (gamma) values to make that color neutral.

- **Enhance Brightness and Contrast** allows Photoshop to use content-aware monochromatic adjustments to produce smoother results across the entire tonal range.

In the **Target Colors & Clipping** options, you can define the target shadow, midtone, and highlight values by clicking the appropriate color swatch. The Clip fields determine how much of the darkest shadow and lightest highlight will be clipped when you apply an automatic adjustment. In other words, a Shadow Clip setting of 1% means Photoshop will ignore the first 1% of the darkest pixels when adjusting the image. If you change the Target Colors & Clipping settings, you can check the Save As Defaults option; you can then apply those settings by clicking the Auto button in the Levels or Curves dialog box.

The Match Color Adjustment

The Match Color adjustment (Image>Adjustments>Match Color) allows you to match colors between multiple RGB images, layers, or selections. In the Match Color dialog box, the Target shows the image, layer, or selection you are modifying. The changes are based on values from the source image and layer selected in the Image Statistics area. You can change the luminance or color intensity of the target image, fade the adjustment, and neutralize color cast caused by the adjustment.

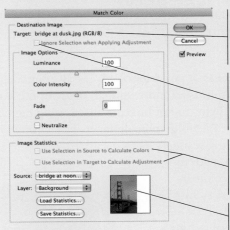

The Destination Image Target is the active image (and selected layer, if applicable) when you open the dialog box.

If the target image has an active selection area, click this check box to apply the change to the entire target image instead of the selected area only.

If the target or source image has an active selection area, click these check boxes to apply changes based on the selected area only.

Choose the source image and layer to which the target will be matched.

- The **Luminance** slider affects the brightness in the target image; higher values lighten the image.
- The **Color Intensity** slider adjusts the color saturation in the target image; higher values increase the color saturation.
- The **Fade** slider changes the amount of adjustment applied to the target image; higher values (i.e., more fade) reduce the amount of the adjustment.
- The **Neutralize** check box automatically removes color cast in the target image.

Stage 4   Preparing Images for Print

You might have noticed that all the images for this project are in the RGB color mode. Printing, however, relies on the CMYK mode to output color images.

Although a full discussion of color science and management can be extremely complex, and is beyond the needs of most graphic designers, applying color management in Photoshop is more intimidating than difficult. We believe this foundational information on color management will make you a more effective and practically grounded designer.

Understanding Gamut

Different color models have different ranges or **gamuts** of possible colors. The RGB model has the largest gamut of the output models. The CMYK gamut is far more limited; many of the brightest and most saturated colors that can be reproduced using light cannot be reproduced using pigmented inks.

This difference in gamut is one of the biggest problems graphic designers face when working with color images. Digital image-capture devices (including scanners and digital cameras) work in the RGB space, which, with its larger gamut, can more closely mirror the range of colors in the original scene. Printing, however, requires images to first be converted or **separated** into the CMYK color space.

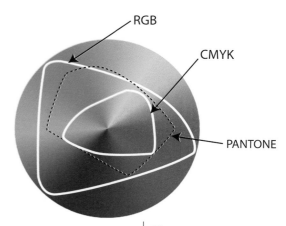

The usual goal in color reproduction is to achieve a color appearance equivalent to the original. Depending on the image, at least some colors in the RGB color model likely cannot be reproduced in the more limited gamut of the CMYK color model. These **out-of-gamut** colors pose a challenge to faithfully reproducing the original image. If the conversion from RGB to CMYK is not carefully controlled, **color shift** can result in drastic differences between the original and printed images.

Color Management in Brief

Color management is intended to preserve color predictability and consistency as a file is moved from one color mode to another throughout the reproduction process. Color management can also eliminate ambiguity when a color is only specified by some numbers. For example, you might create a royal purple in the Photoshop Color Picker; but without color management, that same set of RGB numbers might look more lilac (or even gray) when converted to CMYK for printing. A well-tuned color-management system can translate the numbers that define a color in one space to numbers that can better represent that same color in another space.

It's important to have realistic expectations for color management, and to realize that color management isn't a replacement for a thorough knowledge of the color-reproduction process. Even at its best, color management can't fix bad scans or bad photos — all it can do is introduce consistency and predictability to a process that otherwise rarely has either.

Color management relies on **color profiles**, which are simply data sets that define the reproduction characteristics of a specific device. A profile is essentially a recipe that contains the ingredients for reproducing a specific color in a given color space. The color recipes in profiles are known as **look-up tables** (LUTs), which are essentially cross-reference systems for finding matching color values in different color spaces.

Note:

Color shift can also result when converting from one type of CMYK to another, or (though less likely) from one version of RGB to another. Whatever models are being used, color management gives you better control over the conversion process.

Source profiles are the profiles of the devices (scanner, camera, or monitor in the case of original digital artwork) used to capture or generate the image. Destination profiles are the profiles of output devices used in the process. Most professional-level devices come with profiles you can install when you install the hardware; a number of generic and industry-specific destination profiles are also built into Photoshop.

LAB (or L*a*b*, or CIELAB) is a theoretical color space that represents the full visible spectrum. This device-independent color space can represent any possible color. By moving device-dependent RGB and CMYK colors into LAB as an intermediary space, you can convert color from any one space to any other space.

The Color Management Module (CMM) is the engine that drives color conversions via the LUT numbers. The engine doesn't do much other than look up numbers and cross-reference them to another set of numbers. The mechanics of color-managed conversions are quite simple. Regardless of the specific input and output spaces in use, the same basic process is followed for every pixel:

1. The CMM looks up the color values of a pixel in the input-space profile to find a matching set of LAB values.

2. The CMM looks up the LAB values in the output-space profile to find the matching set of values that will display the color of that pixel most accurately.

Note:

Color profiles are sometimes also called "ICC profiles," named after the International Color Consortium (ICC), which developed the standard for creating color profiles.

Color Management in Theory and Practice

PHOTOSHOP FOUNDATIONS

RGB and CMYK are very different entities. The two color models have distinct capabilities, advantages, and limitations. There is no way to exactly reproduce RGB color using the CMYK gamut because many of the colors in the RGB gamut are simply too bright or too saturated. Rather than claiming to produce an exact (impossible) match from your monitor to a printed page, the true goal of color management is to produce the best possible representation of the color using the gamut of the chosen output device.

A theoretically ideal color-managed workflow resembles the following:

- Image-capture devices (scanners and digital cameras) are profiled to create a look-up table that defines the device's color-capturing characteristics.

- Images are acquired using a calibrated, profiled device. The profile of the capturing device is tagged to every image captured.

- The image is opened in Photoshop and viewed on a calibrated monitor. The monitor's profile is defined in Photoshop as your working space.

- Photoshop translates the image profile to your working space profile.

- You define a destination (CMYK) profile for the calibrated output device that will be used for your final job.

- The image is converted from RGB to CMYK, based on the defined working space and destination profiles.

Notice that three of the "ideal workflow" steps mention a form of the word "calibrate." To **calibrate** something means to check and correct a device's characteristics. Calibration is an essential element in a color-managed workflow; it is fundamentally important to achieving consistent and predictable output.

You cannot check or correct the color characteristics of a device without having something to compare the device against. To calibrate a device, a known target — usually a sequence of distinct and varying color patches — is reproduced using the device. The color values of the reproduction are measured and compared to the values of the known target. Precise calibration requires adjusting the device until the reproduction matches the original.

As long as your devices are accurately calibrated to the same target values, the color acquired by your RGB scanner will exactly match the colors displayed on your RGB monitor and the colors printed by your desktop printer. Of course, most devices (especially consumer-level desktop devices that are gaining a larger market share in the commercial graphics world) are not accurately calibrated, and very few are calibrated to the same set of known target values.

Keeping in mind these ideals and realities, the true goals of color management are to:

- Compensate for variations in the different devices

- Accurately translate one color space to another

- Compensate for limitations in the output process

- Better predict the result when an image is reproduced

Bitmap color reproduces all pixels in the image as either black or white; there are no shades of gray.

Grayscale color reproduces all tones in the file as shades of gray. This type of image has only one channel (you were introduced to color channels in Project 2: African Wildlife Map, and will learn more in subsequent projects).

RGB creates color by combining different intensities of red, green, and blue light (collectively referred to as the "additive primaries"). Computer monitors and television sets display color in RGB, which has a **gamut** or range of more than 16.7 million different colors. An RGB file has three color channels, one for each of the additive primaries.

LAB color is device independent; the colors it describes don't depend upon the characteristics of a particular printer, monitor, or scanner. In theory, LAB bridges the gap between the various color models and devices; it is used in the background when converting images from one color space to another.

CMYK ("process") **color** is based on the absorption and reflection of light. Four process inks — cyan, magenta, yellow, and black — are used in varying combinations and percentages to produce the range of printable colors in most commercial printing. A CMYK file has four color channels, one for each subtractive primary and one for black.

Theoretically, a mixture of equal parts of cyan, magenta, and yellow would produce black. Pigments, however, are not pure, so the result of mixing these colors is a muddy brown (called **hue error**). To obtain vibrant colors (and so elements such as type can be printed cleanly), black ink is added to the three primaries. Black is represented by the letter "K" for "key color."

The problem with using RGB for print jobs is that the RGB colors eventually need to be converted to CMYK separations for a commercial printing press. Photoshop includes sophisticated tools that allow you to control this conversion.

Your client's menu will be printed, which means the image files ultimately have to be in the CMYK color mode. In this stage of the project, you will learn how to control and correct for the conversion process from RGB to CMYK — a very common process in professional graphic design. (In a professional environment, you would actually have to convert all of the images you have used in this project; we are only working with one for the sake of illustration.)

DEFINE COLOR SETTINGS

Photoshop's color management system allows you to set up a fully managed color workflow — from input device through output device. You can use Adobe's predefined color settings or create custom settings that pertain to the equipment you use.

1. **With no file open in Photoshop, choose Edit>Color Settings.**

   The Color Settings dialog box defines default working spaces for RGB, CMYK, gray, and spot colors, as well as general color management policies.

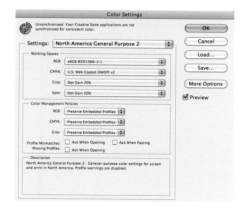

Note:

Your default options might be different than what you see here, depending on what previous users have defined.

2. Choose North America Prepress 2 in the Settings menu.

Photoshop includes four saved groups of options that are common in North America, which can be accessed in the Settings menu. You can also make your own choices and save those settings as a new preset by clicking Save, or you can import settings files created by another user by clicking Load.

3. In the Working Spaces area, choose the RGB profile for your monitor. If your specific monitor isn't available, choose Adobe RGB (1998).

If you use a color-managed workflow, each color mode must be defined as a particular type of color space. Because there are different types of monitors, there are different types of RGB color spaces; the same is true of the other color spaces. The Working Space menus define exactly which version of each space is used to define color within that space.

For color management to work properly, you must have accurate, device-specific profiles for every device in the workflow. However, you can use generic settings such as Adobe RGB (1998) in a "better-than-nothing" color environment — which is almost a direct contradiction to the concept of color management. We're showing you *how* to use the tools in Photoshop, but it's up to you to implement true color management by profiling your devices and using those profiles for specific jobs.

4. In the CMYK menu, choose U.S. Sheetfed Coated v2.

There are many CMYK profiles — each different printer and press has a gamut unique to that individual device.

This is a United States industry-standard profile for a common type of printing (sheetfed printing on coated paper). In a truly color-managed workflow, you would actually use a profile for the specific printing press/paper combination being used for the job. Again, we're using the default profiles to show you how the process works.

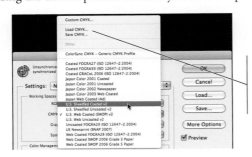

Use the Load CMYK option to access profiles that are supplied by your output provider.

Note:

*In Photoshop, a **working space** is the default profile used for each of the different color modes.*

Note:

When you choose a profile that isn't part of the saved settings, the Settings menu automatically changes to "Custom."

Note:

We assume this menu will be printed on a sheetfed press. However, always ask your output provider what profile to use for a specific job.

Note:

If you convert an image's color space using the Image>Mode menu, Photoshop converts the image to the default working space for the mode you choose.

5. **Leave the Gray and Spot working space menus at their default settings.**

The Gray working space defines how grayscale images will translate when the images are printed. Gray working space options include:

- **ColorSync Gray** (Macintosh only). This is the profile designated as the ColorSync standard for converting monitor space to print.

- **Dot Gain** (of varying percentages). These options compensate for the spread of a halftone dot in a grayscale image.

- **Gray Gamma.** This option allows you to set the monitor's gamma to compensate for differences between the monitor's presentation of an image and the actual grayscale image on press.

The Spot working space is similar to the Gray working space, but you can only specify dot gain percentages (not gamma).

6. **In the Color Management Policies area, make sure RGB is turned off; Preserve Embedded Profiles is selected for CMYK and Gray; and all three check boxes are selected.**

These options tell Photoshop what to do when you open an existing image. When an option here is turned off, color is not managed for that mode. If you choose Preserve Embedded Profiles, images that have a defined profile retain that profile; images with no profile use the current working space. If you choose Convert to Working Space, all images, even those with an embedded profile, are converted to the current working profile; images with no profile are assigned the current working profile as well.

For profile mismatches, you can display a warning when opening or pasting an image with an embedded profile that does not match the working profile. When an image doesn't have an embedded profile, you can display a warning by checking the Missing Profiles Ask When Opening option.

Note:

Web printing is done on larger presses and fed from huge rolls of paper, with the actual pages being cut off the roll only after the ink has been laid down. Although web presses are typically cheaper to operate for long print runs, they generally do not produce the same quality of color as their sheetfed counterparts.

Sheetfed presses place ink on sheets of paper that have already been cut to press-sheet size from a large roll of paper. Sheetfed presses are typically considered higher quality, with appropriately higher costs associated with the job.

Understanding Rendering Intents

PHOTOSHOP FOUNDATIONS

LAB color has the largest gamut, RGB the next largest, and CMYK the smallest. If you need to convert an image from an RGB space to a more limited CMYK space, you need to tell the software how to handle any colors that exist outside the CMYK space. You can do this by specifying the **rendering intent** that will be used when you convert colors.

- **Perceptual** presents a visually pleasing representation of the image, preserving visual relationships between colors. All colors in the image — including those available in the destination gamut — are shifted to maintain the proportional relationship within the image.

- **Saturation** compares the saturation of colors in the source profile and shifts them to the nearest-possible saturated color in the destination profile. The focus is on saturation instead of actual color value, which means this method can produce drastic color shift.

- **Relative Colorimetric** maintains any colors in both the source and destination profiles; source colors outside the destination gamut are shifted to fit. This method adjusts for the whiteness of the media, and is a good choice when most source colors are in-gamut.

- **Absolute Colorimetric** maintains colors in both the source and destination profiles. Colors outside the destination gamut are shifted to a color within the destination gamut, without considering the white point of the media.

7. **Click the More Options button and review your options.**

   The **Engine** option determines the system and color-matching method used to convert between color spaces:

   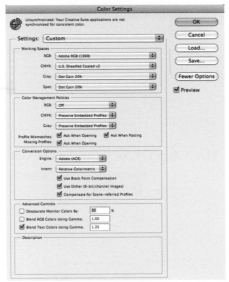

   - **Adobe (ACE)** stands for Adobe Color Engine; this is the default.
   - **Apple CMM** (Macintosh only) uses the Apple ColorSync engine.
   - **Microsoft ICM** (Windows only) uses the Microsoft ICM engine.

   The **Intent** menu defines how the engine translates source colors outside the gamut of the destination profile (see the box on Page 192).

   When **Use Black Point Compensation** is selected, the full range of the source space is mapped into the destination space. This method is most useful when the black point of the source is darker than that of the destination.

   When **Use Dither** is selected, colors in the destination space are mixed to simulate missing colors from the source space. (This can result in larger file sizes for Web images.)

   Compensate for Scene-Referred Profiles relates to the increasingly popular use of Photoshop to perform color correction (and profile matching) for video enhancement.

   Desaturate Monitor Colors is useful for visualizing the full range of color, including colors outside the monitor's range. When the option is deselected, however, colors that were previously distinct might appear as a single color.

   Blend RGB Colors Using Gamma inputs a gamma curve to avoid artifacts. (A gamma of 1.00 is considered "colorimetrically correct.")

   Blend Text Colors Using Gamma applies the defined gamma to text layers.

8. **Click Save in the Color Settings dialog box. In the resulting navigation dialog box, change the Save As field to menus and click Save.**

   Color settings files use the ".csf" extension.

   By default, custom color settings are saved in a Settings folder in a specific location where your system stores user preferences for different applications. Settings files saved in the application's default location are available in the Settings menu of the Color Settings dialog box.

   If you are working on a shared computer or a network where you can't save to the system files, you might want to save the custom Color Settings file in your WIP folder. In this case, you would have to click the Load button to locate the CSF file.

9. In the Color Settings Comment dialog box, type Use this option for PS CS6 Project 3.

10. Click OK to return to the Color Settings dialog box.

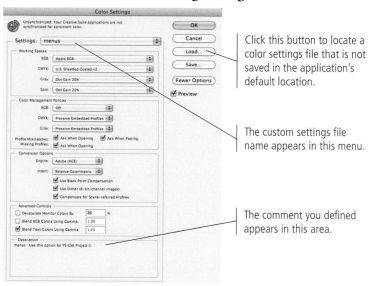

Click this button to locate a color settings file that is not saved in the application's default location.

The custom settings file name appears in this menu.

The comment you defined appears in this area.

11. Click OK to close the Color Settings dialog box and apply your settings, and then continue to the next exercise.

 ## IDENTIFY OUT-OF-GAMUT COLORS

Fortunately, Photoshop contains the necessary tools for previewing out-of-gamut colors, which means you can correct colors *before* converting an image. If you have no out-of-gamut colors, then there is nothing to shift, and you can be fairly confident that your color images will be reproduced as you intended.

1. Open the file salad.jpg from the WIP>Menu folder.

2. If you see a profile mismatch warning, choose Use the Embedded Profile and click OK.

As a general rule, you should use the embedded profile whenever one is available.

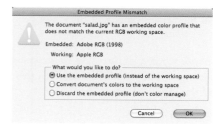

If you do not see a profile mismatch warning, choose Edit>Assign Profile once the image is open. With the Profile option selected, click OK.

You can use this dialog box to change the profile for an image. If an image has an embedded profile, the third radio button is selected and the embedded profile appears in the list. You can choose to not color manage the image, change to your working profile, or choose any other available profile from the Profile menu.

Remember, color management relies on profiles to accurately translate color from one model to another. This dialog box shows you the starting point — the embedded image profile.

3. **Choose View>Proof Colors to toggle that option on.**

This toggle provides a quick preview of what will happen when the image is converted to the CMYK working-space profile — without affecting the actual file data.

View>Proof Colors shows that converting this image will result in a color shift, especially in the red areas.

Original color

Proof color

4. **Choose View>Proof Colors again to toggle the option off.**

5. **Choose View>Gamut Warning.**

The areas that shifted are now highlighted with a gray overlay. This overlay shows you exactly what you need to correct; when this image is printed on a commercial sheetfed press, those regions will not reproduce as expected.

6. **Save the file as `salad.psd`, and continue to the next exercise.**

Note:

Photoshop ships with a large collection of common profiles, which are meant to meet the needs of diverse manufacturing environments in which Photoshop is used for what's commonly called **prepress** *(the process of getting images ready to print).*

Note:

Command/Control-Y toggles the Proof Colors view on or off.

Shift-Command/Control-Y toggles the Gamut Warning View.

Note:

You can change the color of the gamut warning overlay in the the Transparency & Gamut pane of the Preferences dialog box.

For images that will be commercially printed, some allowance must be made in the highlight and shadow areas for the mechanics of the printing process. In CMYK images, shades of gray are reproduced using combinations of four printing inks. In theory, a solid black would be printed as 100% of all four inks, and pure white would be 0% of all four inks. This, however, does not take into consideration the limitations of mechanical printing.

Images are printed as a pattern of closely spaced dots called a **halftone**. Those dots create the illusion of continuous color. Different sizes of dots create different shades of color — larger dots create darker shades and smaller dots create lighter shades.

There is a limit to the smallest size dot that can be faithfully and consistently reproduced. A 1% dot is so small that the mechanical aspect of the printing process causes anything specified as a 1% dot to drop out, resulting in highlights that lack detail and contrast. The **minimum printable dot**, then, is the smallest printable dot, and should be specified for highlights in a CMYK image. There is some debate over the appropriate highlight setting because different presses and imaging equipment have varying capabilities. To be sure your highlights will work on most printing equipment, you should define the highlight as C=5 M=3 Y=3 K=0.

Maximum printable dot is the opposite of minimum printable dot. The paper's absorption rate, speed of the printing press, and other mechanical factors limit the amount of ink that can be placed on the same area of a page. If too much ink is printed, the result is a dark blob with no visible detail; heavy layers of ink also result in drying problems, smearing, and a number of other issues.

Total ink coverage is the largest percentage of ink that can be safely printed on a single area, and therefore dictates the shadow dot you define in Photoshop. This number, similar to minimum printable dot, varies according to the ink/paper/press combination being used for a given job. The Specifications for Web Offset Publications (SWOP) indicates a 300% maximum value. Many sheetfed printers require 280% maximum, while the number for newspapers is usually around 240% because the lower-quality paper absorbs more ink.

Unless your images will be printed in a newspaper, 290% is an acceptable shadow for most applications. You can safely define shadows as C=80 M=70 Y=70 K=70. If you need to adjust a lower or higher number for specific projects, you can do so at any time.

1. **With salad.psd open and the gamut warning visible, choose Image>Adjustments>Curves.**

2. **Double-click the White Point eyedropper.**

3. **In the resulting Color Picker (Target Highlight Color) dialog box, change the CMYK values to C=5 M=3 Y=3 K=0 and click OK.**

Note:

Even though you are working on an RGB image, you can still correct it to target CMYK white and black values.

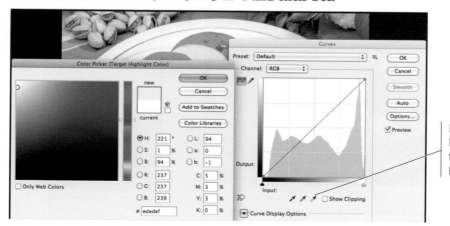

Double-click the White Point eyedropper to open the Color Picker (Target Highlight Color) dialog box.

4. **With the White Point eyedropper selected, click the lightest highlight in the image where you want to maintain detail.**

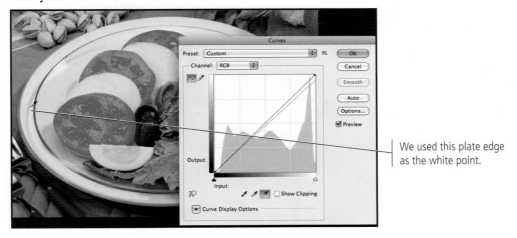

We used this plate edge as the white point.

5. **Double-click the Black Point eyedropper. Change the target CMYK values to C=80 M=70 Y=70 K=70, and then click OK.**

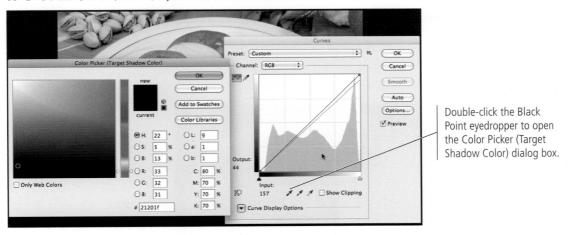

Double-click the Black Point eyedropper to open the Color Picker (Target Shadow Color) dialog box.

6. **With the Black Point eyedropper selected, click the darkest area of the image where you want to maintain shadow detail.**

By defining the target highlight and shadow points in the image, you can see that the gray gamut warning is nearly gone from the green areas, and it's significantly reduced in the red areas.

We used this shadow as the black point.

7. **Display the curve for the Red channel only.**

8. **Add a point near the midpoint, and then drag the point down to steepen the overall Red curve.**

   Just a slight adjustment, from 160 Input to 130 Output, removes nearly all the gamut warning from the tomatoes.

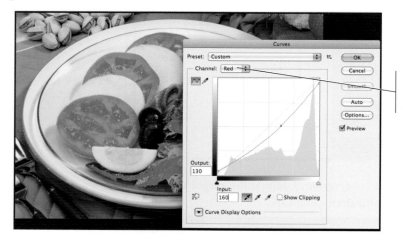

Use this menu to show the curve for only one channel.

Note:

You can turn the gamut warning off and on while the Curves dialog box is open. Simply choose the option from the View menu and toggle the gray overlay off and on.

9. **Display the curve for the Green channel and make adjustments until most or all of the gamut warning is gone.**

   Experiment with points along the curve until you are satisfied with the result.

10. **Click OK to apply your changes.**

11. **Click No in the warning message.**

    If you change the target Black Point, Gray Point, or White Point eyedropper values, Photoshop asks if you want to save the new target values as the default settings when you click OK to close the Curves dialog box.

12. **Choose View>Gamut Warning to toggle that option off.**

13. Save the file and continue to the next exercise.

Because the RGB gamut is so much larger than the CMYK gamut, you can expect colors to be far less brilliant (especially in the outer ranges of saturation) when corrected to the CMYK gamut. It's better to know this will happen and control it, rather than simply allowing the color management engine to shift colors where it deems best.

CONVERTING IMAGE COLOR MODES

Although many modern workflows convert RGB images to CMYK during the output process (called "on-the-fly" or "in-RIP conversion"), there are times when you need to manually convert RGB images to CMYK. This is a fairly simple process, especially if you have corrected your images to meet the requirements of the printing process.

1. With the corrected salad image open from the previous exercise, choose Image>Mode>CMYK Color.

This menu option converts the image to the CMYK color mode using the current working space profile. Since you intentionally defined the working profile and corrected the image to that profile, you can safely use this menu option to convert the RGB image to CMYK.

2. Click OK in the resulting warning dialog box.

If you had not completed the process in the previous series of exercises, you shouldn't convert the image color mode. Color mode is not something that should be simply switched on a whim; rather, it is the final stage of a specific process.

If you didn't precisely follow this workflow, but you are certain the image colors are correct, you can convert an image to a different model by choosing Edit>Convert to Profile and choosing any available profile in the Destination Space Profile menu.

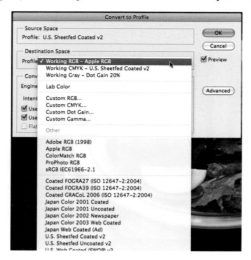

3. **Choose File>Save As. If necessary, navigate to your WIP>Menu folder as the target location.**

4. **Change the Format menu to TIFF, and then add _CMYK to the end of the existing file name (before the extension).**

5. **Macintosh users: In the bottom half of the Save As dialog box, make sure the Embed Color Profile:U.S. Sheetfed Coated v2 option is checked.**

   Windows users: In the bottom half of the Save As dialog box, make sure the ICC Profile: U.S. Sheetfed Coated v2 option is checked.

   This image has been corrected and converted to the U.S. Sheetfed Coated v2 color profile. By embedding the profile into the TIFF file, other applications and devices with color management capabilities will be able to correctly process the image color data in the file, based on the embedded profile.

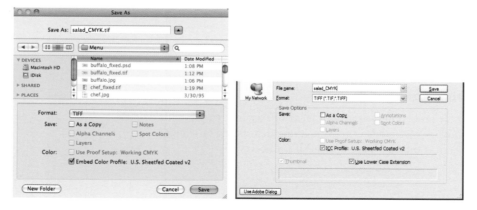

6. **Click Save, and then click OK to accept the default TIFF options.**

7. **Close the file, then continue to the final stage of the project.**

Converting Images to Grayscale

PHOTOSHOP FOUNDATIONS

An RGB image has three channels and a CMYK image has four channels; each channel is a grayscale representation of the tones of that color throughout the image. A grayscale image has only one channel; the grayscale tones in that channel are the tones in the entire image. Choosing Image>Mode>Grayscale simply flattens the component color channels, throwing away the color information to create the gray channel.

The Desaturate adjustment (Image>Adjustments>Desaturate) has a similar effect, but maintains the same number of channels as the original image. This adjustment averages the individual channel values for each pixel and applies the average value in each channel. (Remember, equal values of red, green, and blue combine to create a neutral gray value.)

If you need to convert a color image to grayscale, you might want to carefully consider which data to use for generating the gray channel. The Black & White adjustment (Image>Adjustments>Black & White) enables you to control the conversion process. In the Black and White dialog box, you can either choose one of the built-in presets, or you can drag the individual color sliders to determine how dark that color component will be in the resulting image.

When you move the mouse cursor over the image, it changes to an eyedropper icon. You can click an area in the image to highlight the predominant color in that area. Click within the image and drag to dynamically change the slider associated with that area of the image.

Remember, equal parts red, green, and blue combine to create a neutral gray. Applying the Black & White filter maintains the existing color channels, with the exact same data in all three channels. Because the adjusted

The Reds slider is highlighted, indicating that red is the predominant color where you clicked in the image.

Clicking here and dragging left or right changes the associated Reds slider.

image is still technically in a color mode (not Grayscale), you can also use the Tint options in the Black & White dialog box to apply a hue or saturation tint to the grayscale image. After using the Black & White dialog box to control the conversion of colors to grayscale, you can safely discard the color data by choosing Image>Mode>Grayscale.

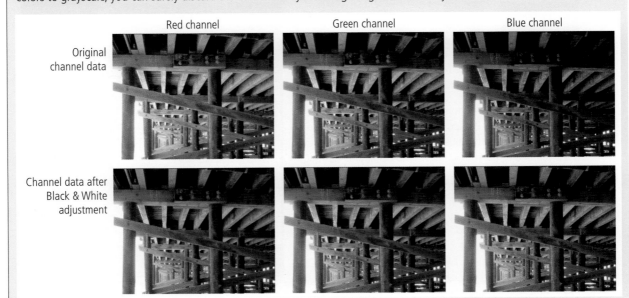

Red channel   Green channel   Blue channel

Original channel data

Channel data after Black & White adjustment

The Channel Mixer Adjustment

You can use the Channel Mixer adjustment to change the values of individual channels in an image, affecting overall color balance and contrast. The Output Channel menu determines which channel you are changing; the Source Channels sliders determine how much of the original channels will be used to create the new output channel values.

Replacing 30% of the Blue channel with information from the Red channel significantly affects the overall color and contrast in the image.

The Constant slider adjusts the overall grayscale value of the output channel. Negative values add more black to the channel (reducing the target color in the overall image), and positive values add more white to the channel (increasing the target color in the overall image).

You can also use the Channel Mixer to control the conversion to grayscale. If you check the Monochrome option, the output channel automatically changes to gray.

When the Monochrome option is checked, you can change the percentage of each component channel that will be used to generate the grayscale values. If the combined channel values are higher than 100%, Photoshop displays a warning icon next to the total.

The "Output Channel:Gray" option is deceptive, since there is no Gray channel in either an RGB or CMYK image. As with the Black and White adjustment, the Channel Mixer results in a color image with the same color channels that it had before you applied the adjustment. All the color channels have equal data, however, so you can safely discard color data by choosing Image>Mode>Grayscale.

Stage 5 **Working with HDR Images**

The human eye is extremely sensitive to subtle changes in light. In general, we can perceive detail in both light and dark areas — and areas in between — with a single glance. Camera sensors, on the other hand, are not so sensitive. If you look at most photographs, they typically have sharp detail in one of the ranges — highlights, midtones, or shadows, depending on the exposure and other settings used to capture the image. If a photograph favors highlights, details in shadow areas are lost (and vice versa).

To solve this problem, the concept of HDR (**high dynamic range**) images combines multiple photographs of different exposures into a single image to enhance the detail throughout the entire image — combining highlight, shadow, and midtone detail from various exposures to create an image more like what the human eye is capable of observing, rather than the more limited range that characterizes a digital camera's sensors.

The phrase "dynamic range" refers to the difference between the darkest shadow and the lightest highlight in an image.

- A regular 8-bit RGB photo has a dynamic range of 0–255 for each color channel (2^8 or 256 possible values). In other words, each pixel can have one of 256 possible values to describe the lightness of that color in that specific location.

- A 16-bit RGB photo allows 16 bits of information to describe the information in each pixel, allowing a dynamic range of 2^{16} or 65,536 possible values in each color channel.

- A 32-bit or HDR image allows 2^{32} possible values — more than 4 billion, which is signficantly larger than the visible spectrum of 16.7 million colors (thus, 32-bit dynamic range is sometimes referred to as "infinite").

USE MERGE TO HDR PRO

The last piece required to complete this project is an image of the antique waterwheel that is one of the hallmarks of the restaurant's exterior. Its location makes it very difficult to capture because the surrounding trees cast shadows even when the sun is at the best lighting angle. The photographer suggested using high dynamic range (HDR) photo techniques to capture the most possible detail in the scene, and has provided you with five photos taken at the same time, using different exposure settings.

1. **With no file open, choose File>Automate>Merge to HDR Pro.**

2. **In the resulting Merge to HDR Pro dialog box, click the Browse button.**

3. **Navigate to WIP>Menu>Mill Photos. Shift-click to select all five images in the folder and click Open.**

Note:

You can merge up to seven images with the Merge to HDR Pro utility.

4. **Make sure the Attempt to Automatically Align Source Images box at the bottom of the dialog box is checked, then click OK.**

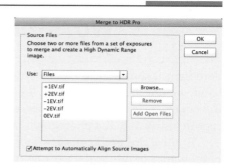

Because you are merging multiple images into a single one, there is a chance that one or more images might be slightly misaligned. (Even using a tripod, a stiff breeze can affect the camera just enough to make the different exposures slightly different.) When Attempt to Automatically Align Source Images is checked, Photoshop compares details in each image and adjusts them as necessary to create the resulting merged image.

5. **Read the resulting message, then click OK.**

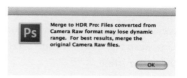

HDR images are best created from Camera RAW files, which can maintain significantly more data than the TIFF or JPEG formats. In many cases, however, you will have to use non-RAW files because that is what your photographer or client will provide to you. The merge process still works very well with JPEG and TIFF files.

6. **If you don't see a histogram on the right side of the dialog box, open the Mode menu and choose 32 Bit.**

The resulting dialog box shows each selected image as a thumbnail at the bottom. By default, all selected images are included in the merge. You can exclude specific exposures by unchecking the box for that image.

If you work with HDR, you need to realize that most computer monitors are not capable of displaying 32-bit image depth. When you merge to a 32-bit image, you can use the White Point Preview slider to change the dynamic range that is visible on your screen, but this has no effect on the actual data in the file — it affects only the current display of the image data.

Note:

The merge process might take a minute or two to complete, so be patient.

7. **Check the Remove Ghosts option on the right side of the dialog box.**

When an HDR image contains movement, merging the individual exposures can blur the areas where that movement occurs — such as the water dripping off the wheel in this image. When you check Remove Ghosts, the software uses one of the exposures (highlighted in green) to define detail in the area of motion; you can change the key exposure by simply clicking a different image in the lower pane.

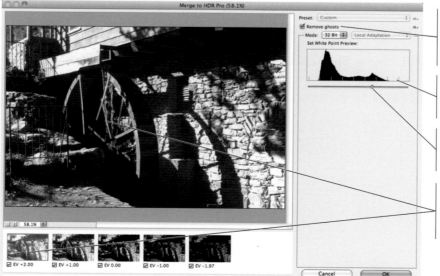

Check Remove Ghosts to eliminate blurring in areas that differ from one exposure to another.

Tones to the right of the white point will be displayed as white.

Drag this slider to change the white point for the active display.

When Remove Ghosts is checked, details in areas of movement are defined by the selected exposure.

8. **Open the Mode menu and choose 8 Bit.**

   32-bit images can store a tremendous amount of information, which creates images with far more detail than you see in a conventional 8-bit photograph. However, one significant disadvantage of such images is that they cannot be separated for commercial printing. If you're going to use an HDR image in a print application — such as the cover of this menu — you need to apply the process of **tone mapping** to define how the high dynamic range will be compressed into the lower dynamic range that is required by the output process.

9. **Leave the secondary menu set to Local Adaptation.**

   You can use the other options to apply less specific tone mapping to the image. Equalize Histogram and Highlight Compression have no further options. The Exposure and Gamma option allows you to define specific values for only those two settings.

   When the Local Adaptation method is selected, you can change the values for a number of specific options to map the tones in the HDR image to a lower dynamic range.

10. **Open the Preset menu and choose Photorealistic.**

    The application includes a number of standard settings, including several variations of monochromatic, photorealistic, and surrealistic. Each preset changes the values of the Local Adaptation sliders to create the desired effect.

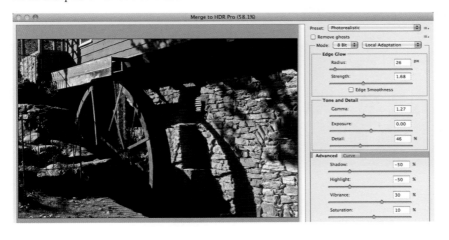

Note:

You can create your own presets by clicking the button to the right of the Preset menu and choosing Save Preset in the resulting menu.

Reducing Dynamic Range for Output

If you choose 32 Bit mode in the Merge to HDR Pro dialog box, you can simply click OK and save the file as a 32-bit HDR image.

If you need to create a 16- or 8-bit image later for a specific application, you can change the image bit depth in the Image>Mode submenu. The HDR Toning dialog box opens with the same options that are available in the Merge to HDR Pro dialog box using the Local Adaptation method. You can define the settings that will be applied to create the smaller-bit-depth image.

11. **Experiment with the different sliders until you are satisfied with the result.**

Tone mapping is a largely subjective process, and different end uses can influence the settings that you apply to a specific image. You should understand the following information as you experiment with the various settings:

- **Radius** defines the size of the glowing effect in areas of localized brightness.

- **Strength** determines the required tolerance between tonal values before pixels are no longer considered part of the same brightness region.

- **Gamma** values lower than 1.0 increase details in the midtones, while higher values emphasize details in the highlights and shadows.

- **Exposure** affects the overall lightness or darkness of the image.

- **Detail** increases or decreases the overall sharpness of the image.

- **Shadow** and **Highlight** affect the amount of detail in those areas of the image. Higher values increase detail and lower values reduce detail.

- **Vibrance** affects the intensity of subtle colors, while minimizing clipping of highly saturated colors.

- **Saturation** affects the intensity of all colors from –100 (monochrome) to +100 (double saturation).

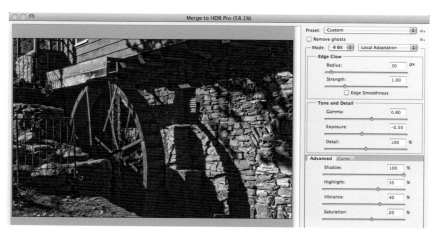

12. **Click OK to finalize the process.**

Because you chose 8 Bit in the Mode menu of the Merge to HDR Pro dialog box, the resulting image is an 8-bit RGB image (as you can see in the document tab).

13. **Save the file in your WIP>Menu>Mill Images folder as a native Photoshop file named mill_merged.psd, then close it.**

1. The _____ filter locates pixels that differ in value from surrounding pixels by the threshold you specify; it sharpens an image by increasing contrast along the edges in an image.

2. _____ is defined as random pixels that stand out from the surrounding pixels.

3. The _____ blends colors from user-defined source pixels with colors in the area where you click.

4. The _____ paints one part of an image over another part, which is useful for duplicating specific objects or removing defects in an image.

5. _____ are direct sources of light such as a light bulb or reflected sunlight on water; they should not be considered the highlights of an image.

6. _____ refers to the tonal variation within an image.

7. A _____ is a visual depiction of the distribution of colors in an image.

8. _____ is defined according to a color's position on a color wheel, beginning from red (0°) and traveling counterclockwise around the wheel.

9. _____ (also called "intensity") refers to the color's difference from neutral gray.

10. _____ (also called "luminance" or "value") is the amount of white or black added to the pure color.

1. Explain the concept of neutral gray.

2. List three important points to remember when working with curves.

3. Briefly explain the concepts of minimum printable dot and maximum ink coverage.

Portfolio Builder Project

Use what you learned in this project to complete the following freeform exercise.
Carefully read the art director and client comments, then create your design to meet the needs of the project.
Use the space below to sketch ideas; when finished, write a brief explanation of the reasoning behind your design.

The tourism board director dined at The Chateau recently. In a conversation with the restaurant owner, he mentioned a new project about local architecture. Mr. Roseman, pleased with your work on the menu images, recommended you for the job.

To complete this project, you should:

❑ Find at least 10 photos of different architectural styles throughout the Los Angeles metropolitan area.

❑ Use photo retouching techniques to clean up any graffiti and trash that is visible in the images.

❑ Use correction techniques to adjust the tonal range and gray balance of the images.

❑ Correct and convert all images based on the U.S. Sheetfed Coated v2 CMYK destination profile.

Over the next year, we're planning on publishing a series of promotional booklets to show tourists that L.A. is more than just Hollywood.

Each booklet in the series will focus on an 'interest area' such as fine art or — for the first one — architecture. The city has a diverse architectural mix, from eighteenth-century Spanish missions to 1920s bungalows to the Walt Disney Concert Hall designed by Frank Gehry in the 1990s.

We'd like at least ten pictures of different landmarks or architectural styles, corrected and optimized for printing on a sheetfed press. If possible, we'd also like some historical images to include in a 'building a metropolis' section on the first couple of pages.

Of course, Los Angeles is a large city, and cities have their problems — not the least of which are graffiti and garbage. We are trying to attract tourists, not turn them away. Make sure none of the images show any graffiti or blatant litter; if these problems are visible in the images you select, give them a good digital cleaning.

As with many other skills, it takes time and practice to master image correction techniques. Understanding the relationship between brightness and contrast, and how these two values affect the quality of reproduction in digital images, is the first and possibly most critical factor in creating a high-quality image. An image that has too much contrast (a "sharp" image) or not enough contrast (a "flat" image) translates to an unsatisfactory print.

A basic understanding of color theory (specifically complementary color) is the foundation of accurate color correction. Effective color correction relies on the numbers, rather than what you think you see on your monitor. As you gain experience in correcting images, you will be better able to predict the corrections required to achieve the best possible output.

Remove photographic grain with blur and sharpen techniques

Use the Healing Brush and Spot Healing Brush tools to correct scratches

Use the Clone Stamp tool to remove major damage

Correct contrast and tonal range using the Levels adjustment

Use Merge to HDR Pro to find detail in multiple exposures

Correct minor color problems using the Brightness/Contrast adjustment

Correct gray balance using the Curves adjustment

Correct lighting problems with the Exposure adjustment

Correct overall color cast using the Color Balance adjustment

Correct contrast with the Curves adjustment

Correct and convert the image using the defined destination CMYK profile

City Promotion Cards

Your client is the Redevelopment Authority for the city of Lancaster, in the California high desert (north of Los Angeles). You have been hired to create a series of promotional postcards featuring the improvements that have been made over the last two years, that will help drive tourism to the area.

This project incorporates the following skills:

❏ Creating new files

❏ Managing missing and mismatched profiles

❏ Working with content-aware tools

❏ Adding effects in the Blur Gallery

❏ Creating and managing different types of text layers

❏ Using paragraph styles to format text

❏ Applying layer styles

❏ Working in 3D

❏ Creating layer comps

client comments

We want to feature two of our proudest achievements in a postcard campaign that we're hoping will help drive tourism to the area.

In the past two years, more than $50 million in public and private funding has been spent revitalizing the downtown Lancaster area. The BLVD, Lancaster's new outdoor shopping and dining destination, is distinguished by its beautiful sidewalk streetscape and ramblas. The BLVD is lined with a unique mix of dining, shopping, arts, and entertainment venues.

The Poppy Festival is attended by more than 20,000 visitors over two days. It's an award-winning festival that celebrates California's state flower, which is fitting since we're also the home of the Antelope Valley Poppy Preserve.

The images you create will be used in digital advertising and on Web sites, but we also plan to print them for inclusion in a larger promotional package that we send to conference coordinators around the country.

art director comments

The client wants to create these files for both digital and print applications, so you should define the file size to meet the print specs:

> Trim: 5″ high × 7″ wide
>
> Bleed requirement: 0.125″ on all four sides

I want each postcard to include two images. The ones we have are excellent, but they will require some manipulation to work in the overall composition.

Although compositing type and images is typically done in a page layout application, there isn't a lot of text to include on these postcards. You can use the Photoshop type tools to do what you need, without requiring a separate file.

I'd also like to see two different versions of each postcard. The 3D options in Photoshop can create the appearance of depth even in a flat file — which might just be the "pop" that the client asked for.

When you're finished, save each version as a JPEG that we can email for approval.

project objectives

To complete this project, you will:

❏ Create a new color-managed file

❏ Apply content-aware scaling

❏ Use the Content-Aware Move tool

❏ Apply a tilt-shift blur effect

❏ Apply an iris blur effect

❏ Place and format point text

❏ Create and control area type

❏ Work with paragraph styles

❏ Create a solid-color fill layer

❏ Apply layer effects

❏ Create a 3D postcard

❏ Create a 3D sphere

❏ Create layer comps

Stage 1 Creating New Files

The basic process of creating a new file is relatively easy. However, you have a number of options that affect what you will see when you begin working. The first stage of this project explores a number of these issues, including color management settings and controlling the background layer.

 CREATE A NEW COLOR-MANAGED FILE

As you learned in Project 3: Menu Image Correction, the Color Settings dialog box defines the default working spaces for RGB, CMYK, Gray, and Spot Color spaces. Once you've made your choices in the Color Settings dialog box, those working spaces are automatically applied when you create a new file.

1. Download **PS6_RF_Project4.zip** from the Student Files Web page.

2. **Expand the ZIP archive in your WIP folder (Macintosh) or copy the archive contents into your WIP folder (Windows).**

   This results in a folder named **Lancaster**, which contains the files you need for this project. You should also use this folder to save the files you create in this project.

3. **In Photoshop, choose Edit>Color Settings.**

4. **In the resulting dialog box, choose the appropriate profile for your monitor in the Working Spaces:RGB menu.**

5. **Set all three Color Management Policies menus to Preserve Embedded Profiles, and check all three boxes for Profile Mismatches and Missing Profiles.**

   You can display a warning when opening or pasting an image with an embedded profile that does not match the working profile. You can also display a warning when opening an image that doesn't have an embedded profile.

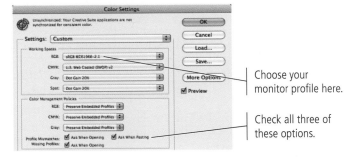

Choose your monitor profile here.

Check all three of these options.

6. **Click OK to apply your changes.**

7. **Choose File>New.**

   The first time Photoshop is used, the New dialog box defaults to the Default Photoshop Size settings.

   If anything exists in the Clipboard (i.e., if you have copied anything in Photoshop or another application), this dialog box defaults to the Clipboard setting in which the size matches the Clipboard contents. (You can clear the Clipboard by choosing Edit>Purge>Clipboard.)

   If the Clipboard is empty, the New dialog box defaults to the last-used settings.

8. **Type festival in the Name field.**

When you save the file, the file name defaults to the name you define here.

9. **Press Tab to highlight the next field (Width) of the dialog box.**

Like most applications, you can press Tab to move through the fields of a dialog box. Pressing Shift-Tab moves to the previous field in the dialog box.

10. **With the Width field highlighted, type 7.25 in the field.**

Because this file will eventually be printed, you are defining the width to include the required bleed (1/8″) area on each side.

As soon as you change any field, the Preset menu switches to "Custom" — you are defining a "custom" file size.

11. **Click the menu to the right of the Width field and choose inches (if it is not already selected).**

When you change one unit of measurement (width), the other (height) changes too.

Note:

If you press Shift when you open the menu, you can change the unit of measurement separately for each dimension.

12. **Press Tab to move the highlight to the Height field. Change the highlighted Height field to 5.25 and press Tab.**

Again, this size includes the require 1/8″ bleed for the top and bottom edges.

13. **Change the Resolution field to 300 pixels/inch.**

Pixels/cm is primarily used in countries that use the metric system of measurement (everywhere except the U.S.). If you inadvertently set the field to 300 pixels/cm, you will create a file that is 762 pixels/inch — far more than you need.

14. **Choose RGB Color in the Color Mode menu.**

The **color mode** (or color space) defines the structure of the colors in your file. Although the file will eventually be printed, you are going to work in the RGB space to preserve the widest-possible color gamut during the development stage.

15. **Choose Transparent in the Background Contents menu.**

If you choose White or Background Color in this menu, the new file will include a default locked Background layer. If you choose Transparent, the new file will have a default unlocked Layer 1.

The Image Size changes dynamically whenever you change an option in this dialog box.

Note:

You can create new files based on a number of included presets, including standard paper sizes (U.S. Paper, International Paper, and Photo) and standard sizes for different devices (Web, Mobile & Devices, and Film & Video).

If you choose one of these presets, the Size menu shows secondary options for the selected preset (such as Letter, Legal, or Tabloid for U.S. Paper). Choosing any of these presets automatically changes the values in the other fields of the dialog box.

16. **Review the options in the Advanced area of the dialog box.**

The Color Profile menu defaults to the working space for the selected color mode; in this case, it automatically shows your defined monitor (RGB) profile. You can also choose a different profile in the menu if you occasionally need to work in a space other than the default working space for a specific color mode.

The options in the Pixel Aspect Ratio menu are primarily used for editing video. Since this is a print project, you don't want to alter the pixel ratio.

Click this button to show or hide the Advanced options.

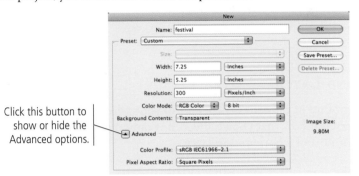

Note:

If you create a file using a profile other than the default working profile for that space, the document tab (or title bar, if you're not using the Macintosh Application frame) shows an asterisk next to the color space information.

× untitled @ 33.3% (Layer 1, RGB/8*)

17. **Click OK to create the new file.**

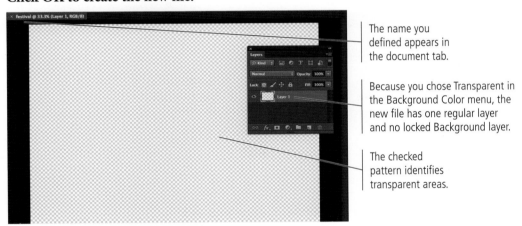

The name you defined appears in the document tab.

Because you chose Transparent in the Background Color menu, the new file has one regular layer and no locked Background layer.

The checked pattern identifies transparent areas.

18. **Choose File>Save As. Navigate to your WIP>Lancaster folder as the location for saving this file.**

Because you named the file when you created it (in the New dialog box), the Save As field is automatically set to the file name you already assigned. The extension is automatically added on both Macintosh and Windows computers.

19. **Make sure Photoshop is selected in the Format menu and click Save.**

20. **Read the resulting warning message, then click OK.**

This warning appears as soon as a file has at least one regular layer. This file has no locked background layer, so the only layer is a regular layer by default.

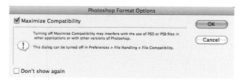

21. **Continue to the next exercise.**

 CONTROL THE BACKGROUND LAYER

When you create a new file, the background of the canvas depends on your selection in the New dialog box. You should understand how that choice affects not only the color of the canvas, but also the existence (or not) of a background layer.

1. **With festival.psd open, make sure rulers are visible (View>Rulers).**

2. **Using any method you prefer, place ruler guides 0.125″ from each edge.**

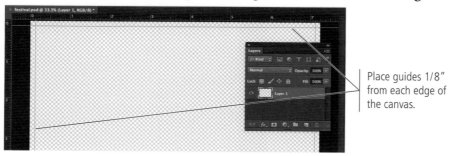

Place guides 1/8″ from each edge of the canvas.

3. **Save the file.**

4. **At the bottom of the Tools panel, click the Default Foreground and Background Colors button, then click the Switch Foreground and Background Colors button.**

5. **With the default Layer 1 selected, choose Layer>Flatten Image.**

When you flatten an image, all layers in the file are flattened into a locked Background layer. Because this file currently has only one layer, the new Background layer is simply a solid white fill. It is important to note that the defined Background color is not applied as the color of the resulting Background layer.

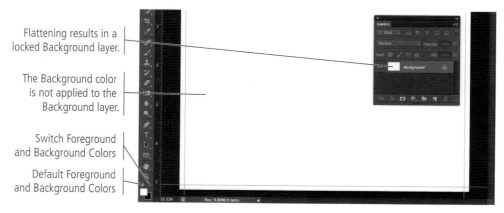

Flattening results in a locked Background layer.

The Background color is not applied to the Background layer.

Switch Foreground and Background Colors

Default Foreground and Background Colors

6. **With the Background layer selected, choose Edit>Fill.**

You can fill a selection with a number of options:

Note:

Press Shift-F5 or Shift-Delete/Backspace to open the Fill dialog box.

- Choose the defined foreground or background color.

- Choose Color to define a specific color in the Color Picker dialog box.

- Choose Content Aware to fill an area with pixels from surrounding image areas.

- Choose Pattern, and then choose a specific pattern in the pop-up menu.

- Choose History to fill the object with a specific history state (if possible).

- Choose Black, 50% Gray, or White.

You can also define a specific blending mode and opacity for the filled pixels. Using layers for different elements, however, is typically a better option than changing the fill transparency settings because you can adjust the layer blending mode and opacity as often as necessary.

7. **In the Fill dialog box, choose Background Color in the Use menu and then click OK.**

Because you did not draw a specific selection area, the entire selected layer (the Background layer) is filled.

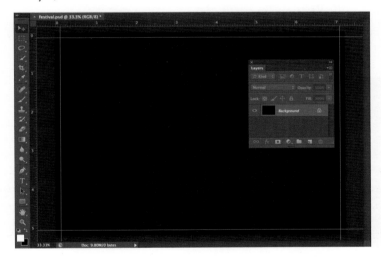

8. **Choose File>Save As. In the Save As dialog box, change the file name to** blvd.psd **and click Save.**

9. **Continue to the next exercise**.

CONTROL MISSING AND MISMATCHED PROFILES

In the Color Settings dialog box, you told Photoshop how to handle images with profiles that don't match your working profiles, as well as images that don't have embedded profiles. These issues become important any time you work with files from more than a single source — and especially with client-supplied images, which often come from a wide variety of sources.

1. **With blvd.psd open, open path.jpg from your WIP>Lancaster folder.**

   This image does not have an embedded profile, so (as you defined in the Color Settings dialog box) Photoshop asks how you want to handle the file.

   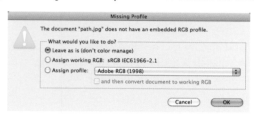

2. **Choose Leave As Is and click OK.**

3. **With path.jpg open, chose Select>All. Choose Edit>Copy, then close the file.**

4. **With blvd.psd active, choose Edit>Paste.**

   Because the file's locked Background layer was selected, the pasted contents are added as a new layer, immediately above the existing (selected) layer. Remember, you can't paste content onto a locked layer.

   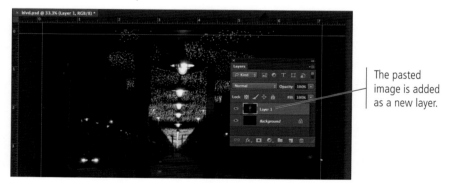

   The pasted image is added as a new layer.

5. **In the Layers panel, rename Layer 1 as Lights.**

6. **Choose File>Save. Click OK in the Maximize Compatibility warning.**

   As we already explained, this warning appears the first time you save a file that has at least one regular layer.

Note:

It's quite common to find images that don't have embedded color profiles, especially when you work with older (legacy) files. In this case, color management will be imperfect at best since you don't know how the image was captured.

Note:

Refer back to Project 1: Composite Movie Ad for a more detailed explanation of the Background layer.

7. **Open the file festival.psd from your WIP>Lancaster folder.**

8. **Open the file bloom.jpg, and read the resulting warning.**

   This file has an embedded profile, but it does not match your defined working RGB profile. Again, you told the application to show a warning when opening a file with a mismatched profile.

9. **Choose the option to use the embedded profile, then click OK.**

10. **Copy the contents of the file, then close it.**

11. **With festival.psd open, choose Edit>Paste.**

    In the Color Setting dialog box, you told the application to warn you if profiles do not match when you paste layer content. Photoshop cannot manage more than one profile for a single color space within the same file.

    The Convert option converts the pasted image colors to the color profile of the file where you're pasting, preserving the color appearance. The Don't Convert option preserves the color data (but not the actual profile) in the pasted information.

12. **In the Paste Profile Mismatch dialog box, choose the Convert option and then click OK.**

    Because this file has no Background layer, the pasted image is pasted into the active Layer 1.

The pasted content is added to the selected Layer 1.

13. **In the Layers panel, rename Layer 1 as Bloom.**

14. **Save the file and continue to the next stage of the project.**

Stage 2 Manipulating Pixels

Before digital image-editing software, a photo was a photo. If you wanted a different angle or arrangement, you simply took another photo. If you completed Project 3: Menu Image Correction, you have already learned a number of techniques for manipulating the color in an image, as well as several retouching methods for removing small imperfections from an image. Digital photo editing also makes it much easier to manipulate the actual content of an image — from scaling specific objects to a different size, to moving them to a new location, to changing the image's entire focal point. In this stage of the project, you will learn a number of techniques for changing the content in the client's supplied images to better meet the needs of the project.

APPLY CONTENT-AWARE SCALING

When you scale a selection, you are stretching or squashing the pixels in that selection. This can produce the result you want, but it can also badly distort the image. Content-aware scaling intends to correct this problem by analyzing the image and preserving areas of detail when you scale the image.

1. **Make blvd.psd the active file.**

   The focus of this image is directly down the center. Because you are going to add type and other images to complete the entire postcard composition, you first need to move the image's focal point to create room for the textual elements.

2. **Choose the Move tool in the Tools panel.**

3. **With the Lights layer selected in the Layers panel, click in the document window to activate it. Press Shift, then click and drag to the left until the path is approximately one-third of the way across the canvas.**

   As you can see, moving a layer's contents reveals the underlying layer. The right edge of the path image creates a harsh line.

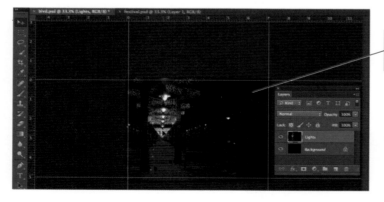

Just moving the layer reveals the content of underlying layers.

Note:

The black background color does not appear as clearly distinct in our screen shots; however, you should be able to see the edge on your monitor.

4. **Choose Edit>Undo Move.**

   Rather than simply moving the image to the position you want, you are going to scale it to fill the entire space — while moving the lighted path into the left half of the image.

5. **With the Lights layer still selected, choose Edit>Transform>Scale.**

   When you enter into transformation mode by calling any of the Transform submenu options, the selection (or entire layer, if you don't have a specific area selected) is surrounded by a bounding box and handles, which you can use to control the transformation. The Options bar also includes fields for numerically transforming the selection.

Note:

These are the same options you saw in Project 1: Composite Movie Ad, when you used the Free Transform command.

6. **Click the left-center handle on the image layer and drag left until the path image is approximately one-third of the way across the canvas.**

   It can be helpful to reduce the view percentage so you can see more area around the defined canvas.

   Transformations alter the pixels in the layer. As you can see, the lights are distorted by scaling the layer in only one direction.

Scaling in only one direction distorts the image content.

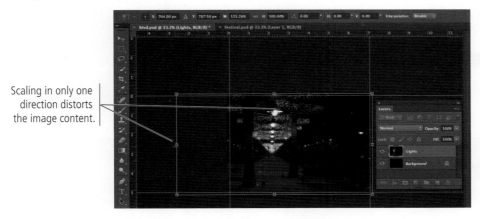

7. **In the Options bar, click the Cancel Transform button (or press ESC).**

   As long as the transformation handles remain visible, you can cancel any changes you made. By cancelling the transformation, the layer is restored to its original state.

8. **With the Lights layer selected, choose Edit>Content-Aware Scale.**

   Again, you see the transformation handles. The process is virtually the same as in regular scaling, but content-aware scaling identifies and tries to protect areas of detail when you scale the image.

9. **Click the left-center handle on the layer and drag left until the path image is approximately one-third of the way across the canvas.**

   As you can see, some distortion still occurs. However, the lights hanging over the path — the most obvious point of detail — are not noticeably distorted. Other areas of detail — the trees and bench, for example — are somewhat distorted, but not nearly as badly as they were from the regular scale transformation.

Content-aware scaling attempts to preserve areas of detail.

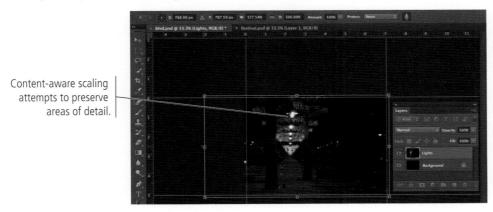

10. **Press Return/Enter to finalize the transformation.**

11. **Save the file and continue to the next exercise.**

More about Content-Aware Scaling

Content-aware scaling identifies areas of detail when it determines what to protect. In some cases, though, the image focus might have little or no detail within the shape areas — the white bird in the following image, for example. To solve this problem, you can identify a specific mask area to protect when you use content-aware scaling.

Use this menu to protect a specific mask area.

Click this button to protect skin tones from scaling.

Original image

Image scaled using
Transform>Scale mode

Image scaled using
Content-Aware Scale mode

Image scaled using
Content-Aware Scale mode, but with
the bird area protected by a mask.

USE THE CONTENT-AWARE MOVE TOOL

Photoshop makes it easy to move content around on the canvas. If an entire layer is selected, you can easily use the Move tool to move all the content on that layer to a different location. If you create a specific selection area using one of the marquee or lasso tools, you can also move only the selected area to another location on the active layer. It's important to realize, however, that this process actually removes the area under the original selection area, which might not be what you want. The Content-Aware Move tool, new in Photoshop CS6, allows you to move a selection and fill the original selection area with detail instead of leaving an empty hole.

1. **Make festival.psd the active file.**

    The main focus of the poppy image is nicely centered in the canvas. To make room for the other pieces of the composition, you need the flower to be on the right side of the image.

2. **Choose the Lasso tool in the Tools panel.**

3. **Draw a marquee that roughly selects the flower in the center of the image.**

Lasso tool

Draw a loose selection around the entire flower.

4. **Choose the Move tool in the Tools panel.**

5. **Click inside the selection area, then drag the selected area to the right side of the canvas.**

When you use the Move tool with a specific selection marquee, you are moving all of the pixels within that selection area. The area of the original selection is removed from that layer, so you can see underlying layers (or transparent gray-and-white checkerboard, if there is no underlying layer).

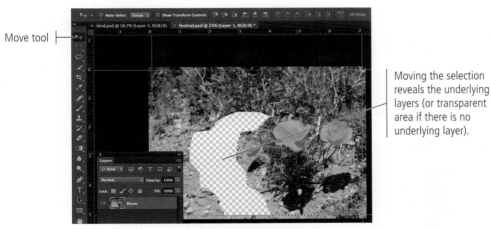

Move tool

Moving the selection reveals the underlying layers (or transparent area if there is no underlying layer).

You should notice that the moved pixels remain on the same layer. As long as the selection marquee remains active, you can continue to move the selected pixels around the same layer without affecting the other pixels on that layer. If you deselect, however, the underlying pixels will be permanently replaced by the pixels you moved.

To get around this problem, it's fairly common practice to move selected pixels to another layer before dragging with the Move tool:

1. Make a selection.
2. Choose Edit>Cut to remove the selected pixels from the original layer, or
3. Choose Edit>Copy to keep the selected pixels on the original layer.
4. Choose Edit>Paste to add the cut/copied pixels onto a new layer.

If you leave the selection marquee in place before choosing Edit>Paste, the cut/copied pixels are pasted in the exact position as they were when you cut/copied them.

More about the Content-Aware Move Tool

You can also use the Content-Aware Move tool in Extend mode to enlarge objects in a linear direction, as you can see in the following images.

Tighter selection marquees generally produce better results than a loose area that includes a lot of background pixels.

In Extend mode, you can make linear adjustments to recompose an object, such as making this bulding taller.

Original image

Image after extending the right building with the Content-Aware Move tool.

6. **Choose Edit>Undo Move to restore all the pixels to their original positions.**

7. **With the same marquee still selected, choose the Content-Aware Move tool (nested under the Spot Healing Brush tool).**

   You can draw a new marquee with the Content-Aware Move tool, but in this case it isn't necessary because you already defined the selection area with the Lasso tool.

8. **In the Options bar, make sure Move is selected in the Mode menu.**

9. **Click inside the selection area and drag the selected flower to the right side of the canvas.**

Content-Aware Move tool

Moving the selection does not reveal the underlying layers.

After you release the mouse button, the process might take a while to complete because Photoshop has to analyze and determine what pixels to create. Be patient.

Note:

The Adaptation menu determines how closely the software analyzes the image and creates results. Stricter adaptation takes longer to process, but can produce more accurate results.

When the process is complete, the original selection area is filled with pixels that seamlessly blend into the surrounding area. The edges of the moved area are also blended into their new surrounding area.

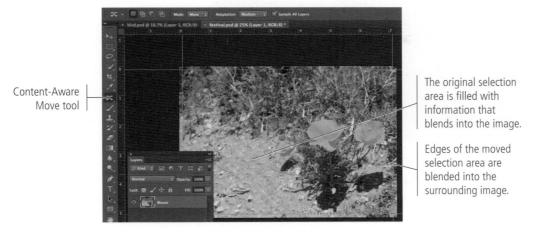

Content-Aware Move tool

The original selection area is filled with information that blends into the image.

Edges of the moved selection area are blended into the surrounding image.

10. **Turn off the active selection (Select>Deselect).**

11. **Save the file and continue to the next exercise.**

 ## APPLY A TILT-SHIFT BLUR EFFECT

Many of the Blur filters can be used for functional purposes, such as removing noise with the Gaussian Blur filter. Others have more artistic purposes, and include far more specific controls than a simple dialog box interface. Photoshop CS6 includes three new blur filters, which are controlled in a specialized workspace that contains only the tools you need to apply the filters.

1. **With blvd.psd active, make sure the Lights layer is selected in the Layers panel.**

2. **Choose Filter>Blur>Tilt-Shift.**

   The Tilt-Shift filter applies a linear blur out from a center line. You can use on-screen controls in the Blur Gallery to change the angle and position of the blur, as well as a number of other options.

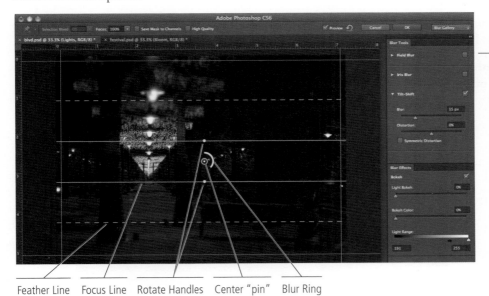

Note:

If nothing appears in the Blur Effects panel, choose Reset Workspace in the Workspace Switcher.

Feather Line   Focus Line   Rotate Handles   Center "pin"   Blur Ring

3. **Move the cursor over either Rotate Handle. Press Shift, then click and drag until the cursor feedback shows the angle of 90°.**

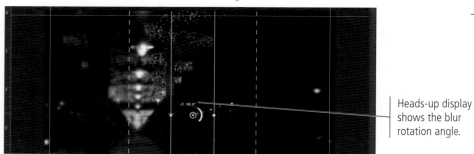

Note:

Pressing Shift constrains the rotation to 22.5° increments.

Heads-up display shows the blur rotation angle.

4. **Click the center "pin" of the blur control and drag left until the row of lights is between the two focus lines.**

   Anything between the two focus lines will be preserved without a blur.

5. **Click the Blur Ring and drag the white area until the cursor feedback shows the Blur: 20.**

   Changing intensity of the blur using the on-screen control applies the same change in the Blur field in the Blur Tools panel.

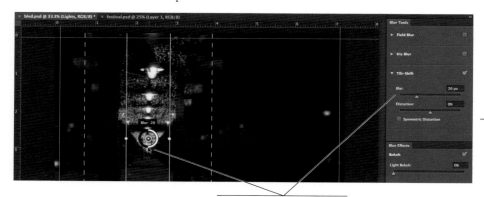

Changing the intensity in the Blur Ring applies the same change in the panel.

Note:

The Distortion option defines the shape of the blur that is applied. You can also check the Symmetric Distortion option to apply the distortion amount to both sides of the blur.

6. **Click the left Focus Line (the solid line) away from the Rotate Handle, and drag left until the line is close to the right side of the left palm tree.**

7. **Click the left Feather Line (the dotted line) and drag until the line is just past the left side of the same palm tree.**

   The Feather Lines define the distance from unblurred (at the Focus Line) and completely blurred pixels.

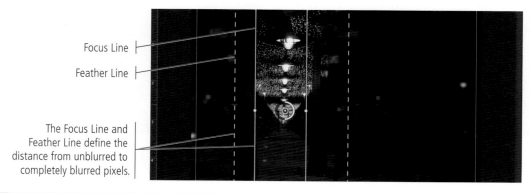

Focus Line

Feather Line

The Focus Line and Feather Line define the distance from unblurred to completely blurred pixels.

8. **Repeat Steps 6–7 to position the right Focus and Feather lines relative to the right palm tree.**

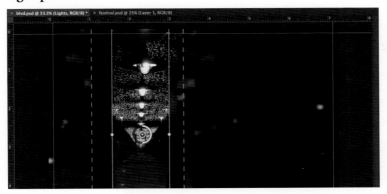

9. **Click OK in the Options bar to apply the blur.**

   When you finalize the blur, the process can take a while to complete. Be patient.

   You cannot apply the Blur Gallery filters to a Smart Object layer, which means these filters are destructive; you can undo them, but you can't turn the effect on or off.

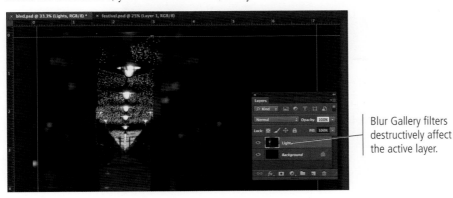

   Blur Gallery filters destructively affect the active layer.

10. **Save the file and continue to the next exercise.**

The Field Blur Filter

In addition to the Tilt-Shift and Iris Blur effects, you can also use the Blur Gallery to apply an overall field blur, which affects the entire layer. Changing the intensity changes the amount of blur that is applied to that layer.

You can also place multiple focus points to change the blur in different areas of the layer. In the image below, we changed the blur intensity in the first pin to 0 px, then added a pin at the back of the bridge with a blur of 30 px.

APPLY AN IRIS BLUR EFFECT

The Iris Blur filter mimics the effect of changing the aperture, focal length, and focus distance with a camera. The blur applies around a central point; you can use on-screen controls to define the shape and size of the blur.

1. **Make the festival.psd file active.**

2. **With the Bloom layer selected, choose Filter>Blur>Iris Blur.**

   The Iris blur is also controlled in the Blur Gallery interface.

Ellipse Handle   Feather Handle   Center "pin"   Blur Ring   Roundness Handle

Note:

You can apply a blur to only certain parts of a layer by drawing a selection marquee before opening the Blur Gallery. In this case, you can use the Selection Bleed option (in the Options bar) to determine how much the selected area blends with the unselected areas.

3. **Click the center "pin" and drag to position the blur so it is approximately centered on the flower.**

   You can click away from the existing blur controls to add a new pin — which means you can define more than one focal point on the same layer.

4. **Click the right ellipse handle and drag in to change the width of the ellipse.**

   If you click the ellipse *away* from the handle, you can enlarge or shrink the existing ellipse without affecting its proportional shape.

Note:

Click the Roundness Handle and drag to make the blur shape more or less rectangular.

Drag the pin to move the focal point of the blur.

Drag the Ellipse Handle to rotate or change the shape of the blur ellipse.

Drag the Ellipse to resize the blur without changing its shape.

5. **Click the top Feather Handle and drag down until it is placed at the top edge of the center flower.**

   The distance between the Feather Handle and the outer ellipse defines the length of the blur. When you click and drag one handle, all four move symmetrically.

Drag any Feather Handle to change the distance from unblurred to entirely blurred pixels.

When you drag one Feather Handle, all four move the same distance.

6. **Press Option/Alt, then click the bottom Feather Handle and drag up to increase the blur distance on only the bottom of the flower.**

   Pressing Option/Alt allows you to move one Feather Handle independently of the others.

Option/Alt-drag a Feather Handle to move it independently of the other handles.

7. **Click the Blur Ring and drag around to increase the intensity to 20 px.**

8. **Click OK in the Options bar to apply the blur.**

9. **Save the file and continue to the next stage of the project.**

When you apply a Tilt-Shift blur, the Focus field in the Options bar defines the blur of the area inside the Focus Lines. For an Iris blur, this field defines the blur inside the Feather Handles.

The Focus option defines the clarity of the area in the focus zone.

You can use the Save Mask to Channels option to create an alpha channel mask from the defined blur. Solid areas in the mask show areas that are unblurred; white areas of the mask show areas that are entirely blurred.

In the Blur Effects panel, you can control **bokeh** effects — the aesthetic qualities of blurred points of light — for any of the three blur types.

- **Light Bokeh** defines the amount of enhancement in blurred areas.

- **Bokeh Color** changes the bokeh highlight from neutral (0%) to colorful (100%).

- **Light Range** determines which brightness values are affected by the Light Bokeh.

Stage 3 Working with Type

Type is naturally a vector-based element. As long as you maintain type as vectors, the letter shapes can be resized and transformed without losing quality. And as you know, Photoshop can combine raster and vector objects into a single composition.

Many Photoshop jobs require some kind of type. Although Photoshop is not a typesetting tool by definition, its type capabilities are robust enough for creating and manipulating type in a variety of ways. To complete these postcards, you are going to create and format several type elements.

The Anatomy of Type

Before we jump into the exercises in this section, you should understand the terms that you will often hear when people talk about type:

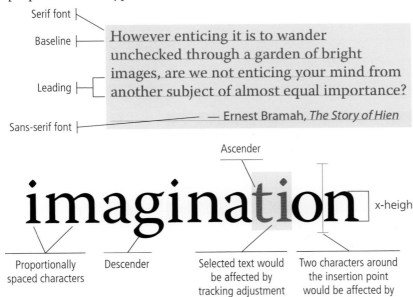

— Ernest Bramah, *The Story of Hien*

Type is typically divided into two basic categories: serif and sans serif. **Serif type** has small flourishes on the ends of the letterforms; **sans-serif** has no such decorations (*sans* is French for "without"). The actual shape of letters is determined by the specific **font** you use; each **character** in a font is referred to as a **glyph**.

Fonts can be monospaced or proportionally spaced. In a monospace font, each character takes up the same amount of space on a line; in other words, a lowercase "i" and "w" will occupy the same horizontal width. In a proportionally spaced font, different characters occupy different amounts of horizontal space as necessary.

When you set type in a digital application, the letters rest on a non-printing line called the **baseline**. If a type element has more than one line in a single paragraph, the distance from one baseline to the next is called **leading** (pronounced "ledding"). Most applications set the default leading as 120% of the type size, but you can change the leading to any value you prefer.

The **x-height** of type is the height of the lowercase letter "x." Elements that extend below the baseline are called **descenders** (as in "g," "j," and "p"); elements that extend above the x-height are called **ascenders** (as in "b," "d," and "k").

The size of type is usually measured in **points** (there are approximately 72 points in an inch). When you define a specific type size, you determine the distance from the bottom of the descenders to the top of the ascenders (plus a small extra space above the ascenders called the **body clearance**).

> **Note:**
>
> *There are other types of special fonts, including script, symbol, dingbat, decorative, and image fonts. These don't fit easily into the serif/sans-serif distinction.*

PLACE AND FORMAT POINT TYPE

You can create two basic kinds of type in Photoshop: point type and area type. **Point type** is created by simply clicking in the image window with one of the Type tools. A point type element can exist on one line or multiple lines. Point type can continue into apparent infinity without starting a new line; if you want to start a new line, you have to manually tell Photoshop where to create the break.

Note:

You must install the ATC fonts from the Student Files Web site to complete the rest of this project.

1. **With festival.psd active, choose the Horizontal Type tool.**

   You can access the basic type options in the Options bar. Additional options are available in the Character and Paragraph panels.

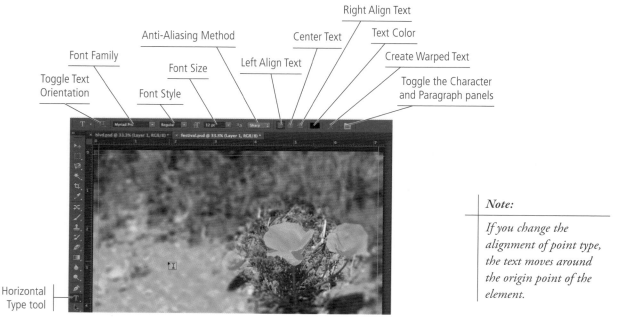

Note:

If you change the alignment of point type, the text moves around the origin point of the element.

2. **In the Tools panel, click the Default Foreground and Background Colors button.**

   Type automatically adopts the active foreground color.

3. **In the Options bar, choose ATC Maple in the Font Family menu, and choose Medium in the Font Style menu. Change the Font Size to 28 pt.**

   If you define type settings before you create a type layer, those settings automatically apply to the layer you create.

4. **Click anywhere in the canvas to create a type layer, then type Antelope Valley.**

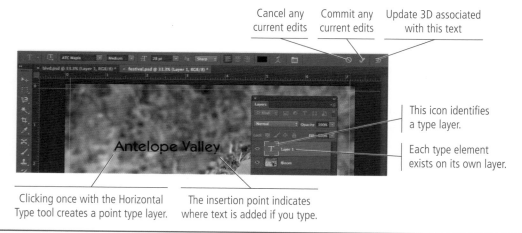

5. **In the Options bar, click the Commit button to finalize your changes to the active the Type layer.**

You can also choose a different tool, or select a different layer to finalize your changes.

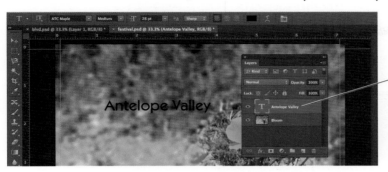

After committing the edits, the type layer adopts its name based on the text in the layer.

6. **Click with the Horizontal Type tool again (away from the existing type) to create a second type layer, then type Poppy Festival.**

Clicking places the insertion point in a new point type element, creating a new type layer.

The Type tools remember the last formatting options you defined.

Clicking again creates a separate type layer.

7. **With the insertion point flashing in the second type layer, choose Select>All.**

When the insertion point is flashing, this command highlights (selects) all of the text in the active type layer.

You can also click and drag to select specific characters, double-click to select an entire word, triple-click to select an entire line, or quadruple-click to select an entire paragraph.

8. **In the Options bar, change the Font Style to [Maple] Ultra, and change the Font Size to 72 pt.**

If you type in the field, you have to Press Return/Enter (or click the Commit button) to finalize the new formatting. If you choose a defined size from the attached menu, you do not need to press Return/Enter.

Note:

If you're working with the insertion point flashing in a type layer, or you have characters on a type layer selected, you can't use the keyboard shortcuts to access different tools.

Character attributes such as font size affect all selected characters.

Point type exists on a single line unless you manually insert a line break.

9. **Press the Left Arrow key to deselect the characters and move the insertion point to the beginning of the type. With the insertion point still flashing in the type, press and hold Command/Control to access the type layer bounding box.**

Pressing Command/Control temporarily switches to the Move tool, so you can move a type layer without switching away from the Horizontal Type tool.

10. **Click inside the bounding box area and drag to place the type approximately 1/4" from the left and top ruler guides.**

Press Command/Control while the insertion point is flashing to access the layer's transformation bounding box.

Click inside the bounding box area and drag to move the layer content.

11. **While still holding the Command/Control key, click the bottom-right bounding-box handle and drag right and down. Resize the type so its right edge is approximately 1/4" from the ruler guide, and the type is approximately 1 1/4" high.**

Even though you resized the type layer (proportionally and disproportionally), it is still live type — you can still place the insertion point and edit as necessary.

Drag the handles to resize the type layer.

Note:

You could accomplish the same thing by selecting the type layer with the Move tool active, then choosing Edit>Free Transform.

12. **When you finish resizing the type, release the Command/Control key.**

13. **Click to place the insertion point between the "F" and "e" in the word Festival.**

14. **In the Options bar, click the button to toggle open the Character and Paragraph panels.**

You can also choose Window>Character or Type>Panels>Character to open the Character panel.

Note:

Changes made in the Character panel apply only to selected text.

Click here to toggle the Character and Paragraph panels.

The Font Size shows the change that was created by scaling the type layer.

15. **In the Character panel, change the Kerning field to −40.**

    Kerning and tracking control the spacing between individual characters. **Kerning** adjusts the spacing between two specific characters (called a **kerning pair**). **Tracking** (also called range kerning) is applied over a range of selected type.

    Kerning values are based by default on the type **metrics** (the values stored in the font data). Professional-quality fonts include predefined kerning and tracking tables in the font data. The **Optical** option in the Kerning menu is useful for fonts that don't have built-in kerning values; Photoshop applies kerning based on how it perceives letter shapes.

    You should always check the letter spacing when you set headline type, use All Caps or Small Caps type styles, or apply any other artificial manipulation such as the stretching you applied in Step 11.

Kerning applies to the space between two characters, where the insertion point is placed.

16. **Continue adjusting the kerning between the letter pairs until you are satisfied with the results.**

    Our solution is shown here:

17. **With the Horizontal Type tool still active, press and hold the Command/Control key to access the layer's bounding box handles, then drag the right-center handle until the right edge of the type is again 1/4″ from the right ruler guide.**

    Reducing the tracking tightened the spacing between specific letter pairs, which reduced the overall width of the type layer. This transformation fixes that problem.

18. **Save the file and continue to the next exercise.**

The Character Panel in Depth

All of the options that are available in the Options bar are also available in the Character panel. However, the Character panel includes a number of other options that control the appearance of type in your document.

Changes to character formatting affect only selected characters. If you make changes before typing, the changes apply to all characters you type from the insertion point.

Font family — Font style
Font size — Leading
Kerning — Tracking
Vertical scale — Horizontal scale
Baseline shift — Text color
Type styles — OpenType attributes
Language — Anti-aliasing

Anti-Aliasing Options for Type

Although type is vector-based, it will eventually be rendered (rasterized) at some point — even if that doesn't happen until the final output. Anti-aliasing produces smooth-edge type by partially filling the edge pixels, which allows the edges of the type to better blend into the background when the type is rendered. (Be aware that anti-aliasing small type might distort the letter shapes.) Photoshop supports five options for anti-aliasing type. The effects of each method are best viewed at higher zoom percentages.

- None applies no anti-aliasing.
- Sharp creates the sharpest type.
- Crisp makes type appear slightly sharp.
- Strong makes type appear heavier.
- Smooth makes type edges appear very smooth.

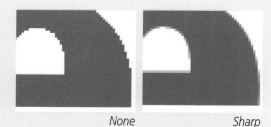

None   *Sharp*

Crisp   *Strong*   *Smooth*

USE THE MOVE TOOL WITH TYPE LAYERS

Type layers in Photoshop are similar to most other layers. You can drag and transform type layers using most of the same tools that you use to transform other kinds of layers. You can scale or skew type layers; change their opacity, fill, and blending mode; apply layer styles; and even add warp effects — while still maintaining the editable type.

1. **With festival.psd active, choose the Move tool.**

2. **In the Layers panel, click the Antelope Valley layer to select it.**

   Using the Move tool, you can move and manipulate type layers like any other layer, but you can't edit the actual type.

3. **In the Character panel, click the Color swatch to open the Color Picker for the type color.**

   The insertion point does not need to be flashing to change the formatting of the active type layer. Keep in mind, however, that any change you make while the insertion point is *not* flashing applies to all type in the layer. If you want to change the formatting of only some type on a layer, you first have to use the Type tool to select the characters you want to affect.

Note:

The only options you can't apply to live text are the Distort and Perspective transformations, custom warps (although you can use the built-in warp shapes), and filters. To use these features, you must rasterize the type layer.

4. **Move the eyedropper cursor over a bright orange color in the poppy image and click to sample that color. Click OK to change the type color.**

When the layer is selected with the Move tool, any formatting change applies to all type on the layer.

Click here to change the color of type on the selected layer.

Use the eyedropper cursor to sample a color from the image.

5. **With the Auto-Select option turned off in the Options bar, click and drag to move the type so the first letter in the layer appears just above the "o" in the word "Poppy".**

If you don't turn off the Auto-Select option, you would have to click exactly on the rather thin letters in the type. When this option is not checked, you can click anywhere in the canvas to drag the selected layer.

Unchecking the Auto-Select option makes it easier to move small type without precisely clicking the letters.

The 28-pt text is too large to fit into this space.

6. **In the Character panel, reduce the font size to 22 pt.**

This layer uses left paragraph alignment, and the origin point of the layer remains in place when you change the formatting.

The type is left-aligned, so the left edge of the type layer does not change when the font size is reduced.

7. **Select the Poppy Festival type layer, then use the Character panel to change the type color to white.**

8. **Save the file and continue to the next exercise.**

 ## CREATE VERTICALLY ORIENTED TYPE

Although most type (in English, at least) is oriented left-to-right, row-to-row, there are times when you want to orient type vertically — each character below the next. You can use the Vertical Type tool to accomplish this goal, whether for foreign-language design or simply for artistic purposes.

1. **Make blvd.psd the active file, then choose the Vertical Type tool (nested under the Horizontal Type tool).**

2. **In the Options bar, choose ATC Maple Ultra as the font, define the size as 72 pt, and choose white as the type color.**

3. **Click to create a new type layer, then type BLVD.**

   When you use the Vertical Type tool, each letter appears below the previous one.

Vertically oriented type can be oriented above, centered, or below the point where you click.

A type layer is created just as it was when you used the Horizontal Type tool.

Vertical Type tool

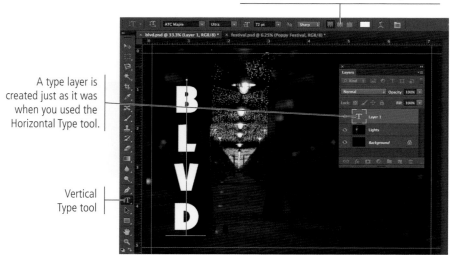

4. With the insertion point flashing, choose Select>All.

5. In the Character panel, change the tracking field to –200.

Even though the type is oriented vertically, tracking and kerning still apply to the spacing between characters. Because this type is oriented vertically, they control the space above and below each letter.

As you can see, the left edges of the letters (especially B and L) do not align. Vertical type orientation does not recognize the edges of lettershapes for the sake of alignment.

In the Options bar, paragraph alignment options affect the position of type relative to the point where you click. You can align the type below, centered on, or above the origin point. You cannot, however, align the left or right edges of the letters.

With vertically oriented type, kerning and tracking apply between the tops and bottoms of characters.

6. With the type layer selected, choose Type>Orientation>Horizontal.

As you can see, the negative tracking that worked for vertical orientation does not work for horizontal orientation.

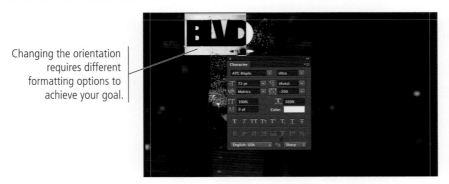

Changing the orientation requires different formatting options to achieve your goal.

7. With all four characters selected, change the tracking back to 0.

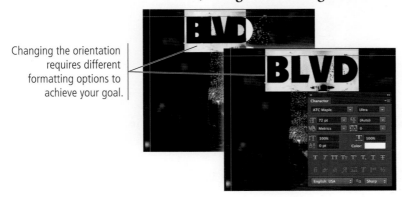

Changing the orientation requires different formatting options to achieve your goal.

8. Place the insertion point after the "B" and press Return/Enter to start a new paragraph.

9. Repeat this process to move each character onto a separate line.

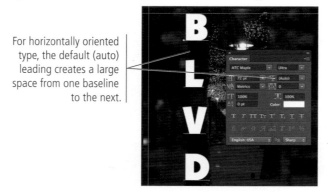

For horizontally oriented type, the default (auto) leading creates a large space from one baseline to the next.

10. Place the insertion point before the "B". In the Options bar, change the type size to 12 pt, then type THE and press Return/Enter.

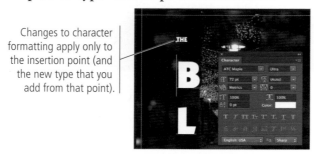

Changes to character formatting apply only to the insertion point (and the new type that you add from that point).

11. Select the four letters in "BLVD". In the Character panel, change the Leading field to 55 pt.

Although leading appears to apply to paragraphs, it is actually a character property. To change the leading for an entire paragraph, you have to select all characters in that paragraph.

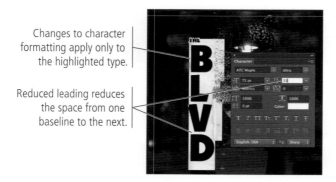

Changes to character formatting apply only to the highlighted type.

Reduced leading reduces the space from one baseline to the next.

12. Choose the Move tool. With the type layer selected, move the layer so the type begins in the top-left corner of the canvas, approximately 1/4″ from the ruler guides.

The Paragraph Panel in Depth

You can change a number of paragraph attributes, including alignment and justification, indents, and space above and below paragraphs. The Justification options are only available when you work with area type (which you will do shortly), and some options are not relevant for point type that only occupies a single line.

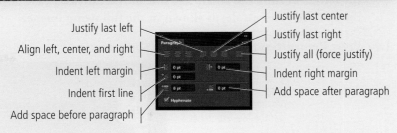

Justify last left
Align left, center, and right
Indent left margin
Indent first line
Add space before paragraph

Justify last center
Justify last right
Justify all (force justify)
Indent right margin
Add space after paragraph

Hyphenation Options

When the Hyphenate option is selected, text in area type hyphenates automatically, based on the Hyphenation options in the Paragraph panel Options menu. You can control the minimum length of a word before it can be hyphenated, as well as the minimum number of characters that must appear before or after a hyphen. Formal rules of typography typically suggest that only words longer than six characters should be hyphenated, and at least three characters should exist before or after a hyphen.

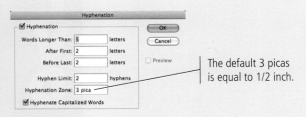

The default 3 picas is equal to 1/2 inch.

The **Hyphen Limit** field defines how many hyphens can appear at the ends of consecutive lines; formal rules of typography recommend limiting consecutive hyphens to three, and preferably no more than two.

The **Hyphenation Zone** determines the distance from the right edge of a type area where automatic hyphens can exist. If this field is set to 1/2″, for example, the automatic hyphen would have to fall within a half inch of the type area edge for a word to be automatically hyphenated.

The final option, **Hyphenate Capitalized Words**, can be turned off to prevent automatic hyphenation in proper names such as corporate or product names (many companies seriously frown on their trademarks being split across lines).

Justification Options

When you work with area type, you can justify paragraphs inside the type area. Justified type stretches horizontally to fill the width of the area. The last line of the paragraph can be aligned left, centered, or right, or it can be stretched based on your choice in the Paragraph panel. When text is justified, it's stretched based on the defined Justification options, which can be changed by choosing Justification in the Paragraph panel Options menu.

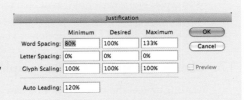

The Minimum and Maximum values define the acceptable spacing for justified paragraphs. The Desired value defines the *preferred* spacing for paragraphs:

- The Word Spacing fields control the space between words (anywhere you press the space bar). A 100% value means the word spacing remains the same when you justify a paragraph.

- The Letter Spacing fields control the space between letters, including kerning and tracking values. A 0% value means the letter spacing remains the same when you justify a paragraph.

- The Glyph Scaling fields control the width of individual characters. A 100% value means they are not stretched.

The Auto Leading field applies to both area type and point type that occupies more than one line. By default, automatic leading is set to 120% of the type size. You can change this automatic value, but it is usually better to change the leading for individual type instances instead of changing the default automatic value.

13. **Choose Edit>Free Transform. Press Shift, then drag the bottom-right handle until the letters occupy the entire left side of the canvas. Leave approximately 1/4″ from the bottom ruler guide, as shown in the following image.**

14. **Press Return/Enter to finalize the transformation.**

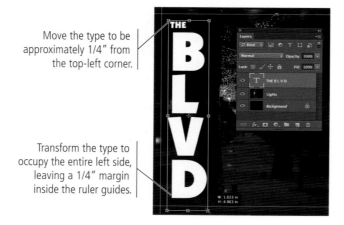

Move the type to be approximately 1/4″ from the top-left corner.

Transform the type to occupy the entire left side, leaving a 1/4″ margin inside the ruler guides.

15. **Choose the Horizontal Type tool, then click to place the insertion point in the word "THE" (the first paragraph).**

    You can choose Window>Paragraph to open the Paragraph panel, or click the Toggle the Character and Paragraph Panels button in the Options bar.

16. **In the Paragraph panel, change the Indent Left Margin field to 5 pt.**

    The Indent values affect the position of the type relative to the layer's orientation point. This better aligns the "T" in "THE" with the left edge of the "B" in "BLVD."

    When you work with point type, paragraph attributes apply to all type on a single line. If you have more than one paragraph — as you do in this type layer — you can apply different paragraph format options to each paragraph.

17. **Change the Space After Paragraph field to –3 pt.**

    Leading affects the space from one baseline to the next, even within a single paragraph. The Space Before Paragraph and Space After Paragraph options relate to an entire paragraph. By reducing this value, you are closing up the space between the first paragraph ("THE") and the second paragraph ("B").

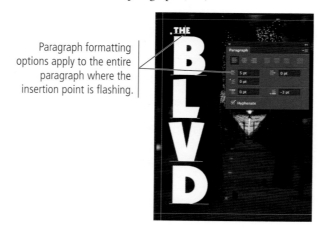

Paragraph formatting options apply to the entire paragraph where the insertion point is flashing.

18. **Save the file and continue to the next exercise.**

CREATE AND CONTROL AREA TYPE

In many cases your clients will provide specific text to include in a design; that text might be part of an email message or saved in a word-processing file. If the client-supplied text is only a couple of words, it's easier to retype the text into your Photoshop file. But when the supplied text is longer, there's no point in making extra work by retyping what has already been typed.

The final type element you need for each postcard is a two- or three-paragraph blurb of promotional copy. You are going to create these as area-type layers so that you can better control the line breaks and alignment, and more easily fit them into a specific amount of space.

1. **On your desktop, double-click the file festival_copy.txt (in your WIP>Lancaster folder) to open the text file in a text-editing application.**

   You can't place or import external text files directly into a Photoshop file. If you want to use text from an external file, you simply open the file in a text editor, copy it, and paste it into a Photoshop type layer.

Note:

We used Macintosh TextEdit as our word processor.

2. **Select all text in the file, copy it, then close the file.**

3. **With festival.psd active in Photoshop, choose the Horizontal Type tool in the Tools panel.**

4. **In Photoshop, click below the "P" in "Poppy", and drag down and right to create a type area (as shown in the following image).**

Click and drag to create a type area.

When you release the mouse button, you have a type area with bounding box handles that you can drag to change the area's shape.

Note:

If the insertion point is not flashing in the top-left corner of the area, make sure the Left Align Text option is selected in the Options bar.

The insertion point flashes at the top-left edge of the type area.

A new type layer is created.

5. **With the insertion point flashing inside the new type area, use either the Character panel or Options bar to define the type formatting as follows:**

> **Font Family: ATC Oak**
> **Font Style: Italic**
> **Font Size: 11 pt.**
> **Leading: 14 pt.**
> **Type Color: white**

6. **With the insertion point still flashing in the type area, choose Edit>Paste.**

Because you defined the type formatting before you pasted the type, it is automatically formatted with the settings you defined.

7. **With the Horizontal Type tool still active, click the right-center bounding box handle of the type area and drag so the right edge of the area is just below the "y" descender.**

When you resize the type area by dragging the bounding box handles, you do not affect the type; you change the type *container*, which allows more (or less, depending on how you drag) of the type to show.

Type also wraps within the type area. You don't have to manually define where new lines begin; simply press Return/Enter to start a new formal paragraph.

Dragging a type area handle with the Horizontal Type tool changes the size of the area without resizing the type.

The Horizontal Type tool is still active.

8. **Click the bottom-center handle and drag down to the bottom ruler guide.**

Note:

Make sure to use the Horizontal Type tool when you want to change the dimensions of a type area. If you press Command/Control-T or choose Edit>Free Transform, stretching or otherwise resizing the type area bounding box resizes the type it contains.

9. **Click and drag to select at least part of all three paragraphs in the area. In the Paragraph panel, change the Space After Paragraph field to 8 pt.**

   Paragraph formatting attributes apply to any paragraph that is even partially selected. If no characters are highlighted, any paragraph formatting changes apply to the paragraph where the insertion point is currently placed.

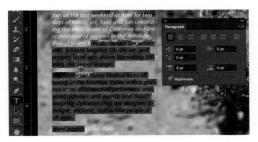

10. **Select the entire last paragraph in the area. In the Character panel, change the font to ATC Oak Normal, and change the size to 13 pt. In the Paragraph panel, click the Center Text button.**

    Remember: character attributes such as font and size apply only to selected characters. To change these for the entire paragraph, you first have to select the entire paragraph.

11. **Save the file and continue to the next exercise.**

 ## CREATE PARAGRAPH STYLES

When you work with longer blocks of text, many of the same formatting options are applied to different text elements throughout the story (such as headings), or to different elements in similar pieces of a campaign. To simplify the workflow, you can use styles to store and apply multiple formatting options in a single click.

Styles also have another powerful benefit: when you change the options applied in a style, any text formatted with that style reflects the newly defined options. In other words, you can change multiple instances of non-contiguous text in a single process, instead of selecting each block and making the same changes repeatedly.

Note:

Photoshop also supports character styles, which can be used to store any character-formatting options that can be applied to selected characters.

1. **With festival.psd active, select any part of the first paragraph in the type area.**

2. **Choose Type>Panels>Paragraph Styles Panel.**

   The Paragraph Styles panel shows that the selected type is formatted with the Basic Paragraph style. The plus sign next to the style name indicates that some formatting is applied other than what is defined by the style.

The *Basic Paragraph* option is included in every file.

The plus sign indicates that formatting other than the style's definition has been applied to the selected type.

3. **Click the Create New Paragraph Style button at the bottom of the panel.**

   When you create a new style, it defaults to include all formatting options that are applied to the currently selected type.

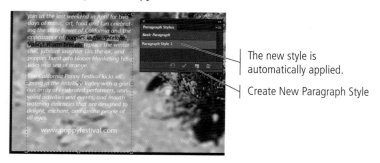

The new style is automatically applied.

Create New Paragraph Style

Note:

You can delete a style by dragging it to the panel Delete button. If the style had been applied, you would see a warning message, asking you to confirm the deletion (you do not have the opportunity to replace the applied style with another one, as you do in Adobe InDesign).

   If you have used type styles in InDesign or Illustrator, you need to be aware of a difference in the way you create styles based on existing formatting. In those applications, a new style adopts the formatting of the current insertion point, which means you do not have to select specific type to create a style.

   In Photoshop, however, you have to select at least part of a paragraph to create a style based on that paragraph's formatting. Also, you cannot select multiple paragraphs with the same formatting to create a style based on those options.

4. **Double-click the new style in the panel to review the style's settings.**

   Double-clicking a style opens the Paragraph Style Options dialog box for that style, where you can edit the settings stored in the style. Different options are available in the right side of the dialog box, depending on what is selected in the list of categories.

Note:

You can also choose Style Options in the panel Options menu to open this dialog box.

   Checking the Preview option allows you to immediately see the effect of your changes in the layout before you finalize the changes.

5. **Change the style name to Body Copy and click OK.**

6. **Select any part of the second paragraph, then click the Body Copy style in the Paragraph Styles panel to apply that style to the active paragraph.**

   This highlights another anomaly in the application. When you apply a style to type that already showed a plus sign, you have to click the Clear Override button to apply only the style's formatting to the selected type.

7. **With the same type selected, click the Clear Override button at the bottom of the Paragraph Styles panel.**

This is an issue that you should be aware of; if you do not clear the overrides, later changes to the applied style might not correctly reflect in type formatted with the style. Whenever you work with styles, check the applied styles to see if a plus sign appears where you know it shouldn't.

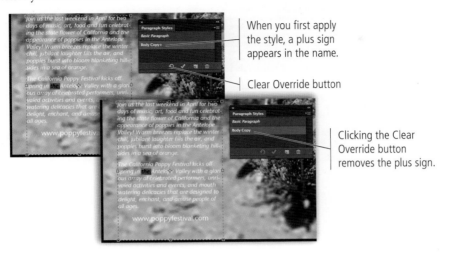

When you first apply the style, a plus sign appears in the name.

Clear Override button

Clicking the Clear Override button removes the plus sign.

Note:

You could also choose Clear Override in the Paragraph panel Options menu.

Note:

If the applied style shows a plus sign in the name, you can click the Redefine button to change the selected style formatting to match the formatting of the current text selection.

8. **Repeat this process to create a new paragraph style named Web Address based on the formatting of the last paragraph in the type area.**

9. **Save the file and continue to the next exercise.**

LOAD PARAGRAPH STYLES FROM ANOTHER FILE

Once you create styles, you can apply them to any text in the file, on any layer. You can also import styles from other Photoshop files so they can be used for different projects.

1. **On your desktop, open the file blvd_copy.txt in a text editor application.**

2. **Select all the text in the file, copy it, then close the file.**

> blvd_copy.txt
>
> The downtown that once served as the heart of the Antelope Valley has been restored to its former glory, with a modern twist! Come see the dramatic transformation and explore more than 40 new shops and restaurants. Don't miss our annual special events, and the weekly farmer's market every Thursday.
> www.theblvdlancaster.com

3. **In Photoshop, open the blvd.psd file if necessary. Using the Horizontal Type tool, click and drag to create a type area in the top-right corner of the canvas.**

4. **With the insertion point in the new area, paste the copy from Step 2.**

   The pasted type adopts the last-applied formatting options, which is not what you want. Because you already defined paragraph styles for the other card in this same campaign, you can load those styles and apply them to the type in this card.

5. **In the Paragraph Styles panel Options menu, choose Load Paragraph Styles. Navigate to `festival.psd` in your (WIP>Lancaster folder) and click Open/Load.**

6. **Click OK in the message that 2 paragraph styles were imported.**

   Remember, the file you selected had only two styles — the ones you defined in the previous exercise. Loading styles from one Photoshop file to another is an all-or-nothing choice; you can't select certain styles to import.

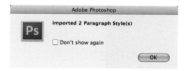

7. **Select the entire first paragraph. Click Body Copy in the Paragraph Styles panel, then click the Clear Override button.**

8. **Repeat Step 7 to apply the Web Address style to the second paragraph.**

9. **If necessary, adjust the handles of the area so all the type in the story appears in the type area.**

10. **Save the file and continue to the next stage of the project.**

In some cases, maintaining a type layer with live text is either unnecessary (e.g., you know the book title isn't going to change) or it prevents you from applying certain changes (e.g., you can't apply filters to a type layer). When you find an effect or change that won't work with live text, you must convert the type layer in one way or another.

You can simply rasterize a type layer by choosing Type>Rasterize Type Layer, which converts the editable, vector-based type to a regular pixel-based layer. Once rasterized, you can't edit the text, but you can apply filters and use the layer as a clipping mask.

Rasterizing type results in a regular, pixel-based layer.

You should understand that type is fundamentally based on vectors. Rather than simply rasterizing type, you can convert a type layer to a vector-based shape layer by choosing Type>Convert to Shape. Converting a type layer to a shape means the type is no longer editable, but you can still manipulate the letterforms as you would any other vector shape layer. By converting type to a shape layer, you can use the Distort or Perspective transformation to create custom warps for the layer. You still can't apply filters, however, since filters work on rasterized layers only. (If you try to apply a filter to a shape layer, you will see a message asking if you want to rasterize the shape layer.)

When you convert a type layer to a vector shape layer, the shape layer adopts the original text color as the fill color.

If you need to apply filters, custom warps, or transformations to type, but you want to maintain the type layer as live (editable) text, you can convert the type layer to a Smart Object in the layer's contextual menu. You can apply the transformations or filters in the main document, but still edit the text in the Smart Object file.

In the master file you can transform and filter the type as a Smart Object.

The Smart Object file maintains the live type.

Finally, you can use the vector information of type to create a work path (Type>Create Work Path), which you can then save as a regular path in the Paths panel. In this case, the type layer is maintained as an editable type layer, but you can use the path for any purpose you choose.

The work path appears in the Paths panel.

The original type layer is maintained.

Creating Type Selections

You can use one of the Type Mask tools (horizontal or vertical) to create a selection in the shape of letters. When you click with one of these tools, you automatically enter a kind of Quick Mask mode; the letters you type are removed from the mask to show what will be selected. (If you press Command/Control while the red mask is visible, you can drag the type selection around in the image window.)

When you have finished typing, switching to the Move tool shows the marching ants that make up the type-shaped selection. This type of selection is similar to any other selection you can make — it just happens to be in the shape of letters. You can manipulate it, create a layer mask with it, save it as an Alpha channel, and so on.

No layer, path, or channel is automatically created when you use the Type Mask tools.

Horizontal Type Mask tool

Stage 4 Creating Style with Layers

In this and earlier projects, you have learned a number of techniques for manipulating layers — isolating specific areas, transforming selections, moving and scaling content while preserving image detail, modifying colors, retouching damage... the list is already extensive. To complete the rest of this project, you will learn several new techniques for adding visual interest to layers, including creating a solid-color overlay and applying layer effects.

 ## CREATE A SOLID-COLOR FILL LAYER

A solid-color fill layer is exactly what it sounds like — a layer of colored pixels, which obscures all underlying layers. Like a vector shape layer (which you used in Project 2: African Wildlife Map), the fill layer's thumbnail shows a swatch of the current fill color; you can double-click that swatch to change the color. A fill layer also has an attached (pixel-based) layer mask, which you can use to define where the fill color will be visible.

1. **With festival.psd open, select the Bloom layer in the Layers panel.**

2. **Click the Create New Fill or Adjustment Layer button at the bottom of the Layers panel and choose Solid Color in the resulting menu.**

Create new fill or adjustment layer

The new layer will be created immediately above the selected layer.

Note:

You will work with adjustment layers in Project 6: Advertising Samples.

3. **Click OK in the Color Picker dialog box to accept the default color value.**

   The fill color defaults to the active foreground color. Don't worry if yours is different than what you see in our images; you will change the color in the next few steps.

The solid color of the fill obscures the underlying image layer.

The Color Picker automatically opens when you add a solid-color fill layer.

4. **In the Layers panel, click the eye icon to hide the Color Fill layer.**

   To sample a color from the underlying image, you first have to hide the fill layer.

5. **Double-click the Color Fill 1 layer's thumbnail to reopen the Color Picker dialog box.**

   You can change the Color Fill layer color even though it isn't currently visible.

6. **With the Color Picker dialog box open, click in the image (behind the dialog box) with the eyedropper cursor to sample a dark green area of the image as the layer's fill color.**

Because the Color Fill layer is hidden, you can sample a color from the underlying layer.

Double-click the color icon to change the layer's fill color.

7. **Click OK to close the Color Picker dialog box, then make the Color Fill layer visible again.**

8. **In the Layers panel, click to select the mask thumbnail for the Color Fill layer.**

   Fill and adjustment layers automatically include a mask, which you can use to define where the fill is visible. This is similar to the vector shape layers, where the vector path(s) define where the color is visible. The fill layer's mask, however, is pixel-based, which means it can include shades of gray.

   Remember from earlier projects: black areas of a mask are transparent and white areas are opaque. In this case, white areas of the mask result in full strength of the fill layer's color; shades of gray indicate varying degrees of the fill color.

9. **Choose the Gradient tool in the Tools panel. Reset the foreground and background colors (so that white is the Foreground and black is the Background Color), then choose the Foreground to Background gradient in the Options bar.**

10. **Make sure the Linear Gradient option is selected. Click at the right edge of the type area, then drag right to the right edge of the canvas.**

Note:

You could have accomplished the same basic goal by creating a new layer, filling it with a solid color, then manually adding a pixel mask. When you add a solid-color fill layer, the mask is automatically added for you; you can also double-click the color swatch in the layer icon to change the color that fills the layer.

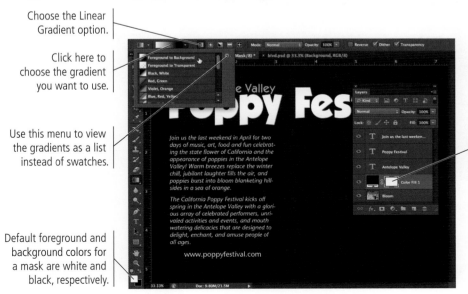

Choose the Linear Gradient option.

Click here to choose the gradient you want to use.

Use this menu to view the gradients as a list instead of swatches.

Default foreground and background colors for a mask are white and black, respectively.

The layer's mask is selected.

11. **Choose Multiply in the Blending Mode menu at the top of the Layers panel.**

Multiplying the dark color with the underlying image allows the white type to stand out more clearly against the background. The result, however, is too dark — almost entirely obscuring the underlying image.

We dragged the gradient from here... ...to here.

The Multiply blending mode mixes the color of the fill layer with colors in the underlying layer.

12. **Change the layer's opacity to 70%.**

Reducing the fill layer's opacity allows more of the underlying image to show through. You can type the new value in the field, use the attached menu, or use the scrubby slider for the field's label.

The **Opacity** percentage changes the opacity of the entire layer, including applied effects and styles. The **Fill** percentage changes the opacity of the actual layer pixels, but none of the applied effects or styles. In this case, the layer doesn't yet have any applied styles or effects, so both controls would have the same effect.

Note:

If the Opacity field is unavailable, check the Lock options. When you use the Lock Position option, you can still affect the opacity of the layer. When you use the Lock All option, however, you can't change the layer opacity.

Reducing the fill layer's opacity reduces the darkness created by the multiplied colors.

13. **Save the file and continue to the next exercise.**

Note:

When a layer is selected and the insertion point is not flashing in a Type layer, you can press the number keys to change the active layer's opacity in 10% increments:

1 = 10%	6 = 60%
2 = 20%	7 = 70%
3 = 30%	8 = 80%
4 = 40%	9 = 90%
5 = 50%	0 = 100%

APPLY LAYER EFFECTS

You worked with layer styles in Project 2: African Wildlife Map, even if you didn't realize it. In that project, you applied predefined styles and textures to the map shape layer using the Photoshop Style libraries. Those styles are simply saved groups of layer style settings that you can apply with a single click. In this project, you're going to learn how to apply and control the individual components that make up those predefined styles.

1. **With `festival.psd` active, select the Bloom layer in the Layers panel.**

2. **Click the Lock All button at the top of the Layers panel.**

   The Bloom layer is technically the postcard background, even though it is not a formal Background layer. By locking all properties, you prevent the layer from being moved, painted on, or otherwise edited.

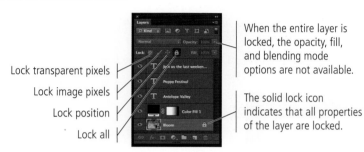

When the entire layer is locked, the opacity, fill, and blending mode options are not available.

Lock transparent pixels
Lock image pixels
Lock position
Lock all

The solid lock icon indicates that all properties of the layer are locked.

Note:

For all but type layers, you can lock three different attributes individually, or you can lock the entire layer at once.

3. **Select the three type layers, then click the Lock Position button.**

   By locking the layers' positions, you prevent them from accidentally being moved as you continue working. Since only the position is locked, however, you can still apply effects that do not affect the position of the layer content.

   You cannot, by definition, lock the image pixels or transparent pixels of a type layer. If you activate the Lock All button for a Type layer, you would not be able to apply styles to those layers in the next steps.

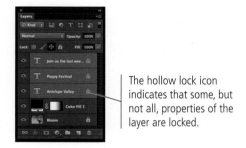

The hollow lock icon indicates that some, but not all, properties of the layer are locked.

4. **In the Layers panel, select only the Poppy Festival layer, then choose Layer>Layer Style>Drop Shadow.**

When you open the Layer Style dialog box, the preview option is automatically checked. You can see the effects of your selections in the image behind the dialog box.

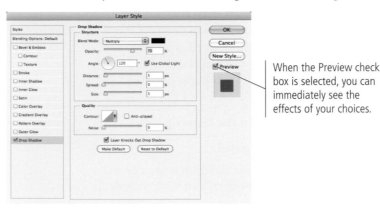

When the Preview check box is selected, you can immediately see the effects of your choices.

5. **Click in the image window (behind the dialog box) and drag until the shadow is fairly heavy, directly below the letters.**

   Dragging on the canvas dynamically changes the Angle and Distance fields of the Layer Style dialog box.

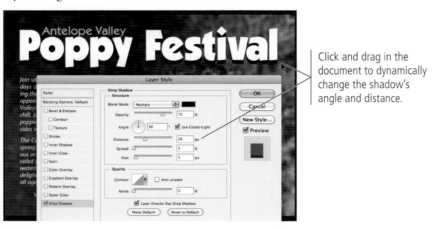

Click and drag in the document to dynamically change the shadow's angle and distance.

6. **With the dialog box still open, select the Bevel and Emboss option in the list on the left. Uncheck the Use Global Light option.**

Click in this list to apply another effect to the same layer.

Turn off the Use Global Light option for the Bevel & Emboss effect.

7. **Click OK to apply both styles to the selected layer.**

   Layer styles are non-destructive, which means you can edit them at any time; double-clicking an effect in the Layers panel reopens the Layer Style dialog box, so you can change the applied settings. You can also use the eye icons in the Layers panel to turn specific styles off or on.

   Double-click a specific effect to open the Layer Styles dialog box and edit the associated settings.

   Layer styles appear in the Layers panel as Effects. You can show or hide these individually or, if more than one is applied, all at once.

8. **Press Option/Alt, then click the Drop Shadow item in the Layers panel and drag onto the Antelope Valley layer.**

   Option/Alt-dragging is an easy way to copy applied styles from one layer to another. You could also Option/Alt-drag the entire Effects heading to copy both applied styles to the second type layer.

   Option/Alt-drag an effect to copy it to another layer in the same file.

9. **In the Layers panel, double-click the Drop Shadow option for the Antelope Valley layer to open the Layer Style dialog box.**

10. **Change the Distance field to 10 px.**

    The smaller characters make a smaller shadow more appropriate. The change in distance does not affect the distance of the other applied shadow.

11. **With the Use Global Light option checked, click the Angle proxy in the dialog box and drag until the type's shadow more closely matches the shadow cast by the flowers.**

    Because both of the drop shadows use the Global Light angle, changing the angle of one shadow applies the same change to the other shadow. The Bevel does not use the global angle, so this does not change the appearance of that effect.

    Changing the angle for one shadow affects the angle for all effects where the Use Global Light option is checked.

12. Click OK to apply the changes and return to the document.

13. Control/right-click the Antelope Valley layer and choose Copy Layer Style from the contextual menu.

14. Click the arrow to the right of the *fx* icon in the Poppy Festival and Antelope Valley layers to collapse the Effects listings.

Clicking this button collapses and expands the Effects list.

15. Save the file, then make **blvd.psd** active.

16. Control/right-click the THE BLVD type layer in the Layers panel, and choose Paste Layer Style in the contextual menu.

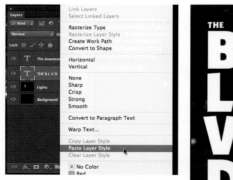

This copy-and-paste technique is an easy way to apply the same layer styles in multiple files. Keep in mind, however, that there is no live link between the styles in the two separate files; changing settings in one — including the global angle — has no effect on the other.

17. Save the file and continue to the final stage of the project.

Photoshop offers ten layer style options, which you can apply individually or in various combinations to create unique flat and dimensional effects for any layer.

Drop Shadow and Inner Shadow

Drop Shadow adds a shadow behind the layer; **Inner Shadow** adds a shadow inside the edges of the layer's content. For both types, you can define the blending mode, color, opacity, angle, distance, and size of the shadow.

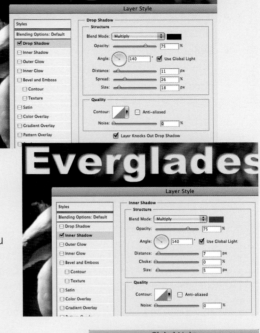

- **Distance** is the offset of the shadow, or how far away the shadow will be from the original layer.

- **Spread** (for Drop Shadows) is the percentage the shadow expands beyond the original layer.

- **Choke** (for Inner Shadows) is the percentage the shadow shrinks into the original layer.

- **Size** is the blur amount applied to the shadow.

You can also adjust the Contour, Anti-aliasing, and Noise settings in the shadow effect. (See the Contours section later in this discussion for further explanation.)

The Layer Knocks Out Drop Shadow option for drop shadows allows you to knock out (remove) or maintain the shadow underneath the original layer area. This option is particularly important if you convert a shadow style to a separate layer that you move to a different position, or if the layer is semi-transparent above its shadow.

Global Light. The Use Global Light check box is available for Drop Shadow, Inner Shadow, and Bevel and Emboss styles. When this option is checked, the style is linked to the "master" light source angle for the entire file. Changing the global light setting affects any linked shadow or bevel style applied to any layer in the entire file. (You can change the Global Light settings in any of the Layer Style fields or by choosing Layer>Layer Style>Global Light.)

Outer Glow and Inner Glow

Outer Glow and **Inner Glow** styles add glow effects to the outside and inside edges (respectively) of the original layer. For either kind of glow, you can define the Blending Mode, Opacity, and Noise values, as well as whether to use a solid color or a gradient.

- For either kind of glow, you can define the **Technique** as Precise or Softer. **Precise** creates a glow at a specific distance; **Softer** creates a blurred glow and does not preserve detail as well as Precise.

- For Inner Glows, you can also define the **Source** of the glow (Center or Edge). **Center** applies a glow starting from the center of the layer; **Edge** applies the glow starting from the inside edges of the layer.

- The **Spread** and **Choke** sliders affect the percentages of the glow effects.

- The **Size** slider makes the effect smaller or larger.

Bevel and Emboss

This style has five variations: Outer Bevel, Inner Bevel, Emboss, Pillow Emboss, and Stroke Emboss:

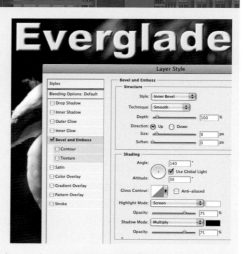

- **Inner Bevel** creates a bevel on the inside edges of the layer contents.
- **Outer Bevel** creates a bevel on the outside edges of the layer contents.
- **Emboss** creates the effect of embossing the layer contents against the underlying layers.
- **Pillow Emboss** creates the effect of stamping the edges of the layer into the underlying layers.
- **Stroke Emboss** applies an embossed effect to a stroke applied to the layer. (The Stroke Emboss effect is not available if you haven't applied a stroke to the layer.)

Any of these styles can be applied as **Smooth** (blurs the edges of the effect), **Chisel Hard** (creates a distinct edge to the effect), or **Chisel Soft** (creates a distinct but slightly blurred edge to the effect).

You can change the **Direction** of the bevel effect. **Up** creates the appearance of the layer coming out of the image; **Down** creates the appearance of something stamped into the image.

The **Size** slider makes the effect smaller or larger, and the **Soften** slider blurs the edges of the effect.

In the Shading area, you can control the light source **Angle** and **Altitude** (think of how shadows differ as the sun moves across the sky). You can also apply a **Gloss Contour** (see the following explanation of Contours). Finally, you can change the Blending Mode, Opacity, and Color settings of both highlights and shadows created in the Bevel or Emboss effect.

When a Bevel and Emboss style is applied, you can also apply Contour and Texture effects.

Contours

Contour options control the shape of the applied styles. Drop Shadow, Inner Shadow, Inner Glow, Outer Glow, Bevel and Emboss, and Satin styles all include Contour options. The default option for all but the Satin style is Linear, which applies a linear effect from solid to 100% transparent.

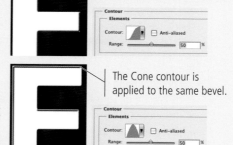

The easiest way to understand the Contour options is through examples. In the following series of images, the same Inner Bevel style was applied in all three examples. In the left image, you can clearly see the size and depth of the bevel. In the right images, the only difference is the applied contour. If you look carefully at the letter edge, you should be able to see how the applied contour shape maps to the beveled edge in the image.

The Gaussian contour is applied to the same bevel.

When you apply a contour, the **Range** slider controls which part of the effect is contoured. For Outer Glow or Inner Glow, you can add variation to the contour color and opacity using the **Jitter** slider.

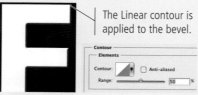

The Linear contour is applied to the bevel.

The Cone contour is applied to the same bevel.

Satin

The Satin options apply interior shading to create a satiny appearance. You can change the Blending Mode, Color, and Opacity settings of the effect, as well as the Angle, Distance, and Size settings.

Textures

The Textures options allow you to create texture effects using the same patterns you worked with in Project 2: African Wildlife Map.

- The **Scale** slider varies the size of the applied pattern.
- The **Depth** slider varies the apparent depth of the applied pattern.
- The **Invert** option (as the name implies) inverts the applied pattern.
- If you check the **Link with Layer** option, the pattern's position is locked to the layer so you can move the two together. If this option is unchecked, different parts of the pattern are visible if you move the associated layer.
- When you create a texture, you can drag in the image window (behind the Layer Style dialog box) to move the texture. When the Link with Layer option is checked, clicking the **Snap to Origin** button positions the pattern origin at the upper-left corner of the layer. If Link with Layers is unchecked, clicking the Snap to Origin button positions the pattern at the image origin point.

Color Overlay, Gradient Overlay, and Pattern Overlay

A **color overlay** is simply a solid color with specific Blending Mode and Opacity value applied. A color overlay can be used to change an entire layer to a solid color (with the Normal blending mode at 100% opacity), or to create unique effects using different Blending Mode and Opacity settings.

A **gradient overlay** is basically the same as a color overlay, except you use a gradient instead of a solid color. You can choose an existing gradient or define a new one (as you did in Project 2), change the Blending Mode and Opacity value of the gradient, apply any of the available gradient styles (Linear, Radial, etc.), and change the Angle and Scale values of the gradient.

A **pattern overlay** is similar to the Texture options for a Bevel and Emboss style. You can choose a specific pattern, change the Blending Mode and Opacity value, and change the applied pattern scale. You can also link the pattern to the layer and snap the pattern to the layer or the file origin.

Stroke

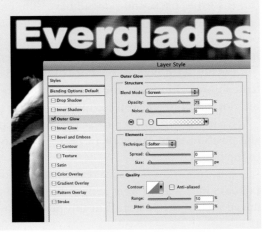

The **Stroke** style adds an outline of a specific number of pixels to the layer. The Stroke effect can be added at the outside or inside of the layer edge, or it can be centered over the edge (half the stroke will be inside and half outside the actual layer edge). You can adjust the Blending Mode and Opacity setting of the stroke, and you can also define a specific color, gradient, or pattern to apply as the stroke.

Stage 5 Working in 3D

Photoshop CS6 Extended includes the ability to create real-time, three-dimensional artwork, either from scratch or by importing wire frames and rendered artwork from industry-standard 3D applications such as Maya or 3D Studio Max.

The following is a brief introduction to Photoshop's 3D functionality. If you have never worked in real three dimensions before, you will almost certainly have to spend some extra time learning the related terminology. We also encourage you to experiment with the various 3D options until you are comfortable manipulating objects in digital space.

You should already be familiar with the concept of the X and Y axes. When you work with 3D files, you also need to understand the concept of the Z axis, which creates the illusion of depth.

Note:

You must have Photoshop Extended to complete the exercises in this stage of the project.

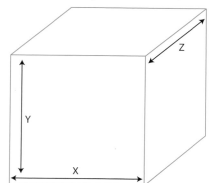

Note:

*In 3D terminology, moving an object in 3D space (near to far) is called a **translation**; rotating an object in 3D space is called a **transformation**.*

- **Meshes** (sometimes called **wireframes**) are the basic skeletons of three-dimensional objects. The mesh defines the underlying shape of the 3D object.

- **Materials** refer to the physical surface of an object (for example, the aluminum of a soda can or the felt of a fedora hat). Photoshop uses a number of texture-map characteristics to create the material appearance of a 3D object; you can also define existing two-dimensional Photoshop layers as the material for a mesh.

- **Lighting** affects the way highlights and shadows are created on and by a 3D object. Photoshop supports four different types of lighting (infinite, spot, point, and image) to create different lighting effects.

- **Camera position** refers to the point of view relative to the object. Photoshop includes the ability to move the camera around an object on all three axes.

To understand digital 3D modeling, you should try to think about the way you interact with the world at large. When you walk around a car, for example, you are able to see the different sides of the car; the front, back, and sides all have different appearances.

You should also understand that what you see depends not only on your position relative to an object, but also on the position of the object. For example, if you stand still but someone backs a car into a parking space, you see a different aspect of the same car.

Finally, what you see on a 3D object also depends on the position of the light. When the garage light shines behind you, for example, you might see your own reflection in the car's window. When the interior lights are on, you see more of the car's interior than your reflection.

It's important to keep these overall concepts in mind: 3D modeling considers the physical shape and position of an object, your position relative to the object, and the position of light sources relative to the object.

It is important to realize that whole books are written about Photoshop's 3D features. The exercises in this stage were designed to introduce you to the possibilities relative to enhancing a static image such as the postcards in this project.

CREATE A 3D POSTCARD

The final piece of the BLVD postcard is a second photo, featuring an HDR image of one of the city's new centerpiece attractions — The Roshambo. Photoshop can open existing 3D files created in other applications and import 3D objects as new 3D Photoshop layers. You can also use built-in functionality to create some 3D objects from scratch. In this case, you're going to create a new 3D object from the simplest built-in shape preset — a postcard.

Note:

The HDR image you are using in this exercise was provided by photographer Charlie Essers.

1. **Open the Performance pane of the Preferences dialog box. Make sure the Use Graphics Processor option is checked and click OK.**

   If this option is not available (grayed out) on your computer, your video card and/or driver does not support OpenGL. If you cannot use OpenGL, your 3D options and functionality will be very limited and very slow; all processes will be performed (if possible) by the Photoshop application instead of the video card in your computer.

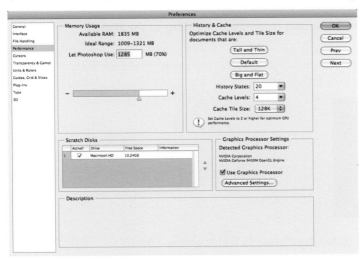

2. **With blvd.psd active, choose File>Place. Select the file roshambo.jpg (in your WIP>Lancaster folder) and click Place.**

3. **Using the Move tool, move the placed layer to the empty area in the bottom-right corner of the canvas. Press Return/Enter to finalize the placement.**

4. **In the Layers panel, Option/Alt-click the Drop Shadow effect for the The BLVD type layer and drag it to the Roshambo layer.**

Option/Alt-drag a specific effect to apply the same effect to a different layer.

5. **Drag the Roshambo layer to the Create a New Layer button at the bottom of the panel.**

   This is an easy way to duplicate a layer. You could also Control/right-click the layer name and choose Duplicate Layer from the contextual menu.

Drag a layer to the Create a New Layer button to duplicate the layer.

Note:

In the final exercise of this project, you will use Layer Comps to export two separate versions of the file using these two separate layers.

   3D extrusions permanently change the layer to a special 3D layer; to maintain the original placed "flat" image and a 3D version of the placed image, you have to use two separate layers.

6. **Click the Effect listing for the Roshambo copy layer and drag to the panel's Delete button.**

   As we explained earlier, effects and styles are non-destructive. You can remove them from a layer by simply dragging to the panel's Delete button.

Drag a layer or effect to the Delete button to permanently remove it from the file.

7. **Change the name of the Roshambo copy layer to Roshambo 3D.**

   This step is simply to make it easier to distinguish one layer from the other. You do not need to include the "3D" tag in a layer that you are using for 3D effects.

8. **Collapse the Effects listings for all layers in the file.**

9. **Hide the Roshambo layer, then select Roshambo 3D as the active layer.**

10. **Choose View>Show>Guides to hide the ruler guides.**

    The 3D workspace has a number of on-screen controls. The ruler guides are no longer necessary, and would simply confuse the visual clarity of the 3D controllers.

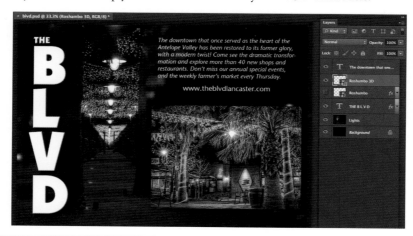

11. Choose 3D>New Mesh from Layer>Postcard.

Photoshop includes a number of prebuilt meshes, which you can add to any file. The most basic mesh — a "postcard" — is simply a two-sided representation of the selected layer. Just like a physical postcard, it has no real depth, but it can be moved in three dimensions to show different aspects of the card.

12. Read the resulting message, then click Yes to automatically switch to the 3D workspace.

Photoshop's built-in 3D workspace includes a number of tools that are useful in controlling a 3D layer. Some of these tools might be intimidating the first time you use the 3D workspace, but they will make more sense when you begin to manipulate the 3D object.

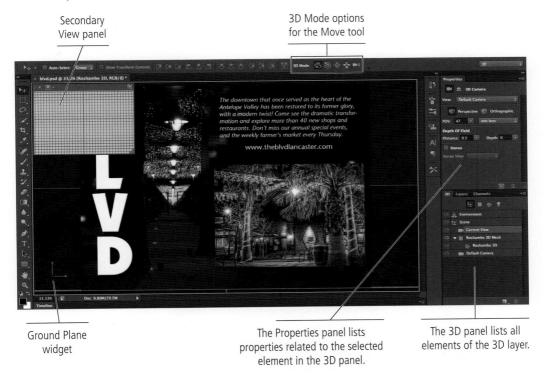

Secondary View panel

3D Mode options for the Move tool

Ground Plane widget

The Properties panel lists properties related to the selected element in the 3D panel.

The 3D panel lists all elements of the 3D layer.

13. **With blⅤd.psd active, review the Roshambo 3D layer in the Layers panel.**

When you create a 3D mesh from an existing layer, that layer shows a number of special attributes. The layer thumbnail includes a 3D icon, and the previous layer content is converted into a material for the active mesh.

This icon identifies a 3D layer.

The selected layer content is converted to a material for the 3D object.

14. **Save the file and continue to the next exercise.**

 ## MOVE AN OBJECT IN 3D

One advantage to working with 3D is the ability to move objects in three directions — left or right, up or down, near or far. You can also rotate the mesh around any axis to change the visible portion of the object.

1. **With blⅤd.psd open, open the menu in the Secondary View panel and choose Default.**

The Default view is the same as what you see in the main document window when you first create the 3D object.

Close View   Select View/Camera   Swap Main and Secondary View

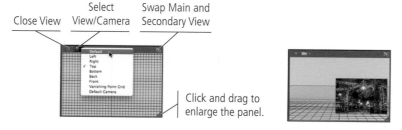

Click and drag to enlarge the panel.

2. **Click and drag in the panel to reposition the mesh and ground plane.**

This panel is a good way to review other aspects of a 3D object without affecting what appears on the canvas. If you find a view you particularly like, you can click the Swap Main and Secondary View button in the top-right corner of the panel to replace the current view on canvas with what you see in the secondary view.

Note:

Press Option and drag in the Secondary View panel to zoom in or out.

Changing the secondary view has no effect on the main document.

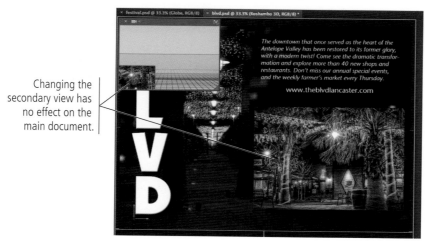

3. **Click the Close View button in the top-left corner of the panel to hide the Secondary View panel.**

4. **Click the 3D Ground Plane widget and drag to reposition the ground plane.**

   As you drag, you can see the ground-plane grid move. The red line in the grid represents the X axis and the blue line represents the Z axis. The gray line behind the image is the theoretical "horizon", which corresponds to the vanishing point for the grid lines.

   When you drag the ground plane on-screen, the Current View is automatically selected in the 3D panel. In the Properties panel (3D Camera mode), the View menu automatically switches to "Custom View".

Note:

You can toggle the visibility of all the 3D on-screen widgets in the View>Show submenu.

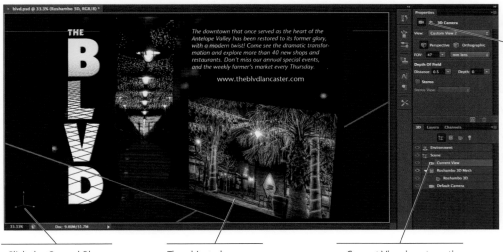

Use these buttons to change modes in the Properties panel.

Click the Ground Plane widget and drag to move the current view.

The object also moves when you change the current view.

Current View is automatically selected when you drag the ground plane.

You should also notice that the 3D object moves along with the ground plane. Basically, rotating the ground plane is like moving the camera to a different location; if you walk around an object with a camera in your hand, the visible area of the object changes with your relative position.

Note:

You can save a specific view preset by choosing Save in the Current View menu.

5. **Click the Coordinates button at the top of the Properties panel.**

   The Properties panel has a number of different modes, depending on what is selected in the 3D panel. The Coordinates mode shows the current position of the camera relative to its original (default) position.

Click here to show the Coordinates.

Note:

Press V to cycle through the modes of the Properties panel.

6. **Click the 3D Camera button at the top of the Properties panel, then choose Default in the View menu to reset the ground plane to its original position.**

   It's important to realize that the changes you make — whether to the scene or to the mesh — are non-destructive; you can reposition either as much as you like, at any time.

7. In the 3D panel, click the Roshambo 3D Mesh.

You could also simply click the mesh on the canvas to select the object.

When the mesh object is selected, the 3D Axis widget appears on screen.

You can apply virtually any changes to the object position using the 3D Axis widget. Each axis in the widget has three different controls:

- **Move Along Axis** changes the position of the object along the selected axis.

- **Rotate Around Axis** changes the rotation of the object around the perpendicular axis. In other words, the control on the red (X) axis rotates the mesh around the green (Y) axis.

- **Scale Along Axis** changes the size of the object along the selected axis.

You can also click the center cube in the widget and drag to scale the object uniformly (on all three axes).

Note:

In the 3D Axis widget, the Y axis is green, the X axis is red, and the Z axis is blue.

Cursor feedback shows the name of the active control.

The active control is yellow.

Y Axis
X Axis
Z Axis

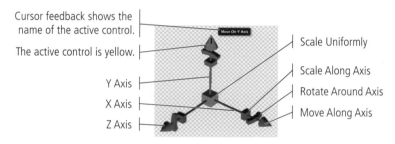

Scale Uniformly

Scale Along Axis

Rotate Around Axis

Move Along Axis

8. In the Properties panel, click the Coordinates button to show the numeric position of the mesh.

9. In the 3D Axis widget, click the Rotate Around Y Axis control (on the red axis) and drag right to rotate the mesh.

When you make changes using the on-screen controls, those changes are reflected in the Coordinates pane of the Properties panel. You can use either method to move, rotate, and scale the selected mesh.

Changes with the on-screen controls are reflected in the Properties panel when you release the mouse button.

Cursor feedback shows the specific transformation as you drag.

10. **Place the cursor over the center cube in the 3D Axis widget. Press Shift, then click and drag up to enlarge the icon.**

Before rotating the mesh in the previous step, it was difficult to see all of the controls in the widget. Making the icon larger makes it easier to access the individual controls.

11. **In the Z Axis (blue) of the widget, click the Rotate Around X Axis control and drag up to rotate the mesh.**

This rotation tilts the mesh front to back.

12. **In the X Axis (red) of the widget, click the Move on X Axis control and drag right to move the mesh until the right edge of the image is past the canvas edge.**

13. **Click the Render button at the bottom of the Properties panel.**

While you work with the 3D mesh, the preview is simply an on-screen representation. Rendering the 3D creates the final, full-resolution version of your 3D object.

Render

This icon moves across the canvas while rendering is being processed.

14. **After the rendering squares have moved across the canvas three times, press ESC to cancel the process.**

For a simple object like this print postcard, three rendering passes generates good-enough quality for the overall project. For complex animation and video applications, you should let the object completely render.

15. **Save the file and continue to the next exercise.**

CREATE A 3D SPHERE

In the previous exercises, you worked with a simple "flat" 3D object. Photoshop includes a number of more complex meshes that allow more flexibility and creativity than a simple postcard. In this exercise, you are going to add a sphere to the festival postcard, with another poppy image as the material on that mesh.

1. **With festival.psd active, create a new empty layer at the top of the layer stack. Change the name of the new layer to Globe.**

2. **In the 3D panel, choose Selected Layer in the Source menu. Choose the Mesh from Preset option, then choose Sphere in the attached menu. Click Create at the bottom of the panel.**

   This has the same general effect as choosing 3D>New Mesh from Layer>Mesh Preset>Sphere. You should try to be aware of your options for accomplishing any particular goal, and determine which is best suited to your personal working preferences.

Note:

If you are not already using the built-in 3D workspace, you will be asked if you want to switch to that workspace before proceeding.

3. **In the 3D panel, select the Sphere_Material.**

4. **In the Properties panel, open the menu next to the Diffuse option and choose Replace Texture.**

Sphere_Material is selected.

5. **Navigate to field.jpg (in your WIP>Lancaster folder) and click Open. If you see a warning about mismatched color profiles, use the embedded profile.**

The selected image becomes the material on the sphere surface.

Understanding 3D Materials Properties

When a 3D object's material is selected in the 3D panel, the top section of the Properties panel defines four types of lights that affect the 3D object:

- **Diffuse** is the color of the surface material, or the file that makes up the reflective surface of the object.

- **Specular** defines the color of areas where the light is 100% reflected (specular highlights).

- **Illumination** is the color of surface areas where the material is transparent; this setting results in the effect of interior lighting, such as a painting on a light bulb.

- **Ambient** defines the color of ambient (environmental) light that is visible on reflective surfaces.

Choose a built-in material from this pop-up panel.

Click these icons to load a texture map for a specific setting.

For each of the types of lighting, you can click the color swatch to change that light's color. For all but Ambient light, you can also use the attached menus to define an existing file (or create a new one) that will be used for that property.

The lower half of the panel defines additional material properties:

- **Shine** defines the dispersion of reflected light. Low values result in more apparent light, and high values result in less apparent light and cleaner highlights.

- **Reflection** increases the strength of reflected objects in the 3D object's surface.

- **Roughness** can be used to cause a surface to appear less polished. Higher roughness makes an object less reflective (think of a chrome bumper that has been scratched by sandpaper).

- **Bump** adds depth in the material surface without altering the actual object mesh. Lighter gray values in the defined texture map create raised areas, and darker gray values create flatter areas.

- **Opacity** determines the transparency of the surface material. If you define a map file for this setting, lighter areas in the map are less transparent, and darker areas are more transparent.

- **Refraction** is the change in light direction that occurs when light strikes a surface (think of the classic "bent pencil in a glass of water" example).

- **Normal** is similar to the Bump option, but can use an RGB image as the texture map file.

- **Environment** stores an image of the environment around the object, which can be seen in reflective areas of the object's surface.

You can load a file to apply as a mesh's surface (as you did in this project). You can also control an object's appearance using a **texture map**, which is (typically) a grayscale image in which different shades determine the strength of a particular setting.

If you choose Edit UV Properties in one of the Texture Map menus, you can control the repeat pattern for the selected texture map. The **Target** menu determines whether changes apply to a specific layer or to the composite image. The **U Scale** and **V Scale** resize the texture; the **U Offset** and **V Offset** values reposition the texture.

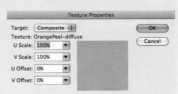

6. **Click the sphere on the canvas to select the mesh object. Using the 3D Axis widget, move the object on the X and Y axes to cover the poppy in the background image.**

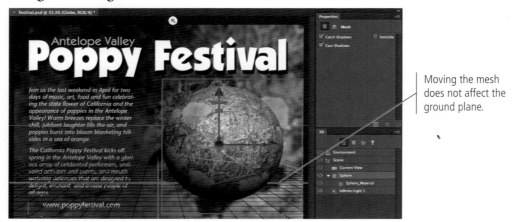

Moving the mesh does not affect the ground plane.

7. **Move the cursor near the vertical edge of the mesh cage. When the cursor feedback shows "Rotate Around Y Axis", click and drag right until the large cluster of poppies is visible on the sphere.**

When the mesh is selected, it is surrounded on the screen by a cage that represents the outer 3D "box" shape. In addition to using the 3D Axis widget, you can also use the mesh cage to make specific changes; cursor feedback shows what you can accomplish by clicking a specific location on the mesh preview.

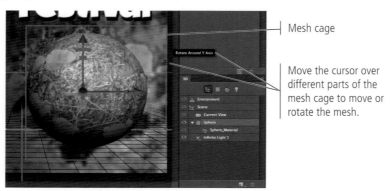

Mesh cage

Move the cursor over different parts of the mesh cage to move or rotate the mesh.

We liked the content that appears when the sphere is rotated almost 180° (as you can see in the Properties panel).

8. **Move the cursor near the top horizontal edge of the mesh cage. When the cursor feedback shows "Rotate Around X Axis", click and drag down until you are satisfied with the image that appears on the sphere surface.**

9. **Click the Scale Uniformly control and drag up to enlarge the sphere proportionally.**

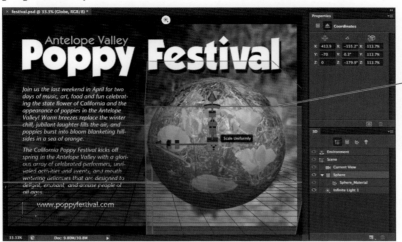

After you rotate around the X axis, you can better see the entire 3D cage.

10. **Click the light widget at the top of the document window.**

   You could also click the Infinite Light 1 option in the 3D panel to select the light.

   The light sources related to a 3D object determine how shadows are cast. The Sphere preset mesh includes one infinite light source, which is a light that shines from a single point far away (like the sun).

Note:

You will learn about all three types of lighting effects in Project 6: Advertising Samples.

11. **Click the light handle in the on-screen preview and drag until the shadow on the bottom of the sphere is strongest on the bottom-right side of the mesh.**

   This position better matches the shadow style that is applied to the type layers.

Click the light widget to select it.

Drag the light handle to change the direction of the light source.

Changing the direction of the light changes the shadows that appear on the sphere and that are cast on the ground plane.

You should notice that the shadow on the ground plane is far behind the sphere, and does not appear natural. This is the result of Step 6, when you moved the object mesh away from the ground plane.

12. **Choose 3D>Snap Object to Ground Plane.**

After snapping the object to the ground plane, the ground plane shadow seems more natural.

13. **Click the ground plane (away from the mesh) to select it.**

14. **Choose the Drag the 3D Object mode in the Options bar.**

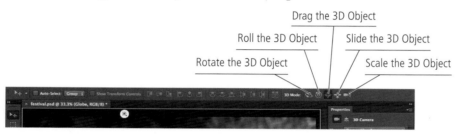

Drag the 3D Object

Roll the 3D Object

Slide the 3D Object

Rotate the 3D Object

Scale the 3D Object

The 3D tool modes can be used to change various properties of the selected scene attribute (the current view or a specific mesh).

Note:

These tools do not work well for the mesh object when the 3D Selection options are showing.

- **3D Object Rotate mode.** Drag up-down to rotate the object around the X axis, or left-right to rotate around the Y axis. Press Option/Alt to rotate the object around the Z axis.

- **3D Object Roll mode.** Drag left-right to rotate the object around the Z axis.

- **3D Object Drag mode.** Drag left-right to move the object horizontally, or up-down to move the object vertically, without affecting its depth or rotation. Press Option/Alt and drag up-down to move the object along the X/Z axis (horizontally far to near).

- **3D Object Slide mode.** Drag left-right to move the object horizontally, or up-down to move the object on the X/Z axis (horizontally far to near). Press Option/Alt and drag up/down to move the object along the X and Y axes simultaneously.

- **3D Object Scale mode.** Drag up-down to make the object proportionally larger or smaller. Press Option/Alt to scale the object along the Z axis only.

15. Click and drag until the sphere is back in the same relative position as before you snapped it to the ground plane.

By moving the ground plane, you are changing the view of the object without changing the actual mesh object. You can see the effect most clearly by observing the shadow that is cast by the sphere.

When you move the ground plane, you also move the object mesh.

16. Click the infinite light widget to select it again. In the Properties panel, change the Shadow Softness slider to 50%.

Now that you can better see the shadow, you can make more informed changes. The Softness option creates a blurrier edge on the ground-plane shadow.

The light is selected in the 3D panel.

Use this option to soften the shadow edges.

17. Select the Environment in the 3D panel. In the Properties panel, change the Ground Plane Shadows Opacity to 75%.

This darkens the shadow that is cast by the sphere onto the ground plane, but does not affect the shadow on the surface of the sphere.

Environment is selected in the 3D panel.

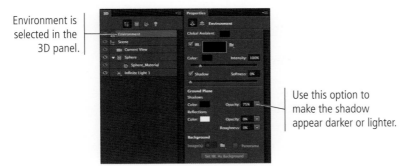

Use this option to make the shadow appear darker or lighter.

18. **Click the Render button at the bottom of the Properties panel.**

The complete rendering process takes a long time, depending on the power of your computer processor. Be patient! The status area at the bottom-left corner of your document window shows the time remaining to complete the rendering process.

When the rendering is complete, the sphere edges and the ground-plane shadow show a distinct improvement over the working on-screen preview.

The status area shows the time remaining in the rendering process.

19. **Save the file and then close it.**

20. **Continue to the final exercise of the project.**

 CREATE LAYER COMPS

The Layer Comps feature allows you to save multiple iterations of a file at one time. A layer comp can store the position and visibility of individual layers, as well as any effects applied. This feature is useful when you want to experiment with the position of specific layers, but you want to keep a record of earlier positions of the layers — or, as in this case, when you want to present two versions of a file: one version with a layer visible, and one version with a layer hidden.

It's important to know that layer comps do not store pixel information. Modifying the actual pixel data on a layer will not be undone by reverting to an earlier layer comp. To undo that kind of change, you must use the History panel and snapshots, assuming you haven't closed the file since you created the snapshots.

1. **With festival.psd open, open the Layer Comps panel (Window>Layer Comps).**

2. **Without changing anything in the file, click the New Layer Comp button.**

3. In the New Layer Comp dialog box, name the comp Final 3D. Make sure the Visibility option is checked, and then click OK.

When you choose the Visibility option, only the currently visible layers (in this case, all of them) will be included in the comp.

New Layer Comp button

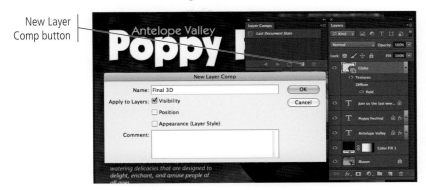

4. In the Layers panel, hide the Globe layer.

5. Create a second layer comp named Final Flat, again including only the layer visibility attributes in the comp.

Because you hid the Globe layer in Step 4, checking the visibility option prevents that layer from being included in the comp.

The Globe layer is hidden.

This icon shows the currently applied comp.

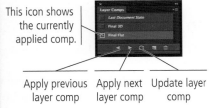

Apply previous layer comp   Apply next layer comp   Update layer comp

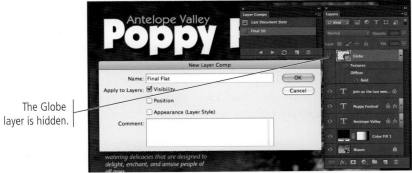

6. Choose File>Scripts>Layer Comps to Files.

7. In the Layer Comps to Files dialog box, choose JPEG in the File Type menu, and leave the remaining options at their default values.

8. **Make sure the WIP>Lancaster folder is selected in the Destination field, and make sure festival appears in the File Name Prefix field.**

   This script creates separate files for each layer comp. The target location defaults to the same location as the working file, and the file name defaults to the current file name.

9. **Click Run.**

   The process could take a while to complete; don't panic and don't get impatient. When the file is done, you will see the message shown here.

   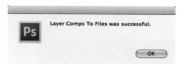

10. **Click OK to close the message, and then save and close the Photoshop file.**

11. **Repeat this process to create two versions of the BLVD postcard. Make sure you show the Roshambo layer when you create the "flat" layer comp. Also make sure the File Name Prefix field accurately reflects the files that you are exporting.**

    There appears to be a bug in the software; when you open this dialog box the second time, the file name defaults to the last-used option. If you don't change it to "blvd", you would overwrite the festival postcard versions.

12. **Save and close the blvd.psd file.**

fill in the blank

1. _____ identifies and tries to protect areas of detail when you scale the image.

2. _____ allows you to move a selection, filling the original selection area with detail instead of leaving an empty hole.

3. A _____ effect applies a consistent blur over the entire selected layer.

4. _____ is created by simply clicking (without dragging) with one of the Type tools.

5. _____ is the distance from one baseline to the next in a paragraph of type.

6. The _____ tools can be used to create selections in the shape of individual characters or entire words.

7. _____ describes the space between individual type characters (where the insertion point is placed).

8. _____ cannot be applied to type layers; you must first rasterize a type layer to apply them.

9. A(n) _____ light source shines as a single point from a seemingly far distance.

10. A(n) _____ stores the visibility of specific layers at a given point.

short answer

1. Briefly describe the result of moving a selection with the Move tool.

2. Briefly explain the difference between point type and area type.

3. Briefly explain the concept of a material, as it relates to a 3D object.

Portfolio Builder Project

Use what you learned in this project to complete the following freeform exercise.
Carefully read the art director and client comments, then create your own design to meet the needs of the project.
Use the space below to sketch ideas; when finished, write a brief explanation of your reasoning behind your final design.

art director comments

Your local chamber of commerce saw the postcards you created for the city of Lancaster, and they would like to create a similar campaign promoting local points of interest.

To complete this project, you should:

❏ Research attractions and points of interest in your community. Choose two areas that you will feature in the postcard series.

❏ Include at least two paragraphs of descriptive text and a Web address for each attraction.

❏ Find or take at least two photos to use in each postcard.

❏ Use the same physical specifications that you used in the Lancaster postcards.

❏ Export all files to JPEG.

client comments

The client wants to do a postcard campaign to promote local tourism, but that's as much information as we have. They didn't provide any content for this project — unfortunately, not an uncommon occurrence.

It will be up to you to write copy and take photos. These are only postcards, so don't use too much copy — one or two paragraphs at most. The Web address is really more important anyway, so that should be prominent.

You don't have to incorporate 3D into the files, but the client did like your other postcards — which means you should definitely consider using 3D in these files. I'd recommend doing versions with and without the 3D, and we can submit both as approval proofs.

project justification

_____

_____

_____

_____

_____

_____

_____

_____

_____

_____

_____

_____

_____

Completing this project required a number of new skills for manipulating layer content — scaling and moving selections, applying blur effects, and working with layer styles. By now you should understand the difference between working with an entire layer and working with only a selected area, and be able to choose the appropriate tools to affect only what you want to change.

You also did a considerable amount of work with type, which can be either created from scratch or pasted from a text editor. Although the type controls in Photoshop are not quite as robust as those in formal page layout applications — which are specifically designed to create and control large blocks of type — they are certainly useful for a range of different applications.

You learned how to create both point and area type, as well as the different formatting options that are available for selected characters or entire paragraphs. You also worked with a number of tools that create unique artistic effects from a Photoshop type layer — sampling colors from an image to format type, applying styles to type layers, and changing layer opacity and blending modes.

Finally, you learned the basics of working with 3D objects. As we already stated, we didn't even come close to explaining everything there is to know about 3D. However, you did experiment with a number of the options that are most relevant to print designers.

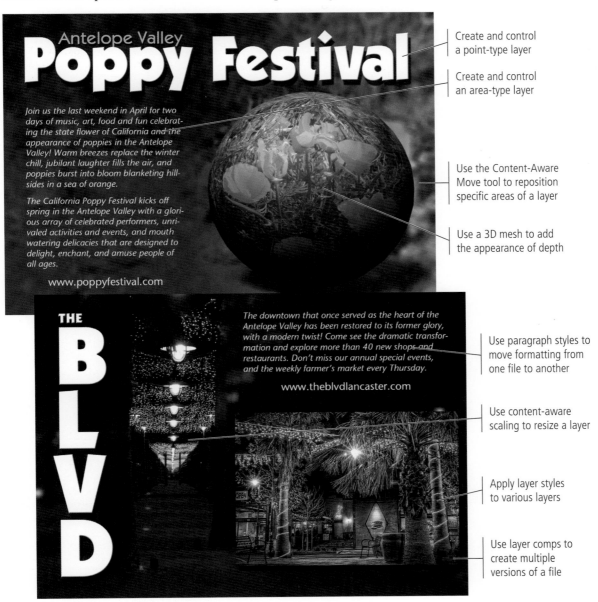

Create and control a point-type layer

Create and control an area-type layer

Use the Content-Aware Move tool to reposition specific areas of a layer

Use a 3D mesh to add the appearance of depth

Use paragraph styles to move formatting from one file to another

Use content-aware scaling to resize a layer

Apply layer styles to various layers

Use layer comps to create multiple versions of a file

Catalog Cover

Your client is a mail-order children's clothing company that sends monthly catalogs to a large mailing list throughout the United States. July is their biggest sales month since parents are buying their children new clothes for the start of the school year. The company hired your agency to create the new fall catalog, which will be mailed in mid-June. Your job is to build the catalog cover.

This project incorporates the following skills:

❑ Using filters and adjustments to identify edges in a complex image

❑ Creating a complex mask by adjusting an Alpha channel

❑ Painting directly on an Alpha channel

❑ Compositing a background image with special effects

❑ Adding layer effects to spot-color objects

❑ Building a spot channel for a special ink color

❑ Creating warped and spot-color type

client comments

We don't have a physical store front, so we depend on mail-order for our business. Although many sales come from our Web site, other customers prefer printed catalogs. And since we get so many orders from those catalogs, we print and mail thousands of every issue.

Each catalog cover features a child wearing an item from our new product line. Our photographer did a great job for this year's back-to-school issue. The model's name is Stephanie and we love her photo. We'd like you to put some kind of image behind the picture of Stephanie that says "school" without being overwhelming or taking too much attention away from the girl's face.

Our catalog covers are printed on a six-color press. Each issue uses a different spot color for our company name and some kind of banner, as well as a flood varnish on the sixth press unit. For the fall, we were thinking of using a yellow "school bus" color.

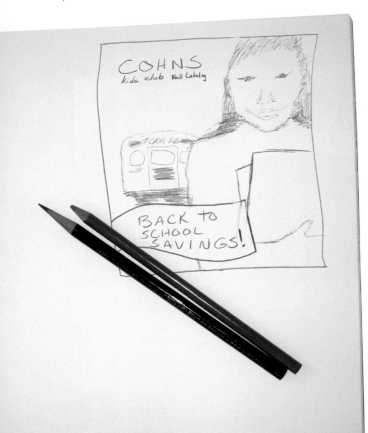

art director comments

The clients were fairly specific about what they want. Since this is the back-to-school issue, I found a good picture of a school bus that will work well as the background image.

The hardest part of this job is going to be isolating Stephanie from her background so you can put the bus behind her. Any time you have a person in a photo, you have to deal with hair — and little wisps can be extremely difficult to isolate in a selection. Photoshop has some good tools for making this task a bit easier, but it still requires manual intervention.

The catalog is 7.75 × 9.75″ trimmed, so you need to build the final file to that size with 1/8″ bleeds. The job will be printed on a web press because of the high volume.

For the fifth color, we will use Pantone 810, which is a warm yellow very much like the color in the bus photo. The yellow type, banner, and bus will contrast nicely with the blue in Stephanie's shirt. Be aware that using spot colors in Photoshop requires a few tricks and workarounds that are different from what you do when you work with regular image channels.

project objectives

To complete this project, you will:

❏ Duplicate an image channel to create an Alpha channel mask

❏ Use effects filters and Levels adjustments to isolate edges in an Alpha channel

❏ Posterize an Alpha channel to remove shading

❏ Use the Brush and Eraser tools to complete a complex mask

❏ Composite a complex image onto a different background image

❏ Edit a background image for visual impact

❏ Create a spot channel for a fifth ink separation, and add design elements to the spot channel

❏ Save the file in the DCS format to preserve spot-color information

Stage 1 Creating a Complex Selection

You have already learned a number of different ways to make selections, from basic shape selections with a marquee to color-based selections using the Color Range options. There are some images, however, that defy these tools. Specifically, images with various colors with thin lines and complex edges can be difficult to isolate. The girl's picture for this project is a perfect example.

You need to isolate the girl from the gray background.

These thin wisps of hair can be very difficult to cleanly separate from a background.

The foreground has too many different hues to allow a color-based selection.

EVALUATE AND DUPLICATE AN EXISTING IMAGE CHANNEL

An Alpha channel based on existing image data is the best option for creating this type of complex mask. Creating that channel is a multi-step process, beginning with evaluating the individual image channels to find the one with the most contrast.

1. Download **PS6_RF_Project5.zip** from the Student Files Web page.

2. **Expand the ZIP archive in your WIP folder (Macintosh) or copy the archive contents into your WIP folder (Windows).**

   This results in a folder named **Catalog**, which contains the files you need for this project. You should also use this folder to save the files you create in this project.

3. **Open the file kid.jpg from your WIP>Catalog folder and display the Channels panel. If you see a warning about mismatched profiles, use the image's embedded profile.**

4. **Open the Channels panel Options menu and choose Panel Options. In the resulting dialog box, select the large thumbnail, and then click OK.**

   Every RGB image has a composite channel and three color channels (one for each primary color), and every CMYK image has a composite channel and four color channels. When working with channels, the larger thumbnail can be helpful.

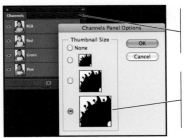

Click here to access the Channels panel Options menu.

The largest thumbnail provides more information directly within the Channels panel.

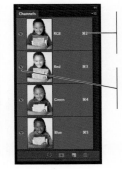

Use these keyboard shortcuts to view individual image channels.

Click these icons to toggle the visibility of individual channels.

5. **Click the Red channel in the panel to view only that channel in the image window.**

Each pixel in an RGB image has a value of 0 to 255 for each of three channels. When you look at individual channels, you see the grayscale representation of tones for that color channel.

6. **Click the Green channel in the panel to view only that channel in the image window.**

Note:

In the Interface pane of the Preferences dialog box, you can check the Show Channels in Color option to show individual channels in color instead of grayscale.

7. **Click the Blue channel in the panel to view only that channel in the image window.**

This channel has the greatest edge contrast; you'll use it to build your Alpha channel.

8. **Click the Blue channel in the panel and drag it to the Create New Channel button at the bottom of the panel.**

Dragging an existing channel onto the Create New Channel button creates an exact copy of the channel. The resulting channel — named "Blue copy" — is automatically created as an Alpha channel.

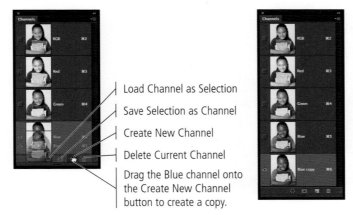

Load Channel as Selection

Save Selection as Channel

Create New Channel

Delete Current Channel

Drag the Blue channel onto the Create New Channel button to create a copy.

Note:

New channels are automatically created as Alpha channels. You can also create a new spot-color channel using the Channels panel Options menu (which you will do later in this project).

9. **In the Channels panel, click the empty space to the left of the RGB composite channel (the location of the eye icon) to make the composite image visible behind the Blue copy Alpha channel.**

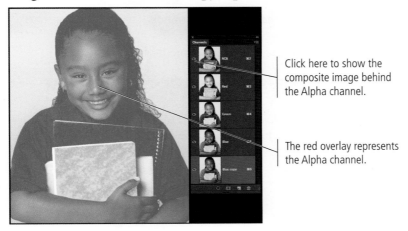

Click here to show the composite image behind the Alpha channel.

The red overlay represents the Alpha channel.

10. **With the Blue copy channel still selected, choose Channel Options from the Channels panel Options menu.**

11. **Change the channel name to Girl Mask and change the Opacity field to 100%.**

12. **Click OK to change the channel options.**

When you're finished with this stage of the project, the 100% opaque mask will entirely obscure the girl, and the background will have no red overlay.

Note:

You can't save an Alpha channel in a JPEG image, so you should use the native Photoshop format (as you should anyway for a work in progress).

13. **Save the file in your WIP>Catalog folder as a native Photoshop file named** girl_masked.psd **using the default options.**

14. **Continue to the next exercise.**

FIND AND ISOLATE EDGES IN THE ALPHA CHANNEL

There are several ways to find the edges in an image, using either image adjustments or filters. The specific image might determine which option is best. In many cases — including this project — the best approach is a combination of two or more methods.

1. **With** girl_masked.psd **open from your WIP>Catalog folder, click the eye icons to hide all but the Girl Mask channel.**

This channel already has fairly good edge contrast, but the channel still shows a large range of shades; the final channel mask, on the other hand, ultimately needs only two shades — masked (black) and not masked (white).

When the RGB channels are not visible, the Alpha channel appears as a grayscale image.

2. **With the Girl Mask channel selected, choose Filter>Other>High Pass.**

The High Pass filter maintains edge details and turns non-edges gray. The Radius value determines the difference in pixels required to define an edge. Lower Radius values result in more edges and less transition detail between the edges and non-edges; higher Radius values result in fewer edges and a pronounced halo effect between edges and non-edges.

3. **Drag the Radius slider right until you see a strong halo around the girl's outline (we used a 75-pixel radius).**

This process could work with a small Radius value, but the halo effect of the higher radius is important here. The white areas behind the wispy hair will become white areas in the Alpha channel mask — eliminating the need to later manually edit out those areas.

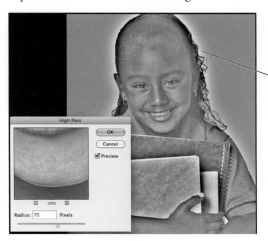

The high Radius value adds a halo large enough to surround the girl's hair, which will become an important part of the Alpha channel mask.

4. **Click OK to apply the filter and return to the image window.**

The next step is to increase the contrast between the edges and the non-edges so you can easily fill in and erase as necessary to create the mask — in essence, you want to turn this Alpha channel into a coloring book that is easy to fill in between the lines. As you learned in Project 3: Menu Image Correction, using Levels is one of the easiest ways to increase contrast.

5. **With the Girl Mask channel still selected in the Channels panel, choose Image>Adjustments>Levels.**

The histogram in the Levels dialog box reflects the distribution of pixels across the available tonal range in the selected channel only. The High Pass filter produced a lot of middle grays, with black edges and white halos.

6. **Drag the Input Shadow slider right until the associated field shows 120.**

7. **Drag the Input Highlight slider left until the associated field shows 136.**

Remember, when you move the Input sliders in the Levels dialog box, you define the available tonal range. Using these settings in the Levels dialog box, you define a tonal range of only 17 possible values. The image shows the result of the settings — most pixels have been pushed to either pure black or pure white; the edges are very pronounced, even in the areas with the wispy hair.

Note:

The Input Shadow slider is on the left end of the histogram.

The Input Highlight slider is on the right end of the histogram.

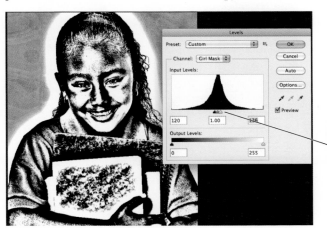

The adjusted Input Shadow and Input Highlight sliders limit the tonal range to only 17 possible values.

"Other" Filters

The Filter>Other submenu includes four options in addition to the High Pass filter. This miscellany of filters really doesn't fit anywhere else, so the filters are lumped together under "Other."

Custom allows you to change the Brightness values of each pixel in the image based on a mathematical operation known as convolution. Each pixel is reassigned a value based on the values of surrounding pixels. You can click Save in this dialog box to save your settings as a custom filter, which you can then reload for any other image.

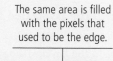

The Custom dialog box displays a grid of fields. The center field represents the pixel being evaluated; each surrounding field represents the pixel in the same position around the pixel being evaluated. The numbers in each field determine how much the brightness of each pixel is being multiplied (from −999 to +999); you don't have to enter values in all the text boxes. The value in the Scale field divides the sum of the Brightness values of the pixels included in the calculation. The value in the Offset field is added to the result of the scale calculation.

The **Maximum** filter has the effect of expanding white areas and shrinking black areas (called a **choke**). The **Minimum** filter has the opposite effect, expanding black areas and shrinking white areas (called a **spread**). These filters replace a pixel's Brightness value with the highest (Maximum) or lowest (Minimum) Brightness value of surrounding pixels within the defined radius.

Offset moves a selection a specified horizontal or vertical amount. (The Offset filter can be applied to any selection — part of a layer, an entire layer, an entire channel, or an entire image.) Moving a selection results in empty areas where the original pixels used to reside; the Undefined Areas options define how those areas will be filled:

- **Set to Background** fills those areas with the current background color.
- **Repeat Edge Pixels** creates a streak-like effect from the pixels at the edge of the moved selection.
- **Wrap Around** creates a tiled effect by filling the empty area with pixels from the moved selection.

The new empty area
is filled with the
background color.

The same area is filled
with the pixels that
used to be the edge.

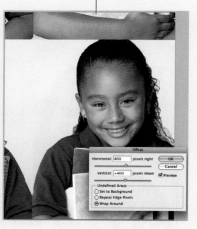

The selection is
wrapped around to
fill the empty areas.

8. **Click OK to close the Levels dialog box and make the RGB composite channel visible behind the Alpha channel.**

   Because you had the Girl Mask channel selected when you made the High Pass and Levels changes, you did not affect the actual image pixels. It's important to remember that you are only editing the mask channel in this stage of the project.

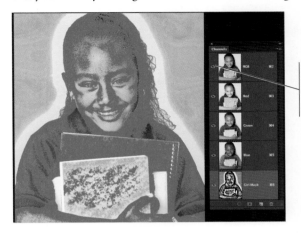

Click here to make the composite image visible behind the mask channel.

9. **Save the file and continue to the next exercise.**

 ## REMOVE SHADING FROM THE ALPHA CHANNEL

When you adjusted the levels of the Girl Mask channel, you reduced the tonal range to 17 possible tones. In Project 2: African Wildlife Map, however, we explained that the values in an Alpha channel are actually degrees of transparency (see page 108). When you view the composite image behind the Alpha channel, you can still see through some of the red mask to the actual image pixels. The complete mask requires pixels to be either solid black (masked) or solid white (not masked) — in other words, the mask channel should have only two tones or levels.

1. **With girl_masked.psd open, hide the composite RGB channel and make sure the Girl Mask channel is selected.**

2. **Choose Image>Adjustments>Posterize.**

   The word "posterize" means to reduce an image to only a few different shades — which is exactly what you need to do in this step.

3. **In the Posterize dialog box, drag the Levels slider all the way to the left until the field shows that the mask channel uses only 2 levels.**

Posterizing to 2 levels means all pixels in the mask are now either solid white or solid black.

4. **Click OK in the Posterize dialog box to apply the adjustment, and then make the RGB composite channel visible behind the Alpha channel.**

Although there are still unfilled areas on the mask, there are no longer any semi-transparent red areas.

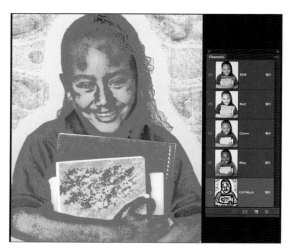

5. **Save the file and continue to the next exercise.**

Special Effects Adjustments

In addition to Posterize, several other options in the Image>Adjustments submenu are used to create special effects that mimic photographic techniques that predate digital image manipulation.

The **Invert** adjustment reverses the color values of the image, creating the effect of a photographic negative.

The **Equalize** adjustment extends the Brightness values of an image so they occupy the entire range of available brightness levels (from 1 to 99%). The lightest part of the image is mapped to full brightness and the darkest part of the image is mapped to black. Although this might sound very similar to extending the tonal range with Levels, the Equalize adjustment typically produces choppy results; it is best used when you want to create special effects rather than fine color adjustments.

Invert

The **Threshold** adjustment converts images to high-contrast bitmap images. Pixels in the resulting image are either black or white; there are no intermediate shades of gray. Any pixels with a value lower than the defined Threshold Level are black; pixels with a value higher than the defined Threshold Level are white.

Equalize

Threshold

ERASE AND PAINT THE ALPHA CHANNEL

Your mask channel still needs a bit of clean-up work to fill in some areas (where the girl is still visible) and remove unwanted parts (in the background area). Combining the High Pass filter with an extreme Levels adjustment created a fairly clear set of edges that will make the final clean-up easier.

1. **With girl_masked.psd open, hide the composite RGB channel and make sure the Girl Mask channel is selected.**

2. **In the Tools panel, click the button to restore the default foreground and background colors to white and black (respectively).**

   When all the color channels are hidden, or when a layer mask is the active selection, the default foreground and background colors are reversed — white is the foreground and black is the background. To fill the solid black areas on the mask channel, you can either use the Eraser tool with the default foreground and background colors, or you can reverse the default foreground and background colors and paint with the Brush tool.

Note:

Be very careful when you paint directly on an Alpha channel.

3. **Select the Eraser tool in the Tools panel.**

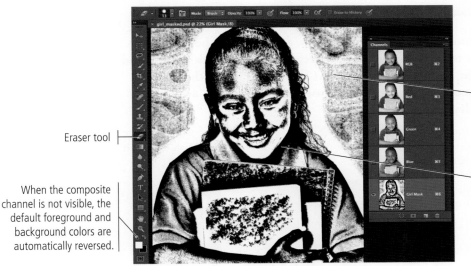

Eraser tool

When the composite channel is not visible, the default foreground and background colors are automatically reversed.

These areas need to be removed from the mask (white).

The area inside the heavy black edges needs to be entirely filled with black.

4. **In the Options bar, choose Brush from the Mode menu.**

   You can use the Eraser tool as a solid square block, using the same settings as the Pencil tool or Brush tool.

Note:

When a specific channel is selected, the Eraser tool basically "paints" the background color on the selected channel.

5. **Choose a large, round brush with 100% hardness, 100% opacity, and 100% flow.**

   Since the areas you need to fill are fairly well defined, you can start with a large brush size, and then use smaller brush sizes when you need to work on more detailed areas.

6. **Click with the Eraser tool to fill in areas of solid black on the mask channel, avoiding any area of fine detail (especially around the girl's ears and neck).**

The following image shows how far we got with the 250-pixel brush. We zoomed in closely to the edges so we could see exactly where the lines appeared. Around the edges, we used individual clicks of the Eraser tool rather than dragging strokes.

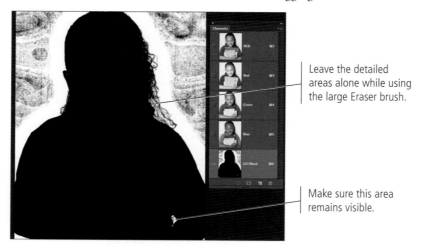

Leave the detailed areas alone while using the large Eraser brush.

Make sure this area remains visible.

7. **Switch the background and foreground colors, and then use the same large-brush Eraser tool to remove the gray areas from the image background. If necessary, use the bracket keys to reduce ([ ) or enlarge ( ]) the brush size so you can remove most of the pixels from the background area. Again, ignore the hair areas for now.**

Because the background color is now white, using the Eraser tool "paints" white in place of the gray background pixels. You can achieve the same result using the Brush tool with the foreground color set to white.

The Eraser tool is still selected.

The background color is now white.

8. **Make the RGB composite channel visible behind the mask channel.**

Viewing both the composite and Alpha channels, you can now clearly see what still needs to be filled.

9. **Zoom in to the girl's face.**

10. **Use either the Brush tool with a black foreground color or the Eraser tool with a black background color to fill in the detailed areas of the mask.**

11. Adjust the brush size as necessary to be as accurate as possible in the detail areas.

When viewing only the Alpha channel, it was difficult to tell exactly what needed to be masked.

When composite color channels are visible, the default foreground color is black and background color is white.

Note:

When using any tool that has a brush size, press [to dynamically decrease the brush size or press] to increase the brush size.

12. When you are satisfied with your mask, save the file and close it, then continue to the next stage of the project.

Stage 2 Compositing Complex Selections

The main goal of this project is to create a catalog cover by compositing two images, several type layers, and a banner shape on a spot channel. The best approach for creating this composite piece is to build a new file where you can place all the pieces.

DEFINE THE COMPOSITE FILE

Because this catalog cover is being designed for print, you should build the main file using the CMYK color mode. The two images you will composite into the cover are in the RGB mode, however, which means you need to evaluate the potential for color shift when you copy the two images into your composite file.

Keep the following job requirements in mind as you complete this exercise:

- Trim size: 7.75″ × 9.75″
- Printing method: Web press
- Bleeds: 0.125″ on all four sides

1. Create a new file (File>New) named `catalog` that is 8″ wide by 10″ high, set to 300 pixels per inch, using the CMYK color mode and a white background. In the Advanced options, choose U.S. Web Coated (SWOP) v2 as the color profile.

2. Click OK to create the new file.

3. **Place a guide at 0.125″ (1/8″) away from each edge of the canvas.**

These guides mark the trim size of the piece.

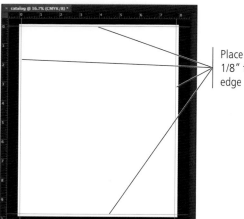

Place ruler guides 1/8″ from each edge of the canvas.

4. **Save the file as a Photoshop file named `catalog_working.psd` in your WIP>Catalog folder, and continue to the next exercise.**

VERIFY COLOR IN THE COMPONENT IMAGES

As we stated in the previous exercise, the two images for this cover are currently in the RGB color mode. When you paste the images into the composite file, they will be converted to the working space of the composite file (U.S. Web Coated (SWOP) v2). Rather than leaving color issues to chance, you should check for potential problem areas in the two images before pasting them into the main file.

1. **Open `girl_masked.psd` from your WIP>Catalog folder. Make sure the Girl Mask channel is hidden and the composite RGB channel is visible and selected.**

As you did in previous projects, if you see a profile mismatch warning, use the image's embedded profile.

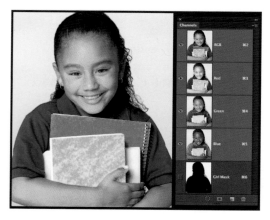

2. **Choose View>Proof Setup>Custom.**

If you continued to this project from Project 3: Menu Image Correction, your defined CMYK working space will be U.S. Sheetfed Coated v2. If you or someone else has changed the color settings, the CMYK working space might be different. By choosing Custom in the View>Proof Setup submenu, you can proof to any destination profile without changing the defined working space.

3. **In the Customize Proof Condition dialog box, choose U.S. Web Coated (SWOP) v2 in the Device to Simulate menu.**

This is the working profile of the composite file you created in the previous exercise, so you should use this profile for proofing colors.

4. **Click OK to close the dialog box.**

5. **Choose View>Gamut Warning.**

You might remember from Project 3: Menu Image Correction that out-of-gamut colors are highlighted with a gray overlay. With the gamut warning turned on, it appears that all colors in this image are within the U.S. Web Coated (SWOP) v2 gamut.

6. **Open the file bus.jpg from the WIP>Catalog folder.**

7. **Choose View>Gamut Warning.**

The Proof Setup menu remembers your previous choice, so you don't need to re-establish the destination profile to simulate.

The gamut warning shows a small area of color that will shift when the file is copied into the composite file. However, you are ultimately going to blur this image as part of the composite background; you are using the image to suggest a theme, not show an exact representation. So in this case, you can accept the small amount of color shift.

You can see areas of this image that are out of gamut, but the shift won't have a negative effect in the composite cover.

8. **Choose View>Gamut Warning to toggle that option off.**

9. **Leave the girl and bus files open and continue to the next exercise.**

COMPOSITE THE COMPONENT IMAGES

You already know how to move pixels from one file to another. You can copy (or simply drag) an entire layer or even a specific selection using the Move tool. Once the two component images are composited into the catalog file, you can start to make adjustments so the two images work together as a single composition.

1. **With all three images open, (bus.jpg, girl_masked.psd, and catalog_working.psd), make catalog_working the active file, then choose Window>Arrange>3-Up Stacked.**

2. **Display the Layers panel.**

3. **Using the Move tool, drag the image layer from the bus file into the catalog_working file.**

4. **Close the bus file.**

5. **Make girl_masked.psd the active file, then choose Select>Load Selection.**

   One advantage of using Alpha channels is that they can be loaded at any time.

   In the Load Selection dialog box, the document menu automatically shows the active document, and the Channel menu defaults to the only available Alpha channel (Girl Mask). If you have more than one Alpha channel, you can use this menu to determine which selection you want to make.

6. Activate the Invert check box.

A mask protects the areas it covers. When you load this Alpha channel as a selection, you are actually selecting anything that is not red when the channel is visible. In this case, you want to select the area that is red (the girl), so you must invert the selection.

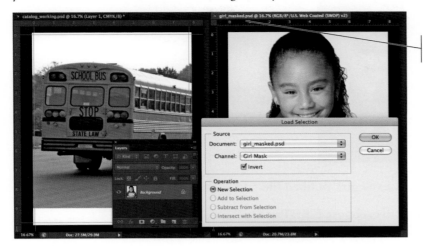

The girl_masked file is active.

Note:

You can also select an Alpha channel in the Channels panel and click the Load Channel as Selection button at the bottom of the panel.

7. Click OK to create the selection.

This type of complex selection often results in halos around fine edges. Modifying the selection slightly will prevent the halo effect from occurring without destroying the edge detail.

8. Choose Select>Modify>Feather.

9. In the Feather Selection dialog box, change the Feather Radius field to 1.5 pixels and click OK.

10. **In the Channels panel, make sure the RGB composite channel — not the Girl Mask channel — is selected.**

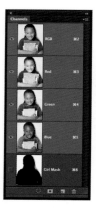

11. **Choose Edit>Copy, and then close the girl_masked file.**

12. **With the catalog_working file active, choose Edit>Paste.**

The original photo was captured at the appropriate size for the catalog cover, so when you paste the photo, it matches the catalog_working file size.

Using Edit>Paste, the girl is pasted into the center of the catalog file.

Because the Alpha channel was not selected in the girl file, the Alpha channel is not pasted into the catalog file.

13. **Save catalog_working.psd. Click OK if you see a warning about maximizing compatibility, and continue to the next exercise.**

Transform the Component Images

Now that the two images are in the main file, you can position and manipulate them to create a unified design. Each image occupies its own layer, making it easy to control the various pieces.

1. **With catalog_working.psd open, rename Layer 1 as Bus and rename Layer 2 as Girl.**

   Meaningful layer names are always a good idea, even if the file has only a few layers.

2. **Select the Girl layer. Using the Move tool, drag right until her head occupies only the right half of the page.**

   It might be helpful if you place a guide to mark the horizontal center of the page, but this isn't necessary.

3. **Select the Bus layer and enter Free Transform mode (Edit>Free Transform or Command/Control-T).**

Note:

You might want to press Shift to constrain the movement to be exactly horizontal.

4. **Scale the layer to 85% proportionally, and drag it so the back end of the bus is directly inside the left trim guide, and the top edge of the bus is about 2.5″ from the top of the image.**

The bus image is still very strong, and it takes too much attention away from the girl.

The girl's positioning leaves the cut-off portion of her arm visible. You'll use a banner to hide that flaw.

Resizing the picture leaves an empty space at the bottom, which needs to be fixed.

5. **Press Return/Enter to finalize the transformation.**

6. **Use the Clone Stamp tool to fill in pavement in the bottom-left corner of the Bus layer.**

7. **With the Bus layer selected, choose Filter>Blur>Motion Blur.**

8. **Apply a blur to the bus so the image becomes less prominent.**

    We applied a 70-pixel blur with a –9° angle.

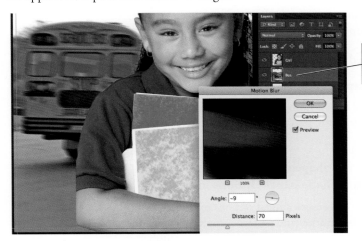

The filter is applied to the selected layer only.

9. **Choose File>Place. Select the file Logotype.ai in the WIP>Catalog folder, then click Place. In the resulting Place PDF dialog box, use the Crop To Bounding Box option, and click OK.**

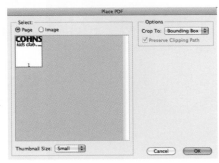

Note:

Recall from Project 1: Composite Movie Ad that Adobe Illustrator uses PDF as its underlying file structure. The Place PDF dialog box shows the options that are available for placing PDF (and Illustrator) files.

10. **Press Return/Enter to finalize the placement.**

11. **Use the Move tool to position the logotype layer content in the white space in the upper-left corner of the image.**

The client provided this logotype, with the season added in the appropriate location. Remember, though, that the company name (COHNS) needs to be set in the fifth color; you'll manage that process in the next stage of this project.

12. **Save the file and continue to the next exercise.**

 ## CREATE A SHAPE LAYER

The only piece of the cover left to create is the banner, which will ultimately be placed on a spot channel. Working with spot channels is one of the few areas of weakness in Photoshop, so the best option is to create the objects as regular layers, and then copy the relevant bits to a spot channel later.

1. **With catalog_working.psd open, click the top layer (Girl) to make it the active layer.**

You want the shape layer to appear at the top of the layer stack. By first selecting the topmost layer, the new shape layer you are about to create will automatically appear directly above the selected layer — at the top of the layer stack.

2. **Choose the Custom Shape tool (nested under the Rectangle tool).**

3. **In the Options bar, make sure the Shape option is selected.**

Like the Pen tool, the shape tools (including the Custom Shape tool) can be used to create a vector-based shape layer, a path, or pixels of a solid color. In this case, you want to create a new shape layer.

4. **Click the arrow button to the right of the Shape menu to open the Custom Shape panel, and then show the Custom Shape panel Options menu.**

The options in this menu should be familiar — you saw similar options in Project 2: African Wildlife Map when you worked with gradients and patterns. You can change the display of the shapes in the panel, load shapes from external files, and access a number of built-in libraries.

The Shape option is selected.

Custom Shape tool

Click here to open the Custom Shape panel.

Click here to access the Options menu for the Custom Shape panel.

5. **Choose Banners and Awards in the panel Options menu. Click OK when asked if you want to replace the current shapes with the new set.**

6. **In the Custom Shape panel (on the Options bar), choose the Flag shape.**

7. **Click the Fill swatch in the Options bar, and choose a bright yellow color.**

Ultimately, the shape you are creating will be moved to a spot channel to reproduce the banner in a specific color of ink, so it really doesn't matter what color you use in this step. We're working with a representative yellow so you can get a feel for the composition before you add the spot-channel information.

We chose this yellow swatch. The color you pick doesn't need to match ours; you will ultimately replace this color with a spot color.

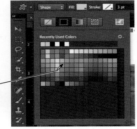

8. **Click and drag to draw the custom shape in the bottom-left corner of the image, wide enough to fill the left half of the file and about 3″ high.**

The Custom Shape tool creates a vector path based on the shape you select. Because you chose the Shape layer option in Step 3, the new shape layer is added to the Layers panel.

The shape layer is added immediately above the previously selected layer.

9. **Using the Direct Selection tool (nested under the Path Selection tool), click the shape edge to reveal the anchor points.**

10. **Adjust the anchor points of the flag shape until the banner covers the flat area where the girl's arm was cut off by the edge of the original photo. Make sure the left edge of the shape extends to the left edge of the image.**

You already know how to edit vector paths, so we won't tell you exactly what to move where. Our solution is shown in the following image. The most important thing is that the flat part of the girl's arm needs to be covered.

Note:

You can choose from a large number of common and special shapes from the built-in shape libraries when you use the Custom Shape tool.

Note:

You can always restore the default shape options by choosing Reset Shapes in the panel Options menu.

11. **When you are satified with your shape, click away from the shape to deselect the anchor points and handles.**

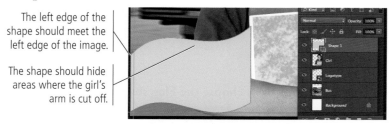

The left edge of the shape should meet the left edge of the image.

The shape should hide areas where the girl's arm is cut off.

12. **With the shape layer selected, choose Layer>Layer Style>Drop Shadow. Define a drop shadow for the shape layer using the following settings, then click OK to apply the style.**

Blend mode:	Multiply Black	Distance:	15 px
Opacity:	75%	Spread:	10%
Angle:	120°	Size:	40 px

13. **Save the file and continue to the next exercise.**

 ## CREATE WARPED TEXT

If you completed Project 4: City Promotion Cards, you have already learned the basics of working with text in Photoshop. In this exercise, you are going to create text that appears to follow the contour of the banner shape you created in the previous exercise. This is easily accomplished with the built-in Warp Text options that change the shape of text without rasterizing it.

1. **With catalog_working.psd open, select the topmost layer (the shape layer).**

   When you create a new type layer, it is placed immediately above the previously selected layer. You are selecting this topmost layer because you want the type layer you create to appear above this shape layer.

2. **In the Tools panel, choose the Horizontal Type tool.**

3. **Click in the image window anywhere other than over the shape layer area to create a type layer with a point-type object, and then type:**

   Back to
   School
   Savings!

   If you click with the Horizontal Type tool *inside* the area of a selected shape layer area, you would convert the shape into a text area that will contain what you type. That isn't what you want, so you need to click outside the shape area and then move the type into the correct position.

4. **Format the type as 60-pt ATC Oak Bold with 48-pt leading, using left paragraph alignment.**

Click outside the shape layer area to add the new type layer.

Use the Character panel to define the font, size, and leading.

5. **Using the Move tool, move the type layer so the text is over the banner shape.**

6. **Select the Type tool again and click inside the existing type to place the insertion point. Click the Create Warped Text button in the Options bar.**

Create Warped Text button

7. **In the Warp Text dialog box, choose Flag from the Style menu.**

As long as text remains editable, your warping options are limited to this list of predefined shapes. When you work with rasterized text (or any other pixel-based selection), you can also create custom warps, which you will do in Project 6: Advertising Samples.

8. **Adjust the Bend settings until you're satisfied with the warped text in relation to your banner shape.**

We changed the Bend setting to −6% and the Horizontal Distortion setting to +13% to match our banner shape.

Note:

Photoshop includes 15 built-in warp styles. The icon next to each style name suggests the result of applying that style.

9. **Click OK to close the Warp Text dialog box.**

10. **Use the Move tool to adjust the position of the type layer (if necessary).**

Note:

If you want to modify the shape layer to better fit the warped type, select the shape layer in the Layers panel and then click the shape edge with the Direct Selection tool to reveal the shape's anchor points.

11. **Save the file and continue to the final stage of the project.**

Stage 3 Working with Spot Channels

Spot colors are frequently used to produce a special look, to match an exact color, or to highlight a certain aspect of a job (for example, with varnish or some other special coating). Spot-color inks are opaque, so they produce the desired result with a single printing unit instead of by combining varying percentages of the four process inks. If you want to create a certain look, or if a color must be the same on every printed job, a spot color is usually the best choice. You should be aware, however, that adding spot color to a process job adds to the cost, and budgets are usually a consideration when designing a print project.

Every designer should own a set of spot-color guides, such as the ones produced by Pantone. (Pantone is the most common spot-color system in the United States, but ask your printer which one they use before building spot colors in any design job.) These printed spot-color guides usually show coated and uncoated samples. Some also show the process-color combination that produces the closest possible match to the spot ink. If you want to approximate a special ink color, you can use those ink percentages to designate the process color in a layout or illustration program.

Note:

Spot colors are typically selected from printed swatch books that show the exact color of the ink. Don't rely on the on-screen previews when you select a spot color.

DEFINE A NEW SPOT CHANNEL

To work with spot colors in Photoshop, you have to create a new channel to include the information for that ink. Anything printed in the spot color needs to be placed or copied onto the spot channel.

1. **With `catalog_working.psd` open, display the Channels panel.**

2. **Open the Channels panel Options menu and choose New Spot Channel.**

3. **In the New Spot Channel dialog box, click the Color swatch to open the Select Spot Color dialog box.**

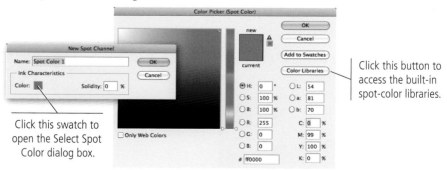

Click this swatch to open the Select Spot Color dialog box.

Click this button to access the built-in spot-color libraries.

4. **Click the Color Libraries button to access the built-in spot-color libraries.**

5. **In the Book menu, choose Pantone Solid Coated. Type 810 to scroll quickly to the color that the client selected for this job.**

Choose the color library in this menu.

Scroll through the swatches or type a number to access the specific color you want to use.

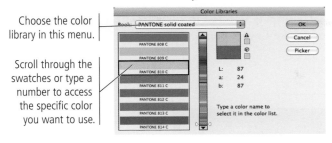

Note:

This is the color your art director defined in the original project meeting.

6. **Click OK to return to the New Spot Channel dialog box.**

7. **Set the Solidity to 100%.**

   Solidity for a spot channel is similar to layer opacity. If the ink channel is not entirely opaque (with a 100% Solidity value), CMYK elements under the spot areas will be visible through the spot ink. In this case, you want the spot-ink areas to completely obscure underlying CMYK elements, so you have to use a 100% Solidity value.

Note:

Double-clicking a spot-color channel thumbnail on the Channels panel opens the same dialog box you see when you first create a new spot channel.

8. **Click OK to add the new spot channel to the file.**

The newly added Pantone spot-color channel doesn't contain anything yet.

9. **Save the file and continue to the next exercise.**

COPY LAYER INFORMATION TO A SPOT CHANNEL

There is no easy way to map specific layer content to a specific spot channel. To ensure that specific objects print in a spot color, you have to manually cut the content from its layer and paste the content directly onto the appropriate spot-color channel. It is also important to understand that there are certain limitations to working with spot colors in Photoshop. You can't apply effects to a spot channel (such as the drop shadow behind the banner on the catalog cover). You also can't store vector information on a spot channel, which means vector shape and type layers must be rasterized if you want to move that content to a spot channel.

1. **With catalog_working.psd open, Control/right-click the Logotype layer and choose Rasterize Layer from the contextual menu.**

   When you placed the logotype file, it was placed as a Smart Object. To move part of this object to the spot-color channel, you first have to rasterize the Smart Object.

2. **With the Logotype layer selected, use the Rectangular Marquee tool to draw a marquee around the word "COHNS".**

    Be careful to select no part of the words "kids club."

3. **Make sure the CMYK composite channel is selected in the Channels panel and the Logotype layer is selected in the Layers panel.**

    Be careful to select nothing but the word "Cohns." Only the logotype should move to the spot-color channel.

    Make sure the CMYK channel is selected.

4. **Choose Edit>Cut.**

    The pixels inside the previous marquee are removed from the Logotype layer and the CMYK channel.

5. **Select the Pantone 810 C channel in the Channels panel, then choose Edit> Paste Special>Paste in Place.**

    This command places the pasted content in the exact position where it was when you cut it, but on the selected Pantone 810 C channel.

    The content is pasted in the exact position where it was when you cut it.

    The pasted content is surrounded by marching ants in the image.

    The pasted content is no longer associated with any layer. It exists only on the Pantone 810 C channel.

6. **Control/right-click the Shape 1 layer in the Layers panel and choose Rasterize Layer from the contextual menu.**

7. **Control/right-click the Back to School Savings type layer and choose Create Work Path from the contextual menu.**

Rather than leaving plain black text, you're going to use this path to remove (knock out) the letter shapes from the banner.

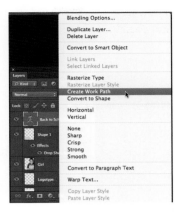

8. **Open the Paths panel. Control/right-click Work Path and choose Make Selection from the contextual menu.**

9. **In the resulting Make Selection dialog box, make sure New Selection is active. Leave the other options at their default values and click OK.**

This dialog box allows you to feather the resulting selection without the need to use the Select>Modify menu.

10. **Hide the Back to School Savings type layer.**

11. **In the Layers panel, select the rasterized Shape 1 layer and press Delete/Backspace.**

Select the Shape 1 layer to delete the selection from the shape area.

You can now see the drop shadow in the knocked out areas of the letter shapes.

12. **In the Layers panel, Control/right-click the Drop Shadow effect for the Shape 1 layer and choose Create Layer from the contextual menu.**

   As we stated at the beginning of this exercise, you can't apply effects to spot-channel content. To maintain the drop shadow after the banner has been moved to the spot channel, you have to create an independent layer from the drop shadow effect.

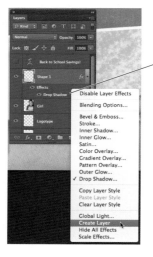

   Control/right-click the Drop Shadow effect to access the contextual menu.

13. **If you see a warning about effects not being reproduced by layers, click OK.**

   Drop shadows can be reproduced with layers, so you can dismiss the warning.

14. **Choose Select>Deselect to turn off the active selection, then draw a rectangular selection marquee around the entire banner shape.**

15. **Make sure the CMYK composite channel is selected in the Channels panel and the Shape 1 layer is selected in the Layers panel.**

Note:

Press Command/Control-D to deselect.

16. **Choose Edit>Cut.**

17. **Select the Pantone 810 C channel in the Channels panel and choose Edit>Paste Special>Paste in Place.**

   The pasted content (which you cut from the Shape 1 layer in Step 16) is not at full strength because the original yellow color maps to a light gray tone on the spot channel.

PHOTOSHOP FOUNDATIONS

Spot colors are sometimes used to print monotone, duotone, tritone, and quadtone images. **Monotones** are grayscale images printed with one ink (typically not black). **Duotones**, **tritones**, and **quadtones** are grayscale images printed with two, three, and four inks (respectively).

Of the four types of images, duotones are the most common. In many cases, duotones are printed with black ink for the shadows and midtones and one other color for the highlights. This technique produces an image with a slight tint that adds visual interest to images in a two-color print job. In Photoshop, duotones are treated as single-channel, 8-bit grayscale images. You can convert any 8-bit grayscale image by choosing Image>Mode>Duotone.

Choose Monotone, Duotone, Tritone, or Quadtone in this menu.

Click these icons to change the curve associated with each ink.

Click these swatches to change the colors of the duotone.

In a duotone image, you can't access the individual ink channels in the Channels panel. You can, however, manipulate the channels through the curves in the Duotone Options dialog box.

You can't use the Channels panel to access the individual inks in a duotone image.

Each ink has a curve that specifies how the color is distributed across shadows and highlights. This curve maps each grayscale value in the original image to a specific ink percentage. The default curve (a straight diagonal line) indicates that the grayscale values in the original image map to an equal percentage of ink. For example, a 50% midtone pixel becomes a 50% tint of the ink.

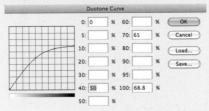

If you need direct access to the individual channels in a duotone, you can convert it to Multichannel mode (Image>Mode>Multichannel).

After converting to Multichannel mode, the individual ink separations are available in the Channels panel.

18. **With the marching ants still showing around the selection, choose Edit>Fill. Choose Black in the Use menu, make sure the Mode is set to Normal, set the Opacity to 100%, and then click OK.**

Remember, each channel is a grayscale representation of one color separation. When you pasted the yellow banner onto the channel, the yellow was converted to a shade of gray as part of that channel data. For the banner to be at full strength of the spot color, it must be filled with solid black on the channel.

19. **Deselect the active selection area, then choose View>Fit on Screen to show the entire image in the document window.**

20. **In the Channels panel, hide the CMYK channels and review the contents of the Pantone 810 C channel.**

The logotype and banner should reproduce as full strength of the spot ink, so they appear as solid black on the spot-color channel.

21. **Show the CMYK channels again, then save the file and continue to the final exercise.**

SAVE THE FILE WITH SPOT-COLOR INFORMATION

When you use spot colors, you have to use a file format that can store the spot-channel information. The native Photoshop format (PSD) obviously stores the spot channels, but not all applications can work with native Photoshop files.

You can also use the DCS (Desktop Color Separation) 2.0 format, which is an extension of the EPS (Encapsulated PostScript) format. DCS is a pre-separated format that can be saved as a single file, or with each separation saved in individual files, which are then combined at the output stage of a job.

1. **With catalog_working.psd open, choose File>Save As.**

2. **Choose Photoshop DCS 2.0 in the Format menu, and change the file name to catalog_final.eps.**

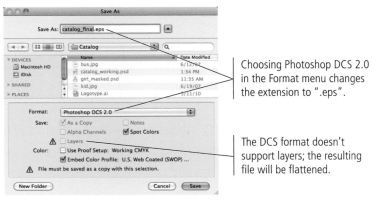

Choosing Photoshop DCS 2.0 in the Format menu changes the extension to ".eps".

The DCS format doesn't support layers; the resulting file will be flattened.

3. **Click Save.**

4. **In the resulting dialog box, choose TIFF (8 bits/pixel) in the Preview menu.**

   The Macintosh options (on Macintosh computers) can't be used on Windows computers. The TIFF preview option can be viewed on any computer. It's always a good idea to be inclusive when you have the option, so use the preview that can be viewed on both platforms.

5. **In the DCS menu, choose Single File with Color Composite (72 pixel/inch).**

   The "72 pixel/inch" refers to the preview only; when the file is printed, the full resolution (300 pixels/inch) will be output.

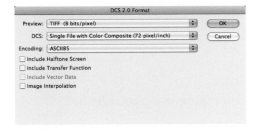

6. **Click OK to save the file.**

7. **When the Save process is complete, close the file.**

1. Duplicating one of the existing color channels results in a _____.

2. The _____ filter maintains edge details and turns non-edges gray.

3. The _____ adjustment reduces images to only a defined number of shades of gray.

4. The _____ adjustment converts images to high-contrast bitmap images; pixels in the resulting image are either black or white.

5. Individual channels are actually _____ representations of the amount of a primary color in different areas of the image.

6. The Custom Shape tool can be used to create _____ from built-in or external libraries.

7. _____ are special inks used to print specific colors, often those that are outside the CMYK gamut.

8. A _____ is an image with only two channels, typically black and one other spot color.

9. Spot-color information is stored in a _____; it is not associated with any Photoshop layer.

10. Images with spot colors must be saved in the _____ or _____ format.

1. Briefly describe the characteristics of an Alpha channel.

2. Briefly explain the process of painting directly on a channel.

3. Briefly explain why spot colors are used in commercial graphic design.

Use what you learned in this project to complete the following freeform exercise.
Carefully read the art director and client comments, then create your design to meet the needs of the project.
Use the space below to sketch ideas; when finished, write a brief explanation of the reasoning behind your design.

art director comments

The Cohn's marketing director is very pleased with the completed back-to-school catalog cover, and would like your agency to take over the ongoing catalog project. The Spring catalog, which will be mailed in early February, is the next issue to design.

To complete this project, you should:

❏ Download the **PS6_PB_Project5.zip** archive from the Student Files Web page to access the client files for this project.

❏ Isolate the child in the client's photograph from her background.

❏ Find an appropriate background image for the "Spring" theme of the catalog.

❏ Composite the different cover elements into a cohesive design.

❏ Build a spot channel with the company name and some kind of banner.

client comments

When the weather starts to get warmer, parents need to buy new clothes to replace the ones their kids have outgrown since the previous year. The Spring catalog is our second biggest seller.

We have an adorable picture of Andrea for the catalog cover. Her shirt is from our new Sweet Sherbet collection, which will include a lot of pastel shades and light cotton fabrics. (We sent the photograph and the logotype for this issue to your art director.)

For this issue's spot color, we were thinking something in a blue shade. We haven't used a blue color for a while, and a blue would contrast well with the peach shirt — in fact, that's one of the reasons we picked this picture for the cover.

Like the Fall catalog, Andrea should fill most of the catalog cover. Find something 'spring-y' to put in the background, but make sure it's subtle.

Use a different shape for the banner this time, with the words 'Spring into Savings!'.

project justification

_____
_____
_____
_____
_____
_____
_____
_____
_____
_____
_____
_____
_____
_____

This project highlighted a number of aesthetic and technical issues associated with building a unified composition from a set of disparate elements. Many on-the-job projects include complex selections such as the one you created in this project. Although the tools available in Photoshop make the process far easier than painting every pixel by hand, you should be prepared to do some manual clean-up to perfect the fine details of a selection mask. Patience and attention to detail separate great work from average work.

In addition to creating and refining a mask to remove the girl from her background, you had to work around the problem of close framing by the original photograph. Although the photo was created to the correct size, moving the girl off center in the final composition left an unnatural edge. Painting the missing part of the girl's arm would be possible for an accomplished artist, but hiding the problem with other design elements is far easier (and more common) for a Photoshop artist.

Create an Alpha channel by duplicating an existing color channel

Use Alpha channel information to create a complex selection

Use a complex selection to isolate an image from its photographic background

Create and warp a type layer

Use the type layer to select and remove pixels from another layer

Rasterize effects and shape layers

Copy elements from regular layers to a spot-color channel

Advertising Samples

You are the in-house designer for a printing company, so your client is the new accounts manager, who is pitching your company's new large-format printing services to a potential customer. She asked you to morph an existing sample ad onto a number of different photos to help promote the company's new "Advertise Anywhere!" services.

This project incorporates the following skills:

- ❏ Patching a photo to remove unwanted elements
- ❏ Replacing specific colors in a photo to change the appearance of an object
- ❏ Using adjustment layers to change hue and saturation values for specific objects in a photo
- ❏ Adjusting an image's shadows and highlights to correct bad lighting
- ❏ Transforming a layer using one-and two-point perspective
- ❏ Warping a layer around irregular, non-flat surfaces
- ❏ Applying lighting effects to unify composite images

client comments

Our new "Advertise Anywhere!" campaign is designed to help our clients promote their products by placing large ads in unusual places — on a bench, on the paint strips in parking lots, wrapped around a city bus, and in other non-traditional locations. The producer of *Nighttime News 6* is very interested, but wants to see some samples. He asked me to do a presentation in two weeks for his superiors, including several network executives. If they like what they see, this contract could evolve into a bigger contract with the entire network.

We already created a sample ad for the news program, and I asked my assistant to gather some photos to use in the presentation. We have pictures of the client's office building, as well as the building where their new production studio will be located — we want to personalize the presentation. We also want to show the client two unusual examples, so we chose pictures of a large water tank by the freeway and a hot air balloon.

art director comments

Since the "Advertise Anywhere!" program is new for our company, the owner is excited about presenting to the first potential client. All the pictures they want to use need some help to make them as attractive as possible.

In the water tank photo, there's a bunch of litter I want you to remove.

The bright yellow in the balloon is going to detract attention from the sample ad. Remove the yellow from the balloon body and mute the other colors a bit so the sample ad stands out.

The studio photo isn't bad, but it has been painted since we took the photo. To personalize the presentation, convert the brown front façade to dark red and clean up any marks.

If you place the ad onto the office building as it is now, most of the ad will end up in dark shadows. Adjust the photo's overall lighting before you wrap the ad around the building.

project objectives

To complete this project, you will:

❏ Use the Patch tool to replace one area of an image with pixels from another area

❏ Use the Replace Color adjustment to change selected colors in an image

❏ Use adjustment layers to apply color changes to specific areas of an image

❏ Use the Shadow/Highlight adjustment to correct a shadow-filled image

❏ Use Free Transform mode to match a layer to the perspective in the background image

❏ Use the Vanishing Point filter to wrap a layer in perspective around a sharp corner

❏ Create a custom warp transformation to morph a sample ad onto a round shape

❏ Use the Lighting Effects filter to unify composited images

Stage 1   Cleaning and Adjusting Images

Photoshop includes a number of tools for creating irregular composite images — such as warping a flat ad around the shape of a water tank along the desert highway, or placing an ad on a hot-air balloon floating in the distance. Before you composite the images for this project, however, you need to do some clean-up work on the background photos. The best approach is to fix the images first, and then morph the ad onto the corrected files.

 ## REMOVE UNWANTED IMAGE ELEMENTS

In Project 3: Menu Image Correction, you learned a number of techniques for retouching damaged images. The Healing Brush and Spot Healing Brush tools are excellent choices for cleaning up marks and blemishes, and the Clone Stamp tool can effectively copy pixels from one location to another. As you have probably already noticed, there is usually more than one way to accomplish the same type of task — and retouching an image is no exception. The Patch tool can be used to replace one area with another and blend the area edges for smoother results.

1. **Download PS6_RF_Project6.zip from the Student Files Web page.**

2. **Expand the ZIP archive in your WIP folder (Macintosh) or copy the archive contents into your WIP folder (Windows).**

    This results in a folder named **Outdoors**, which contains the files you need for this project. You should also use this folder to save the files you create in this project.

3. **In Photoshop, open tanks.jpg from the WIP>Outdoors folder.**
   If you get a warning about a mismatched color profile, choose the option to use the embedded profile.

This image will make a better client sample without the annoying litter along the edge of the road.

4. **Zoom in to the large white object in the bottom center of the image.**

5. **Choose the Patch tool in the Tools panel (nested under the Healing Brush or Spot Healing Brush tool).**

    The Patch tool allows you to repair a selected area with either a texture, with pixels from another specified area, or with a pattern. It matches texture, lighting, and shading of the sampled pixels to the source (selected) pixels. This option gives you more control than the Content-Aware Fill dialog box because you choose the area to be filled *and* the pixels that will be used to fill that area.

6. **Using the Patch tool, draw a selection marquee that entirely surrounds the piece of trash.**

   Because of the texture and detail in the surrounding area, the other repair tools are not the best choices for removing this object from the roadside. The Patch tool, on the other hand, allows you to sample pixels from other areas of the image and blend them smoothly over the selected area.

   Patch tool · Unwanted image area · Selection marquee

7. **In the Options bar, make sure the Source option is selected and the Transparent option is not checked.**

   The Source and Destination options define what the selection marquee represents.

   - If Source is selected, the original marquee represents the area that will be patched.
   - If Destination is selected, the original selection marquee represents the pixels that will be copied to another area.

8. **Place the Patch tool cursor inside the selection marquee, and then click and drag to the left. When you are satisfied with the preview, release the mouse button.**

   The pixels inside the second marquee (where you drag to) will be used to fill the original marquee location. This tool shows a dynamic preview; as you drag the marquee, the original selection changes to show the result that will be created when you release the mouse button.

   When you release the mouse button, the Patch tool blends the selection edge smoothly into the surrounding area, preventing unwanted harsh edges around the patch.

9. **Press Command/Control-D to turn off the selection marquee so you can better review your results.**

Note:

If you aren't satisfied with the result, undo the patch selection and try again. However, keep in mind that deselection is considered a step, so you can't use the one-process Undo command. You have to use the History panel (see Page 21) to go back two steps and restore the original pixels, or use the Step Backward command (Command-Option-Z/ Control-Alt-Z).

10. **Using the same techniques, remove the rest of the litter from the foreground of this image.**

The mechanics of the Patch tool are simple and effective. The most difficult part of this process is determining what to select and what to use as replacement pixels. Keep the following tips in mind when you clean up the rest of the roadside trash from this photo:

- The Source option is best if you want to remove something from an image. The Destination option is best if you want to add or make copies of specific areas.

- It helps to work at 100% view when you use the Patch tool.

- Use the smallest selection area possible to achieve the best results.

- Choose replacement pixels from an area near the pixels you want to replace. This helps avoid obvious differences in color or lighting in the patched area.

- Areas of high contrast outside the selection edge produce a soft blended effect that won't be apparent until you release the mouse button.

Replacement pixels   Original selection

After releasing the mouse button, the unselected part of the litter blends into the original selection area.

- If you want to patch an edge, choose a similar edge as the replacement pixels.

- When you choose the replacement pixels, be careful to avoid creating unwanted patterns or obvious (but unwanted) copies of image elements.

Replacement pixels

These exact spots now appear twice in close proximity, which does not look natural.

11. **Save the file as a native Photoshop file named `tanks_clean.psd` in your WIP>Outdoors folder, and then close the file.**

12. **Continue to the next exercise.**

REPLACE COLORS IN PARTS OF AN IMAGE

The Replace Color adjustment allows you to select and replace a specific range of colors in an image. This adjustment option is a simple method for making overall changes to hue, saturation, or lightness in selected areas without having to experiment with layer blending modes.

1. **Open the file studio.jpg from the WIP>Outdoors folder. If you get a warning about mismatched profiles, choose the option to use the embedded profile.**

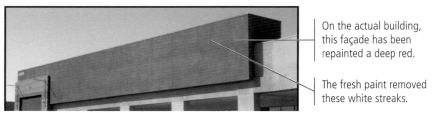

On the actual building, this façade has been repainted a deep red.

The fresh paint removed these white streaks.

2. **Choose Image>Adjustments>Replace Color.**

3. **Using the Eyedropper tool from the Replace Color dialog box, click in the image (behind the dialog box) to select the brown stucco façade of the building.**

Click here to sample the color you want to replace.

Eyedropper tool (selected)

Add to Sample tool

Subtract from Sample tool

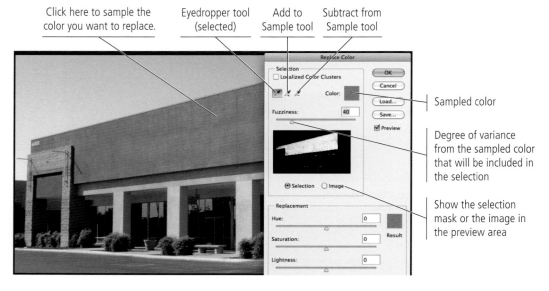

Sampled color

Degree of variance from the sampled color that will be included in the selection

Show the selection mask or the image in the preview area

4. **Drag the Fuzziness slider right to increase the selection tolerance.**

As you increase the fuzziness, you can see other areas of the image being added to the selection. Various areas in this image share many of the same earth tones, which means you can't select the façade color without affecting some other areas of the image — at least, not without a couple of extra steps.

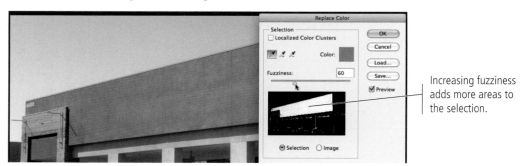

Increasing fuzziness adds more areas to the selection.

5. **Click Cancel to close the Replace Color dialog box.**

6. **In the Layers panel, Control/right-click the Background layer and choose Duplicate Layer from the contextual menu. Click OK in the Duplicate Layer dialog box to accept the default layer name.**

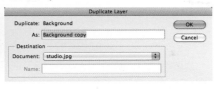

Note:

When you Control/right-click a layer and select Duplicate Layer, you can use the Destination options to place the duplicate layer in the stack for the current (open) image, any open image, or a new image.

7. **With the Background Copy layer selected in the Layers panel, choose Image>Adjustments>Replace Color.**

8. **Click in the image to sample the same brown as the selection color, and then move the Fuzziness slider all the way to the right.**

    The preview shows that a large portion of the image is selected, including areas that you don't want to change. That's okay, since you'll use a layer mask to eliminate those areas from the duplicate layer.

Note:

You can also click the Result color swatch and define a replacement color in the Color Picker dialog box.

9. **In the Replacement area, experiment with the Hue, Saturation, and Lightness sliders until you find a dark red color.**

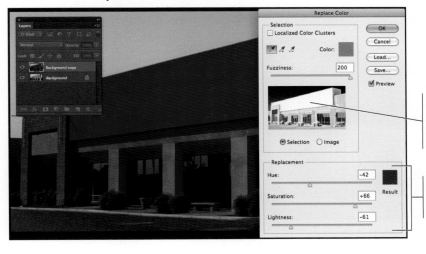

Much of the building has some shade of brown, so full Fuzziness selects most of the building face.

Use these options to change the color of the selected pixels.

10. **Click OK to apply the change to the selected layer.**

11. **Using any method you prefer, draw a selection marquee around the edges of the façade (as shown in the following image).**

Since this selection has straight edges, the Polygonal Lasso tool will do a fine job of creating the selection. You could also draw a work path with the Pen tool, and then make a selection based on the work path.

12. **With the selection active (you can see the marching ants), click the Add Layer Mask button at the bottom of the Layers panel.**

When you add a layer mask with an active selection, the areas outside the selection are automatically masked.

Add Layer Mask button

13. **Zoom in to the edges of the façade and make sure the mask covers exactly what you want it to cover. Use the Brush and/or Eraser tool to clean up the mask edges if necessary.**

Remember, when you paint on a mask, black adds to the mask and white removes areas from the mask. You should also make sure to select the mask in the Layers panel (instead of the layer thumbnail) before painting on the mask, or you will mistakenly paint on the actual image layer.

14. **In the Layers panel, Control/right-click the Background Copy layer name and choose Merge Down from the contextual menu.**

Merge Down combines the selected layer with the next layer down in the Layers panel. **Merge Visible** combines all visible layers into a single layer. **Flatten Image** combines all layers into the Background layer, giving you the option to discard hidden layers.

Note:

In this step, our goal is to teach you about the options for flattening image layers. In many cases, however, it is a better idea to leave the masked layer intact in case you need to make changes later.

Because the next layer down is the Background layer, merging the selected layer down combines the Background Copy layer into the Background layer.

15. **Use any technique you prefer to remove the white streaks from the building's façade.**

The Replace Color function only affected areas of color within the selected range (Step 8). These spots are drastically different than the selected brown shades, so they still need to be corrected.

We used a combination of the Spot Healing tool to clean up the spots on the face and the Clone Stamp and Patch tools to clean up the edges.

16. **Save the file as a native Photoshop file named** `studio_clean.psd` **in your WIP>Outdoors folder, and then close the file.**

17. **Continue to the next exercise.**

Selective Color Adjustment

The **Selective Color** adjustment (Image>Adjustments>Selective Color) allows you to change ink values in specific colors or neutrals without affecting other colors.

For example, if water looks too yellow, you should remove yellow to produce a more inviting blue color. If you reduce the overall amount of yellow, however, you might affect other areas such as the pier and island in the image shown below. The Selective Color option allows you to adjust the yellow component of only blues and greens, so you can fix the water without affecting the pier and island.

The Relative method changes the existing amount of cyan, magenta, yellow, or black by its percentage of the total. For example, if you start with a pixel that is 70% yellow and remove 10%, 7% is removed from the yellow (10% of 70% = 7%). The Absolute method adjusts the color in absolute values. If you start with a pixel that is 70% yellow and remove 10%, the yellow pixel is set to 60%.

Water in the original image has a strong yellow cast.

Adjusting ink percentages of only the greens and blues makes the water more inviting without affecting the pilings in the foreground.

The Preset menu at the top of the Selective Color dialog box is useful if you need to make the same adjustment to multiple images — for example, you know photos from a particular digital camera always have a yellow cast in the blue areas. (The same Preset options are available in all adjustment dialog boxes.)

ADJUST HUE AND SATURATION WITH AN ADJUSTMENT LAYER

Correcting the previous image highlighted one of the potential drawbacks of using image adjustments: you might change areas you don't want to change, requiring a workaround (in this case, a duplicate layer with a mask) to achieve the effect you want.

The process you used in the previous exercise is so common that Photoshop includes built-in options for creating adjustment layers, which effectively achieve the same result that you accomplished manually in the previous exercise. An adjustment layer is an empty layer containing an adjustment (such as a Levels or Curves adjustment) that modifies the layers below it.

1. **Open the file balloon.jpg from the WIP>Outdoors folder. If you get a warning about mismatched color profiles, choose the option to use the embedded profile.**

   The art director wants this yellow balloon to be white so it doesn't distract from the sample ad. The Hue/Saturation adjustment, which allows you to change the Hue, Saturation, and Lightness values of specific primary colors, is perfectly suited for changing this yellow balloon to white.

2. Open the Adjustments panel and click the Hue/Saturation button.

The Hue/Saturation adjustment can be extremely useful for shifting the Hue, Saturation, or Lightness value of an entire image or for selected primary colors.

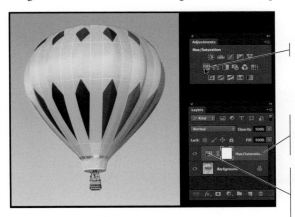

Hue/Saturation button

Clicking creates a new adjustment layer above the selected layer.

The adjustment layer is identified by an icon that matches the Hue/Saturation button in the Adjustments panel.

Note:

You can use adjustment layers for most of the adjustments available in the Image>Adjustments menu. (For some reason, a few adjustments — including the Replace Color adjustment you used in the previous exercise — have been left out of this panel.)

Adding an adjustment layer creates a new layer on top of the currently selected layer (in this case, the Background layer). This allows you to easily show or hide the adjustment, apply multiple adjustments to the same layer, or even delete an adjustment from the file without permanently changing the pixels on the original layer. The adjustment from an adjustment layer is not permanent unless you merge the adjustment layer with one or more underlying layers.

Another advantage of using adjustment layers is that you can change the opacity, order, or blending mode of an adjustment layer, just as you can with a regular layer.

Keep in mind that adjustment layers affect all underlying layers. If you want an adjustment layer to affect only the next layer down, Control/right-click the adjustment layer and choose Create Clipping Mask from the contextual menu.

Note:

You can add adjustment layers using either the Adjustments panel or the menu at the bottom of the Layers panel.

You can also choose from the Layer>New Adjustment Layer submenu.

3. In the Properties panel, choose Yellows in the Edit menu (which defaults to Master) and drag the Lightness slider almost all the way to the right.

The Properties panel contains options specific to the selected adjustment layer.

If you remember from Project 3: Menu Image Correction, lightness is the position of a color along the black/white scale. Lightness of 0 adds no white or black to the hue. Lightness of −100 is solid black (obscuring all other color). Lightness of +100 is pure white (removing all color).

Choose from this Edit menu to adjust the entire image, or individual additive or subtractive primary colors.

Since the balloon was pure yellow, increasing the yellow lightness to +90 converts the yellow parts of the balloon to nearly pure white.

Select the adjustment layer in the Layers panel to show the related settings in the Adjustments panel.

Adjustment layers automatically include an empty layer mask, which you can edit to protect areas of the underlying layers.

4. **In the Layers panel, click the Adjustment Layer Mask thumbnail to select it.**

   Adjustment layers automatically include a layer mask, which allows you to isolate portions of an image for correction. Adjustment layers are also helpful for experimenting with corrections without permanently affecting the underlying layer.

5. **Using the Brush tool with a 70-pixel size and a black foreground color, paint over the area of the basket to protect that area from the increased Lightness setting for yellows.**

The adjustment layer mask is selected.

Painting on the mask restores the original color in the basket.

6. **Save the file as** `balloon_clean.psd` **in your WIP>Outdoors folder. Click OK when asked to maximize compatibility.**

   You were not asked to maximize compatibility with the prevous files, because all of those still have only one layer.

7. **Close the file and continue to the next exercise.**

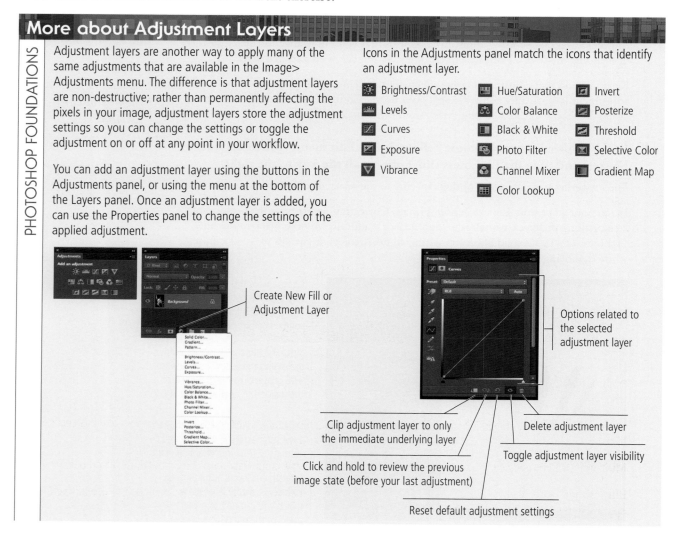

More about Adjustment Layers

PHOTOSHOP FOUNDATIONS

Adjustment layers are another way to apply many of the same adjustments that are available in the Image> Adjustments menu. The difference is that adjustment layers are non-destructive; rather than permanently affecting the pixels in your image, adjustment layers store the adjustment settings so you can change the settings or toggle the adjustment on or off at any point in your workflow.

You can add an adjustment layer using the buttons in the Adjustments panel, or using the menu at the bottom of the Layers panel. Once an adjustment layer is added, you can use the Properties panel to change the settings of the applied adjustment.

Icons in the Adjustments panel match the icons that identify an adjustment layer.

- Brightness/Contrast
- Hue/Saturation
- Invert
- Levels
- Color Balance
- Posterize
- Curves
- Black & White
- Threshold
- Exposure
- Photo Filter
- Selective Color
- Vibrance
- Channel Mixer
- Gradient Map
- Color Lookup

Create New Fill or Adjustment Layer

Options related to the selected adjustment layer

Clip adjustment layer to only the immediate underlying layer

Delete adjustment layer

Toggle adjustment layer visibility

Click and hold to review the previous image state (before your last adjustment)

Reset default adjustment settings

ADJUST IMAGE SHADOWS AND HIGHLIGHTS

The Shadows/Highlights adjustment is well suited for correcting highlight and shadow areas of an image. (Photoshop calculates the changes based on the values of surrounding pixels.) Using the basic settings, you can adjust the values of shadows and highlights independently. If the Show More Options box is checked, you can also exercise finer control over each area.

1. **Open the file office.jpg from the WIP>Outdoors folder. If you get a warning about mismatched profiles, choose the option to use the embedded profile.**

This overall image is extremely dark; most of the building is in shadows.

2. **Choose Image>Adjustments>Shadows/Highlights.**

Extended Control for Shadows/Highlights Adjustments

PHOTOSHOP FOUNDATIONS

When the Show More Options box is checked in the Shadows/Highlights dialog box, you can fine-tune the adjustments for both shadows and highlights, as well as modify the options for color correction and midtone contrast.

Tonal Width defines the part of the tonal range that will be modified by the adjustment. If you set the Tonal Width value to 100%, the adjustment will be applied to half of the entire tonal range. Smaller values restrict the adjustment to smaller regions of the related area (shadows or highlights).

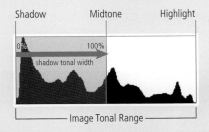

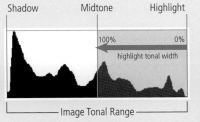

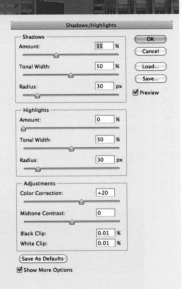

Radius controls the size of the area around each pixel that is used to determine whether a pixel is in the shadows or highlights.

Color Correction fine-tunes the colors in areas that are changed by your choices in the Shadows and Highlights sections of the dialog box. Higher Color Correction values tend to produce more saturated colors.

Midtone Contrast adjusts the contrast in the midtones, similar to the Input Gamma slider in the Levels dialog box.

Black Clip and **White Clip** determine how much of the extreme shadows and highlights are clipped, just as with the Clip options in the Auto Color Correction Options dialog box.

3. **Reduce the Shadow Amount value to 15% to lighten the shadows in the image.**

An Amount value of 0% means no change will be applied to that area; larger values result in lighter shadows or darker highlights.

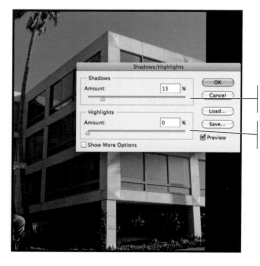

Drag this slider right to lighten the shadows.

Drag this slider right to darken the highlights.

4. **Click OK to apply the change.**

5. **Save the file as a native Photoshop file named** `office_clean.psd` **in your WIP>Outdoors folder, and then close the file.**

6. **Continue to the next stage of the project.**

The Photo Filter Adjustment

The Photo Filter adjustment (Image>Adjustments>Photo Filter, or accessed in the Adjustments panel) creates the effect of taking a photo through colored filters to adjust color balance or to create an artistic effect.

You can choose one of the defined filters in the Filter menu, or you can apply a custom color filter by clicking the Color swatch and choosing from the Color Picker dialog box. For example, you can choose a filter from the Filter menu to create a specific mood (such as a Sepia or Underwater filter), or apply a custom magenta filter to remove a green color cast.

The Density slider adjusts the amount of color applied to the image (higher density means more color). If the Preserve Luminosity option is checked, the color adjustment has no effect on the overall lightness/darkness of the image.

The original image

The image after applying the Cooling Filter (80)

PHOTOSHOP FOUNDATIONS

In addition to the tools you have used throughout this book, a number of tools in the Tools panel can be used to make basic corrections.

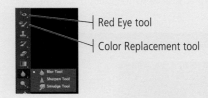

— Red Eye tool

— Color Replacement tool

The **Blur tool** softens hard edges and reduces detail.

The **Sharpen tool** increases contrast at edges to increase apparent sharpness.

The **Smudge tool** allows you to push pixels around in an image, as if you were dragging your finger across wet (digital) paint.

All three of these tools use a selected brush preset to affect the image. You can choose a specific blending mode, as well as the strength of the effect as you paint a brush stroke. Multiple brush strokes increase the tool's effect.

If the Sample All Layers option is checked, you can affect the selected layer using data from all layers in the file. For the Smudge tool, the Finger Painting option adds the foreground color to the beginning of the brush stroke.

The **Red Eye tool** removes the red-eye effect caused by flash photography.

In the Options bar, the Pupil Size menu controls the size of the area affected by the tool. The Darken Amount option sets the darkness of the correction.

Original Image

Blurred

Sharpened

Smudged

The **Color Replacement tool** attempts to simplify replacement of specific colors in your image. You can define the brush you want to use, and then paint over a targeted color to replace it with the foreground color.

You can replace the color, or you can choose Hue, Saturation, or Luminosity in the Mode menu. The sampling options determine how color will be replaced:

- **Continuous** samples colors as you drag.
- **Once** replaces color only in areas of the color that you first click.
- **Background Swatch** replaces only areas of the current background color.

The Limits menu determines how the tool's effect can be constrained:

- **Discontiguous** replaces the sampled color under the brush tip.
- **Contiguous** replaces color contiguous with the color under the brush tip.
- **Find Edges** replaces connected areas of the sampled color, attempting to preserve the sharpness of shape edges.

Tolerance defines how much variance from the sample will be affected. The **Anti-alias** option smoothes edges of the affected areas.

The Color Replacement tool works best for images with high-contrast edges.

Painting Image Exposure and Saturation

The Dodge and Burn tools are used to lighten or darken areas of an image (respectively). These tools are based on traditional photographic techniques for exposing specific areas of a print. Photographers hold back light to lighten an area on the print (**dodging**) or increase the exposure to darken areas on a print (**burning**).

When using the Dodge or Burn tool, you can define a brush tip in the Options bar, as well as the image range you want to affect (highlights, midtones, or shadows) and the degree of exposure.

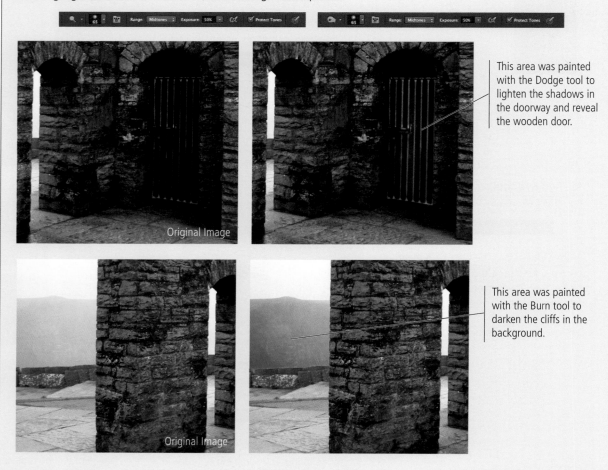

This area was painted with the Dodge tool to lighten the shadows in the doorway and reveal the wooden door.

This area was painted with the Burn tool to darken the cliffs in the background.

The Sponge tool changes the color saturation of an area. As with the Dodge and Burn tools, you can define a specific brush to use. You can also define the mode of the Sponge tool — Saturate or Desaturate — and the flow rate for the tool's effect.

This wall was painted with the Sponge tool in Saturation mode to enhance the green shades in the moss.

Stage 2 Working in Perspective

Many compositing jobs will be straightforward copy-and-paste jobs — putting multiple images together, possibly adjusting size, clipping edges, or blending edges into other elements — such as the work you completed in the earlier projects of this book.

Other jobs are more complex, especially jobs that require you to make one object appear to be a seamless part of another image. When your goal is to merge one element with another existing image, you need to pay close attention to details such as size, angle, and depth so the composited element appears to blend naturally with the background image.

 ## TRANSFORM THE PERSPECTIVE OF A LAYER

Basic transformations such as scale, rotation, skew, and perspective can all be accomplished in Free Transform mode. For skewing a flat ad onto a flat surface, Free Transform mode is the simplest choice.

1. **Open the file studio_clean.psd from your WIP>Outdoors folder.**

2. **Choose File>Place. Select the file banner.tif from the WIP>Outdoors folder and click Place.**

   As you should remember if you completed Project 1: Composite Movie Ad or Project 2: African Wildlife Map, the Place command adds the selected file as a Smart Object layer.

Note:

Whenever you open a file throughout the rest of this project, maintain the embedded profile if you get a warning about mismatched profiles.

3. **Using the Options bar, scale the layer to 73% proportionally, and then drag the banner so its top-right corner is near the top-right corner of the studio façade.**

Use the W and H fields to resize the banner graphic to 73% of its original size.

Position the top-right corner near the top-right corner of the façade.

When you choose one of the Transform options, handles appear around the selection or layer so you can control the transformation.

Note:

Press Shift while Command/Control-dragging to skew the object exactly vertical or exactly horizontal.

4. **Command/Control-click the center-left transformation handle and drag down to skew the layer.**

   Simply dragging a center handle stretches or shrinks the selection. Pressing the Command/Control key allows you to skew a selection instead of changing its horizontal or vertical size.

Press Command/ Control and drag the center handle to skew the selection.

Note:

Press Shift while Command/Control-dragging to constrain the movement of the transformation handle to 45° angles.

5. **Command/Control-click the top-left transformation handle and drag down to distort the perspective of the layer.**

   Simply dragging a corner handle stretches or shrinks the selection. Pressing the Command/Control key allows you to distort the image's shape, which affects perspective when you drag straight corners in this manner.

Press Command/ Control and drag the corner handle to alter the perspective of the selection.

6. **Adjust the bottom corner handles so the banner fits entirely within the front of the façade.**

7. **When you're satisfied with the position, size, and perspective of the banner, press Return/Enter to finalize the transformation.**

8. **Apply a slight drop shadow to the ad layer (Layer>Layer Style>Drop Shadow). We used the following settings:**

Blend Mode:	Multiply Black	Opacity:	75%
Angle:	125°	Distance:	10
Spread:	0	Size:	5

Note:

We used the 125° angle for the drop shadow to approximate the angle of shadows that already exist in the image.

9. **Save the file as `studio_ad.psd` in your WIP>Outdoors folder. If asked, click OK in the Photoshop Format Options dialog box to maximize file compatibility.**

10. **Close the file, and then continue to the next exercise.**

Free Transform Options

You can transform any layer or selection using the options in the Edit>Transform menu or by choosing Edit>Free Transform. (Most of the options in the Edit>Transform submenu — Scale, Rotate, Skew, and Distort — can actually be applied using the Free Transform option, making these choices redundant.)

When you choose Edit>Free Transform, the selection is surrounded by handles that allow you to control the transformation. Use the following images as a guide for controlling your transformations.

Click a center handle to stretch or shrink the selection in one direction.

Command/Control-click a center handle to skew the selection.

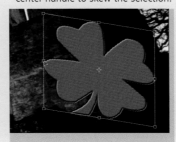

Click slightly outside a corner handle to rotate the selection.

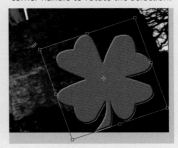

Click a corner handle to stretch or shrink the selection horizontally and vertically at the same time.

Command/Control-click a corner handle to distort the selection.

Press Option/Alt while making any free transformation to apply it equally on both sides of the selection center.

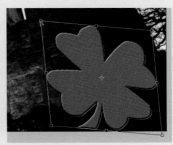

Pressing Shift with any of the transformations constrains the transformation to 45-degree increments. For example, if you press Shift while skewing a selection, the skew will be constrained to exactly horizontal or vertical.

If you choose Edit>Transform>Perspective, dragging a corner handle has the same effect as pressing Command-Option-Shift/Control-Alt-Shift when working in Free Transform mode. Dragging a side handle has the same effect as pressing Command/Control-Shift when in Free Transform mode.

The advantage to Perspective transformation mode is that you don't have to use the modifier keys. The disadvantage is that you can't change anything other than the horizontal or vertical skew and the reflective horizontal or vertical distortion of the selection.

Drag a corner handle to shrink or expand that side of the selection around the center point.

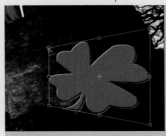

Drag a center handle to skew the selection.

Use the Vanishing Point Filter

The previous exercise used **one-point perspective** — an artistic principle in which all lines in an image ultimately meet at a single invisible vanishing point outside the edges of the image. To effectively merge one image into another, the new image must be adjusted to use the same vanishing point as the original. The Free Transform option is usually enough to combine images in one-point perspective.

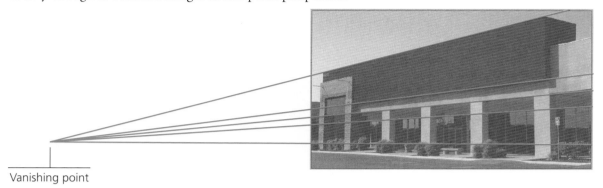

Vanishing point

Many images have more than one side (or plane), where lines go off in two different directions. This type of image has **two-point perspective** because there are two different vanishing points. Combining images in two-point perspective (such as wrapping a selection around a corner) is a bit more difficult to manage using the Free Transform option. Fortunately, the Vanishing Point filter makes the process relatively easy — once you understand how it works.

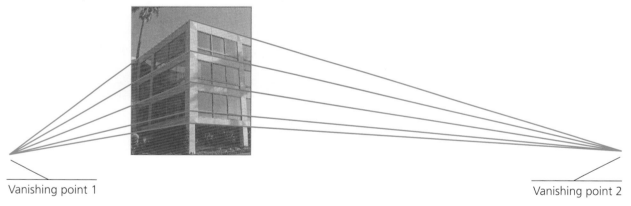

Vanishing point 1   Vanishing point 2

1. **Open the file banner.tif from the WIP>Outdoors folder.**

2. **Select the entire banner file (Command/Control-A) and copy it to the Clipboard.**

   The object that you want to put into perspective — whether from the active file or any other file — needs to be copied before you open the Vanishing Point filter. In this case, you can't place the banner artwork into the office file for the filter to work properly.

3. **Close the banner file, then open the file office_clean.psd from your WIP>Outdoors folder.**

PHOTOSHOP FOUNDATIONS

The Vanishing Point dialog box might seem intimidating at first, but it's fairly easy to use once you understand the tools. Most of these tools perform the same functions as in the main Photoshop interface; the Marquee tool, however, is the most notable difference.

Edit Plane tool
Create Plane tool
Marquee tool
Stamp tool
Brush tool
Transform tool
Eyedropper tool
Measure tool
Hand tool
Zoom tool

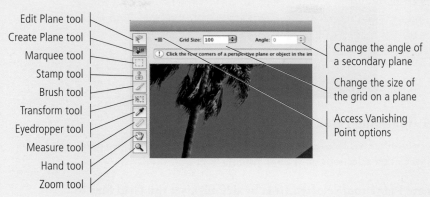

Change the angle of a secondary plane

Change the size of the grid on a plane

Access Vanishing Point options

In addition to pasting a selection from the Clipboard, you can use the Marquee tool to make selections within the perspective planes in the Vanishing Point dialog box. Once you've drawn a selection, a number of options become available above the preview.

- The **Feather** option defines how many pixels at the selection edges are blurred to help smooth the transition from the copied pixels to the original pixels.

- The **Opacity** option allows you to adjust the opacity of moved pixels, which is useful if you aren't building the filter onto a new layer.

- The **Heal** menu defines the blending mode for moved pixels, which is also useful if you aren't building the filter onto a new layer.

- The **Move Mode** menu is similar to the Patch tool Source and Destination options.

  - If Destination is selected, clicking inside a selection marquee and dragging moves the marquee to a new position, maintaining the same perspective defined in the plane. (You can press Command/Control and drag from inside a Destination mode marquee to fill the selection with pixels from another area.)

  - If Source is selected, clicking inside a selection marquee and dragging fills the marquee with pixels from the destination area.

- Once you have moved pixels into a selection, you can use the Transform tool to rotate or scale the selection, as well as flip it horizontally or vertically using the check boxes that appear over the preview image.

Defined perspective plane

Using the Marquee tool, we defined the original selection to be large enough to copy the entire shutter.

With the marquee set to Destination Move mode, we clicked inside the original marquee and dragged to the place we wanted to create a new shutter. (Notice the size and shape of the marquee, which is altered to match the defined perspective plane.)

We then switched to Source Move mode and dragged back over the original selection to create a second shutter.

4. **Add a new empty layer to the file and make sure it is selected in the Layers panel.**

   The results of the Vanishing Point filter will become part of the selected layer. If you don't add a new layer before using the filter, the sample ad will be automatically flattened into the background.

   Click here to create a new layer.

5. **Choose Filter>Vanishing Point.**

   The Vanishing Point filter has its own interface, where you can define the perspective in an image and place other selections onto those planes.

6. **With the Create Plane tool selected (it is by default), set the Grid Size to 200 pixels.**

7. **Click at the top corner where the two sides of the building meet, and drag to the right (following the top edge of the building). Click above the second window to anchor the plane. Use the lines in the image to draw the rest of the perspective plane (as shown in the following image).**

   The Create Plane tool defines the first perspective plane of the image. When you define the perspective plane, make sure you follow the path of lines in the image so the vanishing point of your plane matches the vanishing point in the image.

   When you define the third corner of the plane, lines automatically connect the first and third points with the mouse cursor. Simply click to anchor the fourth corner point.

   Create Plane tool

   Click here first…

   …then click here…

   …then click here…

   …and then click here.

8. **With the Edit Plane tool selected, drag the top-, bottom-, and right-center handles in toward the center of the concrete surrounding the first section of windows, so the plane edges are about halfway between the surrounding windows. (Leave the left edge at the building corner.)**

   Edit Plane tool

   Drag the top, right, and bottom handles in toward the center of the concrete blocks surrounding the first bank of windows.

9. **Press Command/Control, click the left-center handle, and then drag left to create a secondary plane that's perpendicular to the first plane.**

If you click the handle before pressing Command/Control, this step won't work. Make sure you press the modifier key before you click and drag the handle.

Press Command/ Control, and then drag this handle to add a secondary plane.

10. **Drag the top- and bottom-corner handles on the left side of the secondary plane until the plane more closely matches the perspective of lines on the left face of the building.**

Drag these handles up or down to adjust the perspective of the secondary plane.

11. **Press Command/Control-V to paste the copied pixels from the Clipboard (the banner file that you copied in Step 2).**

The pasted pixels appear in the top-left corner of the preview, surrounded by a selection marquee.

12. **Click inside the selection marquee and drag onto any part of the perspective plane.**

The selection is dropped into the perspective plane, cleanly wrapped around both sides of the building.

13. Drag the selection inside the plane until the ad fills the entire defined plane area.

14. Select the Transform tool in the left side of the Vanishing Point filter dialog box.

15. In the Vanishing Point filter Options menu, turn off the Clip Operations to Surface Edges option (it should be unchecked).

Transform tool

This option should be unchecked (turned off).

You can now see the entire selection, including areas outside the defined perspective plane.

16. Drag the top, bottom, and side handles of the selection until all of the banner text fits within the plane edge.

The perspective planes still produce a very good result, even though you are scaling out of proportion to fit the banner within the allowed space.

17. Reactivate the Clip Operations to Surface Edges option, and then click OK to apply the Vanishing Point filter.

18. **Apply a drop shadow using the following settings:**

Blend mode:	Multiply Black	Opacity:	75%
Angle:	40°	Distance:	5
Spread:	0	Size:	10

Note:

The 40° angle helps match the drop shadow angle to the apparent light source in the office image.

19. **Save the file as `office_ad.psd` in your WIP>Outdoors folder, close the file, and then continue to the next exercise.**

 ## WARP THE SAMPLE AD

Linear perspective, such as the two examples you just created, is fairly easy to adjust (especially using the Vanishing Point filter). However, the world is not entirely linear; objects with curves also have depth and perspective. Compositing onto rounded objects is slightly more complicated than linear perspective, but you can accomplish the task with patience and attention to detail.

1. **Open the file `tanks_clean.psd` from your WIP>Outdoors folder.**

2. **Place the banner.tif file as a Smart Object layer into the tanks file.**

3. **Scale the placed ad to 35% and position it in the center of the front water tank (above the top of the fence).**

4. **With the banner layer selected, choose Edit>Transform>Warp.**

   This is the same option you used in Project 5: Catalog Cover to warp text. However, when you warp anything other than text, you have more options and better control over the warp.

Click here to finalize the transformation.

Click here to cancel the transformation.

When transforming anything other than text, a grid and handles appear for controlling the warp.

5. In the Options bar, choose Arc Upper from the Warp menu.

As for warping text, the same predefined warp options are available for warping an object.

The background image — the water tank — is only slightly curved. A minor Arc Upper warp should be enough to add perspective to the ad layer.

The default Bend value (50%) is obviously too much for compositing these two images.

6. Experiment with Bend values until you're satisfied with the result. (We used a 4.5% bend.)

The Bend value changes only the edges affected by the warp you apply; in the case of Arc Upper, only the top edge changes when you modify the Bend value.

7. In the Options bar, click the Commit button to finalize the transformation (or press Return/Enter).

8. Apply a drop shadow to the layer using the following settings:

Blend mode:	Multiply Black	Opacity:	75%
Angle:	90°	Distance:	2
Spread:	0	Size:	5

Note:

The 90° angle helps match the drop shadow angle to the apparent light source in the tanks image.

9. Save the file as `tanks_ad.psd` **in your WIP>Outdoors folder and close the file.**

10. Continue to the next exercise.

APPLY A CUSTOM WARP

In some cases, the predefined warp styles are adequate. In other cases — such as warping the ad around the balloon in this exercise — the existing styles do not work. In these cases, Photoshop provides a powerful toolset for defining custom warp shapes.

1. **Open the file `balloon_clean.psd` from your WIP>Outdoors folder.**

2. **Place the banner.tif file into the balloon file as a Smart Object.**

3. **Scale the banner layer to 40% proportionally and position it as shown in the following image:**

4. **Choose Edit>Transform>Warp. Apply the Arch warp to the ad layer with a 12% bend.**

5. **If necessary, drag the layer (still in Warp Transform mode) so the banner appears within the white area (as shown here).**

   As you can see, this warp shape is flat; it does not reflect the roundness of the balloon.

6. **Choose Custom in the Warp menu on the Options bar.**

   Anchor points (and their attached handles) are now visible at the corners of the warped shape; you can move these points and handles to adjust the exact shape of the warp to better align it to the balloon's shape.

These handles control the warp curves between points on the grid.

Beginning from the Arch warp style gives you a better starting point than the basic Custom warp.

7. **Drag the corner points on the left side of the warp grid to be directly inside the second seam line on the balloon.**

8. **Drag the handles on the left side of the grid to bloat the left edge of the ad layer.**

   Handles on a warp grid are just like handles on a vector path (created with the Pen tool). Curves follow the direction in which you drag the connected handles.

Position the left corner points directly inside this seam line.

Drag these two handles left so the left edge of the ad follows the line of the seam.

9. **Repeat Steps 7–8 for the right side of the ad.**

10. **Adjust the top and bottom handles to fit the edges vertically within the area between the color patches.**

Use this seam to align the ad's top edge.

Use this seam to align the ad's right edge.

Use this seam to align the ad's bottom edge.

11. **Press Return/Enter to finalize the transformation, and then apply a drop shadow using the following settings:**

Blend mode:	Multiply Black	Opacity:	75%
Angle:	120°	Distance:	3
Spread:	0	Size:	5

> *Note:*
>
> *The 120° angle helps match the drop shadow angle to the apparent light source in the balloon image.*

12. **Save the file as `balloon_ad.psd` in your WIP>Outdoors folder, and then close the file.**

13. **Continue to the next stage of the project.**

Stage 3 Working with Lighting

Photoshop provides extremely powerful tools for creating one composite image from a number of separate components. Although the tools and techniques for doing this type of work are fairly mechanical, some degree of human judgment is required to ensure the separate pieces blend together seamlessly.

In extreme cases of mismatched lighting, a composited image might contain both one person in a photo squinting into the bright sunlight and everyone else in cooler shadows. Of course, not all lighting problems are this obvious, but even subtle differences can make good technical composites appear "off" to even the casual observer. Whenever you composite images, you need to be careful that the lighting is consistent across the entire composition.

The lighting in the original photo is evenly lighting the surface, so the composited ad is fine as is.

The shadows on this side of the building should also affect the composited ad.

The bright sun glare on this spot of the balloon should also affect the composited ad.

This ad is too bright for the apparent position of the sun (directly overhead).

In Photoshop CS6, the Lighting Effects filter (Filter>Render>Lighting Effects) allows you to create different lighting effects in RGB images. The filter opens a separate gallery-like interface, with only the tools you need to apply lighting effects:

- **Options bar** for adding light sources, controlling the overall preview, and cancelling or finalizing the filter.

- **Preview area**, which includes widgets for all applied light sources.

- **Properties panel**, which defines a number of settings for the selected light.

- **Lights panel**, which lists all light sources that exist on the current layer.

The Lighting Effects filter supports three basic types of light sources. The appearance of different light widgets indicates the way each type casts light:

- **Point lights** shine in all directions, such as light that shines from a light bulb.

- **Spot lights** cast an elliptical beam of light, such as the beam from a flashlight.

- **Infinite lights** shine in a single direction from a far distance, such as the sun.

You can select a specific light by clicking in the Lights panel, or simply clicking the related light's widget in the preview area. When a specific light is selected in the preview area, you can use the on-screen controls to change various properties of the selected light.

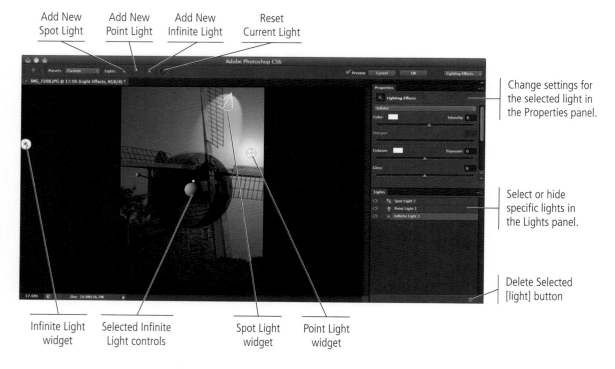

Add New Spot Light
Add New Point Light
Add New Infinite Light
Reset Current Light

Change settings for the selected light in the Properties panel.

Select or hide specific lights in the Lights panel.

Delete Selected [light] button

Infinite Light widget
Selected Infinite Light controls
Spot Light widget
Point Light widget

APPLY A POINT LIGHTING EFFECT

Point light shines in all directions from a single source point. This is a good option when you want to place a highlight point and blend the shadow away from that spot — as in the case of the balloon ad.

1. **Open the Performance pane of the Preferences dialog box. Make sure the Use Graphics Processor option is checked and click OK.**

   If this option is not available (grayed out) on your computer, your video card and/or driver does not support OpenGL. If you cannot use OpenGL, you will not be able to use the Lighting Effects filter.

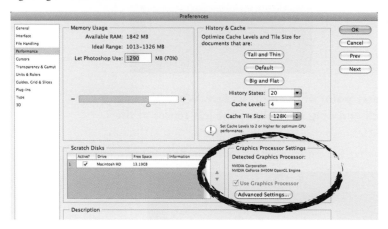

2. **Open balloon_ad.psd from your WIP>Outdoors folder.**

3. **With the banner layer selected in the Layers panel, choose Filter>Render> Lighting Effects.**

   By default, the last-applied light(s) is applied to the active layer.

4. **In the Options bar, choose Default from the Preset menu.**

   Photoshop includes a number of default lighting styles, which you can apply to any image. The default light source is a single spot light.

The Default light source is a single spot light in the center of the image.

Note:

You can also save your own lighting styles by clicking Save in the Preset menu; all defined light sources (and their properties) will be saved in the style so you can call it again later for another image.

5. **With the only light selected in the Lights panel, choose Point in the menu at the top of the Properties panel.**

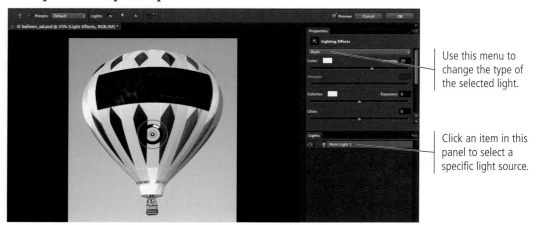

Use this menu to change the type of the selected light.

Click an item in this panel to select a specific light source.

6. **Place the cursor over the center point of the light widget. When the cursor feedback shows "Move", click and drag the light to the left center of the banner.**

   For a point light, you can simply drag the center point to reposition the light's position.

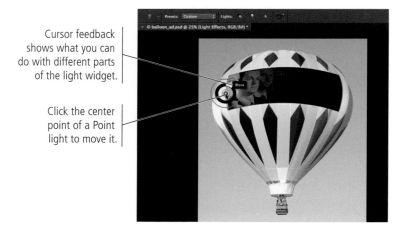

Cursor feedback shows what you can do with different parts of the light widget.

Click the center point of a Point light to move it.

7. **Move the mouse cursor over the green line that surrounds the point light source. When the cursor feedback shows "Scale", click and drag out to enlarge the light source.**

   We enlarged the light to enclose all three faces in the banner ad.

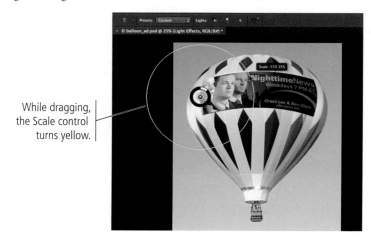

While dragging, the Scale control turns yellow.

8. **In the Options bar, click the button to add a new Point light.**

9. **In the preview area, move the second point light to the bottom-center of the banner.**

10. **Move the cursor to the heavy black circle around the light point. When the cursor feedback shows "Intensity", click and drag left until the heads-up display (HUD) shows Intensity: 10.**

    Intensity determines how bright the light appears; full intensity (100) is the brightest light, while negative values (down to –100) remove light.

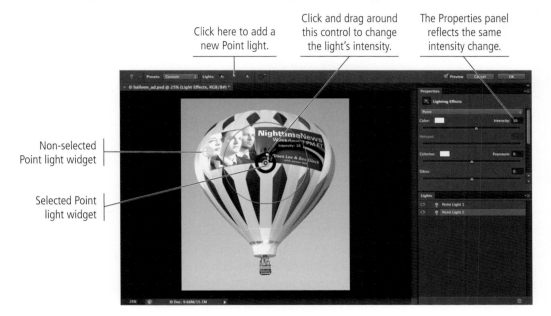

Click here to add a new Point light.

Click and drag around this control to change the light's intensity.

The Properties panel reflects the same intensity change.

Non-selected Point light widget

Selected Point light widget

11. **In the Options bar, toggle the Preview checkbox off and then back on.**

    When you turn off the preview, you toggle the visibility of all lights at once. You can also use the Lights panel to turn individual lights off and on.

    The change is subtle, but you should be able to see how the two light sources change the banner to more realistically match the lighting that exists in the balloon photo.

Click here to toggle all lights on and off.

Click here to toggle a specific light on and off.

12. **Click OK in the Options bar to apply the lighting effect.**

In the Layers panel, you can see that the Lighting Effects have been applied as a Smart Filter. You can turn the effect off or on using the eye icon, or double-click the Lighting Effects item in the panel to reopen the filter interface and change the applied lighting.

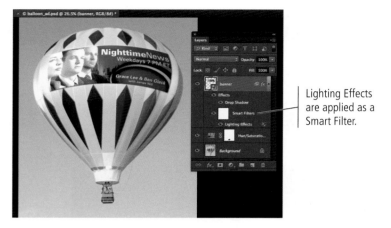

Lighting Effects are applied as a Smart Filter.

13. **Save the file as** `balloon_final.tif` **in your WIP>Outdoors folder.**

14. **Close the file and continue to the next exercise.**

 ## APPLY AN INFINITE LIGHT LIGHTING EFFECT

The light in the water tank photo is striking the top of the tanks; without adjusting the lighting that affects the banner ad, it seems unnaturally bright. To correct this problem, you are going to use the Lighting Effects filter to position the "sun" that is striking the banner layer from the correct position.

1. **Open the file** `tanks_ad.psd` **from your WIP>Outdoors folder.**

2. **Make sure the banner layer is selected in the Layers panel, then choose Filter>Render>Lighting Effects.**

The Lighting Effects filter defaults to the last-used settings. If you continued directly from the previous exercise, your layer has two Point lights.

3. **In the Options bar, make sure the Preview option is checked.**

When you open the Lighting Effects filter, the last-applied lights are still in place.

4. **Click the Point Light 2 in the Lights panel, then click the panel's Delete button.**

You can delete all but one light source from a layer.

5. **With Point Light 1 selected in the Lights panel, choose Infinite from the menu at the top of the Properties panel.**

Infinite light shines from far away, so the overall light angle remains the same throughout an image. The widget in the preview area identifies the position of the light.

An Infinite light defaults to shine from directly in front of the image.

6. **Click the light source handle and drag up to rotate the light source.**

By dragging the light's handle, you are directing the angle of the infinite light — think of positioning the sun relative to the photo. You have to try to think in three dimensions when you reposition an infinite light; use the open hemisphere as a guide.

Drag the light handle to redirect the light source.

The open face of the hemisphere indicates the direction of the light source.

7. **Move the cursor over the Intensity control, then click and drag to change the light's intensity to 30.**

You can see that the infinite light actually darkens the banner layer — which is what you need to make the two layers blend together into a more natural composite.

8. **Click OK in the Options bar to apply the filter.**

9. **Save the file as tanks_final.tif in your WIP>Outdoors folder, and then close the file.**

10. **Continue to the next exercise.**

APPLY A SPOT LIGHT LIGHTING EFFECT

Spot lights cast an elliptical beam of light from a specific direction. This type of light is a good choice for lighting the right half of the office building ad, while leaving the left half of the ad in shadow.

1. **Open the file office_ad.psd from your WIP>Outdoors folder.**

2. **Make sure Layer 1 is selected in the Layers panel and choose Filter>Render>Lighting Effects.**

    Remember, you didn't place the banner into this file; instead, you pasted the banner into the Vanishing Point filter. In this file, the banner exists on Layer 1.

3. **With the existing light selected in the Lights panel, choose Spot in the menu at the top of the Properties panel.**

A Spot light casts an elliptical beam of light.

Hotspot Angle control

Intensity control

Move control

Scale Length control

Scale Width control

4. **Click the Move control of the light widget and drag to the corner of the building, near the bottom of the banner area.**

    As with a point light, you can easily reposition the light by dragging the center point in the widget control.

5. **Move the cursor outside the darker gray line. When you see "Rotate" in the cursor feedback, click and drag right until the light is approximately horizontal.**

    If you click outside the darker (outside) gray line, you can rotate the light. You can also use the handles on that line to scale the width and length of the light.

    The lighter (inside) gray line defines the hotspot angle of the light.

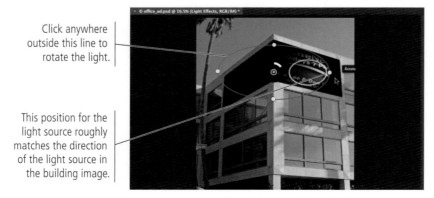

Click anywhere outside this line to rotate the light.

This position for the light source roughly matches the direction of the light source in the building image.

6. **Click the Scale Width handle and drag out past the edge of the banner ad.**

Click the handle on either end of the oval to change the scale width.

7. **Click the top Scale Length handle and drag up to near the top of the image.**

Click the handle on either side of the oval to change the scale length.

8. **Click the Intensity control and drag to change the Intensity to 50.**

   The light striking the right side of the building is relatively bright, so you are increasing the banner's light intensity to more closely match.

9. **Click the Hotspot Angle control and drag out past the building corner.**

   Increasing the hotspot angle increases the area that is affected by the light. Again, think of holding a flashlight — if you shine it directly at your feet, the spot is a small circle; if you shine it farther away from your feet, the beam becomes more elliptical and illuminates a larger area.

   This is very close to realistic lighting based on the shadows in the building image. Keep in mind, however, that your job is to highlight your company's ad placement; in this case it might be good to "cheat" a bit to make the ad slightly more prominent.

This hotspot angle matches the building lighting...

...but half of the ad is very dark.

10. Click the Hotspot Angle control and drag out past the building edge.

This extends the light to the left side of the ad — artificially, but it helps to meet both goals of highlighting your company's capabilities and making the two separate layers blend more naturally together.

Extending the hotspot lightens the ad, but does not adversely affect the overall lighting.

11. Click OK in the Options bar to apply the lighting effect.

12. Save the file as `office_final.tif` in your WIP>Outdoors folder, and then close the file.

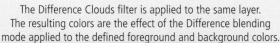

The Rendering Filters

PHOTOSHOP FOUNDATIONS

The **Clouds** filter (Filters>Render>Clouds) fills the currently selected layer with a random cloud-like pattern that varies between the foreground and background colors. The **Difference Clouds** filter (Filters>Render>Difference Clouds) does the same thing but returns a cloud pattern that looks as though it were affected by the Difference blending mode. Because these filters replace the content of the current layer, they are best applied on a separate layer that you can mask and blend to create the look you want.

The Clouds filter is applied to a separate layer behind the masked foreground layer. The clouds are a mixture of the defined foreground and background colors.

The Difference Clouds filter is applied to the same layer. The resulting colors are the effect of the Difference blending mode applied to the defined foreground and background colors.

The **Fibers** filter (Filters>Render>Fibers) fills the currently selected layer with a pattern that looks like woven fibers of the foreground and background colors. The Variance option controls how the colors vary (a low value produces long streaks of color, and a high value results in very short fibers). The Strength option controls how each fiber looks; low strength produces a loose weave, and high strength produces a tighter weave. The Randomize button changes the pattern randomly; you can keep clicking the button to generate new patterns until you find one that you like.

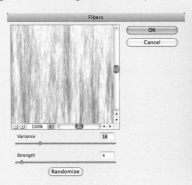

The **Lens Flare** filter (Filters> Render>Lens Flare) simulates the refraction caused by shining a bright light into a camera lens. You can drag the crosshair in the small preview image to change the position of the flare center, change the brightness of the flare, and define the type of lens to simulate.

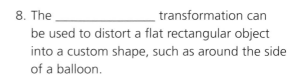
fill in the blank

1. When using the Patch tool, choose the _____ option to select an area that will be copied to another area (where you drag the marquee).

2. The _____ adjustment allows you to change the ink values in specific primary colors or neutrals without affecting other colors.

3. The _____ adjustment allows you to change the Hue, Saturation, and Lightness values of specific primary colors.

4. The _____ tool attempts to simplify replacement of specific colors in your image; you can paint over a targeted color to replace it with the foreground color.

5. The _____ tool mimics a process used in traditional photo development, and is used to lighten an area of a photograph.

6. In _____ perspective, all lines in an image move toward a single spot on the horizon.

7. The _____ provides an easy interface for transforming layer content onto a perspective plane.

8. The _____ transformation can be used to distort a flat rectangular object into a custom shape, such as around the side of a balloon.

9. A(n) _____ light source casts an elliptical beam of light, such as the beam from a flashlight.

10. A(n) _____ light source shines light in all directions from directly above the image.

short answer

1. Briefly explain the advantages to using adjustment layers rather than applying adjustments to regular layers from the Image>Adjustments menu.

2. Briefly explain the concept of a vanishing point.

3. Briefly explain the three types of lighting that can be created using the Lighting Effects filter.

Portfolio Builder Project

Use what you learned in this project to complete the following freeform exercise.
Carefully read the art director and client comments, then create your own design to meet the needs of the project.
Use the space below to sketch ideas; when finished, write a brief explanation of your reasoning behind your final design.

art director comments

Your company's sales manager has another potential client for the Advertise Anywhere! program, and would like to build a personalized presentation similar to the one you did for the Nighttime News show.

To complete this project, you should:

❏ Build a sample ad for the Go Green clean energy initiative.

❏ Find background images on which you can composite the sample ad.

❏ Clean up or adjust the background images as necessary to create the best possible samples.

❏ Composite the sample ad onto the different backgrounds; adjust perspective and lighting as necessary to make the samples appear as natural as possible.

client comments

The director of the Go Green clean energy initiative saw the Nighttime News ads that we placed around the city, and called the show's marketing director to find out where they were created. I just got off the phone with her, and we have a meeting scheduled next week to present some ideas for advertising the Go Green 2013 campaign.

I need you to create a sample ad at the same size as the news show sample. It should include imagery that supports the idea of clean energy — hydroelectricity, windmills, or whatever. The only text for the ad should be the words 'Go Green!', and the Web site address (www.ggenergy.org).

For the background images, find a variety of different types of images. Methods of public transportation, buildings, and large outdoor signs are all good options, but we also want to highlight the 'anywhere' part of Advertise Anywhere! services. Get creative with these sample backgrounds — think up unusual locations where ads might be seen by large numbers of people.

project justification

_____

_____

_____

_____

_____

_____

_____

_____

_____

_____

_____

_____

_____

Compositing images such as the ones in this project is part skill (applying necessary corrections), part judgment (determining the perspective and light source in the background images), and part experimentation (exploring the transformation and filter options to find the best possible solution to the specific problem). Being able to manipulate images — including the correction and transformation tools you used to create these samples — will be invaluable during your graphic design career.

Composite the ad layer with a built-in warp transformation

Composite the ad layer with the Vanishing Point filter

Use the Patch tool to clean up digital garbage

Apply an Infinite lighting effect to unify the layers

Correct lighting with the Shadow/Highlight adjustment

Apply a Spot lighting effect to unify the layers

Apply a Point lighting effect to unify the layers

Use a Hue/Saturation adjustment layer to change the balloon color

Use the Replace Color adjustment to apply a fresh coat of digital paint

Composite the ad layer in Free Transform mode

Composite the ad layer with a custom warp transformation

House Painting

Your client, a real estate developer, is planning a new pre-sales campaign for the company's latest master plan community. He has line-art sketches of the completed houses, but he wants color "paintings" to show prospective buyers what the finished houses might look like. You were hired to create a full-color digital rendering based on one of the artist's black-and-white sketches.

This project incorporates the following skills:

❑ Converting an image from bitmap to RGB color mode

❑ Loading a custom swatch panel to access approved colors

❑ Using fill and stroke techniques to create the basic shapes in the artwork

❑ Using hard and soft brushes to create detail in the painting

❑ Using brush blending modes to achieve special effects such as deep shadows

❑ Creating and applying custom patterns to create large areas of consistent texture

❑ Setting brush options to randomize brush strokes and paint "natural" scenes

Project Meeting

client comments

In three months we break ground on a new master plan community targeted for middle-income families. We are installing an on-site sales office soon so we can start preselling, and we want to be able to show potential buyers what finished houses will look like.

Our architect gave us pen-and-ink renderings, but we want something more realistic — like a painting — in color. If you can create a painting, we can print several copies to frame and hang around the office. When we get closer to building the houses, we might also launch a direct mail sales campaign and do some other print advertising. It depends on how many plots we can presell.

We have worked with an environmental designer to create the community master plan, and have finalized everything from the site map to the stucco and trim colors that will be used for the finished houses. I showed your art director swatches of the paint chips, and we're hoping you can use those to create the actual painting.

art director comments

Most people in our field will tell you that high-quality art is part creativity and part technique. Your role in this project is to provide technique, since the actual artwork was already drawn by the architect.

The client isn't sure what he's going to do with the final artwork. He knows it's going to be printed, definitely as a framed print in the sales office, possibly in brochures and newspapers, and probably on his Web site as well.

With all these possible uses, you need to produce a versatile file that can support many file formats. The RGB color space is larger than CMYK, so create the painting in RGB and start with high enough resolution for print.

The large-format output company has switched to an all-PDF workflow for output. They don't accept any native application files, so you'll have to save the final painting as a high-resolution PDF file. The service rep also said their output devices convert color on the fly, and they get better results from RGB images than images already converted to CMYK.

project objectives

To complete this project, you will:

- ❏ Convert a bitmap image to RGB
- ❏ Import custom swatches
- ❏ Create fill shapes
- ❏ Fill areas with the Paint Bucket tool
- ❏ Use hard- and soft-edge brushes
- ❏ Clone repeating drawing elements
- ❏ Create texture with a faux-finish brush
- ❏ Use opacity and blending modes to create deep shadows
- ❏ Define and save a custom pattern
- ❏ Change brush settings to paint random elements
- ❏ Create and save a brush preset
- ❏ Export a PDF file for print

Stage 1 Preparing the Workspace

This project differs from the ones you have completed so far. In this project, you use Photoshop to create original artwork — that is, rather than compositing images and text to create a finished job, you use Photoshop tools to create the actual pixels that make up the finished artwork.

Some of the skills you learn in this project (including painting with brushes) are normally used by creative designers to develop original digital artwork — starting with nothing other than an idea. By starting with an existing line-art drawing, however, you can use the same tools and techniques to build a full-color artistic rendering, even if you don't have the natural painting ability of da Vinci.

CONVERT A BITMAP TO RGB

The provided sketch is a bitmap (or line art) image, which you learned about in Project 1: Composite Movie Ad. It contains only two tonal values — black and white. Any apparent shading was created using traditional artistic techniques such as crosshatching and pointillism.

Line-art images are typically scanned between 1200 and 2400 pixels per inch to provide enough data for cleanly outputting the images on a high-resolution output device. The first task in creating a color image from a line-art drawing is converting the scanned bitmap image to RGB, which actually requires two separate steps.

1. **Download PS6_RF_Project7.zip from the Student Files Web page.**

2. **Expand the ZIP archive in your WIP folder (Macintosh) or copy the archive contents into your WIP folder (Windows).**

   This results in a folder named **Realty**, which contains the files you need for this project. You should also use this folder to save the files you create in this project.

3. **Open the file house.tif from the WIP>Realty folder.**

4. **Choose Image>Mode>Grayscale.**

   You can't convert a bitmap image directly to RGB because the Bitmap mode has only two possible tonal values (black and white). You first have to convert the image to grayscale, and then convert it to RGB so you can paint it in full color.

5. **In the Grayscale dialog box, make sure the Size Ratio field is set to 1 (the default value), and then click OK.**

   Because bitmap images are typically at much higher resolution than necessary for grayscale or color images, you could scale the image at the same time that you convert it to grayscale. The Size Ratio option is the factor for scaling down the bitmap image (for example, a Size Ratio value of 2 reduces the grayscale image by 50%). We prefer to convert using a 1-to-1 ratio, and then manually resize or resample the image using the Image Size dialog box.

   After you click OK, the conversion process might take a few minutes to complete, depending on the speed of your computer. Photoshop has to calculate a lot of pixel data to turn this bitmap image into a grayscale image.

6. Choose Image>Image Size.

The original image was scanned at 1200 pixels per inch, which is appropriate for bitmap images. As you can see, converting the bitmap image to grayscale at a 1-to-1 ratio resulted in 99.9 megabytes — a huge size that might be unmanageable, depending on your computer.

For grayscale and RGB, you need only 300 pixels per inch. You can simply resample the file to discard the unnecessary resolution.

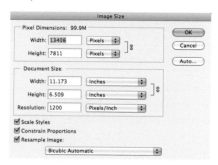

7. With the Resample Image option checked, type 300 in the Resolution field, leave the units set to pixels/inch, and then click OK.

At 300 ppi, you can see the dramatic reduction in file size — down to 6.24 megabytes.

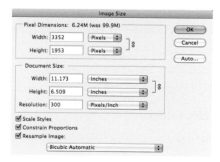

8. Choose View>Fit On Screen.

The change in resolution dramatically reduces the view of the image in the document window. (The view percentage is not changed by resampling the image.)

9. Choose Image>Mode>RGB Color.

Note:

You could have converted to RGB before resampling the image, but you would have been working with a file of about 400 megabytes before resampling. By resampling first, you have a more manageable file size to convert to RGB.

After the conversion is complete, the file is around 19 megabytes — large, but workable.

10. **Rename the Background layer** Sketch **and lock the layer.**

You're going to use this layer as a template for your painting. Locking the layer prevents you from accidentally moving or altering the original artwork.

Click here to
lock the layer.

11. **Save the file as** house_working.psd **in your WIP>Realty folder and continue to the next exercise.**

 IMPORT CUSTOM SWATCHES

The Swatches panel stores colors that you use frequently; you can access a color by simply clicking a swatch in the panel. You can use swatches from a number of built-in libraries commonly used in the graphics industry, or you can create custom swatch libraries that can be shared with other applications in the Adobe Creative Suite.

Rather than randomly picking colors for the various elements of the house, you will use a set of custom swatches based on the color scheme defined in the community master plan.

1. **With** house_working.psd **open, display the Swatches panel (Window>Swatches).**

Photoshop includes a default set of swatches chosen from the various built-in swatch libraries.

2. **In the Swatches panel Options menu, choose Replace Swatches.**

The options in this menu are similar to the ones you used for patterns, gradients, and styles in Project 2: African Wildlife Map. You can create a new swatch, change the panel view, manage visible swatch sets, or open built-in swatch libraries.

Note:

You can always restore the default swatches by choosing Reset Swatches in the panel Options menu.

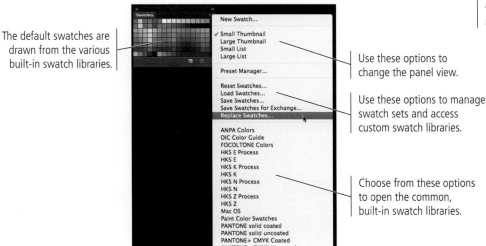

The default swatches are drawn from the various built-in swatch libraries.

Use these options to change the panel view.

Use these options to manage swatch sets and access custom swatch libraries.

Choose from these options to open the common, built-in swatch libraries.

3. **Windows users: Choose Swatch Exchange (*.ASE) in the Files of Type menu.**

4. **Navigate to the file home color.ase in the WIP>Realty folder, then click Open/Load.**

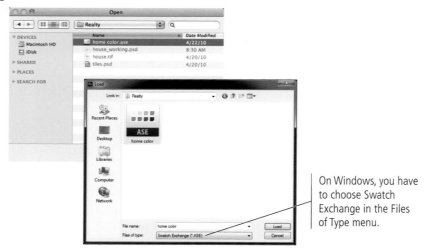

On Windows, you have to choose Swatch Exchange in the Files of Type menu.

Note:

Creative Suite users: If you are sharing swatches between applications, Photoshop doesn't recognize pattern swatches, gradient swatches, or the Registration swatch from Illustrator or InDesign, nor does Photoshop transfer "book color" references such as HSB, XYZ, duotone, Monitor RGB, opacity, totally ink, or webRGB from within the application.

The ASE extension identifies an Adobe Swatch Exchange file, which is a special format for sharing swatch libraries between applications in the Adobe Creative Suite.

You can save custom swatch sets to be used in other Adobe applications by choosing Save Swatches for Exchange in the Swatches panel Options menu. To save a swatch library for only Photoshop, you can use the Save Swatches command to save the swatch library with the ".aco" extension.

5. **Using the Swatches panel Options menu, change the panel to Small List view.**

Because you chose Replace Swatches in the panel Options menu in Step 2, the new panel contains only the swatches from the ASE file. These swatches were created specifically for this project, using basic names that will make it easier to complete the house painting.

Click and drag this corner to resize the panel.

6. **Continue to the next stage of the project.**

Stage 2 Filling Solid Areas

The easiest way to start a painting such as this one is to create the basic shapes that make up the object you are painting. You can make a basic selection and simply fill it with a color, use the Paint Bucket tool to fill areas of similar color, or use brushes and painting techniques to color specific areas. When you combine these techniques with Photoshop layers, you can also use transparency and blending modes to create images that appear as though they were painted with a traditional canvas and brushes.

 ## CREATE FILL SHAPES

In this exercise, you use standard selection tools to paint the front walls of the house — large and relatively simple areas that you can fill with "stucco" colored paint.

1. **With house_working.psd open, create a new layer named Walls.**

2. **With the Walls layer selected, use the Rectangular Marquee tool to draw a selection around the front of the garage face (including the pillars to the left and right of the garage door).**

   Don't worry if your selection covers parts of the bushes and doesn't include the pieces that stick out from the basic rectangular shape. You will refine the selection in the following steps, and you will paint the bushes on higher layers later in this project.

   Note:

   As hard as we tried to get this image exactly square on the scanner bed, no scans are perfect. There's a chance that the straight lines, paths, and guides you create in Photoshop will not exactly match the horizontal, vertical, or angled lines in your scans. A very slight difference is nothing to worry about. The finished product will look fine because the original scan will ultimately be deleted.

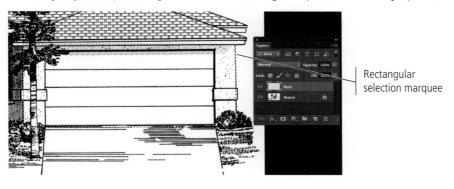

Rectangular selection marquee

3. **Using the Add to Selection and Subtract from Selection options, draw additional selection marquees to select the entire face of the house.**

   Zooming in might make it easier to refine the selection, especially in the smaller areas where the house shape extends slightly.

Add to Selection   Subtract from Selection

We outlined the selection in red to make it easy to see in this screen capture. Yours will be visible as "marching ants."

4. **Click the Stucco 2 swatch in the Swatches panel to define that swatch as the foreground color.**

Clicking a color in the Swatches panel changes the active foreground color.

5. **Choose Edit>Fill. Choose Foreground Color in the Use menu of the Fill dialog box.**

6. **Click OK to fill the wall selection.**

7. **With the Walls layer selected in the Layers panel, change the Opacity setting to 80%.**

Semi-transparent fills make it possible to see and continue painting the elements of the original artwork. When you're finished with the project, you can return this layer to 100% opacity. If you had changed the fill opacity to 80% in the Fill dialog box, you would be unable to change it back to 100%.

Note:

The finished artwork will be at full opacity. While you're working, however, it helps to see through various layers.

8. **Turn off the current selection (Select>Deselect), save the file, and then continue to the next exercise.**

FILL AREAS WITH THE PAINT BUCKET TOOL

The Paint Bucket tool has the same basic functionality as the Fill dialog box — you click the tool cursor to fill an area with the current foreground color. In the Options bar, you can choose the color, blending mode, and opacity of the fill.

1. **With `house_working.psd` open, hide the Walls layer and add a new layer named `Front Trim` at the top of the layer stack.**

2. **Choose the Paint Bucket tool (nested under the Gradient tool) in the Tools panel. In the Options bar, type `30` in the Tolerance field, and activate the Contiguous and All Layers options.**

   Unlike the Fill dialog box, the Paint Bucket tool creates fills based on the defined sample tolerance (like the settings used to create a selection based on a color range).

   In addition to the fill color, blending mode, and opacity, the Options bar includes settings for tool tolerance and anti-aliasing, as well as whether to fill only contiguous pixels within the defined tolerance. The All Layers option allows you to sample pixels from all visible layers instead of only the selected layer.

3. **Change the foreground color to the Trim 1 swatch.**

4. **Click the Paint Bucket tool on a white area of the trim board on the left side of the house.**

   The Paint Bucket tool fills areas with the selected foreground color. Because the Contiguous option is checked in the Options bar, only the area inside the "board" edges is filled.

   The tool's cursor can be confusing. Watch the top of the pointer in the cursor — not the drop of paint falling from the bucket — to identify the area that will be filled.

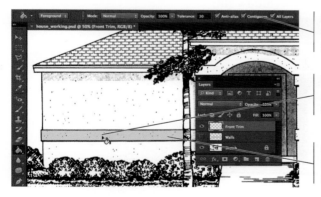

Use these settings to determine the sensitivity of the Paint Bucket tool.

Use the arrow tip to determine which area will be filled.

Contiguous white pixels are filled with the current foreground color.

5. **Click inside each of the trim areas in the front of the house. (Use the following image as a guide for the areas you should fill.)**

   Make sure you click on both sides of the trees, and don't forget the window sill. In some segments, you might need to click several times to fill the primary shapes.

6. **Zoom into the trim on the right side of the window.**

   Because of the way the illustrator created shadows, you need to use a slightly different method to fill in the shadowed pieces of trim.

   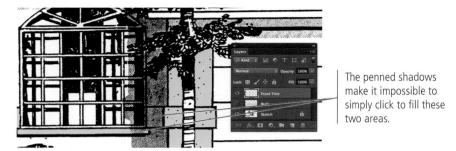

   The penned shadows make it impossible to simply click to fill these two areas.

7. **Draw a rectangle marquee around the shadowed trim. Select the Paint Bucket tool, turn off the All Layers option in the Options bar, then click inside the selection marquee.**

   Select this shadowed area, then turn off the All Layers option and click to fill the selection.

8. **Repeat Step 7 to fill the shadowed section of the window sill.**

9. **Hide the Sketch layer.**

   Because of the points used to create texture in the sketch, the Paint Bucket tool did not fill all the shapes. That's okay, though, because you will later use the empty spots to create texture of your own. Also, don't worry about the areas where trees and bushes cover the house; you're going to paint trees that will cover those areas.

   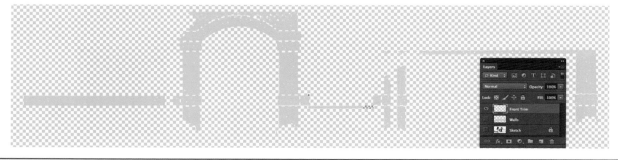

10. Show the Sketch layer again.

11. Create a new layer named `Fascia` at the top of the layer stack. Select the new layer as the active one.

12. Using the Paint Bucket tool with the All Layers option active, fill the upper parts of the fascia boards with the Trim 2 swatch.

13. Fill the lower parts of the fascia boards with the Trim 3 swatch.

These are the fascia boards.

14. Create a new layer named `Garage Door` at the top of the layer stack and select it. Use the Paint Bucket tool with the All Layers option active to fill the four panels on the garage door with the Doors 3 swatch.

Because of the sketched shading, you might need to increase the tool's tolerance to fill most of the the top garage door panel. Alternatively, you can use the selection marquee technique to fill the appropriate area.

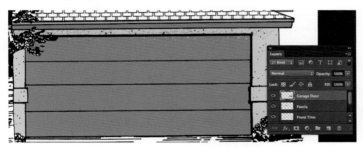

15. Create a new layer named `Pavement` at the top of the layer stack and select it. Use the Polygonal Lasso tool to draw a marquee around the sidewalk and driveway areas, then fill the selected area with the Pavement 1 swatch.

In the sketch, the driveway area doesn't have a solid edge, so simply clicking with the Paint Bucket tool would fill most of the layer with gray. If you have defined a selection area, clicking inside the selection marquee only fills the selected area.

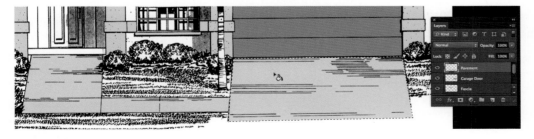

16. Deselect the active marquee, then save the file and continue to the next stage of the project.

Stage 3 Painting with Brushes

Filling a selection area is one of the more basic techniques for painting in Photoshop. To create complex custom artwork, you can use Photoshop brushes in the digital workspace just as you would use traditional brushes on canvas. The built-in brushes come in hundreds of shapes and sizes; combining these brushes with options such as opacity, flow, and blending mode provides an almost infinite array of choices for painting pixels in a Photoshop layout.

By this point you should be familiar with using Photoshop brushes to paint and erase areas of a layer mask — but there is far more to using brushes than what you have already learned throughout this book's earlier projects. Painting the house in this project requires several different types of brushes, as well as controlling the brush options to complete various areas of the painting.

When you choose the Brush tool, you must first select a specific brush. You can choose one of the built-in brush presets from the Options bar, or you can define your own brush by changing the Size and Hardness settings. You can also use the Options bar to change the blending mode, opacity, and flow of the current brush, as well as work in Airbrush mode.

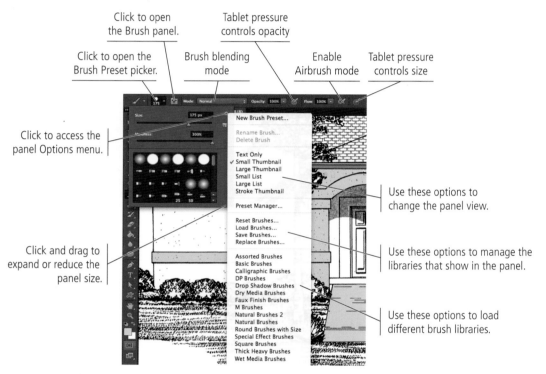

You learned about blending modes and opacity in an earlier project. The other brush options require a little bit of explanation.

- **Size** is the size of the brush tip, measured in pixels.

- **Hardness** is the percentage of the brush that's completely opaque. For example, a Hardness setting of 50% for a brush with a 10-pixel diameter means 5 pixels in the brush center are hard, and the remaining diameter has a feathered edge.

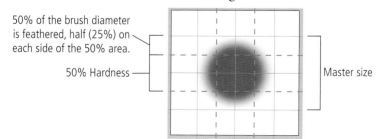

> **Note:**
>
> *Pressure sensitivity becomes an issue when you use a drawing tablet. The harder you press, the more "paint" is applied. Many of the painting tools in Photoshop — including the Brush tool — include options to allow pressure sensitivity while you paint.*

- **Flow** sets the rate at which color is applied as you paint repeatedly over the same area. As you continue painting over the same area (while holding down the mouse button), the amount of color "builds up."

In the following example, we set the brush color to C=100 M=50, with a Flow setting of 50%. Each successive click moved the color values 50% closer to the brush color.

Contrary to what many people think, the Flow setting does not apply hard percentages of the brush color. The first click resulted in 25% magenta, or 50% of the brush color value. The second click produced 38% magenta, which is the result of adding 50% of the difference between the first click (25% magenta) and the brush color (50% magenta) — or one half of the difference between 25 and 50 (25 / 2 = 12.5).

For the third click, 50% of the difference between 38 (the previous value) and 50 (the brush value) is added: 50 − 38 = 12 / 2 = 6 + 38 = 44

Note:

Press the Left Bracket key ([ ) or Right Bracket key ( ]) to decrease or increase (respectively) the current brush diameter to the next predetermined size.

Press Shift-[to decrease brush hardness, and press Shift-] to increase the brush hardness in 25% increments.

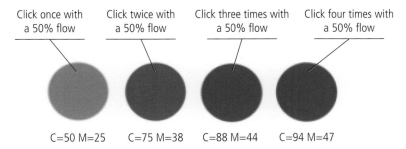

Click once with a 50% flow — Click twice with a 50% flow — Click three times with a 50% flow — Click four times with a 50% flow

C=50 M=25 | C=75 M=38 | C=88 M=44 | C=94 M=47

Note:

Color values are always whole numbers, which is why the magenta value is rounded to 38 instead of the mathematical 50% value of 37.5.

- **Airbrush mode** simulates painting with an airbrush. If you hold down the mouse button or move the cursor back and forth over the same area, more color builds up in the same location. (Brush hardness, opacity, and flow options control how fast and how much "paint" is applied.)

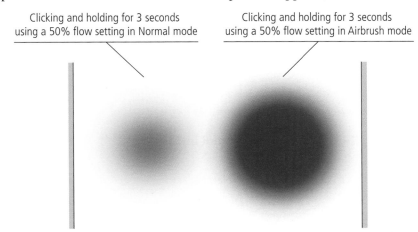

Clicking and holding for 3 seconds using a 50% flow setting in Normal mode — Clicking and holding for 3 seconds using a 50% flow setting in Airbrush mode

Note:

Press a number key to define the brush opacity setting in increments of 10% (e.g., pressing 6 sets the opacity to 60%).

Note:

Press Shift and a number key to define the brush flow setting in increments of 10% (e.g., pressing Shift-6 sets the flow to 60%).

USE HARD BRUSHES

The brush Hardness setting allows you to paint either sharp lines or soft, feathered edges. Most painting projects — including this one — require a combination of hard- and soft-edge brushes.

1. **With house_working.psd open, hide all but the Sketch layer. Create two new layers at the top of the layer stack — one named Front Door and one named FD Panels. Make sure the FD Panels layer is higher in the layer stack.**

   The Front Door layer will hold the overall door area; the FD Panels layer will hold the painted lines that form the shapes of the raised panels within the front door.

2. **Open the Cursors pane of the Preferences dialog box (in the Photoshop menu on Macintosh or the Edit menu on Windows).**

3. **In the Painting Cursors area, choose the Full Size Brush Tip option and activate the Show Crosshair in Brush Tip option. Click OK to apply the change.**

   The Full Size Brush Tip option changes the cursor to include the entire brush area, including the feathered part of soft-edge brushes.

Note:

When using the Brush tool, you can activate Caps Lock on your keyboard to temporarily switch to the Precise cursor mode. If you are already in Precise cursor mode, activating the Caps Lock key switches to the Normal Brush Tip cursor.

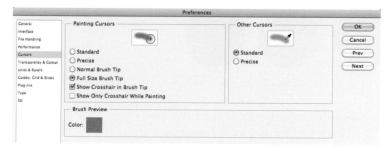

4. **Make the Front Door layer active, then draw a rectangular selection around the front door. Make sure all door edges are included in the selection.**

5. **Change the foreground color to the Doors 3 swatch, then choose the Paint Bucket tool in the Tools panel. Uncheck the All Layers option in the Options bar.**

   If the All Layers option is selected, clicking with the Paint Bucket tool would sample from the Sketch layer, and some of the selected area wouldn't be entirely filled.

6. **With the Front Door layer active, click the Paint Bucket tool inside the selection marquee.**

   Since the active layer (Front Door) has no current content, the Tolerance setting is irrelevant. The entire selection area fills with the Doors 3 color.

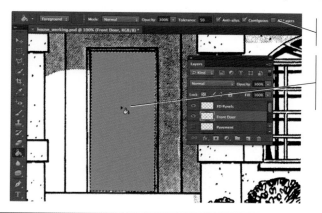

The All Layers option is turned off.

The Front Door layer has no content yet, so clicking paints all pixels inside the selection area.

7. **Deselect the active selection marquee. Change the Front Door layer Opacity value to 50% so you can see the underlying sketch.**

8. **Make the FD Panels layer active, and then choose the Brush tool in the Tools panel.**

9. **Change the foreground color to the Doors 4 swatch.**

10. **In the Options bar, click the Brush button to open the Brush Preset picker. Open the panel Options menu and choose Small List view.**

Click to open the Brush Preset picker. Click to open the Brush panel.

11. **Select the Hard Round shape option, and define its Size as 10 px. Press Return/Enter to close the Brush Preset picker.**

12. **Place the cursor over the inset line on the top-left panel of the front door.**

The default brush cursor shows the size of the selected brush tip. In this case, the 10-pixel brush is clearly wider than the line you want to paint.

Brush tool cursor

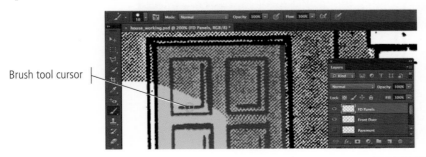

13. **Press [six times to reduce the brush size to 4 pixels.**

You can press [and] to decrease or increase the brush size to the next defined preset. Under ten pixels, the key shortcuts change the brush size by 1 pixel at a time.

14. **Click at the top of the panel inset, press Shift, and then click at the lower-right corner of the panel inset.**

15. **Press Shift and click at the lower-left corner of the panel inset.**

Pressing Shift and then clicking again connects the first and second points with a straight line of the brush color. You can also press Shift while dragging to paint a perfectly horizontal or vertical line.

Note:

Zooming in helps when you're working on the smaller details of a painting (such as the door inset panels).

Click here...
...then Shift-click here...
...then Shift-click here.

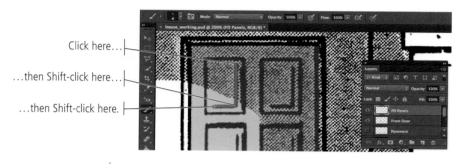

16. **Save the file and continue to the next exercise.**

USE SOFT BRUSHES

Painting with a hard brush results in colored pixels edged by white pixels. In the real world, however, there are very few perfectly hard edges with no variation in shades. Soft-edge brushes are far more useful for creating artwork that includes the subtle color variations found in a real object.

1. **With house_working.psd open, draw a rectangular selection marquee around the front door panel where you painted the inset.**

2. **Make sure the FD Panels layer is selected and Doors 4 is the current foreground color.**

3. **Choose the Brush tool. Using the Options bar, open the Brush Preset picker and change the brush Size to 15 px and the Hardness to 0%. Press Return/Enter to finalize your selections and close the Brush Preset picker.**

4. **Place the cursor so the crosshairs are exactly on top of the selection marquee.**

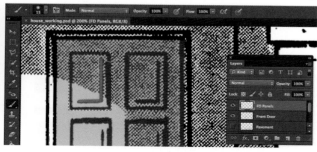

5. **Click at the top-right corner of the selection marquee, press Shift, and drag down to paint the panel's right edge.**

   Even though half the cursor is outside the selection marquee, areas outside the marquee are not painted; the reduced hardness results in a softer edge to the brush stroke.

Click here...

...and Shift-drag to here.

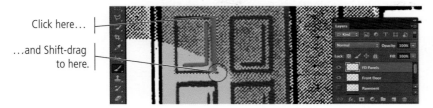

6. **Using the same technique, paint the stroke that makes up the top edge of the panel.**

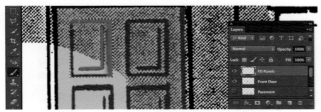

Note:

Always remember that when you have an active selection, you can only affect the area inside the selection.

7. **Change the foreground color to Doors 2, and reduce the brush size to 10 px. Paint the left and bottom edges of the panel.**

8. **Turn off the active selection.**

9. **Use the same processes outlined in this and the previous exercise to create the lower-left inset panel of the door.**

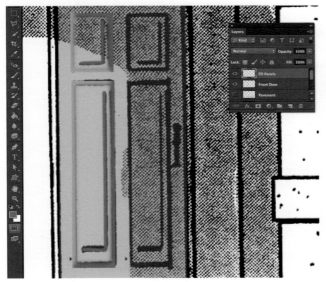

Note:

Even though these screen shots show the art at 200%, which naturally causes even hard edges to appear soft, you should be able to see the difference between the hard-edge line and the soft-edge line.

10. **Deeslect the active marquue, save the file, and then continue to the next exercise.**

When you're painting something like this house, you start with spaces defined by sharp, black lines drawn on white paper. In the case of the bitmap scan provided by your client, there are plenty of lines to define the objects in the drawing. But as you can guess, real-world objects rarely contain sharp black lines.

In addition to the techniques you have already applied, a number of other options can be used to paint color into a digital file. In this exercise, you will use the Stroke dialog box to outline the front door.

1. **With house_working.psd open, make sure the FD Panels layer is selected.**

2. **With the Move tool active, press Option/Alt-Shift, and then click-drag right.**

   This method of copying a selection (or layer, if there is no specific selection marquee) is called **cloning**. When you clone an entire layer, the result is a copy of the existing layer. If you clone a selection marquee, the cloned content becomes part of the active layer.

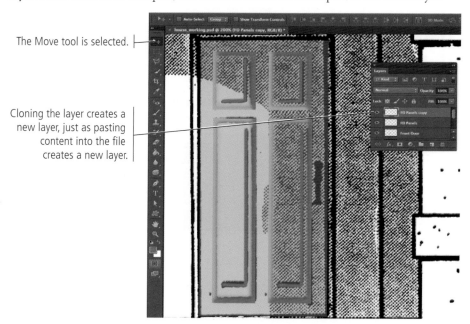

The Move tool is selected.

Cloning the layer creates a new layer, just as pasting content into the file creates a new layer.

Note:

Press Option/Alt and click-drag to clone the current selection.

Press Shift to constrain movement to 45° increments.

3. **Use a small hard brush with a black foreground color to create the door handle.**

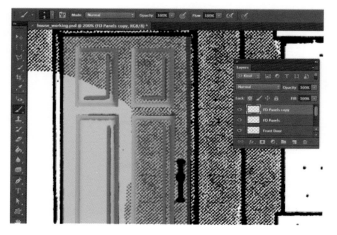

4. **Change the Front Door layer opacity back to 100%.**

5. **Select the FD Panels copy, FD Panels, and Front Door layers. Open the Layers panel Options menu and choose New Group from Layers.**

   The merged layer adopts the attributes (name, opacity, etc.) of the topmost layer included in the merge.

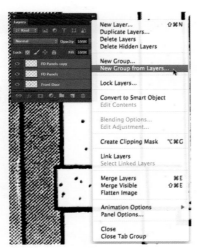

   You could also merge the selected layers into a single layer using the Merge Layers command. However, that option permanently flattens the merged layers, so you can no longer edit the individual component layers. In many real-world projects, professionals often prefer to maintain individual components as long as possible in case changes need to be made at a later time.

6. **In the resulting dialog box, type `Front Door` as the group name and then click OK.**

7. **In the Layers panel, expand the Front Door layer group.**

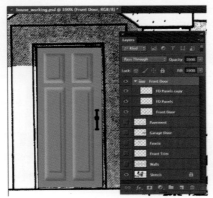

8. **Choose the Magic Wand tool (nested under the Quick Selection tool). In the Options bar, choose the New Selection option and make sure the Sample All Layers option is turned off.**

   You can use the Magic Wand tool to create a selection based on the content of all visible layers in the file. In this case, you want to base your selection on the Front Door layer only, so the Sample All Layers option needs to be turned off. You can use whatever sample size you prefer for this exercise.

9. With the Front Door layer (inside the Front Door layer group) selected, click anywhere outside the door area.

Because the door is the only object on the layer, the only area that gets selected is the empty portion of the layer.

Marching ants surround the entire image…

…and the painted front door area.

Everything but the front door is selected.

10. Choose Select>Inverse to select only the filled area of the layer (the door).

Only the front door is selected.

11. **Change the foreground color to the Doors 4 swatch.**

12. **Choose Edit>Stroke. In the Stroke dialog box, set the Width value to 3 px and the Location to Center. Leave the Blending Mode menu set to Normal, then click OK to apply the stroke.**

   The Stroke dialog box is similar to the Fill dialog box, except you use it to define the stroke for the current selection.

   Note:

   The Location value of the stroke determines the placement of the stroke width in relation to the selection marquee.

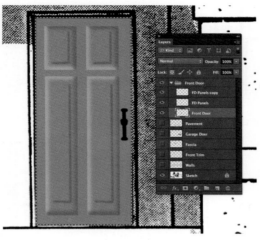

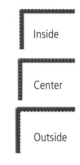

13. **Using the Rectangular Marquee tool, draw a new selection area around the outer door area. Use the Stroke dialog box to apply a 5-px stroke to the new selection.**

14. **Deselect the current selection.**

15. **Choose the Brush tool, and define a 5-px brush with 100% hardness.**

16. **Place the cursor over the bottom-left corner of the stroke created in Step 13. Click, then Shift-drag left to create the line that marks the top of the stoop.**

Use the brush cursor preview to align the brush with the existing stroke.

Use the brush cursor to align the new stroke with the bottom of the existing stroke.

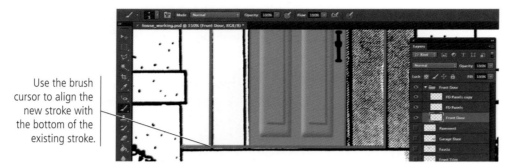

17. **Repeat Step 16 to create the line on the right side of the door.**

18. **In the Layers panel, collapse the Front Door layer group.**

19. **Save the file and continue to the next exercise.**

APPLY STROKES TO CLOSED PATHS

The window on the front of the house includes a bit more detail than most other elements in this painting. To create this detail, you will use a combination of methods to add strokes to both closed and open paths.

1. **With house_working.psd open, create a new layer named Window at the top of the layer stack. Select it as the active layer.**

2. **Choose the Pen tool. In the Options bar, choose Path in the left menu. Open the Geometry Options menu and make sure the Rubber Band option is not checked.**

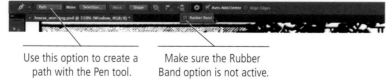

Use this option to create a path with the Pen tool.

Make sure the Rubber Band option is not active.

3. Draw the top curved portion of the window.

The Pen tool makes it easier to draw a path that matches the window curve. You can then use this path to create a selection that you can use to apply a stroke.

Draw this path.

The path is stored in the Paths panel as a work path.

4. With the work path selected in the Paths panel (Window>Paths), click the Load Path as Selection button at the bottom of the panel.

Load Path as Selection

5. Choose Edit>Stroke. Apply a 6-px black stroke centered on the selection marquee and click OK.

It's obscured by the sketch, but the selection is already outlined with a 6-px black stroke.

6. Immediately choose Edit>Stroke again, and apply a 3-px white stroke centered on the selection marquee.

7. Turn off the active selection marquee.

8. Use the same 6-px-black/3-px-white sequence of strokes to create the outer frame of the square window.

In this case, you can simply use the Rectangular Marquee tool to draw the selection.

9. **Hide the Sketch layer and review your work.**

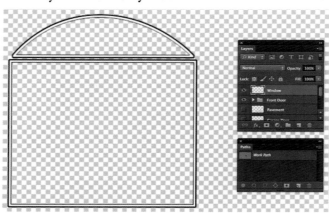

10. **Save the file and continue to the next exercise.**

 APPLY STROKES TO OPEN PATHS

The rest of the lines in the window are basically straight lines, which are easy to create; however, these straight lines do not create closed shapes from which you can make a selection, so you will use a slightly different technique to create the inner lines of the window.

1. **With `house_working.psd` open, show the Sketch layer, and then create a new layer immediately above the Window layer.**

   You will use this layer as a temporary workspace, so it isn't necessary to name it.

2. **Choose the Pencil tool (nested under the Brush tool in the Tools panel), and then reset the default foreground and background colors.**

3. **In the Options bar, open the Brush Preset picker. Choose the Hard Round brush and change the size to 5 px. Press Retun/Enter to close the picker.**

   The Pencil tool is very similar to the Brush tool, except it only creates hard edges (just like an actual pencil). In the Options bar, you can select a brush preset from any of the available hard-edge brushes; you can also define the blending mode and opacity to use for the pencil stroke.

Note:

*If the **Auto Erase** option is checked, the Pencil tool paints based on the defined foreground and background colors in the Tools panel, as compared to the color of pixels under the tool cursor. If you draw over an area that contains the foreground color, that area is erased to the background color. If you draw over an area that does not include the foreground color, the Pencil tool simply applies the foreground color.*

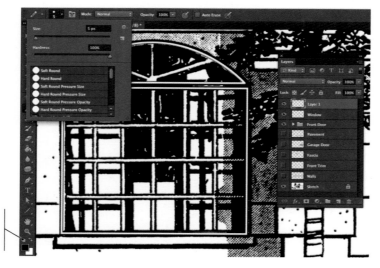

Click here to reset the default foreground and background colors.

Although you are not going to use the Pencil tool to draw in this exercise, you need to set the tool's attributes so you can apply them later in this exercise.

4. **Use the Pen tool in Path mode to draw a horizontal line that represents the middle division of the window.**

   Because this is an open path (i.e., it doesn't create an actual shape), creating the black-and-white effect requires a slightly different method.

5. **With the work path selected in the Paths panel, choose Stroke Path from the panel Options menu.**

   Draw this line as the path.

6. **In the resulting Stroke Path dialog box, choose Pencil, and then click OK.**

   Using this method, you can define a specific tool to use for the stroke. The current characteristics of the selected tool will be applied, which is why you set the Pencil tool options in Steps 2 and 3.

7. **Choose the Pencil tool again, change the brush size to 3 px, and then swap the foreground and background colors.**

   The brush size is now 3 px.

   The Pencil tool is selected again.

   The same work path is still active.

   Click here to swap the foreground and background colors.

   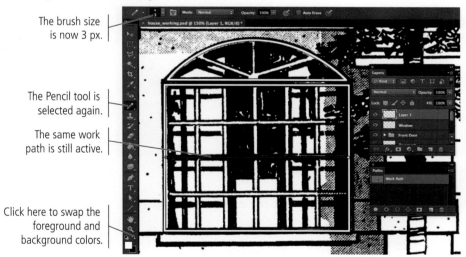

8. **With the work path still selected in the Paths panel, choose Stroke Path from the panel Options menu.**

9. **Choose Pencil in the resulting dialog box and click OK. Hide the Sketch layer and review your work.**

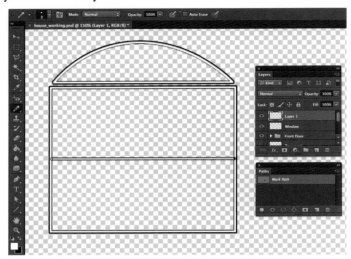

10. **Click the empty area of the Paths panel to turn off the work path.**

11. **Select the Move tool. With the Layer 1 layer active in the Layers panel, press Option/Alt-Shift, and then click and drag up to clone the horizontal line.**

   If you had not deselected in Step 10, this step would create the cloned line on the existing Layer 1 instead of creating a new layer.

Using the Move tool, Option/Alt-Shift-click-drag to clone the layer with the horizontal line.

The work path should not be selected when you clone the layer.

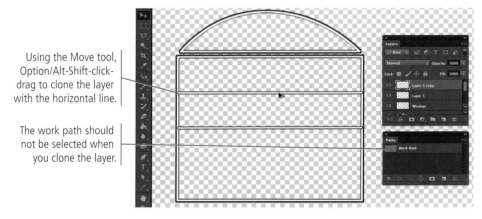

12. **Repeat Step 11 (dragging down this time) to create the remaining horizontal line.**

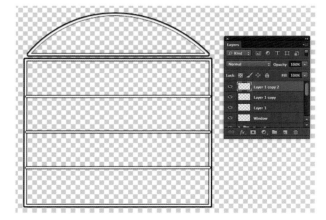

13. **Use any method you prefer to create the remaining lines of the window, including the lines in the arched window area.**

Whenever possible, clone elements to save yourself work. For example, you could clone one of the layers with a horizontal line, then transform (rotate and scale) that clone to create a vertical line — which you can then clone to create all the necessary vertical lines.

You can use the same process to create the angled lines in the arched window, rotating the layers as necessary to approximate the correct angles.

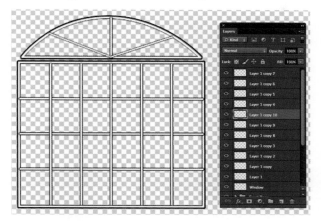

14. **Move the Window layer to the top of the layer stack.**

This hides the ends of the open lines behind the closed paths. If any line ends are visible, select the appropriate layer with the Move tool and use the Arrow keys to nudge it into place.

15. **Select all temporary layers and the Window layer. Open the Layers panel Options menu and choose Merge Layers.**

The topmost layer attributes — including the name — are applied to the merged layer. The entire element is now contained on the single Window layer.

As with the Front Door layer, you might prefer to store the component layers in a layer group so you could more easily make changes to the component layers at a later point. In this case, it really isn't necessary so you are merging all the component layers into a single Window layer.

Note:

The document tab displays the name of the active layer. This tab can be very helpful when you're working on complex files with multiple layers.

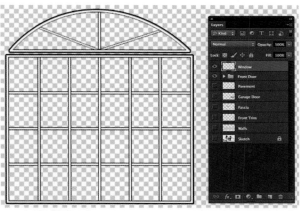

16. **Save the file and continue to the next exercise.**

PAINT BEHIND EXISTING COLOR

The Behind blending mode is only available when you are creating pixels (painting, adding a fill or stroke to a selection, and so on). This blending mode adds new pixels behind the existing pixels; any existing pixels that are fully opaque will entirely hide the new pixels. This technique is extremely useful for filling spaces and lining edges of existing areas. In this exercise, you will use the Behind method to create the lines that surround the garage door panels.

1. **With `house_working.psd` open, hide all but the Sketch and Garage Door layers, and then select the Garage Door layer as the active layer.**

2. **Change the foreground color to the Doors 4 swatch.**

3. **Choose the Brush tool. In the Options bar, select the Hard Round brush preset and change the size to 25 px. Open the Blending Mode menu and choose Behind.**

4. **Click and drag across the top dividing line in the garage door.**

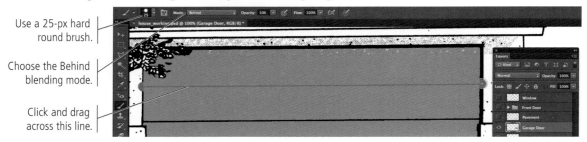

Use a 25-px hard round brush.

Choose the Behind blending mode.

Click and drag across this line.

5. **Repeat Step 4 to fill in the other dividing lines in the door, the space above the door, and the space on the right and left sides of the door.**

6. **Show the Front Trim layer, then drag it to the top of the layer stack.**

   The Behind blending mode only applies to the active layer; other layers are obscured by painted areas. To create the appropriate effect, you have to change the layer stacking order so the trim appears in front of the entire Garage Door layer.

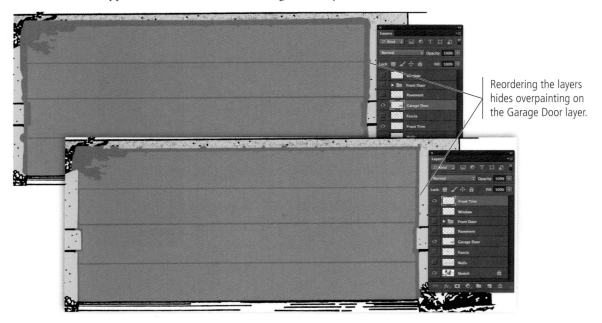

Reordering the layers hides overpainting on the Garage Door layer.

7. **Save the file and continue to the next exercise.**

MODIFY SELECTIONS TO FILL BEHIND COLOR

Much of the remaining work is more of the same — you need to fill in the empty areas and apply a stroke around the house trim, fascia, and pavement. You could accomplish this with brushes, carefully painting individual strokes as necessary to all the different pieces. However, another method based on selections can accomplish the same general result in a fraction of the time.

1. **With `house_working.psd` open, make sure the Front Trim layer is selected.**

2. **Create a selection that contains only the filled area of the Front Trim layer.**

   To accomplish this, use the Magic Wand tool to select the unpainted area of the layer, then choose Select>Inverse to invert the active selection (just as you did earlier to apply a stroke to the front door).

The selection excludes
all of the inner areas.

3. **Choose Select>Modify>Expand. In the resulting dialog box, type 4 in the field and click OK.**

   This enlarges the original selection area by 4 pixels. When you fill the enlarged selection, the result will be an apparent edge around the objects on the Front Trim layer.

Expanding the selection includes
most of the inner areas of the trim.

4. **Choose Select>Modify>Feather. In the resulting dialog box, type 3 in the field and click OK.**

   Feathering the selection creates a softer edge, which will result in a more natural shadow effect.

5. **Change the foreground color to Doors 4.**

6. **With the selection active, choose Edit>Fill. In the Fill dialog box, choose Behind in the Blending Mode menu and then click OK.**

   The Behind blending mode in this dialog box has the same effect as painting with the Brush tool using the Behind blending mode.

7. **Deselect the active selection, then hide the Sketch layer and review the results.**

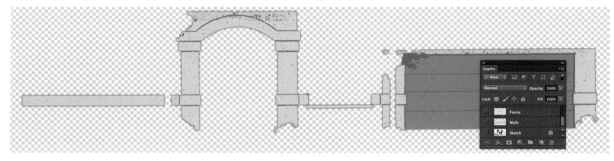

8. **Show the Fascia layer, and then drag it to the top of the layer stack.**

9. **Repeat Steps 2–7 for the Fascia layer using the same Doors 4 color.**

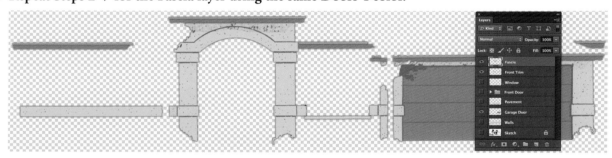

10. **Show the Pavement layer, and then drag it below the Garage Door layer.**

11. **Repeat the same general process (without the feathering) for the Pavement layer, using the Pavement 2 swatch as the fill color.**

   We did not feather this selection before filling it because pavement typically does not have a softened edge.

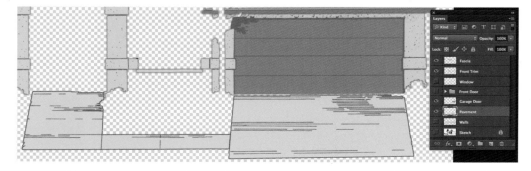

12. Deselect the active marquee.

13. **Choose the Brush tool and define a hard round brush. Using the Behind blending mode, fill in the pavement areas that were not filled in by Step 11.**

Click-Shift-click to create straight lines that connect the two points where you click; this method allows you to cleanly paint the pavement edges. You can then more easily fill in the empty areas.

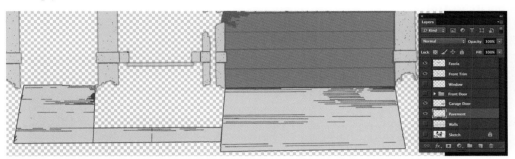

Note:

You could also use the Polygonal Lasso tool to draw a straight-edged, angled selection area; you can then use the Fill dialog box to fill behind the existing areas.

14. Save the file and continue to the next exercise.

Painting with the Mixer Brush

The Mixer Brush simulates realistic painting techniques such as mixing colors on a canvas, combining colors on a brush, and varying paint wetness across a stroke.

In the Options bar, the **Current Brush Load** shows what color(s) are currently loaded in the brush. You can Option/Alt click the screen to sample a load color from the existing image, or click the swatch to open the color picker.

If you click the arrow button to the right of the Current Brush Load swatch, you can choose **Clean Brush** to empty all color from the brush, or choose **Load Brush** to fill the brush with the defined load color. You can also toggle the **Load Solid Colors Only** option to prevent the brush from loading multiple "paint" colors.

If **Load Brush After Each Stroke** is toggled on, the brush load is restored to full capacity after each stroke.

If the **Clean Brush After Each Stroke** option is toggled on, the brush is restored to only the load color after each stroke. When this option is toggled off, the brush "picks up" and holds color from the canvas, just as it would if you painted with oils on a traditional canvas; that pick-up color is then transferred to the canvas on the next stroke.

The **Wet** setting defines how much paint the brush picks up from the canvas; higher settings produce longer paint streaks.

The **Load** setting defines the amount of paint loaded in the reservoir. At low values, strokes dry out more quickly.

The **Mix** setting defines the ratio of canvas paint to reservoir paint. At 100%, all paint is picked up from the canvas; at 0%, all paint comes from the reservoir.

Load Brush After
Each Stroke

Current
Brush Load

Clean Brush After
Each Stroke

Choose common presets
of Mixer Brush options.

Mixer Brush tool

Painting mixes the Load
color with the existing
color based on Wet, Load,
Mix, and Flow settings.

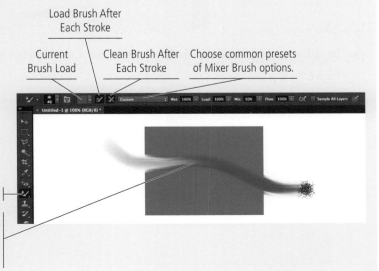

PHOTOSHOP FOUNDATIONS

CREATE TEXTURE WITH A FAUX FINISH BRUSH

Textures can be sampled from other images, copied and pasted into place, and created from scratch using combinations of brush styles and options. In this exercise, you use a textured brush to turn what are now simple brown walls into realistic-looking stone.

1. With **house_working.psd** open, hide all but the Walls layer. Change the Walls layer opacity to 100%.

2. Make a selection area that includes only the filled area of the Walls layer.

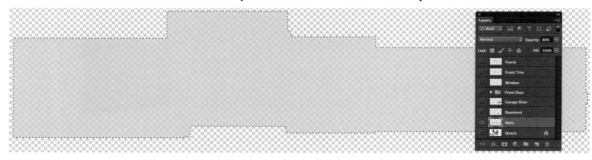

3. Choose the Brush tool. In the Options bar, set the brush blending mode to Normal.

4. Open the Brush Preset picker from the Options bar, and then choose Faux Finish Brushes in the panel Options menu.

Note:

You can Command/ Control-click a layer thumbnail to select all pixels on that layer.

5. In the warning message, click OK to replace the current brushes with the new set.

Note:

You could append the new brush set, but we prefer to keep the list small by replacing the previous brushes with the new set.

6. **Select the Stencil Sponge – Wet preset. Make the brush size large enough to cover the highest part of the fill in the Walls layer.**

   At 50% view percentage, a 700-px brush is large enough to cover the entire area in one brush stroke.

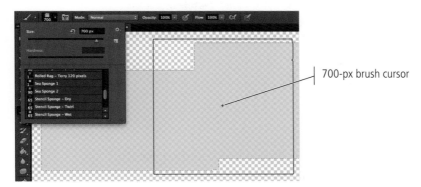

700-px brush cursor

7. **Change the foreground color to the Stucco 3 swatch, and then click and drag from left to right to paint the texture into the selection area.**

8. **Deselect off the active selection, save the file, and continue to the next exercise.**

 ## USE OPACITY AND BLENDING MODES TO CREATE SHADOWS

In many cases, it works well to paint on a separate layer and adjust the layer's blend options (blending mode and opacity). In other cases, however, adjusting the settings for the specific brush makes it easier to create subtle elements such as the shadows on the front of the house.

1. **With `house_working.psd` open, make all layers visible.**

2. **Reduce the Walls layer opacity to 50% so you can see the sketch through the walls.**

3. **Create a new layer named `House Shadows` immediately below the Front Trim layer.**

4. **Choose the Brush tool and set the foreground color to Doors 3.**

5. **In the Options bar, use the Brush Preset picker Options menu to reset the brushes, replacing (not appending) the existing brushes.**

6. **Using the Brush Preset picker, choose the Soft Round brush and set the size to 100 px.**

7. **Change the brush Opacity to 25%, change the Blending Mode to Multiply, and click the button to Enable Airbrush-Style Build-Up Effects.**

8. **Use the shadows in the Sketch layer as a guide to paint the shadow strokes on the House Shadows layer.**

   Because you are using Airbrush mode, each successive brush stroke applies more color. Use multiple strokes to build darker shadows near the house edges that cast the shadows.

   Using reduced brush opacity and the Multiply blending mode, you can build darker shadows without completely obscuring the color and texture of the wall — just as actual shadows appear in real life.

   Click this button to enable airbrush-style build-up effects.

   The shadows on the Sketch layer define where you need to paint shadows on the House Shadows layer.

9. **Hide the Sketch layer and review your results.**

   It can be helpful to frequently toggle the visibility of the Sketch layer as you paint in the shadows, so you can see where your shadows still need work.

The **History Brush tool** allows you to restore specific areas of an image back to a previous state. In the Options bar, you can choose the brush preset and brush settings that you want to use. When you paint with the History Brush tool, areas where you paint return to the target state or snapshot in the History panel. (The same effect can be achieved using any of the regular Eraser tools with the Erase to History option active.)

In the image shown here, we opened a file and made a Levels adjustment to lighten the image. We then applied some painting and touch-ups, as well as a filter to make the image look like a line-art drawing. In the final step, we selected the adjusted, unfiltered state and used the History Brush tool to restore only the clock tower back to the photographic pixels.

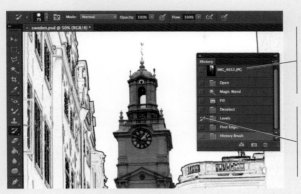

By default, the History panel includes a snapshot of the original file, which is the default target state for the History Brush tool.

By targeting the adjusted state (before filtering) and painting with the History Brush tool, we restored the clock tower to the unfiltered pixels.

The **Art History Brush tool** paints with stylized strokes, using the targeted history state (or snapshot) as the source data for the painting. (We can't say the tool "restores" the data, because results from the artistic style of the brush could hardly be called "restorative.")

In the Options bar, you can define the brush preset, blending mode, and opacity, as well as a specific style that will be used for the brush marks. The Area option defines the area that will be covered with the brush marks; larger area values result in a greater area covered, as well as more brush marks created by the stroke. Tolerance limits the area where brush strokes can be applied; higher tolerance values limit painting to areas that significantly differ from colors in the targeted state of the snapshot.

In the series of images shown here, we targeted the original image snapshot in the History panel, and then restored the clock tower by using the Art History Brush with different style settings.

Restored with the Tight Short style

Restored with the Loose Medium style

Restored with the Dab style

Restored with the Tight Curl style

10. Continue painting the shadows until you are satisfied with your result.

11. Create a new layer named Window Inside below the Window layer. Fill the window area with black, and set the layer opacity to 35%.

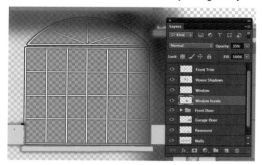

12. Create another new layer named Window Shadows below the Window layer but above the Window Inside layer.

13. Use a soft round brush with a low Flow setting, and use black as the foreground color to paint the shadows that fall inside the house. Change the brush size, flow, and opacity as necessary to create the shadows.

   We used a 20-px brush with 50% hardness and 25% flow to create these shadows.

14. Show all layers, and set the Walls layer to 100% opacity.

15. Save the file and continue to the next stage of the project.

Stage 4 Working with Patterns

The only element of the house left to paint is the roof. Manually drawing every shingle would take hours, and it would be difficult (if not impossible) to create the uniformity that is an actual part of real roofing shingles. A better solution is to use a pattern fill. Unfortunately, the built-in Photoshop pattern sets do not include a roof tile pattern, so in this exercise, you will create your own. Fortunately, you can create a pattern from anything you can paint.

DEFINE A PATTERN FROM EXISTING ARTWORK

The trick to creating a good repeating tile is placing or creating elements in such a way that apparent edges align properly when the pattern is tiled. Once you have defined the tile, creating and applying the pattern is fairly easy.

1. **Open the file tiles.psd from the WIP>Realty folder. If you receive a color profile mismatch warning, use the embedded profile.**

   This file was created as a 1-inch square. Each edge of the square has half of the blurred lines that make up the tile edges in the second and fourth rows.

2. **Choose Edit>Define Pattern.**

3. **In the Pattern Name dialog box, type Shingles and click OK.**

4. **Make the house_working.psd file active in the document window.**

5. **Create a new layer named Roof 1 at the top of the layer stack.**

6. **Using the Polygonal Lasso tool, draw a selection around the main roof area.**

   You might have to make some assumptions in the top corners, where the sketched trees obscure the roof corners.

   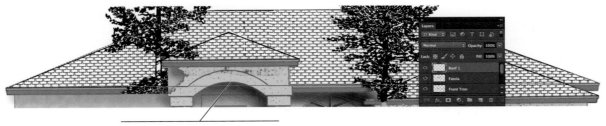

   Don't worry if the selection covers some of the house. You'll rearrange layers to fix any potential problems.

7. **Choose Edit>Fill, and choose Pattern in the Use menu. Open the Custom Pattern menu and choose the Shingles pattern.**

   This pattern you created was added to the existing options in the Patterns panel.

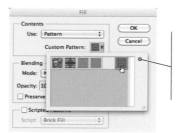

   As with other types of panels, you can use this menu to view the patterns as thumbnails or in a list.

8. **Make sure the Blending Mode menu is set to Normal, then click OK to fill the selection area with the pattern.**

   As you can see, the lines on the pattern tile align seamlessly when you create the pattern fill, but the 1″ square pattern tile is far too large for this image.

The Pattern Stamp Tool

The Pattern Stamp tool (nested under the Clone Stamp tool) is used to paint patterns onto selected areas of an image. In the Options bar, you can define the specific brush settings and the pattern you want to apply.

The Impressionist option creates an artistic interpretation of the pattern; you have no control over the results, other than the specific brush and options being used.

If the Aligned option is checked, the pattern is basically locked to the layer; clicking and dragging reveals the part of the pattern that exists where you drag. Think of the Aligned option this way: The entire layer is theoretically "filled" with the selected pattern; when you paint with the Pattern Stamp tool, the pattern fill is revealed in those areas where you paint — in other words, the pattern is aligned in each successive stroke.

If the Aligned option is checked, each stroke reveals more of the same continuous pattern.

If the Aligned option is not checked, each stroke paints the pattern without respect to the pattern in previous strokes.

When the Aligned option is not checked, each stroke of the Pattern Stamp tool paints the pattern onto the selected layer. The pattern is not aligned from one stroke to the next.

9. Make the `tiles.psd` file active in the document window and open the Image Size dialog box (Image>Image Size). With the Resample Image option turned on, resample the image to 0.25″ by 0.25″ and click OK.

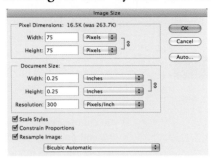

10. Choose Edit>Define Pattern. Name the new pattern Small Shingles and click OK.

11. Close the tiles image without saving it.

12. With the main roof area still selected in the house_working file, choose Edit>Fill. Choose the new Small Shingles pattern, then click OK.

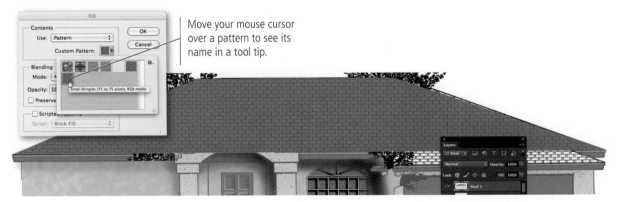

Move your mouse cursor over a pattern to see its name in a tool tip.

13. Deselect the active selection, then hide the Roof 1 layer.

14. Use the same process to create the two remaining sections of the roof, each on its own layer (named Roof 2 and Roof 3).

    Use the Polygonal Lasso tool to make a selection, then use the Fill dialog box to add the pattern fill.

15. Show the Roof 1 layer.

    With all three roof sections showing, you can now see two problems. First, the main roof is obscuring the porch covering and fascia. Second, all three pieces of the roof were created with the same pattern, so all three pieces merge seamlessly together.

PHOTOSHOP FOUNDATIONS

The **Eraser tool** removes pixels where you click. If you erase from the Background layer or in a regular layer with transparency locked, the background color shows through where you erased.

If the **Erase to History** option is checked, dragging with the Eraser tool (in any mode) reveals the selected state in the History panel.

- The default Block mode simply erases the area under the square cursor; you can't control the size, shape, opacity, or flow of the tool. When using the Eraser tool, the opacity setting determines the strength of the tool; 100% opacity entirely erases pixels.

- If you choose Brush mode, you can define the specific brush preset, opacity, and flow, as well as use the Eraser brush in Airbrush mode.

- If you choose Pencil mode, you can define the specific brush and opacity; Pencil mode does not offer flow control or Airbrush mode.

The **Magic Eraser tool** (nested under the Eraser tool) works on the same principle as the Magic Wand tool. Clicking with the tool erases all pixels within the defined tolerance.

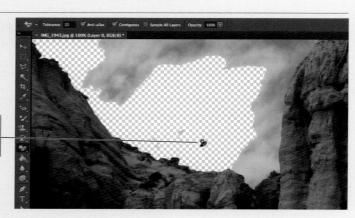

Clicking with the Magic Eraser tool removes all pixels within the defined tolerance.

The **Background Eraser tool** (nested under the Eraser tool) erases pixels while attempting to maintain the edges of an object in the foreground. The Background Eraser samples color at the brush center, and deletes that color where it appears inside the brush. In the Options bar, you can define the brush size and settings. You can also specify different sampling and tolerance options to control the range of pixels that are affected.

The sampling options determine how color will be replaced:

- **Continuous** samples colors as you drag.
- **Once** erases color only in areas containing the color that you first click.
- **Background Swatch** erases only areas containing the current background color.

The Limits menu constrains the tool's effect:

- **Discontiguous** erases the sampled color where it occurs under the brush.
- **Contiguous** erases colors that are contiguous with the color immediately under the brush tip.
- **Find Edges** erases connected areas of the sampled color, attempting to preserve edge sharpness.

Tolerance defines how much variance from the sample will be affected. If the **Protect Foreground Color** option is checked, pixels of the defined foreground color in the Tools panel will be protected from erasure.

Clicking and dragging with the Background Eraser tool removes pixels within the defined tolerance; the high-contrast edge of the foreground object (the rocks) remains unaffected.

16. **Drag the Fascia and Front Trim layers to the top of the layer stack.**

    It's common to lock, hide, and move layers as necessary when working on a complex assignment like this one. At times, the position of specific layers becomes critical; so, too, does making sure you're working on the correct layer. When you work on a complex file, plan your work and then carefully follow those plans.

17. **Use any method you prefer to add a dark, soft edge around each roof section. Sample the dark color in the tile pattern to use as the edge color.**

    You can use the Paint Behind method with a soft-edge brush, or use the modified-selection fill technique you used for the front trim.

18. **Choose the Eraser tool in the Tools panel. In the Options bar, choose Brush in the Mode menu. Open the Brush Preset picker and define a hard round brush with a medium size.**

19. **With the Roof 1 layer active, click and drag to remove the section of roof tile that falls below the porch archway.**

    The Eraser tool can function as a brush, pencil, or block.

    Eraser tool

    Erase any pixels from the Roof 1 layer that appear below the front trim.

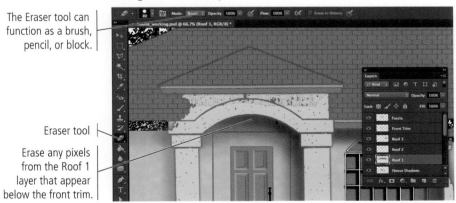

20. **Save the file and continue to the next exercise.**

SAVE CUSTOM PATTERNS

You never know when a particular pattern or other asset might be useful. By default, when you quit Photoshop you lose any custom assets unless you intentionally save them. Since you have taken the time to create the pattern for a tiled roof, it's a good idea to save it so you can use it again later.

1. **With house_working.psd open, choose Edit>Presets>Preset Manager.**

   You can use the Preset Manager to control built-in and custom assets, including brushes, swatches, gradients, styles, patterns, contours, custom shapes, and tools.

    Click here to change the view of the presets, reset or replace current assets, or access built-in sets of the selected preset type.

2. **Choose Patterns in the Preset Type menu.**

3. **Shift-click to select all patterns except the two custom patterns you created.**

Note:

Your panel might have more than the patterns shown in our screen shots. Select everything except the two shingle patterns.

4. **Click Delete to remove the selected patterns from the dialog box.**

   You're deleting these patterns from the panel only. Because they are part of one of the built-in sets (in this case, the Patterns 2 set), you can always load them again by choosing that set in the Patterns panel Options menu.

5. **Select the two remaining pattern swatches and click the Save Set button.**

6. **In the Save dialog box, name the set Portfolio Patterns.pat and click Save.**

   When you save a custom pattern set, the Save dialog box defaults to the application's Presets>Patterns folder. The extension ("pat") is automatically added for you.

Note:

After the pattern set has been saved, you can access those patterns again by clicking the Load button in the Preset Manager or by opening the Patterns panel Options menu.

   If you are using a shared computer, you might not be able to save files in the application's default location. If this is the case, navigate to your WIP>Realty folder to save the Portfolio Patterns.pat file.

7. **Click Done to close the Preset Manager, and then continue to the next stage of the project.**

Stage 5 Painting Nature

Some elements of this painting are far less structured than the house. The trees, bushes, grass, and other natural elements can't be created by filling and painting with basic brushes — or at least, you can't make them look natural with the tools you have learned so far. These elements should be painted more randomly so they look as natural as possible.

PAINT SHADES OF NATURE

When it comes to painting the landscaping, it helps to have an eye for art in general (moreso than for any other component of this project). That's not to say, however, that you need to be Michelangelo to finish this project. The easiest place to start is by creating the "solid" elements such as the tree trunks and sidewalks, using skills that you learned in earlier exercises.

1. **With house_working.psd open, create a new layer named Trees at the top of the layer stack. Hide all other layers except the Sketch layer.**

   You're going to use a series of different layers to create the various landscaping elements. Doing so will allow you to control the different pieces, including rearranging or merging them together as necessary to create the best possible result. These layers should be on top of the layer stack because most of the trees and bushes are in the sketch foreground (i.e., in front of the house).

2. **Use the Paint Bucket tool to fill the white areas of the two tree trunks with the Trim 1 swatch.**

   Remember, clicking with the Paint Bucket tool fills contiguous pixels of the same color. If you activate the All Layers option in the Options bar, the tool recognizes the black lines in the sketch layer and fills the white areas of the tree trunks.

3. **Change the foreground color to the Trim 3 swatch, and select a small round brush with 100% hardness, with both opacity and flow set to 100%. Using the Behind blending mode, paint in the dark areas of the tree trunks and add an edge to the outside edges of the trunks.**

   We used a 20-px brush to create the required effect. (The modified fill method is not as effective in this case because so much of the trunk area is painted by the Paint Bucket tool.)

4. **Save the file and continue to the next exercise.**

CHANGE BRUSH SETTINGS TO PAINT RANDOM ELEMENTS

The randomness of shapes, colors, and textures occurring in nature simply cannot be painted using basic lines, regardless of the brush size, flow, opacity, and other options. For this reason, we can't provide specific step-by-step instructions to create every required brush stroke in this exercise. Every person will end up with different results.

To create the leaves, shrubs, and grass, we can only provide advice on how to select the best tool settings for the job. You should experiment with the different brush settings as you paint these elements. Use layers liberally as you create the various elements so you can easily turn off or delete objects and try again.

1. **With house_working.psd open, select the Brush tool.**

2. **In the Options bar, make sure Normal is selected in the Mode menu, and the Opacity and Flow are set to 100%.**

3. **Open the Brush Preset picker in the Options bar, then open the panel Options menu. Choose the Natural Brushes 2 set, and then click OK to replace the existing set.**

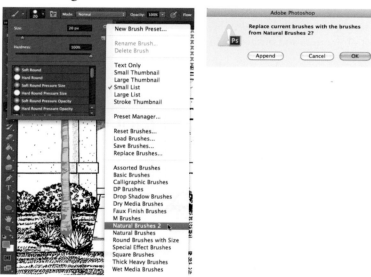

4. **Open the Brush Preset picker and choose Wet Brush 60 Pixels.**

   This brush is the starting point; you will change the settings based on this selected preset.

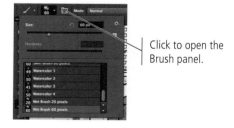

Click to open the Brush panel.

5. **In the Options bar, click the button to open the stand-alone Brush panel.**

6. **Choose Brush Tip Shape in the list of options. Change the Angle to –30°.**

Leaves are rarely straight up and down, so your brush strokes shouldn't be either.

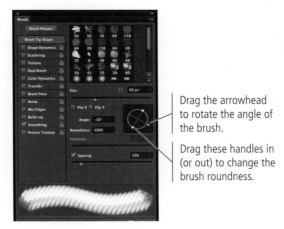

Drag the arrowhead to rotate the angle of the brush.

Drag these handles in (or out) to change the brush roundness.

7. **Select Shape Dynamics in the list on the left. Change all the Jitter sliders to values near the middle of the scale, and then set all the Control menus to Off.**

Real leaves come in many different shapes and sizes. By jittering all these settings, you allow Photoshop to randomize the brush marks that will create the leaves.

Notice the new preview, which dynamically shows the results of your settings.

8. **In the Scattering options, allow Photoshop to scatter the marks along both axes using a medium setting (we used 250%).**

By scattering along both axes, you get a more random result than if brush marks only move perpendicularly from the brush stroke. Watch the preview to evaluate the results of different scatter values.

9. **Set the Count value to 2 to prevent overloading the brush marks in any particular area.**

You can use multiple brush strokes to build up more marks in the same space.

Using the Brush panel, you can control an extensive array of brush settings. Clicking a category in the left side of the panel shows the related options. The bottom area of the panel shows a dynamic preview of your choices.

Brush Tip Shape

Size controls the diameter (in pixels) of the brush.

Flip X and **Flip Y** change the direction of a brush tip on the X (horizontal) or Y (vertical) axis.

Angle defines the angle for an elliptical brush.

Roundness controls the ratio between the short and long axes of the brush; 100% creates a round brush, 0% creates a linear brush, and middle values create elliptical brushes.

Hardness controls the size of the brush's hard center. (This is the same as the Hardness setting in the Options bar.)

Spacing controls the distance between brush marks in a stroke. The spacing is a percentage of the brush diameter.

Scattering

Scatter controls how brush marks are distributed in a stroke, based on the maximum percentage defined here. If Both Axes is active, brush marks are distributed radially; if Both Axes is not active, brush marks are distributed perpendicular to the stroke path.

Count defines the number of brush marks applied at each spacing interval.

Count Jitter varies the number of brush marks for each spacing interval, based on the maximum percentage defined here.

Brush Pose

These options allow you to define settings that mimic the behavior of a drawing tablet/stylus — Tilt X, Tilt Y, Rotation, and Pressure — if you are using a mouse. If you are using a digital drawing tablet, you can check the Override options to prevent stylus properties from affecting the brush stroke.

Shape Dynamics

Size Jitter varies the size of brush marks in a stroke, based on the maximum percentage defined here. You can also use the Control menu to vary the size of brush marks:

- Off provides no control over the variation.

- Fade varies the size of brush marks between the initial diameter and the minimum diameter in a specified number of steps (from 1 to 9999).

- Pen Pressure, Pen Tilt, Stylus Wheel, and Rotation vary the size of brush marks, based on the way a user draws with a drawing tablet/pen.

Minimum Diameter defines the minimum brush (as a percentage of brush diameter) when Size Jitter is used.

Tilt Scale specifies the scale factor for brush height when Pen Tilt is active in the Control menu.

Angle Jitter varies the angle of brush marks in a stroke (as a percentage of 360°). The Control menu specifies how you control the angle variance of brush marks:

- Off, Fade, Pen Pressure, Pen Tilt, and Stylus Wheel have the same meanings as for Size Jitter (above).

- Initial Direction bases the angle of brush marks on the initial direction of the brush stroke.

- Direction bases the angle of brush marks on the overall direction of the brush stroke.

Roundness Jitter varies the roundness of brush marks in a stroke (as a percentage of the ratio between the brush height and width).

Minimum Roundness specifies the minimum roundness for brush marks when Roundness Jitter is enabled.

Flip X Jitter and **Flip Y Jitter** allow the flip behavior (when enabled) to be randomized.

Texture

Textured brushes use patterns to make strokes look as though they were painted on paper or canvas. After you choose a pattern from the palette, you can set many of the same options that are available when applying a texture effect to a layer.

Invert reverses the high (light) and low (dark) points in the texture; when Invert is selected, the lightest areas are the low points and the darkest areas are the high points.

Scale defines the size of the pattern texture as a percentage of the pattern size.

Texture Each Tip applies the selected texture to each brush mark, rather than to the brush stroke as a whole.

Mode defines the blending mode that combines the brush and the pattern.

Depth defines how deeply color affects the texture. At 0%, all points receive the same amount of color, which obscures the texture; at 100%, low points are not painted.

Minimum Depth specifies the minimum depth to which color can penetrate.

Depth Jitter varies the depth (when Texture Each Tip is selected), based on the maximum percentage defined here.

Dual Brush

A dual brush combines two brush tips. The second brush texture is applied within the brush stroke of the primary brush; only the areas where both brush strokes intersect are painted.

Mode defines the blending mode that will combine marks from the two brushes.

Size defines the diameter of the dual tip (in pixels).

Spacing defines the distance between the dual-tip brush marks in a stroke, as a percentage of the brush diameter.

Scatter determines how dual-tip brush marks are distributed in a stroke, based on the maximum percentage defined here. If Both Axes is active, dual-tip brush marks are distributed radially; if Both Axes is not checked, dual-tip brush marks are distributed perpendicular to the stroke path.

Count defines the number of dual-tip brush marks at each spacing interval.

Color Dynamics

Color dynamics determine how the color of paint changes over the course of a stroke.

Foreground/Background Jitter varies between the foreground and background colors, based on the percentage of allowable variation defined here.

Hue Jitter varies the hue in the stroke; lower percentages in this setting create less hue variation across the stroke.

Saturation Jitter varies the saturation in a brush stroke; lower percentages in this setting create less saturation variation across the stroke.

Brightness Jitter varies the brightness in a brush stroke; lower percentages in this setting create less brightness variation across the stroke.

Purity increases or decreases the saturation of the color, between −100% and 100%. (At −100%, the color is fully desaturated; at 100%, the color is fully saturated.)

Transfer

Opacity Jitter varies the opacity of color in a stroke, up to the opacity value defined in the Options bar.

Flow Jitter varies the flow of color in a brush stroke.

Wetness Jitter varies the wetness setting of a Wet Mixer brush.

Mix Jitter varies the mixing quality of a Wet Mixer brush.

Other Brush Options

Noise adds randomness to brush tips that contain shades of gray (e.g., soft tips).

Wet Edges causes paint to build up along the edges of the brush stroke, creating a watercolor effect.

Build-up applies gradual tones to an image, simulating traditional airbrush techniques (this is the same as the Airbrush button in the Options bar).

Smoothing, which creates smoother curves in brush strokes, is most useful if you are using a drawing tablet.

Protect Texture applies the same pattern and scale to all textured brushes to simulate a consistent canvas texture throughout the entire image.

10. **In the Color Dynamics options, apply a high Foreground/Background Jitter setting.**

You could manually vary the colors by frequently switching the foreground color, but this option speeds the process by varying the colors in a single brush stroke without choosing new paint colors.

Note:

As you paint, don't forget about the History panel. You can step back up to 20 brush strokes, or you can create new History snapshots at regular intervals so you can return to earlier stages of your work.

11. **In the Transfer options, apply a small amount of opacity jitter.**

A slight variation in the stroke opacity will further increase the randomness of the brush marks. Because some marks will be semi-transparent, overlapping areas will produce an even broader range of color without manually changing the brush color.

12. **Set the foreground color to the Foliage 5 swatch and the background color to the Foliage 7 swatch.**

13. **Click with the brush and drag around the leafy area of the tree to the left of the garage door.**

The settings you applied allow you to easily create a random set of brush marks, differing in size, angle, roundness, position, color, and opacity.

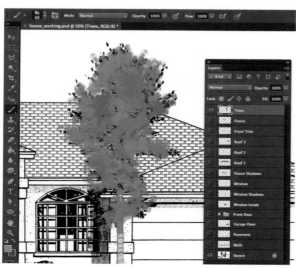

Note:

Applying multiple brush strokes, rather than a single stroke, helps to vary the color throughout the leafy area.

14. Show all layers in the file and review your work. Paint leaves over any areas where the house is not perfectly painted.

15. Using the same brush, paint the leaves on the other tree.

16. Save the file and continue to the next exercise.

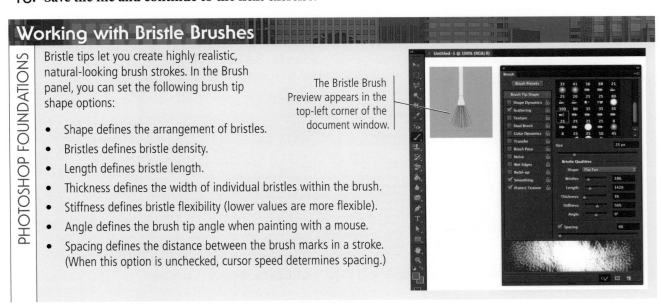

CREATE A BRUSH PRESET

As with custom patterns, you must save custom brush presets if you want to be able to use them again later (after quitting and relaunching Photoshop). You have a lot of leaves to paint in this image, so it's a good idea to save the brush you defined in the previous exercise.

1. **With house_working.psd open, open the Brush panel Options menu and choose New Brush Preset.**

Note:

If you changed your Brush panel or quit Photoshop since the previous exercise, you might have to go back and re-create the Leafy Scatter brush for this exercise to work properly.

2. **In the Brush Name dialog box, name the new preset Leafy Scatter and click OK.**

3. **Choose Edit>Presets>Preset Manager.**

4. **With Brushes showing in Small List view, select everything other than the Leafy Scatter brush you created in Step 2, and then click Delete.**

5. **Select the remaining brush and click Save Set.**

6. **Name the new set Portfolio Brushes.abr and click Save.**

   New brush sets are saved by default in the Presets>Brushes folder in your Photoshop application folder. The extension ".abr" is automatically added, so you only need to type the file name.

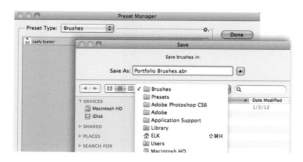

Note:

If you are using a shared computer, you might not be able to save files in the application's default location. If this is the case, navigate to your WIP>Realty folder to save the Portfolio Brushes.abr file.

7. **Click Done to close the Preset Manager, and then continue to the next exercise.**

FINISH THE PAINTING

Using the skills and techniques you just learned, paint the rest of the landscaping in the image. Keep the following tips in mind as you paint these elements.

1. Create, rearrange, and merge layers as necessary to produce the best result.

2. Grass — especially new sod — has far less randomness than leaves.

   - Choose foreground and background colors that are only slightly different (try Foliage 6 and Foliage 7).

   - Start with a brush preset that looks like a blade of grass (try one of the veining brushes in the Faux Finish Brushes set).

   - Use a small brush size with a small amount of size and angle jitter, and allow the marks to flip horizontally (Flip X Jitter option).

   - Experiment with different settings for foreground/background and opacity jitter.

3. As with the tree leaves, the bushes also need variation.

   - Try the Stencil Sponge–Twirl brush from the Faux Finish Brushes set, using the Foliage 1 and Foliage 2 swatches as the foreground and background colors.

   - Use a small brush size with relatively low roundness.

   - Apply a small amount of size and angle jitter, and a medium-to-high roundness jitter.

   - Scatter the marks along both axes at a lower percentage, and increase the count to add more brush marks in the same space.

   - Use medium jitter between the foreground and background colors, as well as the color brightness.

4. When you're finished, add a new layer immediately above the Sketch layer, and fill it with solid white.

5. Save the file as house_final.psd in your WIP>Realty folder and continue to the final exercise.

PHOTOSHOP FOUNDATIONS

Just as saving a custom brush preset allows you to access that brush again later, tool presets allow you to save and reuse settings for any Photoshop tool. Tool presets can be accessed in the Options bar or in the Tool Presets panel (Window>Tool Presets). The structure of the panel Options menu offers the same options as other asset panels — you can control what is visible in the panel, load and save custom sets of tool presets, and access built-in sets of tool presets.

To save your own tool presets, simply choose New Tool Preset from the panel Options menu or click the Create New Tool Preset button at the bottom of the panel. The new tool preset will include whatever tool and options are currently selected.

Click here to access tool presets.

View presets for all tools or for only the currently selected tool.

Use these options to manage the view of tool presets in the panel.

Use these options to reset tools to the default application settings.

Use these options to load built-in sets of tool presets.

Create New Tool Preset

EXPORT A PDF FILE FOR PRINT

The Portable Document Format (PDF) was created by Adobe to facilitate cross-platform transportation of documents, independent of the fonts used, linked files, or even the originating application. The format offers a number of advantages:

- PDF files can contain all the information needed to successfully output a job.

- Data in a PDF file can be high or low resolution, and it can be compressed to reduce file size.

- PDF files are device-independent, which means you don't need the originating application or the same platform to open and print the file.

- PDF files are also page-independent, which means a PDF document can contain rotated pages and even pages of different sizes. (You can't create multi-page PDF files in Photoshop, but you can combine individual pages created in Photoshop using Adobe Acrobat.)

1. **With house_final.psd open, choose File>Save As.**

2. **Navigate to your WIP>Realty folder as the target destination and choose Photoshop PDF in the Format menu.**

3. Uncheck the Layers check box.

The As a Copy option is checked when you turn off the Layers option; since you are saving as a different format with a different file name, nothing else changes.

4. Click Save, and then click OK in the warning message.

Before the PDF is saved, you have to define the settings that will be used to generate the PDF file. Some options (such as color profile information) can be changed in the Save Adobe PDF dialog box; those choices will override the selections in the Save As dialog box.

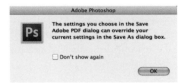

5. Choose High Quality Print in the Adobe PDF Preset menu.

The Adobe PDF Preset menu includes six PDF presets (in brackets) that meet common industry output requirements. Other options might also be available if another user created custom presets in Photoshop or another Creative Suite application.

Because there are so many ways to create a PDF — and not all of them are optimized for commercial printing — the potential benefits of the file format are often undermined. The PDF/X specification was created to help solve some of the problems associated with bad PDF files entering the prepress workflow. PDF/X is a subset of PDF, specifically designed to ensure that files have the information necessary for and available to the digital prepress output process. Ask your output provider whether you should apply a PDF/X standard to your files, and if so, which version to use.

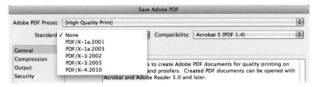

The Compatibility menu determines which version of the PDF format you will create. This is particularly important if your layout uses transparency. PDF 1.3 does not support transparency, so the file will require flattening. If you save the file to be compatible with PDF 1.4 or later, the transparency information will be maintained in the PDF file; it will have to be flattened later in the output process (after it leaves your desk).

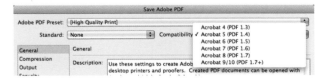

6. In the General pane, uncheck all but Optimize for Fast Web Preview.

As soon as you change an option away from the defined preset, the menu changes to [High Quality Print] (Modified).

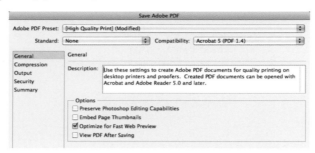

7. Review the Compression options.

The Compression options determine what — and how much — data will be included in the PDF file. This set of options is one of the most important when creating PDFs, since too-low resolution results in bad-quality printing, and too-high resolution results in extremely long download times.

Before you choose compression settings, you need to consider your final goal. If you're creating a file for commercial printing, resolution is more important than file size. If your goal is a PDF for posting on the Web for general consumption, file size and image quality are equally important.

You can define a specific compression scheme for color, grayscale, and monochrome images. Different options are available, depending on the image type:

- ZIP compression is lossless, which means all file data is maintained in the compressed file.

- JPEG compression options are lossy, which means data is discarded to create a smaller file. When you use one of the JPEG options, you can also define an Image Quality option (from Low to Maximum).

If you don't compress the file, your PDF file might be extremely large. For a commercial printing workflow, large file size is preferable to poor image quality. If you don't have to submit the PDF file via modem transmission, large file size is not an issue. If you must compress the file, ask your service provider what settings they prefer you to use.

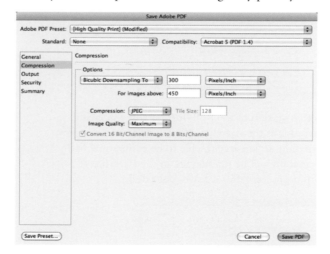

8. Click Save PDF. When the process is finished, close the Photoshop file.

> *Note:*
>
> *Since you chose the High Quality Print preset, these options default to settings that will produce the best results for most commercial printing applications.*

> *Note:*
>
> *The Output options relate to color management and PDF/X settings. Ask your output provider if you need to change anything for those options.*

Project Review

fill in the blank

1. The _____ dialog box can be used to change the resolution of an image without affecting its physical size.

2. The _____ command can be used to share color swatches between Photoshop and other Creative Suite applications.

3. The _____ tool is used to fill areas with a solid color or pattern by clicking the area you want to fill.

4. _____ is the percentage of a brush's diameter that is completely opaque.

5. The _____ brush mode option is useful for filling gaps left by other painting methods.

6. The _____ removes pixels from an image while attempting to maintain edges of an object in the foreground.

7. The _____ can be used to restore specific areas of an image back to a previous state.

8. The _____ tool is similar to the Brush tool, but can only create hard edges.

9. The _____ tool is used to paint with patterns, either painting a stroke of the pattern or revealing more of the solid pattern with each brush stroke.

10. _____ store specific settings for a specific tool; they can be accessed in the menu on the left end of the Options bar.

short answer

1. Briefly explain the difference between the Size, Hardness, and Flow settings when using the Brush tool.

2. Briefly explain how layers made it easier to complete this complex project.

3. Briefly explain three advantages of the PDF file format.

Use what you learned in this project to complete the following freeform exercise.
Carefully read the art director and client comments, then create your own design to meet the needs of the project.
Use the space below to sketch ideas; when finished, write a brief explanation of your reasoning behind your final design.

art director comments

The client is very happy with the house painting, and would like to hire you again to create color renderings of the other two models that will be available in the complex.

To complete this project, you should:

❏ Download the **PS6_PB_Project7.zip** archive from the Student Files Web page to access the client sketches for this project.

❏ Convert the bitmap sketches to RGB mode at 300 pixels/inch.

❏ Create a custom pattern to fill in the roof areas of the houses.

❏ Experiment with custom brushes to create realistic looking grass and trees around the houses.

client comments

Buyers for the new community will actually have three models to choose from. We would like to have paintings for the other two models as well so buyers can compare apples to apples when they're choosing which model they prefer. We would be happy with one more color rendering, but we would be thrilled if you could do both of the other two house sketches.

When you paint the other houses, use colors from the same color palette, but none of the houses should look exactly the same. Buyers are shown the same paint swatches as those in the palette you used to paint the first house; they can pick any combinations of those colors for the main stucco and up to two shades for the trim.

Remember, these houses are all going to be in the same development, so try to be consistent with the plant life. We can't have one house look like it's in a rainforest and another surrounded by desert scrub.

project justification

_____

_____

_____

_____

_____

_____

_____

_____

_____

_____

_____

_____

_____

Project Summary

Drawing and painting from scratch requires some degree of creativity and natural artistic talent; however, learning the technical aspects of drawing and painting will help you as you complete many different types of projects — and might even help you to develop and refine natural artistic skills.

Creating original artwork in Photoshop — including artwork that starts as a black-and-white pen sketch — can be a time-consuming and sometimes repetitive process. If you learn how to use the painting and drawing tools, you will have a unique advantage when you need something unique. Mastering these skills also gives you an advantage because few people take the time to learn the intricacies of creating original digital artwork.

Fill solid areas using selection tools

Fill color-based selections with the Paint Bucket tool

Paint different effects with hard- and soft-edge brushes

Clone layers to create repetitive design elements

Apply a stroke to a selection

Use the Behind blending mode to fill gaps in color

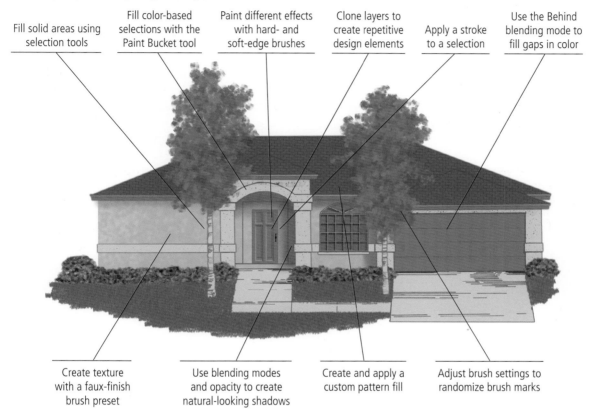

Create texture with a faux-finish brush preset

Use blending modes and opacity to create natural-looking shadows

Create and apply a custom pattern fill

Adjust brush settings to randomize brush marks

Photo Gallery Web Page

Your client is a photographer in the San Francisco Bay area who has hired you to create a digital portfolio Web page. Your job is to take the first draft and add a number of finishing touches to create a visually appealing and functional photo gallery that provides links to larger versions of a number of the client's photographs.

This project incorporates the following skills:

❏ Using actions and batches to automate repetitive processes and improve productivity

❏ Adding depth and visual interest with 3D extrusion and puppet warping

❏ Creating and optimizing frame-based animation in a Photoshop file

❏ Slicing a page into pieces and defining settings for individual slices

❏ Saving images and pages in appropriate format for display on the Web

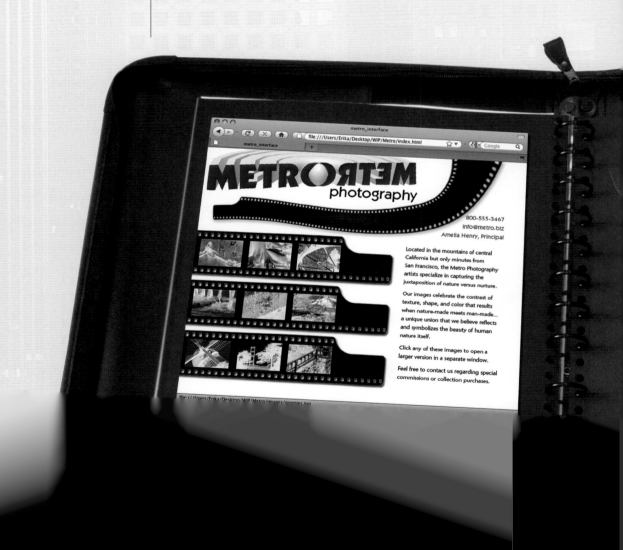

client comments

I really like the general idea that you created. I sorted through some photos and selected nine that I want to include as samples on the filmstrips. I think they're a good representation of the type of photography I enjoy most.

My only real complaint is that the top part is rather bland. Right now everything is just too horizontal. I don't have a real logo at this point, but is there anything you can do with the word "Metro" to make it a bit more visually interesting? And maybe something to make the longer filmstrip less horizontal too.

I was also hoping for some type of movement, at least when the page first opens. How about making the three filmstrips with the thumbnails slide onto the page instead of just sitting there?

art director comments

All of the client's points are reasonable, and you can use Photoshop's built-in tools to meet each of her specific goals.

First, you need to scale down her images to make them fit as thumbnails onto the filmstrips. I also think it would be a nice touch to convert them to "negatives." Keep in mind, though, that you need to keep the original images because users should be able to click the thumbnails to see the larger versions.

For the top, I want you to bend the filmstrip a bit. That will break the horizontal syndrome, and create a sort of frame around her studio name. Then you can use the 3D functionality to add some depth to the studio name itself.

Her last request will require a relatively simple frame animation, but I think it should be in three steps — each strip coming in *after* the previous one is in place. It shouldn't take very long, though, for everything to be in place because site users typically have very short attention spans.

project objectives

To complete this project, you will:

- ❏ Create and save an action
- ❏ Batch-process multiple files
- ❏ Use puppet warping to bend a straight object into a custom shape
- ❏ Create a 3D extrusion from a type layer
- ❏ Create individual animation frames
- ❏ Create an animated tween
- ❏ Control animation timing
- ❏ Create slices from guides
- ❏ Create manual slices
- ❏ Create slices from layers
- ❏ Test your page in a Web browser
- ❏ Define slice and page export options

Stage 1 **Automating Repetitive Tasks**

Actions are some of the most powerful (yet underused) productivity tools in Photoshop. In the simplest terms, actions are miniature programs that run a sequence of commands on a particular image or selected area. An action can initiate most of the commands available in Photoshop — alone or in sequence — to automate repetitive and potentially time-consuming tasks.

Running an action is a fairly simple process: highlight the appropriate action in the Actions panel and click the Play button at the bottom of the panel. Some actions work on an entire image, while others require some initial selection. If you use the actions that shipped with the Photoshop application, the action name tells you (in parentheses) what type of element the action was designed to affect; in most cases, however, you can run an action on other elements without a problem.

The Actions Panel in Depth

The default Actions panel (Window>Actions) shows the Default Actions set, which contains several pre-built actions. A folder icon indicates an **action set**, which is used to create logical groupings of actions. You can expand an action set to show the actions contained within that set, and you can expand a specific action to show the steps that are saved in that action; any step in an action marked with an arrow can be further expanded to see the details of that step.

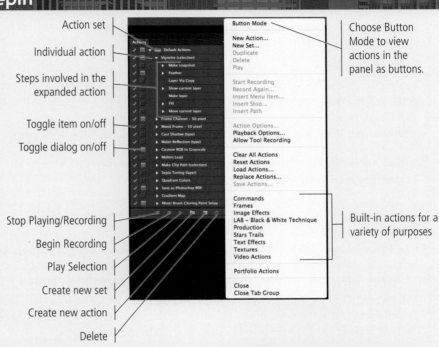

The left column of the Actions panel shows a checkmark next to each action set, individual action, and step within an expanded action. All elements of pre-recorded actions are active by default, which means that playing an action initiates each step within the action. You can deactivate specific steps of an action by clicking the related checkmark. (If the checkmark next to an action is black, all elements of that action are active. If the checkmark is red, one or more steps of that action are inactive.)

Modal Controls

The second column in the Actions panel controls the degree of user interaction required when running an action. If an icon appears in this column, the Photoshop dialog box relevant to that step opens when the action runs. These are called **modal controls**; the action pauses until you take some required action. You can deactivate modal controls for:

- An entire action set by clicking the dialog box icon next to a set name
- An individual action by clicking the icon next to the action name
- A single step by clicking the icon next to the step

If the modal controls are turned off, Photoshop applies the values that were used when the action was recorded. This increases the automatic functionality of the action, but also offers less control over the action's behavior.

Some actions require a certain degree of user interaction, in which case the modal controls can't be entirely deactivated. In this case, the dialog box icon appears grayed out in the panel, even when the remaining modal controls are turned off. (If an action shows a black dialog box icon, all modal controls within the action are active. If an action shows a red dialog box icon, one or more modal controls within the action have been turned off.)

Button Mode

Choosing Button Mode in the panel Options menu makes running an action one step easier. Each action is represented as a colored button, which you can simply click to run the action.

SAVE AN ACTION SET

Whenever you need to perform the same task more than two times, it's a good idea to automate as much of the process as possible. This project requires you to create thumbnails from nine images. Creating a single "negative" thumbnail for this project requires at least five steps:

1. Open the file (any number of clicks, depending on the default location in the Open dialog box).

2. Resize the image to 72 pixels high (at least two clicks, possibly three if the Resample check box is active), as well as typing the new dimensions.

3. Convert the reduced image to a negative representation.

4. Save the file in a new folder with a revised file name (any number of clicks, depending on the default location in the Save dialog box), as well as typing the new file name.

5. Close the file.

This process can be streamlined by using an action, which you have to record only once.

1. **Download PS6_RF_Project8.zip from the Student Files Web page.**

2. **Expand the ZIP archive in your WIP folder (Macintosh) or copy the archive contents into your WIP folder (Windows).**

   This results in a folder named **Metro**, which contains the files you need for this project. You should also use this folder to save the files you create in this project.

3. **In Photoshop with no file open, open the Actions panel (Window>Actions).**

4. **Choose Clear All Actions from the Actions panel Options menu.**

   Rather than editing an existing action set, you are going to create your own action set to store the action you define. If you did not clear the existing actions, the set you define would include all of the default actions as well as the one you create.

5. **Click OK in the warning message dialog box.**

   Clear All Actions removes everything from the Actions panel. You can also remove a specific action or set from the panel by highlighting the item in the panel and clicking the Delete button, or by choosing Delete from the Actions panel Options menu. These commands remove the actions or sets from the panel, but they do not permanently delete saved actions or sets. If you delete an action from one of the built-in sets, you can reload the set to restore all items that originally existed in the set.

Note:

It's important to remember when creating actions that, "just because you can, doesn't mean you should." There are many powerful tools in Photoshop that require human judgment and intervention if they are to be effective. Color correction, for example, is different for every image, and should never be left entirely to a computer to implement.

Note:

*You can add actions to the Actions panel by choosing a defined set or by choosing **Load Actions** in the panel Options menu.*

***Reset Actions** restores the default set to the Actions panel. You have the option to replace the existing actions or append the default set to the current sets.*

***Replace Actions** replaces the current action sets with whatever set you load in the resulting dialog box.*

6. **Click the Create New Set button at the bottom of the Actions panel.**

7. **In the New Set dialog box, name the new set Portfolio Actions, and then click OK.**

You can name the set whatever you prefer, but the action set name should indicate what the set contains, whether it's a set of actions for a specific type of project, for a specific client, or any other logical group.

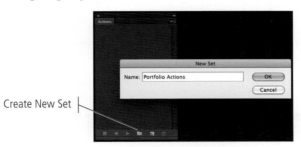

Create New Set

Note:

You don't need to have a file open in Photoshop to change the Actions that are available in the Actions panel.

8. **With the Portfolio Actions set highlighted in the Actions panel, choose Save Actions from the panel Options menu.**

9. **In the Save dialog box, make sure the Save As field shows Portfolio Actions.atn and click Save.**

Action sets are saved by default in the Photoshop>Presets>Actions folder with the extension ".atn" (which is automatically added for you). If you are using a shared computer, you might not be able to save files in the application's default location. If this is the case, navigate to your WIP>Metro folder to save the Portfolio Actions.atn file.

Note:

Action sets are stored by default in the Presets>Actions folder in the Photoshop Application folder on your computer. You can also load an action from another location, such as when someone sends you an action that was created on another computer.

If you make changes to a set — whether you delete an existing action from the set or add your own custom actions — without saving the altered set, you will have to repeat your work the next time you launch Photoshop.

10. **Continue to the next exercise.**

CREATE A NEW ACTION

Recording an action is a fairly simple process: open a file, click the Record button in the Actions panel, and perform the steps you want to save in the action. Click the Stop button to stop recording, either permanently when you're done or temporarily if you need to do something else in the middle of creating the action. (If you stop recording, you can later select the last step in the existing action and start recording again by clicking the Record button.)

Note:

You can change the name, keyboard shortcut, and/or button color of any action by selecting it in the Actions panel and choosing Action Options from the panel Options menu.

1. **In Photoshop, open poppies.jpg from your WIP>Metro>images folder. If you get a profile mismatch warning, use the embedded profile.**

   When you apply this action in the next exercise, you can determine how color profile problems are managed by the automated batch processing.

   Create New Action
   Play Selection
   Begin Recording
   Stop Playing/Recording

2. **Click the Create New Action button at the bottom of the Actions panel.**

3. **In the New Action dialog box, type Create Web Thumbnail in the Name field.**

   By default, new actions are added to the currently selected set. You can add the action to any open set by choosing from the Set menu. The Function Key menu allows you to assign a keyboard shortcut to the action, so an "F" key (with or without modifiers) can initiate that action. The Color menu defines the color of the button when the Actions panel is viewed in Button mode.

Note:

As with any user-defined element, you should use descriptive names for your actions.

4. **Click the Record button.**

   Anything you do from this point forward is recorded as a step in the action until you intentionally stop the recording by clicking the Stop button at the bottom of the Actions panel.

   The red button shows that the action is currently being recorded.

5. **With poppies.jpg open, choose Image>Image Size.**

6. **Make sure the Constrain Proportions and Resample Image options are checked.**

   You want the thumbnails to be proportionally sized, and you want them to remain at 72 ppi.

7. **Change the Pixel Dimensions height to 72 pixels.**

Because the Resample Image option is checked, changing one field in this dialog box affects others; reducing the number of pixels results in a proportionally smaller document size.

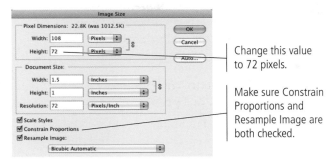

Change this value to 72 pixels.

Make sure Constrain Proportions and Resample Image are both checked.

8. **Click OK to close the Image Size dialog box and apply the change.**

9. **Choose Image>Adjustments>Invert.**

The open image has been resized to 72 pixels high.

Pixel color data has been inverted to appear as a photo negative.

The two things you did in Steps 5–9 are included in the action.

Note:

Press Command/ Control-I to apply the Invert adjustment.

10. **In the Actions panel, click the Stop Recording button.**

11. **Expand the Image Size item in the Create Web Thumbnail action.**

12. **Close the poppies.jpg file without saving.**

You don't need to save the changes since this file will be processed when you run the action on the entire images folder.

13. **Select the Portfolio Actions set in the Actions panel and choose Save Actions in the panel Options menu.**

14. Accept the default options in the Save dialog box and click Save. When asked if you want to replace the existing set of the same name, click Replace.

If you don't resave the set after adding the action, the Create Web Thumbnail action will be lost when you quit Photoshop.

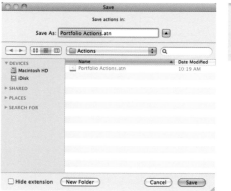 

15. Continue to the next exercise.

Inserting Action Stops and Menu Options

When you record actions, you can insert an intentional pause by choosing **Insert Stop** from the Actions panel Options menu. When you insert a stop, the Record Stop dialog box allows you to type a message that displays when the action runs. This message can include specific instructions or reminders to the user, such as a prompt to make a selection before the remainder of the action runs.

When the action reaches a stop, the message you entered into the Record Stop dialog box displays. The user must click Stop, perform the required step, and then click the Play button in the Actions panel to complete the rest of the action. The Allow Continue option in the Record Stop dialog box adds a Continue button to the Stop message; if the user clicks Continue, the action resumes.

You can also cause an action to open a specific dialog box or execute a menu command by choosing **Insert Menu Item** from the Actions panel Options menu. When the Insert Menu Item dialog box appears, you can make a selection from the application menu, and then click OK. When the action runs, the specified dialog box opens or the menu command executes.

When you insert a menu item that opens a dialog box (such as Select>Color Range), you are adding a modal command that can't be turned off. When the action runs, even with modal commands turned off, the dialog box opens and requires user interaction. Although an action can automate many steps in a repetitive process, there are still some things that can't be entirely automatic.

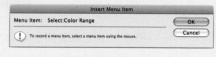

BATCH-PROCESS FILES

The ability to batch-process files further enhances and automates productivity. If you have a large group of files that all require the same adjustments, you can build an action, set up a batch, and go to lunch (or, depending on your computer processor and number of files, go home for the night).

For example, when we write the Portfolio books, we take screen shots in RGB mode at 100%. Before the books are laid out for print production, the screen shots are converted to the U.S. Web Coated (SWOP) v2 CMYK profile and resized (not resampled) to 40%. As you have probably noticed, there are a lot of screen shots in these books. Rather than sitting for several days and modifying each file (or even sitting for one full day and running an action on each file), we set up a batch that converts all screen shots for an entire book in about 25 minutes.

1. **In Photoshop, choose File>Automate>Batch.**

   At the top of the Batch dialog box, the Set and Action menus default to the active selection in the Actions panel. In this case, there is only one available choice, so the Create Web Thumbnail action is already selected. You can choose to run a batch for any action in any open set.

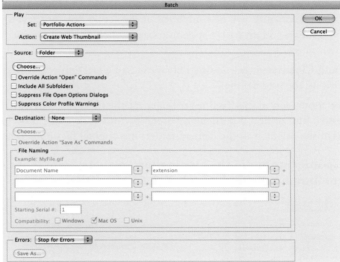

2. **Choose Folder in the Source menu.**

   The Source menu allows you to choose which files are batched:

   - **Folder** processes a complete group of images arranged within a single folder on your computer.

   - **Import** acquires and processes a group of images from a scanner or digital camera.

   - **Open Files** processes all files currently open in the application.

   - **File Browser** processes files selected in the File Browser.

   When Folder is selected, you can also choose to override "Open" commands that are recorded in the selected action, include subfolders within the selected folder, and suppress color profile warnings for the files being processed.

3. **Click the Choose button and navigate to the WIP>Metro>images folder and click Choose/OK to return to the Batch dialog box.**

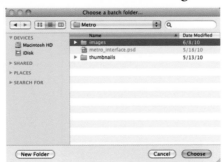

4. **Make sure the Suppress Color Profile Warnings option is checked to prevent the batch from stopping if color management policies are violated.**

   This is a matter of some debate, but when processing images for the Web, color management is not considered as critical as it is for print.

5. **Choose Folder in the Destination menu.**

   The Destination menu in the Batch dialog box presents three options:

   - **None** simply means that the action will be run. If the action saves and closes the files, those commands will be completed. If the action does not save and close the files, you might end up with a large number of open files and eventually crash your computer.

   - **Save and Close** saves the modified file in the same location with the same name, overwriting the original file.

   - **Folder** allows you to specify a target folder for the files after they have been processed. This option is particularly useful because it saves the processed files as copies of the originals in the defined folder; the original files remain intact.

6. **Click the Choose button (in the Destination area), navigate to the WIP>Metro>thumbnails folder, and click Choose/OK.**

7. **In the File Naming area, open the menu for the first field and choose document name (lowercase) from the menu.**

   The File Naming fields allow you to redefine file names for the modified files. You can choose a variable from the pop-up menu, type specific text in a field, or use a combination of both. The example in the File Naming area shows the result of your choices in these menus.

Note:

*You can create a **droplet** from an action, which allows you to run the action using a basic drag-and-drop technique (as long as Photoshop is running). The Create Droplet dialog box (File>Automate>Create Droplet) presents most of the same options as the Batch dialog box, with a few exceptions. Clicking Choose at the top of the dialog box allows you to define the name of the droplet and the location to save it. The dialog box does not include Source options because the source is defined when you drag files onto the droplet.*

8. **In the second field, type _sm.**

   This identifies the images as thumbnails, differentiating them from the full-size images with the same names.

9. **Choose extension (lowercase) from the menu for the third field.**

Note:

These options are only available when Folder is selected in the Destination menu.

10. **Click OK to run the batch.**

    When the process is complete, you will have nine thumbnail images in your WIP>Metro>thumbnails folder.

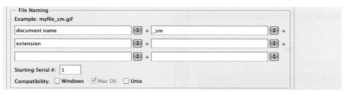

Note:

*The last section of the Batch dialog box determines what happens if an error occurs during a batch. **Stop for Errors** (the default setting) interrupts the batch and displays a warning dialog box. **Log Errors to File** batch-processes every file and saves a record of all problems.*

11. **Continue to the next exercise.**

 PLACE AND ALIGN THUMBNAILS ON THE PAGE

Now that the thumbnail images have been created, you can arrange them in the gallery file so it can be animated, sliced, and saved for the Web.

1. **Open the file metro_interface.psd from the WIP>Metro folder.**
   If you receive a profile mismatch warning, choose the option to not color manage this file.

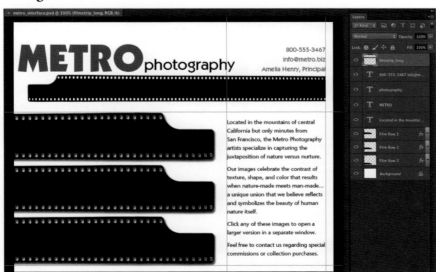

2. **Open the Mini Bridge panel and navigate to the WIP>Metro>thumbnails folder. Select all nine images in the folder, and then click the thumbnail of any selected item and drag into the interface file.**

The Mini Bridge panel makes this process far easier than using the File>Place command, which only allows placement of a single image at once.

The Mini Bridge panel makes it possible to place all nine images in one step.

Note:

Refer to Project 1: Composite Movie Ad for more information about Mini Bridge.

3. **Press Return/Enter nine times to finalize the placement of each image.**

4. **In the Layers panel, drag the postpile_sm, poppies_sm, and rust_sm layers immediately above the Film Row 1 layer.**

The names of the thumbnail layers are based on the names of the thumbnail files you placed, which makes it easy to find exactly what you need.

Although not strictly necessary, it is easier to work with complex files when you organize your Layers panel logically. By placing the relevant thumbnail images above the filmstrip layer that will serve as their background, you will be better able to manage the individual layers.

Note:

Shift-click to select contiguous layers; Command/Control-click to select non-contiguous layers.

5. **Drag the shamrocks_sm, waves_sm, and starfish_sm layers immediately above the Film Row 2 layer.**

6. **Drag the sunset_bridge_sm, stairs_sm, and windmill_sm layers immediately above the Film Row 3 layer.**

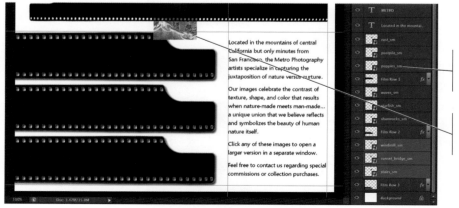

Three thumbnail images should appear directly above each filmstrip layer.

The placed images all appear in the same spot, directly on top of each other.

7. **Select the Film Row 1 layer and the three image layers immediately above it. Open the panel Options menu and choose New Group from Layers.**

8. **Name the new group `Filmstrip1` and then click OK.**

   Grouping each row of thumbnails with the appropriate background layer will make it easier to manage the set as a single object later in this project.

9. **Repeat this process to create two more layer groups, one for each row of thumbnail images (named `Filmstrip2` and `Filmstrip3`).**

10. **Save the file and continue to the next exercise.**

ARRANGE THE THUMBNAIL IMAGES

The Align and Distribute options in the Options bar offer the easiest solution when you need to arrange the content of multiple layers in relation to one another. You can simply select the layers you want to arrange, and then click the appropriate buttons to align edges or centers; or you can distribute layers across a specific amount of space.

1. **With `metro_interface.psd` open, make sure the Snap option is toggled on in the View menu.**

2. **Open the View>Snap To submenu and make sure Layers is selected.**

   When the Snap options are turned on, arranging layers relative to one another is fairly easy (as you will see in the next few steps).

   Make sure Snap is toggled on. | Make sure the Layers option is toggled on.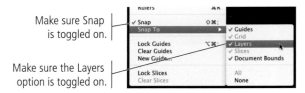

3. **Select the Move tool in the Tools panel. In the Options bar, uncheck the Auto-Select option.**

   By turning off Auto-Select, you can click anywhere in the document window to move the contents of the selected layer. Turning this option off prevents you from accidentally moving the content of a different layer.

4. **Expand the Filmstrip1 layer group in the Layers panel, and then select the rust_sm image layer.**

5. **Drag the layer contents until the left edge snaps to the left edge of the word Metro, and the thumbnail is approximately centered within the first filmstrip.**

   We found it necessary to select the Move tool and use the Arrow keys to nudge the image layer down a bit because we weren't satisfied with the vertical position within the filmstrip that resulted from the layer snapping to other elements in the file.

   Drag until the left edge of the thumbnail snaps to the left edge of the word "Metro".

   Manually nudge the thumbnail to be centered vertically in the filmstrip area.

   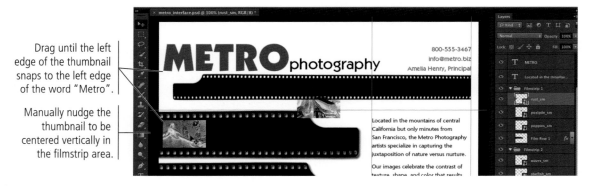

6. **Click the postpile_sm layer in the Layers panel, and use the Move tool to drag the layer content until the top edge snaps to align with the top edge of the rust thumbnail. Leave a small amount of space between the two images.**

   Drag until the top edge of the thumbnail snaps to the top of the first thumbnail.

7. **Repeat Step 6 for the poppies_sm layer.**

8. With the poppies_sm layer selected, press Shift and drag right until the right edge of the thumbnail appears below the last sprocket hole in the filmstrip.

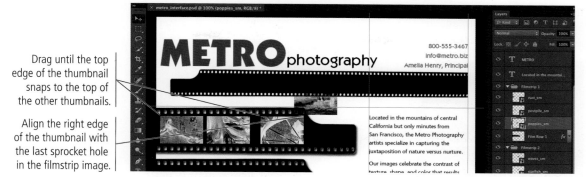

Drag until the top edge of the thumbnail snaps to the top of the other thumbnails.

Align the right edge of the thumbnail with the last sprocket hole in the filmstrip image.

9. In the Layers panel, Shift-click to select all three image layers in the Filmstrip1 layer group.

When multiple layers are selected in the Layers panel, a number of alignment options become available in the Options bar. These are very useful for aligning or distributing the content of multiple layers relative to one another.

10. Click the Distribute Horizontal Centers button in the Options bar.

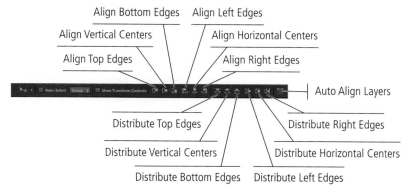

Align Bottom Edges Align Left Edges
Align Vertical Centers Align Horizontal Centers
Align Top Edges Align Right Edges

Auto Align Layers

Distribute Top Edges Distribute Right Edges
Distribute Vertical Centers Distribute Horizontal Centers
Distribute Bottom Edges Distribute Left Edges

This option places an equal amount of space between the horizontal center point of each selected layer. Because these three thumbnails have the same width (caused by your earlier batch-processed action), the images are exactly spaced in relation to one another.

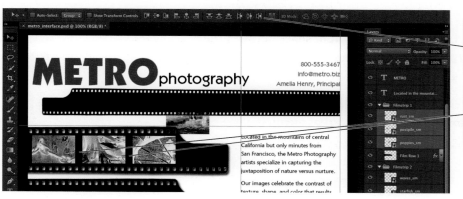

Selecting multiple layers allows you to access the Align functions in the Options bar.

Clicking Distribute Horizontal Centers creates equal space between the content of selected layers.

11. **Repeat this process to align the three thumbnail images on each of the remaining two filmstrips.**

In this case, you can simply drag the layers to arrange them. Because the Snap To Layers option is active, the thumbnails in the second and third rows will snap to the edges of the thumbnails in the first row to create the rows in even columns.

12. **Save the file and continue to the next stage of the project.**

Stage 2 Editing Layers for Visual Effect

At the meeting, your client asked for some way to break up the horizontal homogeneity in the top half of the interface design. Photoshop offers a number of tools for distorting layers, from simple scaling to the Free Transform mode to the Liquify filter. If you completed the other projects in this book, you have already used all of these techniques to fulfill specific project goals. In this stage of this project, you will learn two more methods for transforming layer content — puppet warping and 3D extrusion — to achieve effects that can't easily be created with other methods.

USE PUPPET WARP TO TRANSFORM A LAYER

Puppet Warp provides a way to transform and distort specific areas of a layer without affecting other areas of the same layer. It is called "puppet" warp because it's based on the concept of pinning certain areas in place and then bending other areas around those pin locations — mimicking the way a puppet's joints pivot. In this exercise, you use puppet warping to bend and distort the top filmstrip image layer.

> **Note:**
>
> *Puppet warping can be applied to image, shape, and text layers, as well as layer and vector masks.*

1. **With metro_interface.psd open, make sure guides are visible (View>Show>Guides)**

2. **Control/right-click the filmstrip_long layer in the Layers panel. Choose Convert to Smart Object from the contextual menu.**

By first converting this layer to a Smart Object, you can apply the puppet warp non-destructively.

3. **Choose Edit>Puppet Warp.**

When you enter Puppet Warp mode, a mesh overlays the active layer content. This mesh represents the joints in the shape that can bend when you warp the layer content.

In the Options bar, you can change the mesh density from the default Normal to show Fewer Points (which decreases precision in the warp) or More Points (which increases the warp precision, but can require longer processing time).

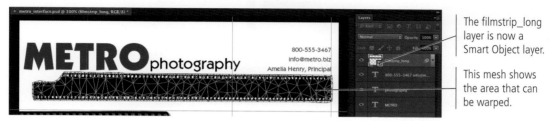

The filmstrip_long layer is now a Smart Object layer.

This mesh shows the area that can be warped.

4. **Click the mesh on the vertical guide near the top edge of the filmstrip.**

Clicking the mesh places a pin, which anchors the layer at that location.

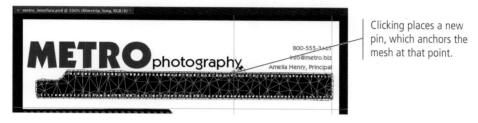

Clicking places a new pin, which anchors the mesh at that point.

5. **Click the top-right corner of the mesh and, without releasing the mouse button, drag up above the top edge of the image.**

Clicking and dragging places a new pin and rotates the image around the location of the existing pin. Because you have placed placed one other pin on the layer, the entire shape rotates around the first pin location.

Clicking and dragging places a new pin, and rotates the layer around the existing pin.

This is the pin you placed in Step 4.

6. **Press Command/Control-Z to undo the pin/movement from Step 5.**

Pressing Command/Control-Z while working in Puppet Warp mode undoes the last action you performed inside the puppet warp mesh. You can only undo one action; after you finalize the warp, the Undo command undoes the entire warp — everything you did since you entered Puppet Warp mode.

7. **Click to place pins in the top-left and bottom-left corners of the mesh, as shown in the following image.**

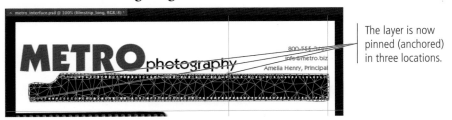

The layer is now pinned (anchored) in three locations.

8. **Click the top-right corner and drag up above the top edge of the image.**

Because you have now anchored the left corners of the mesh, only the right side of the object is significantly affected. The bottom edge warps the entire way across because you didn't add a pin anywhere along the bottom edge.

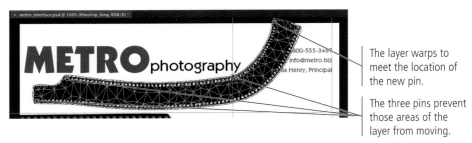

The layer warps to meet the location of the new pin.

The three pins prevent those areas of the layer from moving.

9. **In the Options bar, choose the Distort option in the Mode menu.**

As you can see, Distort mode warps the object based on the position and angle of existing pins.

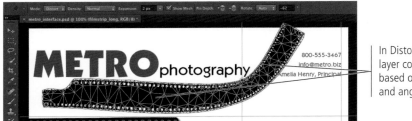

In Distort mode, the layer content distorts based on the position and angle of pins.

10. **Click the top-right corner of the mesh and drag right.**

This enlarges the distortion between the two pins on the right end of the filmstrip.

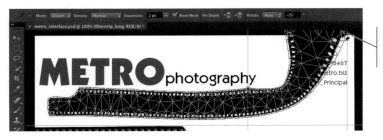

Adding a new pin changes the overall shape distortion.

11. Click the top-left pin to select it, then press Option/Alt. Move the cursor slightly away from the pin until you see a curved-arrow icon. While still pressing Option/Alt, click and drag to change the angle of the selected pin.

As soon as you press Option/Alt, the pin changes from an Auto rotation angle to a Fixed rotation angle. By dragging, you change the angle of the pin — and the position of the distortion around that pin.

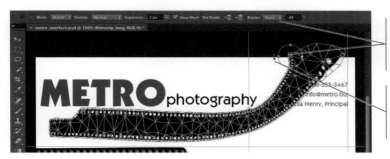

Pressing Option/Alt over an existing pin changes that pin to Fixed rotation instead of Auto.

You can click and drag the rotation proxy around the pin to change its angle.

12. Continue manipulating the filmstrip warp until you are satisfied with the result. Keep the following points in mind:

- Click to add new pins at any point in the process.
- Option/Alt click an existing, selected pin to remove it from the mesh.
- With a specific pin selected, press Option/Alt, then click the rotation proxy and drag to change the angle of that pin.
- Uncheck the Show Mesh option to get a better preview of your warp.

Our solution is shown here. (We achieved a more satisfying result by changing the mesh to show More Points.)

Note:

The Expansion option in the Options bar determines how far the mesh extends beyond the edge of the layer content.

Note:

If you warp a layer so that the mesh overlaps, you can use the Pin Depth buttons in the Options bar to show pins on underlying layers.

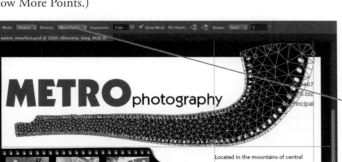

With More Points in the mesh, we were able to create a more precise warp.

Uncheck the Show Mesh option to get a better preview of your warped layer.

13. Press Return/Enter to finalize the warp.

14. Select the layer containing the client's phone number, and position and scale it (if necessary) so it is not obscured by the warped filmstrip.

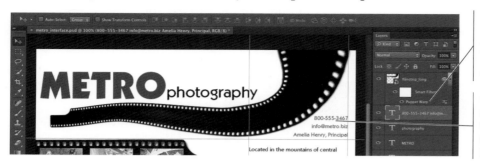

Because you converted the layer to a Smart Object, you can double-click the Puppet Warp effect to change the warp settings.

Reposition and scale (if necessary) the type layer with the contact information so it is not obscured by the warped filmstrip.

15. Save the file and continue to the next exercise.

 ## EXTRUDE A TEXT LAYER TO 3D

If you completed Project 4: City Promotion Cards, you already experimented with some of the 3D options that are built into Photoshop Extended. In addition to wrapping an object around a mesh shape, you can also create three-dimensional shapes from certain types of layer content — specifically, text.

As we explained in Project 4, we are only touching the surface of what you can do when you work in three dimensions; our goal is to show you some of the options that will be useful for creating 3D effects in a 2D medium such as print or Web design.

1. With **metro_interface.psd** open, hide the filmstrip_long, photography, and phone number layers.

2. Using the Type tool, place the insertion point anywhere in the Metro type layer, and click the 3D button in the Options bar.

You could also select the layer in the panel, and than choose 3D>New 3D Extrusion from Selected Layer. The Options bar button simply provides easy access to extrusion for the active text layer.

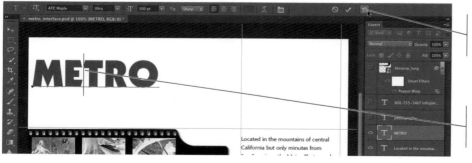

Click here to make a 3D extrusion from the active text layer.

The insertion point is placed in this layer.

3. Read the resulting message and then click Yes.

To work effectively with 3D objects, you need (at least) the Layers panel, the 3D panel, and the Properties panel. The built-in 3D workspace automatically shows those panels.

When you create a 3D layer from the existing Type layer, Photoshop automatically asks if you want to switch to that workspace.

4. **Open the View>Show submenu. Turn off the 3D Secondary View and 3D Ground Plane options, and turn on the 3D Lights and 3D Selection options.**

You're only manipulating a single word of type, so the secondary view and ground plane aren't particularly helpful in this instance. The lights and selection options, however, can be very helpful for manipulating the 3D shape on screen.

Because 3D Selection options are showing, you can use on-screen proxies to change a number of settings.

Move the mouse over various parts of the on-screen mesh to change different properties.

Options related to the new 3D layer are available in the 3D and Properties panels.

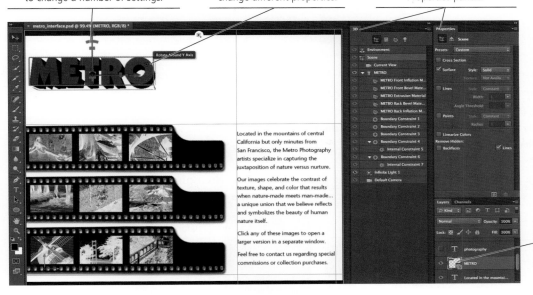

The Type layer now shows the 3D layer icon.

If you completed Project 4: City Promotion Cards, you were already introduced to some of the 3D capabilities that are available in Photoshop CS6. As you complete this exercise, keep in mind that the 3D panel lists all of the elements that make up a 3D object:

- The Environment is everything around the 3D object.

- The Scene is basically everything that makes up the 3D effect.

    - Current View defines properties of the camera, or the perspective from which the scene is being viewed.

    - Object defines properties related to the actual 3D model, including:

        ° Materials, which are the appearances of the surfaces

        ° Constraints, which are the shapes that make up the 3D mesh

    - Light defines the specific light sources that shine on the 3D model. (These are the same light sources that you used in Project 6: Advertising Samples.)

5. **With the Metro object selected in the 3D panel, review the options in the Properties panel.**

When the 3D type object is selected, the Properties panel has four modes:

Note:

Press V to toggle through various modes of the Properties panel.

- Mesh options relate to the overall 3D shape. You can change how the mesh casts and catches shadows, and choose a shape preset to distort the 3D mesh.

  At the bottom of the Properties panel, you can use the Text swatch and Character Panel buttons to make changes to the type formatting. Clicking the Edit Source button opens a separate file with the live type layer — which means you can edit the text (and its formatting) even after converting it to a 3D layer.

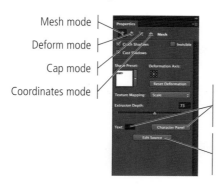

Mesh mode
Deform mode
Cap mode
Coordinates mode

Use these options to change the formatting of the actual text.

Click here to edit the live text in a separate window.

- Deform options control the depth, twist, taper, bend, and shear of the 3D extrusion.
- Cap options control the beveling and inflation effects that are applied to the front and/or back surfaces of a 3D shape.
- Coordinates options are the same as for the Scene, but apply only to the selected object.

6. **Click the Deform button at the top of the Properties panel, then place the mouse cursor over the Bend control of the on-screen Deform proxy.**

Twist
Bend
Extrude
Taper

Deform mode of the Properties panel controls the same options that are available in the on-screen proxy.

Note:

In either the Mesh or Deform properties, you can apply a predefined group of shape options using the Shape Preset menu. Different presets change the Extrude options, which define the shape that is created.

7. **Click and drag right until the cursor feedback shows the Bend X: 180°.**

Dragging right or left changes the horizontal bend (Bend X). Dragging up or down changes the vertical bend (Bend Y).

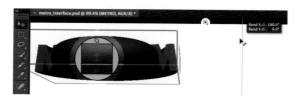

8. **In the Properties panel, click the right-center point in the Deformation Axis proxy.**

   The registration point defines the origin of the bend or shear. As you can see in this example, the bend is now applied around the right-center point of the original object.

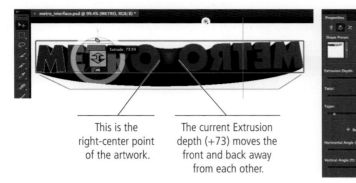

The Deformation Axis defines how the bend is applied, relative to the original shape.

This is the right-center point of the artwork.

The current Extrusion depth (+73) moves the front and back away from each other.

9. **Place the cursor over the Extrude control of the on-screen Deform proxy. Click and drag down until the two "o" shapes overlap, as shown in the following image.**

   Changing the Extrusion Depth moves the front and back sides closer together or farther apart.

Decreasing the Extrusion Depth moves the front and back sides closer together.

Note:

Sometimes the 3D panel changes automatically to select the scene instead of the object; this appears to be a bug in the software. You should make sure the correct element is selected in the 3D panel.

10. **With the Metro object still selected in the 3D panel, click the Cap button at the top of the Properties panel.**

11. **Place the mouse cursor over the Bevel Width control in the on-screen Cap proxy. Click and drag right to apply a 15% bevel.**

    Bevel options change the contour map for the front and/or back of the shape. The Inflate options can be used to create a bubble effect; a positive angle creates an outer bubble effect.

12. **In the Properties panel, choose Front and Back in the Sides menu.**

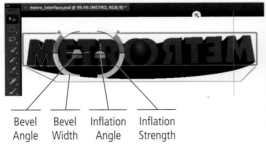

Cap mode of the Properties panel controls the same options that are available in the on-screen proxy.

Cap settings can be changed for the front or the back (or both).

Bevel Angle   Bevel Width   Inflation Angle   Inflation Strength

13. **In the 3D panel, click METRO Extrusion Material to select only that mesh.**

    When a specific material is selected, you can change the color and texture that apply to the selected material.

14. **In the Properties panel, open the Material Picker. Scroll down to find the No Texture option, then click it to remove the texture from the extrusion mesh.**

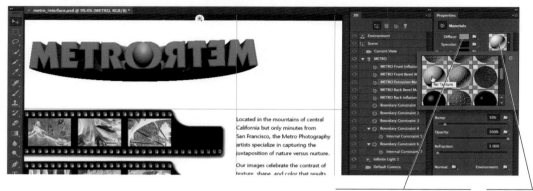

Click these swatches to change the color of the various lights that affect the material.

Click here to change the texture for the selected material.

15. **Click the Diffuse color swatch. Choose White as the new diffuse color, then click OK.**

    The color of various lights changes the appearance of the selected material:

    - Diffuse is the color of the surface material, or the file that makes up the reflective surface of the object.

    - Specular defines the color of specular highlights (i.e., areas where the light is 100% reflected).

    - Illumination is the color of surface areas where the material is transparent; this setting results in the effect of interior lighting, such as a painting on a light bulb.

    - Ambient defines the color of ambient light that's visible on reflective surfaces.

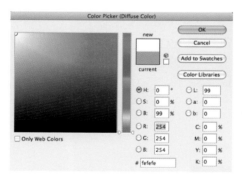

Changing the Diffuse color of the material changes the material's overall appearance.

Other shades on the material are caused by shadows that are cast by the mesh.

16. **In the 3D panel, click Scene to select it.**

Note:

When Scene properties are visible in the Properties panel, you can define a number of rendering options.

17. In the Properties panel, click the Coordinates button. Change the X Rotation field to –25°.

Depending on the existing position, it can be difficult to find the exact control you want in the on-screen proxy. The Properties panel provides an easy way to change exactly the property you want.

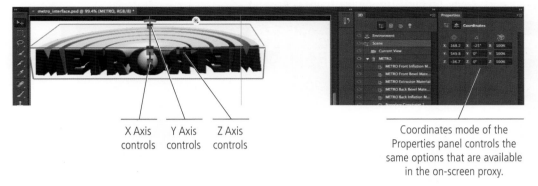

X Axis controls · Y Axis controls · Z Axis controls

Coordinates mode of the Properties panel controls the same options that are available in the on-screen proxy.

18. In the on-screen 3D Axis, click the Rotate Around Z Axis control and drag left.

In the on-screen proxy, each axis has three controls: Move, Rotate, and Scale.

Move On Axis
Rotate Around Axis
Scale Along Axis

19. In the Layers panel, make the filmstrip_long, photography, and phone number layers visible.

You hid these layers earlier to better focus on the 3D object. Now you need to scale the 3D object to fit into the available space, so you have to make those layers visible again.

20. Place the mouse cursor over the Scale Uniformly control in the on-screen 3D Axis. Click and drag down to reduce the size of the 3D object to about 80%.

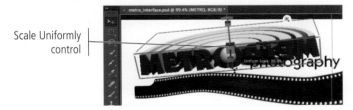

Scale Uniformly control

21. Move the mouse cursor over the 3D object until the cursor feedback shows "Move on XY Plane". Click and drag to reposition the object so it does not overlap with any of the other objects in the file.

Move the mouse over different parts of the mesh to move or rotate on a particular axis.

Cursor feedback shows what you can do by clicking and dragging.

22. **Click the Light proxy at the top of the screen to select the applied light source. In the Infinite Light mode of the Properties panel, click the Move to View button.**

When a specific light is selected, you can change the properties of that light. (These are the same as the properties you used in Project 6: Advertising Samples.) In this case, changing the light source changes the way the object casts shadows, which in turn changes the apparent colors on the extrusion materials.

23. **Save the file and continue to the next stage of the project.**

Stage 3 Building Frame Animations

Animating objects on Web pages can be an effective way to hold visitors' interest. In Photoshop, animation is created as a series of frames displayed in rapid succession, creating the illusion of movement. For each frame in the animation, you can change the position of objects, the opacity and visibility of a layer, the color of objects, the applied styles, and other options.

 ## PREPARE LAYERS FOR ANIMATION

In this stage of the project, you're going to create a three-stage animation in which each row of thumbnails moves onto the screen after the previous one is already in place. As the filmstrips are moving, the main block of introductory text will fade into view.

Photoshop combines layers with frames to create the illusion of movement. For each frame in an animation, you can change the position, opacity, visibility, and effects applied to a layer, as well as add new layers, paint on existing layers, and more. In short, what is visible in the Layers panel for a selected frame is what you see when the animation reaches that frame during playback.

1. **With metro_interface.psd open, open the Timeline panel (Window>Timeline).**

When you first open the Timeline panel, you have to determine what you want to create. Photoshop supports both video timelines and frame animation. In this project, you are going to create a frame animation.

2. **If the button in the middle of the panel says "Create Video Timeline", click the arrow button in the middle of the panel and choose Create Frame Animation in the menu.**

3. **Click the Create Frame Animation button.**

When you create a frame animation, you can create or delete frames; control looping options, frame delay, and tweening; and preview the animation within Photoshop.

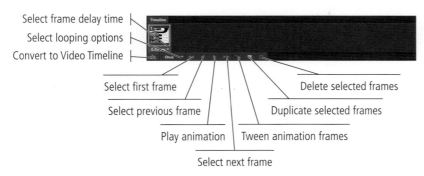

Select frame delay time
Select looping options
Convert to Video Timeline

Select first frame
Select previous frame
Play animation
Select next frame

Delete selected frames
Duplicate selected frames
Tween animation frames

- The **looping** option determines how many times the animation plays. You can choose Once, Forever, or Other (a specific number of times).

- The **frame delay** for each frame determines the amount of time before the next frame appears. Short or no delays help create smoother transitions; longer delays create a more choppy flow (which might not be what you want).

- **Tweening** creates intermediary frames between two selected frames to smooth transitions from one frame to the next.

4. **In the Layers panel, Shift-click to select the three Filmstrip layer goups.**

5. **With the Move tool active, press Shift, then click and drag the selected layer groups left until none of the filmstrips are visible within the image boundaries.**

   To reveal these layer groups, you will move them from this location and back into place, and then animate the change in position.

6. **Select the main text layer ("Located in the...") in the Layers panel and change the opacity field to 0%.**

   To reveal this layer, you will set the opacity back to 100% and animate the change in opacity.

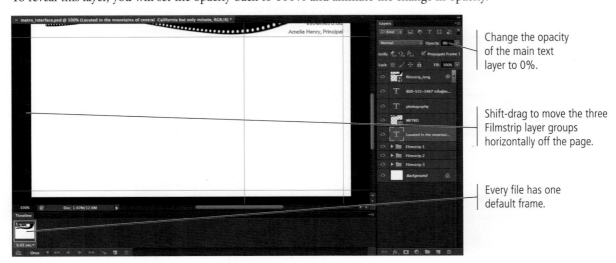

Change the opacity of the main text layer to 0%.

Shift-drag to move the three Filmstrip layer groups horizontally off the page.

Every file has one default frame.

7. **Save the file and continue to the next exercise.**

CREATE NEW FRAMES

When you build a frame-based animation, you need to add a new frame every time you want something to change. For the animation in this project, you need four frames in addition to the default frame that appears when you open the file.

1. **With `metro_interface.psd` open, click the Duplicate Selected Frames button at the bottom of the Timeline panel.**

   The second frame is an exact duplicate of the first.

2. **With Frame 2 selected in the Timeline panel, select the Filmstrip1 layer group in the Layers panel. Press Shift and drag the group right until it is in the same position as before you moved it in the previous exercise.**

3. **Select the main text layer in the Layers panel and change the opacity to 33%.**

   You're revealing one-third of the text opacity in each part of a three-stage animation.

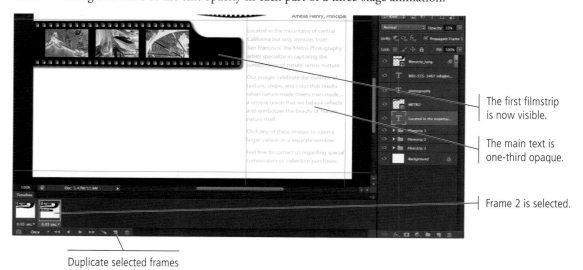

The first filmstrip is now visible.

The main text is one-third opaque.

Frame 2 is selected.

Duplicate selected frames

4. **Duplicate Frame 2 in the Timeline panel.**

5. **With the new Frame 3 selected, repeat Step 2 for the Filmstrip2 layer group, and then change the main-text layer opacity to 66%.**

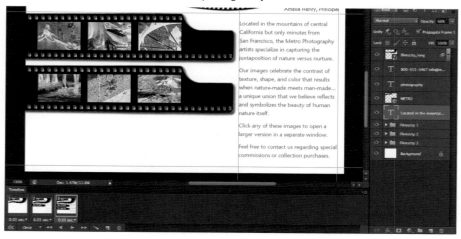

6. **Duplicate Frame 3 in the Timeline panel.**

7. **With the new Frame 4 selected, repeat Step 2 for the Filmstrip3 layer group, and then change the main-text layer opacity to 100%.**

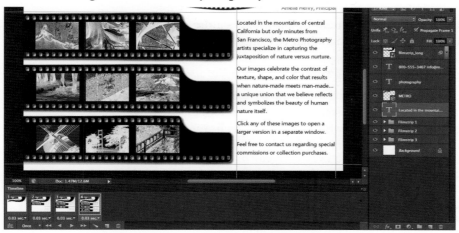

8. **In the Timeline panel, Shift-click to select all four frames in the animation.**

9. **Click the Select Frame Delay Time menu for any of the selected frames, and choose 0.5 [seconds] in the menu.**

    Frame delay is the length of time between the appearance of frames in the animation. You can set this value for all frames to control the overall speed of the animation (as you did in this step), or change the frame delay for individual frames to create different effects.

Note:

By selecting all four frames, you can change the delay for all four frames at once.

10. **Make sure Once is selected in the Select Looping Option menu.**

    You don't want this animation to occur repeatedly. Setting this option to Once makes the filmstrips slide in as the text fades in.

11. **Click Frame 1 to select it, and then click the Play Animation button to preview your animation.**

    When the animation plays, each frame is revealed sequentially. Each filmstrip simply pops into view, and there is no smooth transition in the text opacity. You will fix these problems in the next exercise.

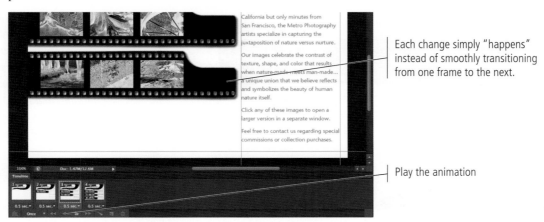

Each change simply "happens" instead of smoothly transitioning from one frame to the next.

Play the animation

12. **Save the file and continue to the next exercise.**

CREATE TWEENS

To create the appearance of movement, such as a filmstrip sliding onto the page or a block of text fading in, you have to use a sequence of frames between the starting position and the ending position. Each intermediary frame changes the object slightly; when the frames play in quick succession, the objects appear to make a smooth transition from their original state to their ending state.

For very precise control, you could create each intermediary frame manually, but that method would be very time consuming for even a simple animation. Fortunately, Photoshop includes an option to **tween** frames, which means the application creates intermediary frames for you based on specific parameters.

1. **With `metro_interface.psd` open, Shift-click to select Frames 1 and 2 in the Timeline panel.**

2. **Click the Tween Animation Frames button at the bottom of the Timeline panel.**

   In the Tween dialog box, Selection is automatically chosen in the Tween With menu. Using this option, the new frames will be placed between (hence the name) the two selected frames.

3. **Change the Frames to Add field to 5, make sure All Layers is selected in the Layers area, and check the Position and Opacity options in the Parameters area.**

   A tween can create transitions for layer position, opacity, and effects — and any combination of those three attributes. You have not applied any effects, so that option is not relevant in this project.

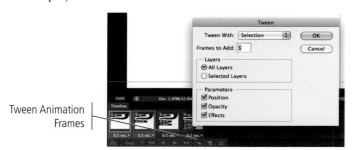

Tween Animation Frames

Note:

If only one frame were selected in the Timeline panel, you could choose Tween With Next Frame or Previous Frame to determine where the tween would be created.

4. **Click OK to create the tween frames.**

   When Photoshop creates the tween, the specified number of frames is added to the animation. Each frame varies the selected parameters (in this case, the position of the first filmstrip and the opacity of the main text) slightly to create the transition.

Note:

If the Selected Layers option is active, the tween frames will include only the layers currently selected in the Layers panel; the rest of the page (the background, buttons, and so on) will not be visible during the tween frames' playback.

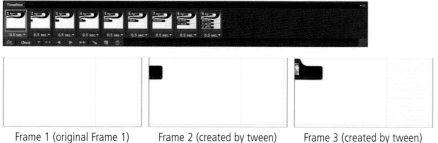

Frame 1 (original Frame 1)   Frame 2 (created by tween)   Frame 3 (created by tween)

Frame 4 (created by tween)   Frame 5 (created by tween)   Frame 6 (created by tween)   Frame 7 (original Frame 2)

5. **Create another tween between Frames 7 and 8, adding 5 frames that change the position and opacity parameters.**

Each new frame moves the second filmstrip group further into place and increases the opacity of the text layer from 33% to 66%.

6. **Create another tween between Frames 13 and 14, adding 5 frames that change the position and opacity parameters.**

At Frame 19, all three filmstrips are now in place, and the text layer is fully opaque.

7. **Select Frame 1 in the Timeline panel and play the animation.**

As it stands now, the animation is very choppy because each frame has a half-second delay; in other words, each frame appears for half a second before the next frame appears. Some animations might actually require longer delay times, but in other cases (like the tweens you created in this file), a long delay can ruin the effect.

8. **Click Frame 1, then Shift-click Frame 19 to select all frames in the animation.**

9. **Click the arrow next to the current delay interval for any of the selected frames, and choose 0.2 [seconds] from the resulting menu.**

Click here to open the Delay menu.

10. **Select Frame 1 in the Timeline panel and play the animation.**

The transitions move much more smoothly now. If you see a slight delay between frames, don't worry; it will be less apparent when the final animation file is exported. Photoshop is a good tool for building this type of animation, but its previewing capabilities are limited.

11. **Save the file and continue to the next stage of the project.**

Optimizing Animations

If bandwidth is a concern (and it should be) you might want to optimize animations to reduce the size of the file that will be exported. Frame disposal and overall optimization options are built into the Photoshop Timeline panel. Control/right-clicking a frame in the Timeline panel displays three options for frame disposal; these choices determine what happens to the current frame during a transition.

- **Automatic** discards the current frame if the next frame contains layer transparency. This is the default setting, and it is desirable for many animations. This method must be used when optimizing images using the Redundant Pixel Removal optimization option.

- **Do Not Dispose** preserves the current frame as the next frame is added, allowing the current frame to show through transparent areas of the next frame. To preview an animation accurately, you should use a browser with this option.

- **Dispose** deletes the current frame before the next frame loads. The current frame does not appear through transparent areas of the following frame.

You can also reduce the final file size by cropping frames until you are left with only the important parts of the animation.

Photoshop can move through the frames of an animation, looking for identical information in two sequential frames; when it finds such a situation, it crops the frames so they include only the information that changes from frame to frame. Static areas are eliminated, saving system resources.

If you choose Optimize Animation from the Timeline panel Options menu, you have two choices. The Bounding Box option crops each frame to include only the areas that have changed. The Redundant Pixel Removal option replaces every static pixel with transparency.

Stage 4 Slicing the Page

Now that you have finished designing your page and building the animation, the next step is to cut the image into pieces (called **slices**) that can work properly on a Web page. At the very least, each element that needs to link to a different location should become a slice, as should any element that requires unique output options (such as file format).

When you export the page, Photoshop can create an HTML file with the necessary information for assembling the slices into a functional Web page — which is useful for previewing your work. However, Photoshop is not a Web-design application. A more common workflow for developing live Web sites is to create the pieces in Photoshop, and then hand them off to a Web developer who uses specialized products (such as Adobe Dreamweaver) to reassemble the pieces using proper HTML structure and code.

CREATE SLICES FROM GUIDES

Photoshop includes three options for creating slices: based on guides, based on layers, and based on a manually defined area. Each of these methods has its own advantages, which you will see as you use all three techniques to slice the photo gallery page.

1. **With `metro_interface.psd` open, make sure guides are visible (View>Show>Guides). In the Timeline panel, make sure the last frame in the animation is selected.**

2. **Choose the Slice tool (nested under the Crop tool) in the Tools panel.**

3. **In the Options bar, click the Slices From Guides button.**

   Each resulting slice is identified by a number and icon in the top-left corner. Slices are automatically numbered from left to right, top to bottom.

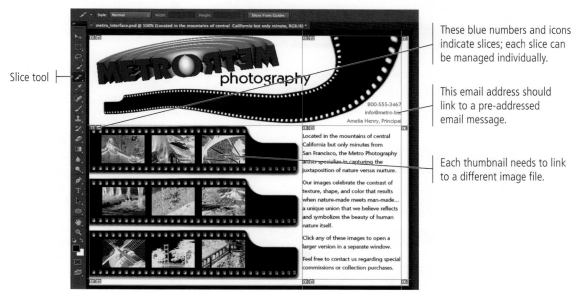

4. **Choose the Slice Select tool in the Tools panel (nested under the Slice tool).**

5. **Click Slice 2 and then press Delete/Backspace.**

6. **Click the Show Auto Slices button in the Options bar.**

Note:

If the button reads "Hide Auto Slices" then the auto slices are already visible in your file.

It is important to realize that the resulting HTML file will reassemble the sliced images with a table. To reassemble the table correctly, all areas of the image must be created as slices. If you delete a user-created slice, Photoshop creates the necessary auto slices to allow the table to work properly.

Slices that you create (**user slices**) have bright blue tags; the ones Photoshop generates to support your manual slices (**auto slices**) have gray tags. You can convert an auto slice to a user slice by double-clicking it with the Slice Select tool and defining slice options, or by selecting an auto slice and clicking Promote in the Options bar.

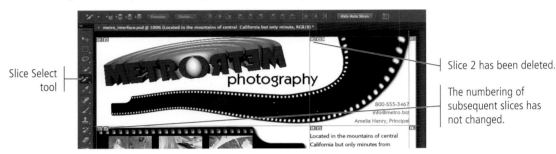

Slice Select tool

Slice 2 has been deleted.

The numbering of subsequent slices has not changed.

7. **Select and delete Slice 3 from the first row.**

The entire area of the former Slice 2 and 3 is now combined into a single auto slice.

The numbering of subsequent slices changes to reflect the new number of slices in the first row.

8. **Using the Slice Select tool, click Slice 1 to select it. Click the right-center handle of the slice and drag to the right edge of the image.**

Because you resized Slice 1 to fill the space that had been occupied by Slices 2 and 3, the auto slice is no longer required.

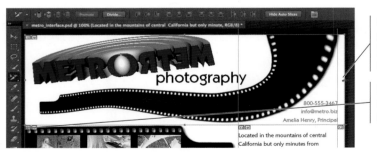

Click and drag the slice handle to extend it across the entire top of the page.

Subsequent slice numbers change to reflect the single slice in the first row.

9. **Click the Hide Auto Slices button in the Options bar.**

10. **Save the file and continue to the next exercise.**

CREATE SLICES FROM LAYERS

You can also create slices based on selected layers, which can be far easier than manually drawing slices around individual images (such as the thumbnail images that make up this photo gallery).

1. **With metro_interface.psd open, expand all three Filmstrip layer groups.**

2. **Click any of the thumbnail layers to select it, then press Command/Control and click each thumbnail image layer to select all nine thumbnails at once.**

3. **Choose Layer>New Layer Based Slices.**

The filmstrips are automatically cut into a number of slices. The important slices are the ones that surround each thumbnail; the other slices are necessary to align the thumbnail slices in the exported HTML file.

Each thumbnail image is now a separate slice.

Several other slices are created to maintain the table structure.

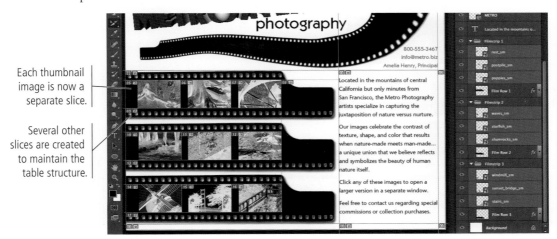

4. **Using the Slice Select tool, double-click any of the resulting thumbnail slices to open the Slice Options dialog box.**

For every slice, you can define a number of settings:

- **Name** is the file name that will be used when you save the slice for the Web.

- **URL** is the file that opens if a user clicks the slice. (Slices don't have to be links; if you don't want a slice to link to something, simply leave the URL field blank.)

- **Target** is the location where the URL opens when a user clicks the slice. Although there are other options available in full-scale HTML development applications such as Dreamweaver, you will primarily use "_self" to open the link in the same window or "_blank" to open the link in a new window.

- **Message Text** appears in the browser's status bar. If you don't type a specific message, the URL link will display.

- **Alt Tag** appears in place of an image when image display is disabled in the browser, or when a Web page is being read by screen-reader software.

Because all nine of the slices are technically selected because they were just created, you are simultaneously editing the options for all nine thumbnail slices. This is useful because a number of the settings will be the same for each slice; you can minimize your workload by adding the common information to all nine slices at once.

5. **Define the following information in the Slice Options dialog box and then click OK.**

Name:	_thumb
URL:	images/
Target:	_blank

These settings apply to all nine selected thumbnail slices.

6. **Using the Slice Select tool, click in the page head area (Slice 1) to deselect the new layer-based slices.**

7. **With the Slice Select tool, double-click the top-left thumbnail slice (Slice 5 in our example) to open the Slice Options dialog box for only that slice.**

The same information you just defined already appears in the Slice Options dialog box. You now need to add the unique information for the specific slice you are editing.

Note:

You need to use the Slice Select tool to access the Set Options for the Current Slice button in the Options bar.

Note:

The "images/" part of the URL tells the HTML code to look in the folder named "images" within the folder where you export the HTML page. All the full-size images, as you may remember from the batch-processing exercise, are saved as JPEG files in the images folder.

Note:

The _blank target opens the defined URL in a new browser window.

8. **Place the insertion point before the existing name (_thumb) and type `rust`.**

When you placed these images into the interface file, each was placed onto a separate layer named after the original file name. To name each slice, you simply replace the _sm from the layer name with _thumb.

9. **Place the insertion point after the existing URL and type `rust.jpg`.**

Again, this is the same as the layer name, minus the "_sm", and with the extension ".jpg" added. Be very careful to type the exact image names here; if you enter a file name incorrectly, links in the Web page will not work properly.

You are adding slice-specific information to the one selected slice.

10. **Click OK to apply the changes to the selected slice.**

11. **Repeat Steps 7–10 for the rest of the thumbnail slices, naming each slice and URL according to the selected layer name.**

12. **Save the file and continue to the next exercise.**

 ## CREATE MANUAL SLICES

In some cases, guide- and layer-based slices simply can't create what you need. In this case, you can create a specific slice by simply drawing the slice area with the Slice tool. When you manually create a slice, Photoshop automatically creates extra slices as necessary to support the ones you create.

1. **With `metro_interface.psd` open, choose the Slice tool in the Tools panel.**

2. **Click and drag an area around the email address in the header area.**

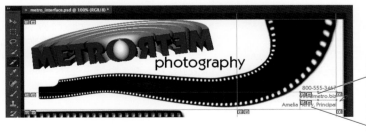

Use the Slice tool to create a manual slice at a precise location.

Other slices are created as necessary to support the slice you draw.

3. Using either the Slice or the Slice Select tool, double-click the new slice around the email address to open the Slice Options dialog box.

4. Define the following settings for the slice, then click OK.

Name:	email
URL:	**mailto:info@metro.biz**
Target:	[None]
Message Text:	[None]
Alt Tag:	**Send email to Metro Photography**

5. Save the file and continue to the next exercise.

Creating No Image Slices

In the Slice Options dialog box, you can change the slice type to No Image, which is useful if you want to create a slice to contain editable HTML text instead of a graphic representation of text. When No Image is selected in the Slice Type menu, you can define the HTML text that will appear in the slice after the page is exported. (If you convert a slice to a No Image slice, any animation included in that slice area will not be visible in the exported file.)

Double-clicking a slice in the Save For Web preview opens the Slice Options dialog box with most of the same options as in the main interface. Two additional menus allow you to define the alignment of text within the exported slice (the word "cell" is used because the exported text area is actually a table cell rather than an image slice).

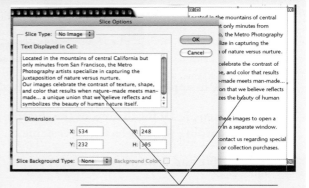

We converted the main text slice, and pasted the text from the layer into the dialog box.

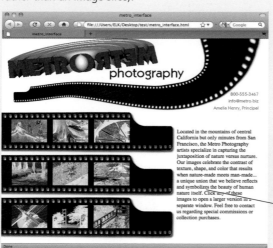

The defined text appears as selectable text in the cell when the page is viewed in a browser.

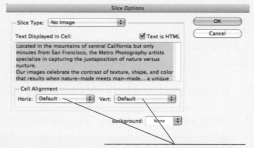

If you open this dialog box from the Save For Web dialog box, you can define the position of text within the HTML cell.

PHOTOSHOP FOUNDATIONS

You can click the Divide button in the Options bar to create a grid of slices within the area of an existing selected slice. You can use this dialog box to divide the slice horizontally, vertically, or both.

If you use the Slices Down/Across option, the selected slice will be divided into equally sized slices in the selected direction.

If you choose the Pixels Per Slice option, the selected slice will be divided into equally-sized slices in the selected direction. This creates as many slices as will fit into the area of the original selected slice.

Using the Preview option, you can see the result of your grid choices before you finalize the process.

REVIEW IMAGE SETTINGS AND EXPORT HTML

Once all the slices have been defined, you can safely export the page and all the necessary image files for the Web. Before exporting, however, you should define the file formats, compression, and color settings that will work best for each slice. This process is made easier using the File>Save For Web command.

1. **With the file metro_interface.psd open, choose File>Save For Web.**

    By default, the dialog box shows the optimization settings that will be used for all slices in the file. You can also click a specific slice with the Slice Select tool to define different options for that slice.

2. **Review the optimization settings in the right side of the dialog box.**

    Animated files must be saved using the GIF format. Because most of this interface includes animation, you are going to export the entire file as GIF.

Note:

The tools in the Save For Web dialog box serve the same purpose as the related tools in the main interface.

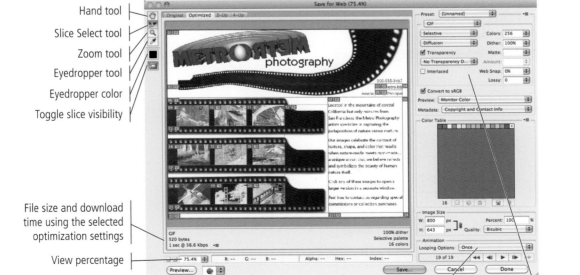

Hand tool
Slice Select tool
Zoom tool
Eyedropper tool
Eyedropper color
Toggle slice visibility

File size and download time using the selected optimization settings

View percentage

Preview the image or page in a browser

Change looping options for animated GIF slices

Slice optimization settings

3. **Using the Slice Select tool, click and drag to select all slices in the file.**

4. **In the right side of the dialog box, make sure GIF is selected in the Preset menu, and uncheck the Transparency option.**

   Although GIF files support transparency, the transparency can cause obvious degradation around the edges of certain design elements. It can also cause the resulting animation to be choppy. You know you want all of these images to appear on a white background, so you do not need to include transparency in the exported images.

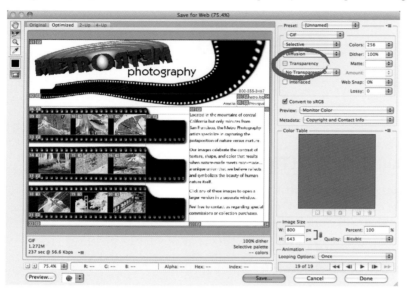

Note:

The dialog box defaults to show the optimized version of the image. You can use the tabs at the top of the preview to show the original image or split the window into two or four panes; each pane can have different settings for experimentation/ comparison.

Note:

Clicking Done closes the dialog box and saves your slice optimization settings. Clicking Cancel simply closes the dialog box; your choices are not saved.

Note:

You can double-click a slice in the dialog box to edit the slice options for that slice.

5. **Click the Save button and navigate to your WIP>Metro folder as the location for saving.**

6. **Change the file name to `index.html`.**

   This is the standard naming convention for the file that opens by default when a user navigates to a specific Web address.

7. **Make sure HTML and Images is selected in the Format menu, and All Slices is selected in the Slices menu.**

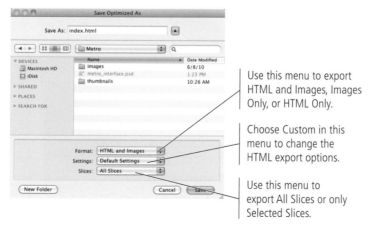

Use this menu to export HTML and Images, Images Only, or HTML Only.

Choose Custom in this menu to change the HTML export options.

Use this menu to export All Slices or only Selected Slices.

Note:

Don't assume that all users have high-speed Internet access. Many people, especially in the general consumer and international markets, still use dial-up modems. If your target audience is one of these, you should optimize your files for slower download speeds.

8. **Click Save to generate the HTML and image files for the photo gallery page.**

When optimizing files for the Web, the format you use will affect the display of the colors in the exported file, as well as compression and transparency capabilities. The Save For Web dialog box allows you to save images or slices in one of five formats (JPEG, GIF, PNG-8, PNG-24, or WBMP), and then define options specific to the format you choose.

JPEG

JPEG is the format of choice for continuous-tone images (such as photos) since it can store up to 24-bit color. The JPEG format compresses information using lossy compression, which means information is lost in the resulting file. It is not well suited for text or graphics, since its compression method introduces a blurring effect to the graphics.

You can choose a predefined compression level (Low, Medium, High, Very High, or Maximum) or define a specific quality percentage. These choices refer to the quality of the resulting image, not the amount of compression applied; the higher quality you want, the less compression you should apply.

- The **Optimized** check box creates an enhanced JPEG with a slightly smaller file size. Some older browsers don't support this feature.

- The **Progressive** option allows the image to appear in stages as more data downloads; this option is only available if the Optimized check box is selected.

- The **Blur** option applies a Gaussian blur to the exported image, which allows higher compression without destroying the image.

- The **Embed Color Profile** preserves the profile of the image in the exported file.

- The **Matte** option defines a color for any pixels that were transparent in the original image. The JPEG format does not support transparency.

PNG-8 and PNG-24

PNG is another format used for Web graphics and images. Two versions of the format — PNG-8 and PNG-24 — support 8-bit and 24-bit color respectively. For the PNG-8 format, the options are the same as for the GIF format, except that PNG-8 files cannot be compressed. PNG-24 can support continuous-tone color as well as transparency.

GIF

GIF is an 8-bit format typically used for graphics and artwork that don't have a large range of color. It is ideally suited for files with large areas of solid color, but it is ill suited for continuous-tone images that have subtle color variations.

When you save a file in the GIF format, all the colors are mapped to a color table (called **indexed color**). Indexed color is an 8-bit color model in which the specific 256 values are based on the colors in the image. You can remap the indexed colors using a number of options:

- **Perceptual** gives priority to colors to which the human eye is more sensitive.

- **Selective** is similar to Perceptual, but favors broad areas of color. This usually produces the best results.

- **Adaptive** samples colors appearing most commonly in the image.

- **Restrictive (Web)** uses a standard 216-color Web-safe color table. This option can result in drastic color shift.

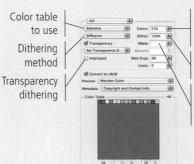

The **Lossy** option reduces file size by selectively discarding data; higher settings result in more data being discarded.

The **Dithering Method** option applies **dithering**, which blends two available colors to simulate additional colors. A higher dithering percentage creates the appearance of more colors and more detail, but can also increase the file size.

The **Transparency** and **Matte** options determine how transparent pixels are treated. If Transparency is checked, semi-transparent pixels blend into the defined Matte color.

The **Transparency Dithering** option allows you to dither transparency in a similar manner as dithering colors.

The **Interlace** option allows the image to display in stages as more data downloads (similar to progressive JPEG files).

The **Web Snap** option specifies a tolerance level for shifting colors to the closest Web palette equivalents.

You can change the options for the resulting HTML by choosing Other in the Settings menu of the Save Optimized As dialog box. The four panes of the Output Settings dialog box are accessed in the menu below the Settings menu. Most of these options require a good understanding of HTML and/or CSS; if you don't understand these concepts, you can safely use the default settings for most basic pages you design in Photoshop.

HTML Options

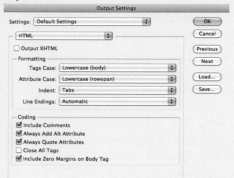

The **Output XHTML** option creates Web pages that meet the XHTML standard. This option disables options that might conflict with this standard; when this is selected, the Tags Case and Attribute Case options are automatically set.

The **Formatting** options determine how the resulting HTML code will be formatted. The **Coding** options determine what will be included in the resulting code.

Slices Options

The **Generate Table** option creates an HTML table to reassemble the slices in the exported Web page.

- **Empty Cells** defines how empty slices are converted to table cells.

- **TD W&H** defines when to include width and height attributes for table data.

- **Spacer Cells** defines when to add empty spacer cells around the generated table.

The **Generate CSS** option creates a cascading style sheet to reassemble the slices in the exported page. The **Referenced** menu defines how slice positions are referenced in the HTML file (By ID, Inline, or By Class).

The **Default Slice Naming** options are like the options that you used to name batch-processed files.

Background Options

The **View Document As** option defines a specific image or color to use as the Web page background. If Image is selected, the page displays an image or color as the background behind the image or page you are exporting. If Background is selected, the page will display the optimized image as a tiled background.

In the **Background Image** field, you can define an image to use as the page background. The background image will be tiled behind the optimized image on the Web page.

The **Color** field and menu allow you to define a color that will be used as the background of the exported page.

Saving Files Options

The **File Naming** options change the default file naming conventions for files created when you export an image or page for the Web. These options are similar to those that you used to assign names to batch-processed files.

The **Filename Compatibility** options make the file name compatible with Windows, Mac OS, or Unix servers.

The **Put Images In Folder** option defaults to "images", which is a standard convention for Web site folder structure. If a folder named "images" does not exist where you save the optimized file, the images folder will be created for you.

The **Copy Background Image When Saving** option preserves a defined background image as a single image.

9. On your desktop, double-click the **index.html** file in your WIP>Metro folder to open the file in a browser.

10. Click any thumbnail image to view the larger image.

The large image opens in a new window (or tab) because you used the _blank target.

11. Close the browser windows and return to Photoshop.

12. Save the Photoshop file, and then close it.

Using the Save For Web dialog box does not save your work in the native Photoshop file. You have to save the Photoshop file separately after the HTML and images have been exported.

Project Review

1. The _____ command can be used to run an action on all files in a specific folder without user intervention.

2. Align options are available in the _____ when multiple layers are selected in the Layers panel.

3. _____ is the process of automatically creating frames to animate a change between the beginning and ending states of a layer.

4. The _____ for each frame determines the amount of time before the next frame appears.

5. When defining slice settings, the _____ option defines the file that should open when a user clicks that slice.

6. The _____ is used in place of an image when a Web page is being read by screen-reader software.

7. The _____ tool is used to manually cut apart a page into smaller pieces for Web delivery.

8. When setting image optimization settings in the Save For Web dialog box, the _____ format allows lossy compression and does not support transparency; it is best used for photos.

9. The _____ format supports transparency but not a large number of colors; it is best used for artwork or graphics with large areas of solid color.

10. The _____ format supports both continuous-tone color and transparency, but is not universally supported by Web browsers.

1. Briefly explain how actions can be used to improve workflow.

2. Briefly explain the concept of a tween.

3. Briefly explain the difference between an image slice and a no-image slice.

Portfolio Builder Project

Use what you learned in this project to complete the following freeform exercise.
Carefully read the art director and client comments, then create your own design to meet the needs of the project.
Use the space below to sketch ideas; when finished, write a brief explanation of your reasoning behind your final design.

art director comments

Every professional designer needs a portfolio of their work. If you have completed the projects in this book, you should now have a number of different examples to show off your skills using Photoshop CS6.

The projects in this book were specifically designed to include a broad range of *types* of projects; your portfolio should use the same principle.

Using the following suggestions, gather your best work and create printed and digital versions of your portfolio.

client comments

❏ Include as many different types of work as possible — book covers, image retouching, art projects, etc.

❏ Print clean copies of each finished piece that you want to include.

❏ For correction or compositing jobs, include the "before" image as part of the sample.

❏ For each example in your portfolio, write a brief (one or two paragraphs) synopsis of the project. Explain the purpose of the piece, as well as your role in the creative and production process.

❏ Design an interactive Web page with thumbnails of your work; link the thumbnails to larger versions of the files so potential employers can review your work digitally.

❏ Create a portable version of your digital portfolio so you can present your work even when an Internet connection is not available — you never know when you might meet a potential employer.

project justification

_____

_____

_____

_____

_____

_____

_____

_____

_____

_____

_____

_____

_____

_____

The graphic design workflow typically revolves around extremely short turnaround times, which means that any possible automation will only be a benefit. Photoshop actions can be useful whenever you need to apply the same sets of options to more than one or two images. Every click you save will allow you to do other work, meet tight deadlines, and satisfy your clients. In the case of running a batch on multiple images, you are completely freed to work on other projects, be in other places, or even (technically) "work" while you're gone for the evening.

Although many developers use dedicated Web-design software like Adobe Dreamweaver to build sophisticated Web sites, the images for those sites have to come from somewhere. It is very common for a designer to build the "look and feel" of a site in Photoshop, then slice and export the pieces so the developer can reassemble them in the Web-design application. As you saw by completing this project, Photoshop can even be used to create complete (although basic) pages including frame animation and hyperlinks.

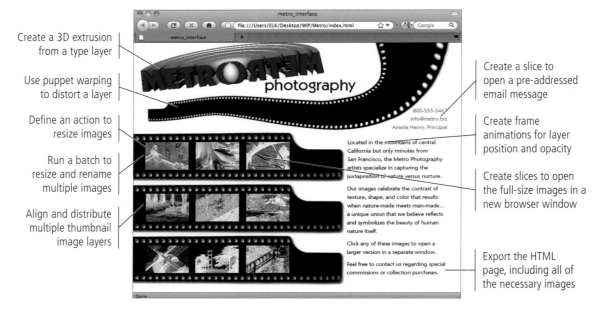

Create a 3D extrusion from a type layer

Use puppet warping to distort a layer

Define an action to resize images

Run a batch to resize and rename multiple images

Align and distribute multiple thumbnail image layers

Create a slice to open a pre-addressed email message

Create frame animations for layer position and opacity

Create slices to open the full-size images in a new browser window

Export the HTML page, including all of the necessary images

Index